Portrait Photography

Selected from the Graphis Annuals

PAGE ONE PUBLISHING

Cover: Sharon Stone photographed by Albert Watson

Distributed worldwide by
Könemann Verlagsgesellschaft mbH
Bonner Str. 126, D - 50968 Köln

Designed by Peter Feierabend, Berlin
Foreword by Carola Stoiber, Berlin
English translation by Karen Williams, Wall
French translation by Sylvie Adam-Kuenen, Cologne
Typesetting by Zentralsatz Dieter Noe, Cologne
Printed and bound by Toppan Printing

Printed in Singapore
ISBN 981-00-5720-2

Foreword

The man wears a thick woollen cap. His beard is more than three days old, and tiredness and resignation are written in his eyes. Homeless, living on the streets of Kansas City, he is captured by Nick Vedros in a portrait which leaves half of his face in shadow (p. 115).

Hers, on the other hand, is sharply lit, setting off to perfection the fine contours of her nose and mouth. Her penetrating gaze bores through the viewer. With her wildly styled blonde hair and her slashed costume exposing the flesh beneath, she is tranformed into a seductive vampire – at least in this photo. This is Sharon Stone, the »hottest« film star of 1992, posed by Albert Watson for the cover of *Rolling Stone* (p.45).

Just as people see each other through different eyes, so too camera artists produce different likenesses of their models – all depending on the circumstances and their underlying aim at the time. Some take photographs to make a magazine, a dress or a beauty cream sell better. Others emphasize the structure of a face, capture a grimace or a smile, in order to document a person's mood, attitude to life, or characteristic traits.

This book presents a cross-section of contemporary portrait photography. It shows the wide-ranging artistic and technical possibilities of the genre, as well as the differing aesthetic principles it includes. And of course it shows faces. Faces of the old and the young; of women, men, children and groups; of actors such as Dustin Hoffman and Catherine Deneuve, musicians such as Elton John and Chet Baker, politicians such as Arafat, and artists such as Andy Warhol.

Many of these portraits have been grouped together on the basis of certain common characteristics. Thus some share lines of vision, while others make similar gestures. Others again are juxtaposed in glaring contrasts. The shots by Volkmann and Walisiewicz on pp. 102/103, for example, both show two men posing. Each photographer employs the whole body to create his specific image – in one case a classical statue, and in the other a cockroach. In another instance on pp. 152/153, the four most expensive models in the world – Cindy Crawford, Stephanie Seymour, Tatiana Patitz and Naomi Campbell – appear alongside grimy coalmen from Schwerin. Here and elsewhere, the viewer is abruptly confronted by the discrepancy between society's ideal of beauty, as dictated to us by the world of advertising, and the daily lives of the people next door.

Some of those portrayed have no wrinkles channelling rivers beneath their eyes, no folds of fat doubling under their chin, no pimples rising from the flawless surface of their cheeks. They know how to act in front of the camera, and they play their role perfectly. Others are visibly marked by the trials of life. Their appearance testifies to long working days, to nights of toil, to the heavy burden of responsibility, to fear, anger, sadness and wisdom. Their unmade-up faces are the mirrors of their souls.

Every person exercises a different fascination on his or her fellows. Which face looks friendly, which face we would like to spend more or less time with – these are decisions which ultimately we can only make for ourselves. Every day afresh. And so it is with the photographs in this book: drawn from many different countries, cultures and milieux, these portraits will speak to each viewer individually, and to none alike.

Vorwort

Er trägt eine dicke Wollmütze. Der Bart ist älter als drei Tage und in seinen Augen liegt Müdigkeit, Resignation. Er ist ein Obdachloser in Kansas City, porträtiert von Nick Vedros, der die eine Hälfte dieses Gesichtes im Schatten läßt (S.115).

Das ihre dagegen ist so ausgeleuchtet, daß die feinen Konturen von Nase und Mund perfekt zur Geltung kommen. Der stechende Blick will den Betrachter durchbohren. Das Zusammenspiel der wild gestylten, blonden Haare mit dem zerrissenen Fetzen an ihrem Leib macht sie zum verführerischen Vamp – zumindest auf diesem Foto. Es zeigt Sharon Stone, den »heißesten Filmstar« des Jahres 1992, in Szene gesetzt von Albert Watson für den Titel des *Rolling Stone* (S. 45).

So unterschiedlich Menschen andere Menschen wahrnehmen, schaffen Kamerakünstler Abbilder ihrer Modelle – je nachdem unter welchen Umständen und mit welcher Intention sie arbeiten. Die einen fotografieren, damit sich ein Magazin, ein Kleid oder eine Creme besser verkauft. Die anderen betonen Strukturen eines Gesichtes, halten eine Grimasse oder ein Lächeln fest, um die Stimmung, Lebensauffassung oder charakterlichen Eigenheiten einer Person zu dokumentieren.

Dieser Band liefert einen Querschnitt der zeitgenössischen Porträt-Fotografie und zeigt die vielfältigen künstlerischen und technischen Möglichkeiten wie auch die differierenden Auffassungen von Ästhetik in diesem Genre. Und natürlich Gesichter. Alte und junge; von Frauen, Männern, Kindern und Gruppen; von Schauspielern wie Dustin Hoffman oder Catherine Deneuve, Musikern wie Elton John oder Chet Baker, Politikern wie Arafat oder Künstlern wie Andy Warhol.

Oft sind die Porträtierten durch Blickrichtungen, Bewegungen oder auch krasse Gegensätze miteinander in Beziehung gesetzt. So zeigen die Arbeiten von Volkmann und Walisiewicz auf S. 102/103 zwei »Männer in Posen«. Der ganze Körper kommt zum Einsatz, um eine Figur darzustellen: antike Statue und Küchenschabe. Auf S. 152/153 tauchen die vier teuersten Models der Welt, Cindy Crawford, Stephanie Seymour, Tatjana Patitz und Naomi Campbell, neben dreckigen Kohlenschleppern aus Schwerin auf. Nicht nur an dieser Stelle wird der Betrachter mit der Diskrepanz zwischen dem in unserer Gesellschaft angestrebten, von der Werbung diktierten Schönheitsideal und dem Alltag der Menschen von nebenan konfrontiert.

Bei den einen bilden keine Falten ein Netz um die Augen, keine Doppelung macht sich unter dem Kinn bemerkbar und nicht eine rote Pustel erhebt sich aus der ebenmäßigen Fläche der Wangen. Sie wissen, wie sie vor einer Kamera agieren müssen, spielen ihre Rolle perfekt. Bei den anderen hat das Leben sichtbare Spuren hinterlassen. Ihr Aussehen berichtet von langen Arbeitstagen, durchgemachten Nächten, der schweren Last der Verantwortung, von Angst, Wut, Trauer und Weisheit. Ihre ungeschminkten Gesichter sind die Spiegelbilder ihrer Seelen.

Aber jede Person übt auf ihr Gegenüber eine andere Faszination aus. Die Entscheidung, welches Gesicht einem sympathisch ist, welchem man mehr oder weniger Aufmerksamkeit und Zeit schenken möchte, trifft jeder selbst. Jeden Tag von neuem. Und so wird der Betrachter auch hier mit sehr unterschiedlichen Menschen aus vielen Ländern, Kulturen und Milieus flüchtige oder intensivere Begegnungen haben.

Préface

Il porte un épais bonnet de laine. Sa barbe est d'au moins trois jours; dans ses yeux se lisent la fatigue, la résignation. C'est un sans-abri à Kansas City. Nick Vedros fait son portrait en lui laissant la moitié du visage dans l'ombre (page 115).

Le sien, par contre, est abondamment éclairé, de manière à mettre parfaitement en valeur les contours fins du nez et de la bouche. Le regard perçant veut vriller le spectateur. Avec ses cheveux blonds coiffés sauvagement et ses vêtements en lambeaux, elle fait femme fatale – tout du moins sur cette photographie. C'est Sharon Stone, la «vedette de cinéma la plus excitante» en 1992, dans une mise en scène d'Albert Watson pour la couverture du magazine *Rolling Stone* (page 45).

Autant les gens perçoivent les autres de façon différente, autant les artistes photographes arrivent à transformer l'image de leurs modèles en fonction des circonstances et de leurs intentions. Les uns photographient en vue d'améliorer les ventes d'un magazine, d'un vêtement ou d'une crème. Les autres insistent sur les structures d'un visage, fixent une grimace ou un sourire afin de faire part de l'état d'esprit, de la philosophie ou des traits de caractère de quelqu'un.

Cet album présente un échantillon de portraits photographiques contemporains. Il montre à la fois les multiples possibilités artistiques, techniques et les conceptions esthétiques diverses dans ce genre. Et bien sûr des visages. Des vieux et des jeunes; ceux de femmes, d'hommes, d'enfants et ceux de groupes; ceux d'acteurs comme Dustin Hoffman ou Catherine Deneuve, de musiciens tels Elton John ou Chet Baker, d'hommes politiques comme Arafat ou d'artistes tel Andy Warhol.

Souvent les personnes représentées sont liées entre elles par la direction du regard, par un mouvement ou tout simplement par leur contraste. Ainsi les travaux de Volkmann et de Walisiewicz, pages 102/103, montrent deux «hommes posant». C'est tout le corps qui se mobilise en représentant une statue antique et un cancrelat. Pages 152/153, les quatre modèles les plus chers du monde, Cindy Crawford, Stephanie Seymour, Tatjana Patitz et Naomi Campbell posent à côté des herscheurs tout sales de Schwerin. Ce n'est pas la seule fois où le spectateur se trouve confronté à la disparité existant entre l'idéal de beauté que dicte la publicité et auquel aspire notre société, et la vie quotidienne des gens d' à-côté.

Chez les unes pas l'ombre d'une ride n'apparaît autour des yeux, point de double menton, aucune pustule rouge ne vient rompre l'uniformité lisse des joues. Elles savent se comporter devant un objectif; elles jouent leur rôle à la perfection. Chez les autres, la vie a laissé des marques visibles. Leur apparence fait le récit des longues journées de travail, des nuits blanches, du fardeau des responsabilités, de la peur, de la colère, du deuil et de la sagesse. Leurs visages sans fard est le reflet fidèle de leur âme.

Cependant chaque personne exerce sur qui la regarde une fascination différente. Il appartiendra à chacun de décider quel visage lui est sympathique, quel est celui auquel il voudra accorder plus ou moins d'attention et de temps. Et cela chaque jour à nouveau. De cette manière, le spectateur se trouve ici aussi confronté à des gens extrêmement différents, issus d'un grand nombre de pays, de cultures et de milieux, le temps d'une rencontre fugace ou plus intense.

Jean-Paul Goude

Grace Jones on the sleeve of her album »Slave to the Rhythm«, taken by Jean-Paul Goude.

Grace Jones für die Hülle ihrer Schallplatte »Slave to the Rhythm«, fotografiert von Jean-Paul Goude.

Grace Jones sur la pochette de son disque «Slave to the Rhythm», photographiée par Jean-Paul Goude.

Herb Ritts

Portrait to accompany an article on Madonna in *Rolling Stone* magazine.

Porträt für einen Beitrag über Madonna in der Zeitschrift *Rolling Stone*.

Portrait destiné à un article du magazine *Rolling Stone* consacré à Madonna.

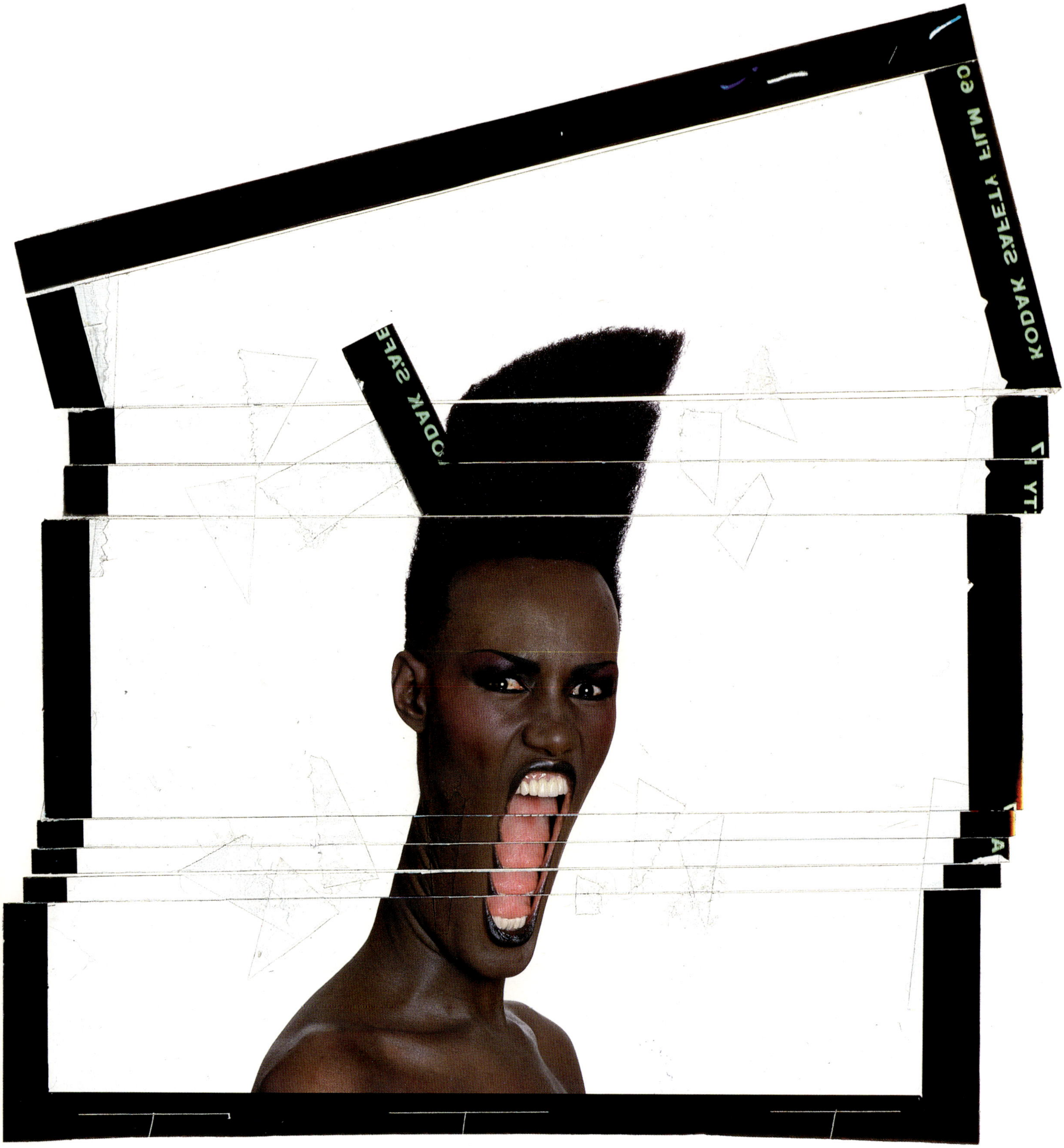

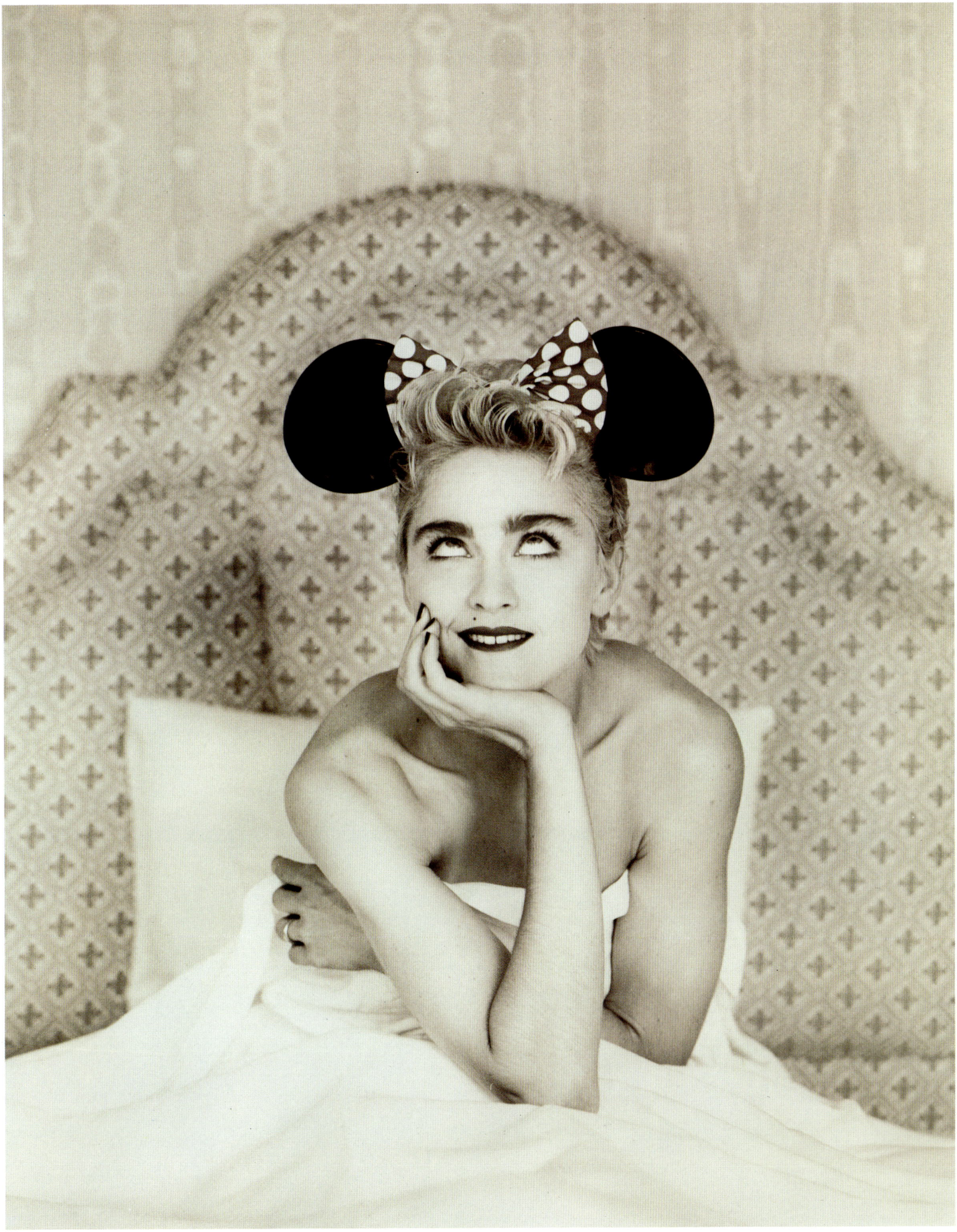

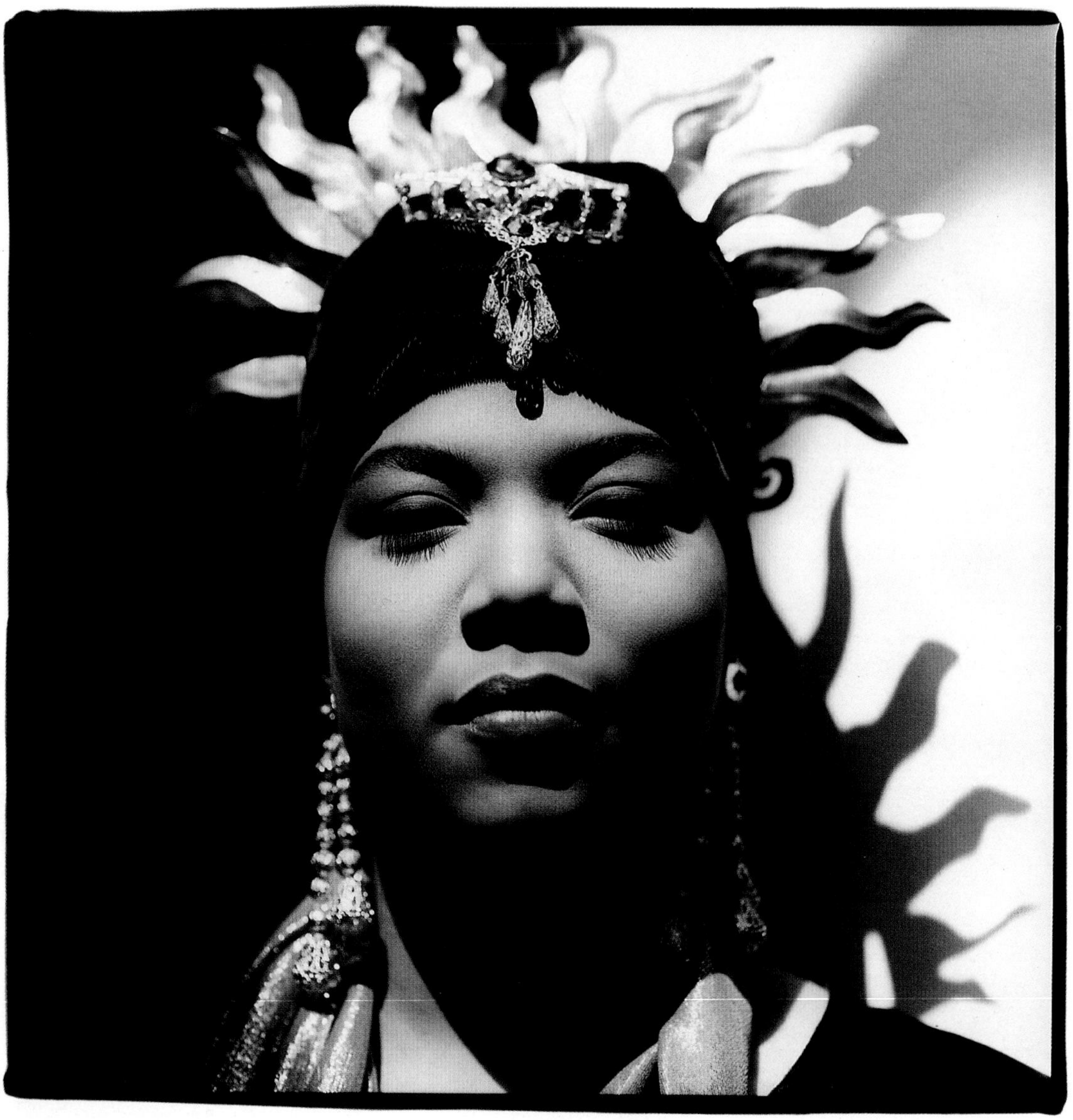

Frank Ockenfels 3

»Queen Latifah«, for a series on female rap artists in *Vanity Fair*. The photographer and Rasscale Lewis, the hair and make-up stylist, tried out various pieces of jewellery and fabric. The crown is actually a necklace which held the fabric in place. A natural ray of light from a skylight came at just the right moment.

»Queen Latifah«, Porträt für eine Reihe über Raperinnen in der Zeitschrift *Vanity Fair*. Der Fotograf und die Make-up und Haar-Stylistin, Rasscale Lewis, probierten verschiedenen Schmuck und Stoff – die Krone ist eigentlich ein Halsschmuck, der hier den Stoff hält. Ein Strahl natürlichen Lichtes fiel im richtigen Moment von oben ein.

«Queen Latifah», portrait d'une série sur les vedettes féminines du rap parue dans *Vanity Fair*. Le photographe et le maquilleur-coiffeur-styliste, Rasscale Lewis, ont expérimenté divers bijoux et étoffes. La couronne est en réalité un collier: ce dernier maintient l'étoffe en place. Un rayon de lumière naturelle tombe à point nommé.

Albert Watson

Portrait of actress Ellen Barkin, that appeared in *Rolling Stone* magazine under the column »New Faces«.

Porträt der Schauspielerin Ellen Barkin, die unter der Rubrik »Neue Gesichter« in *Rolling Stone* vorgestellt wurde.

Portrait de la comédienne Ellen Barkin, paru dans la rubrique «Nouveaux Visages» du magazine *Rolling Stone*.

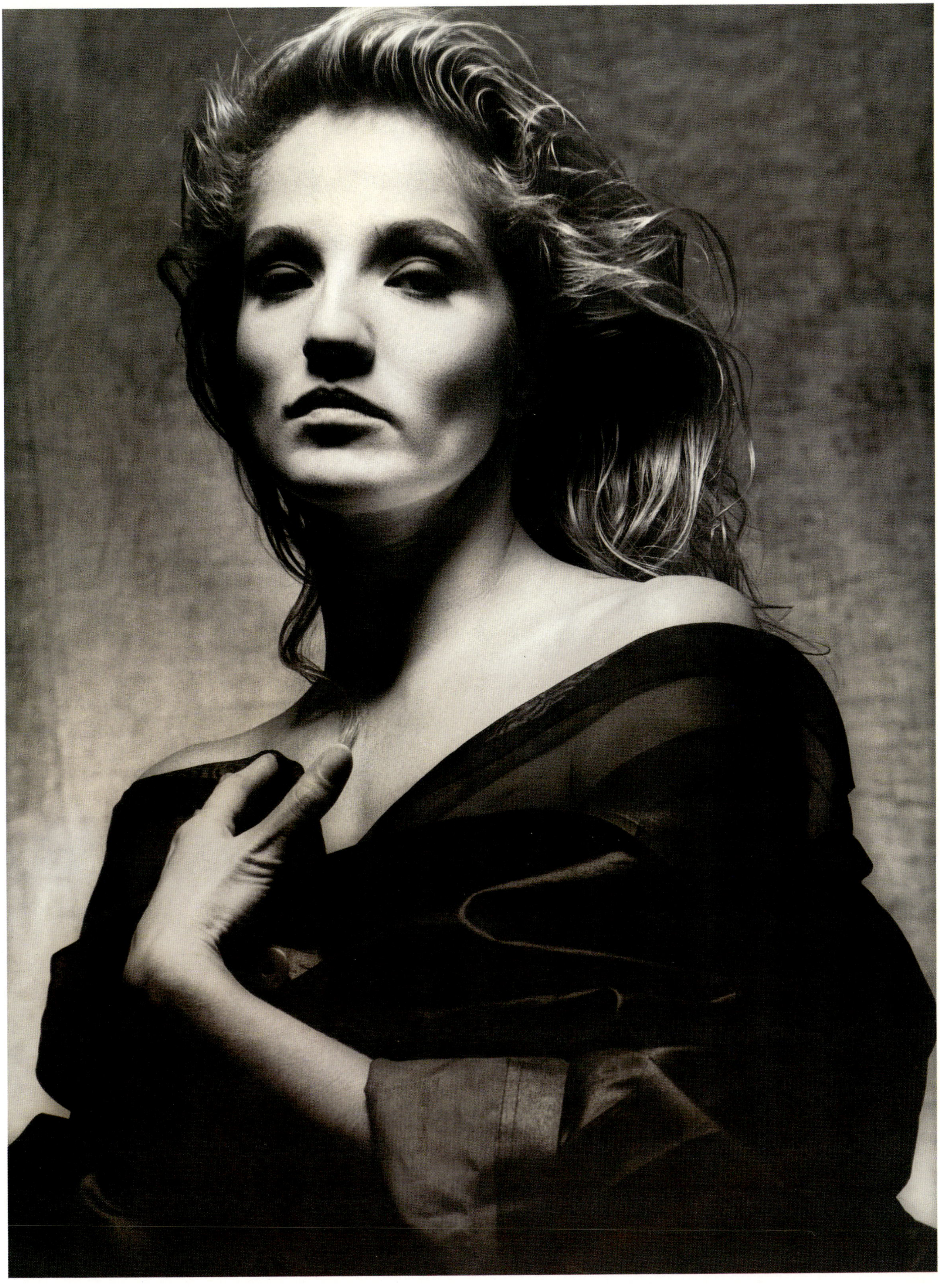

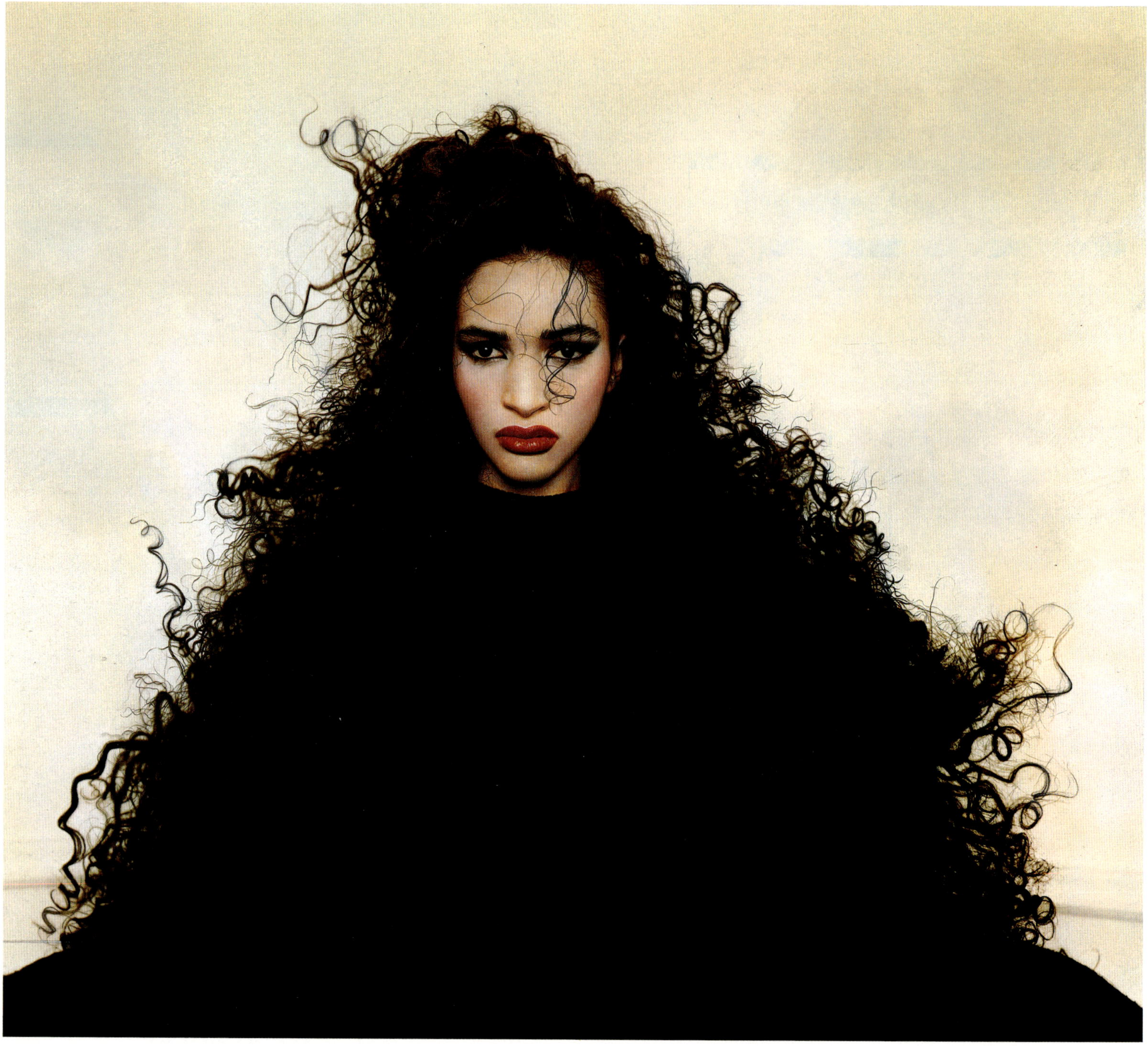

Jean-Paul Goude

»Farida«, portrait by Jean-Paul Goude, published in *Männer Vogue* magazine.

»Farida«, Porträtaufnahme von Jean-Paul Goude, aus der *Männer Vogue*.

«Farida», portrait par Jean-Paul Goude, paru dans le magazine *Männer Vogue*.

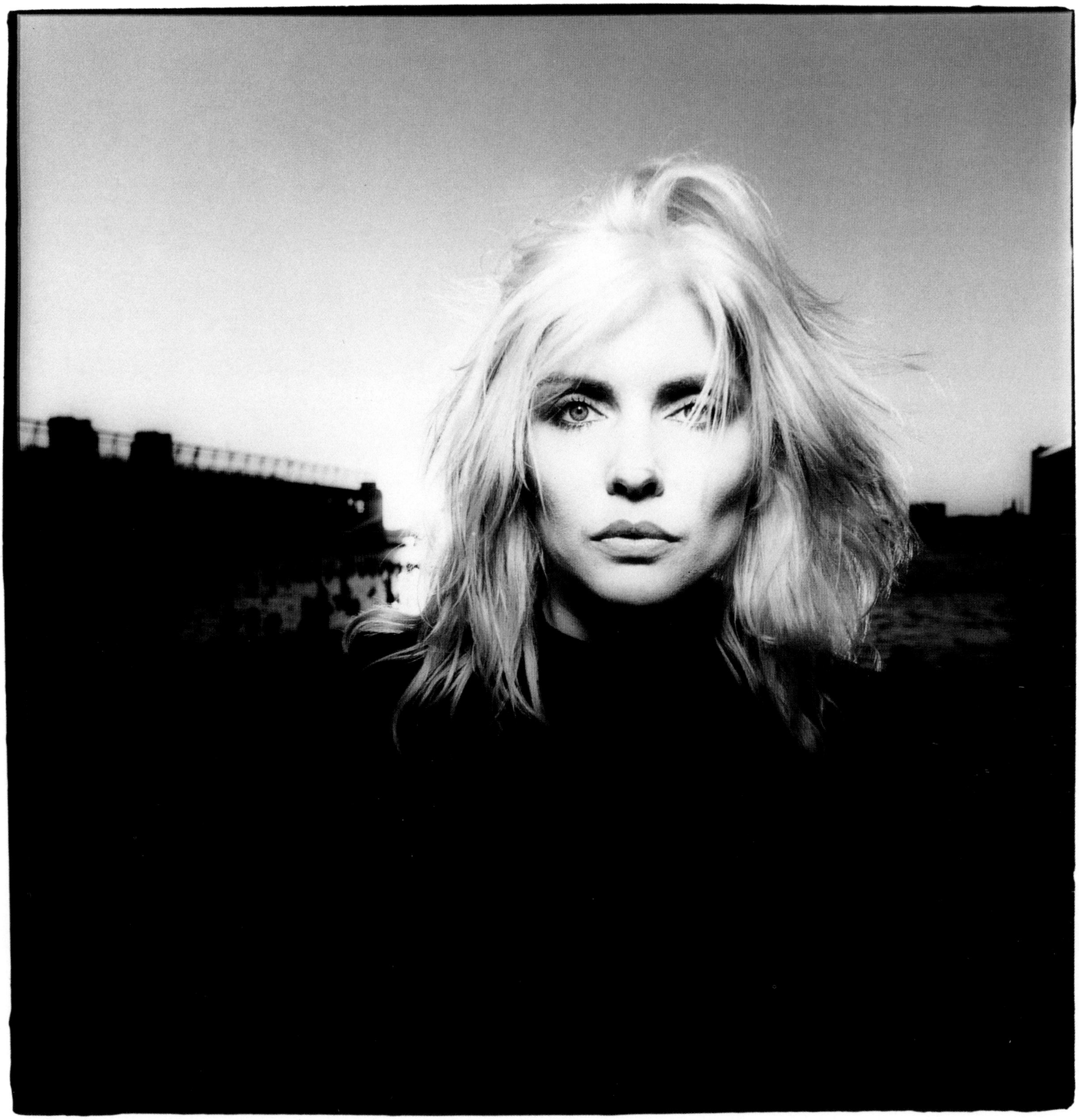

David Michael Kennedy

Rock star Deborah Harry, photograph from a series of black-and-white portraits shot by photographer David Michael Kennedy for a worldwide campaign for *Hasselblad* cameras.

Rockstar Deborah Harry, Aufnahme aus einer Serie von Schwarzweissporträts des Fotografen David Michael Kennedy für eine weltweite Kampagne für *Hasselblad*-Kameras.

La vedette de rock Deborah Harry. Portrait tiré d'une série noir et blanc que le photographe David Michael Kennedy avait prise en vue d'une campagne mondiale destinée à promouvoir les appareils photo *Hasselblad*.

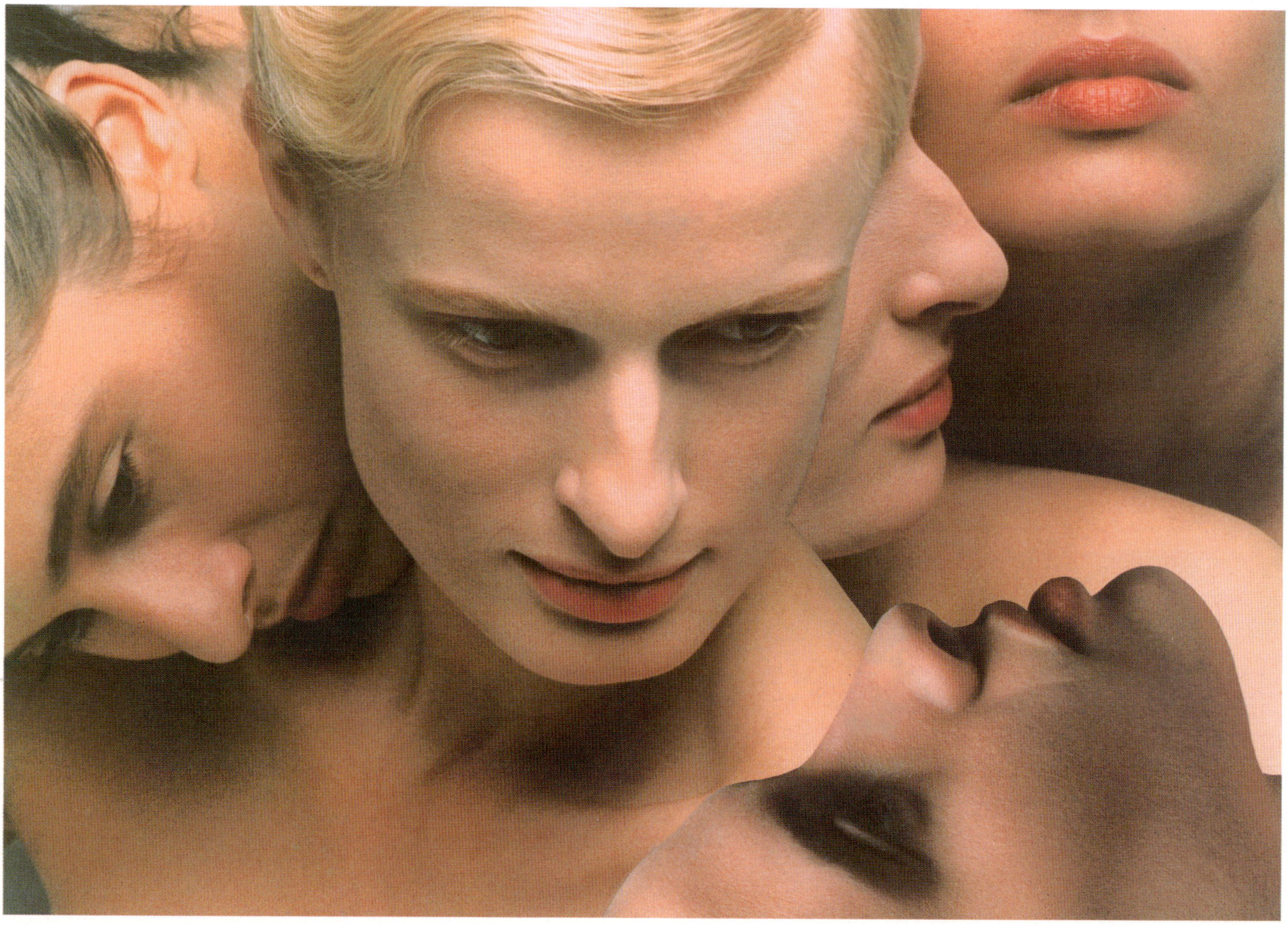

John Chan

Photograph to be included in the »Beauty« column of *Taxi* magazine.

Für die Rubrik »Schönheit« verwendete Aufnahme im *Taxi*-Magazin.

Photographie destinée à la rubrique Beauté du magazine *Taxi*.

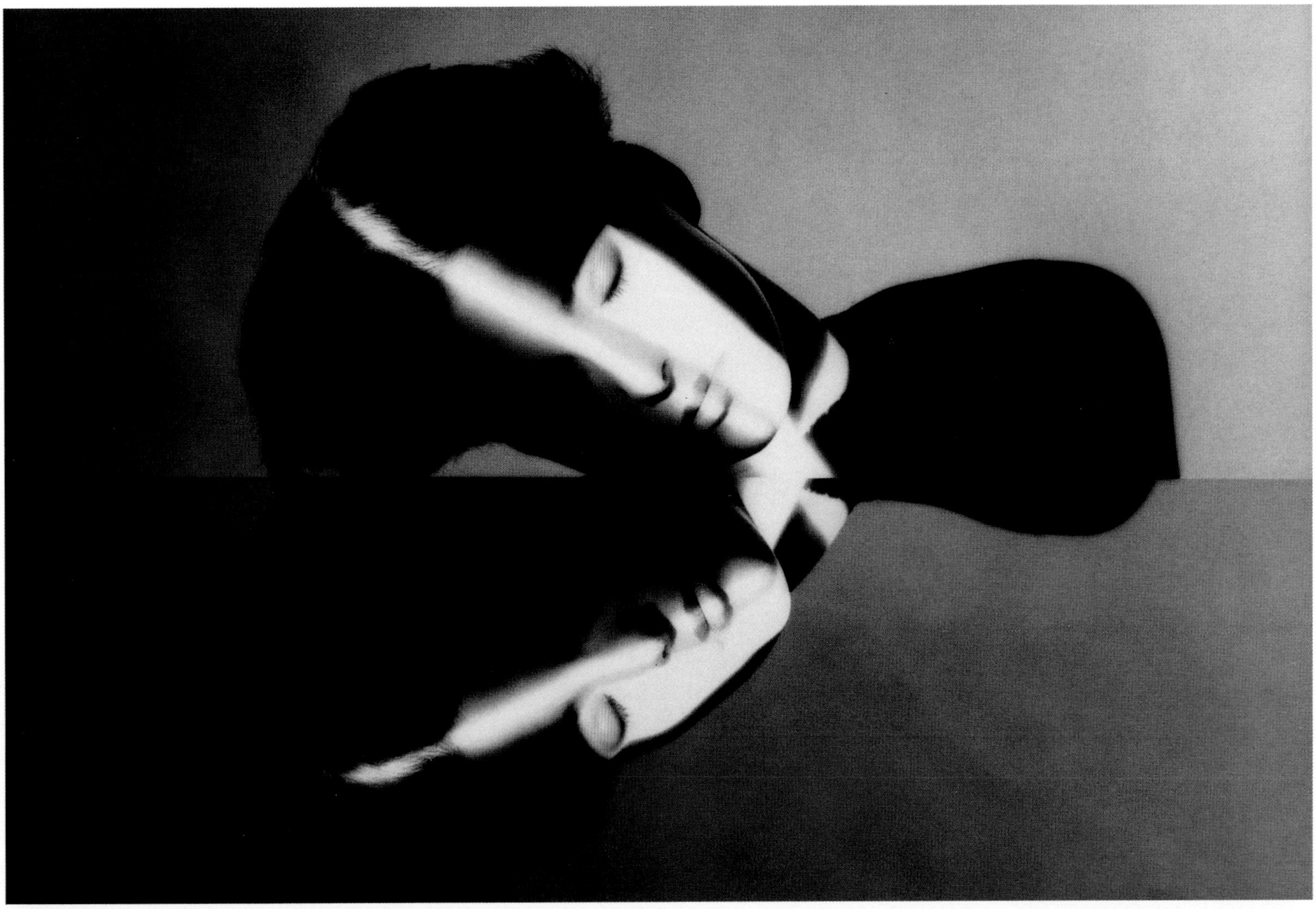

Francis Giacobetti

Photograph by Francis Giacobetti, from an article about this photographer in *Camera* magazine.

Aufnahme von Francis Giacobetti, aus einem Beitrag über diesen Fotografen in der Zeitschrift *Camera.*

Photographie prise par Francis Giacobetti, extraite d' un article consacré à ce photographe dans le magazine *Camera.*

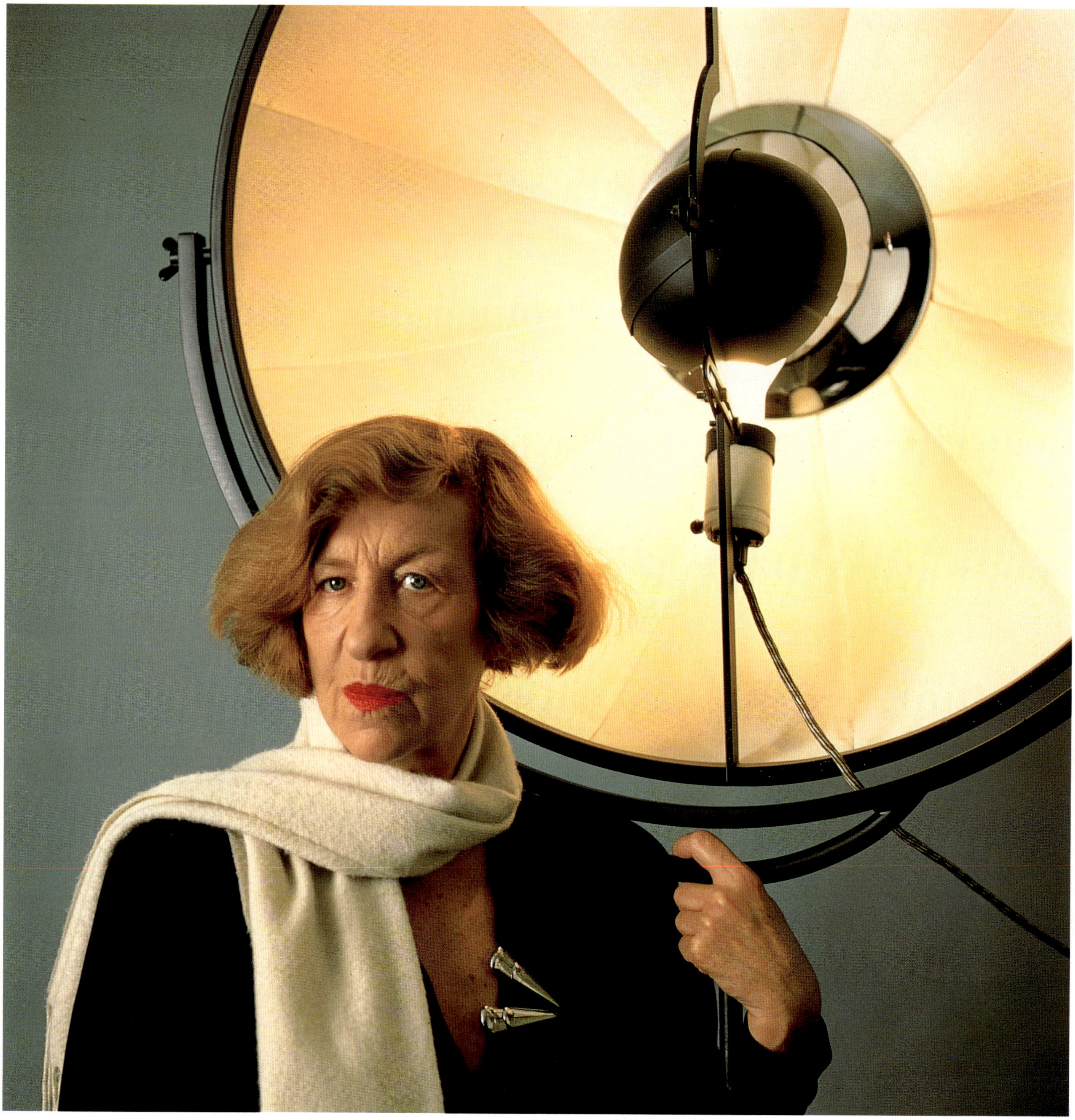

Abe Frajndlich

Portrait of interior architect Andrée Putman, shown here with a lamp created by the Italian Mariano Fortuny.

Porträt der Innenarchitektin Andrée Putman, hier mit einer Lampe des Italieners Mariano Fortuny.

Portrait de la décoratrice d'intérieurs Andrée Putman avec une lampe créée par l'Italien Mariano Fortuny.

Noritsune Nose

In this personal study, the photographer shows the current fashion trend of mixing old and new, and under and outer wear.

In dieser persönlichen Studie einer Japanerin kommentiert der Fotograf den gegenwärtigen Modetrend, Altes mit Neuem zu kombinieren.

Dans cette étude personnelle, le photographe montre une tendance actuelle de la mode qui consiste à mélanger l'ancien et le moderne, les vêtements de dessous et les vêtements de dessus.

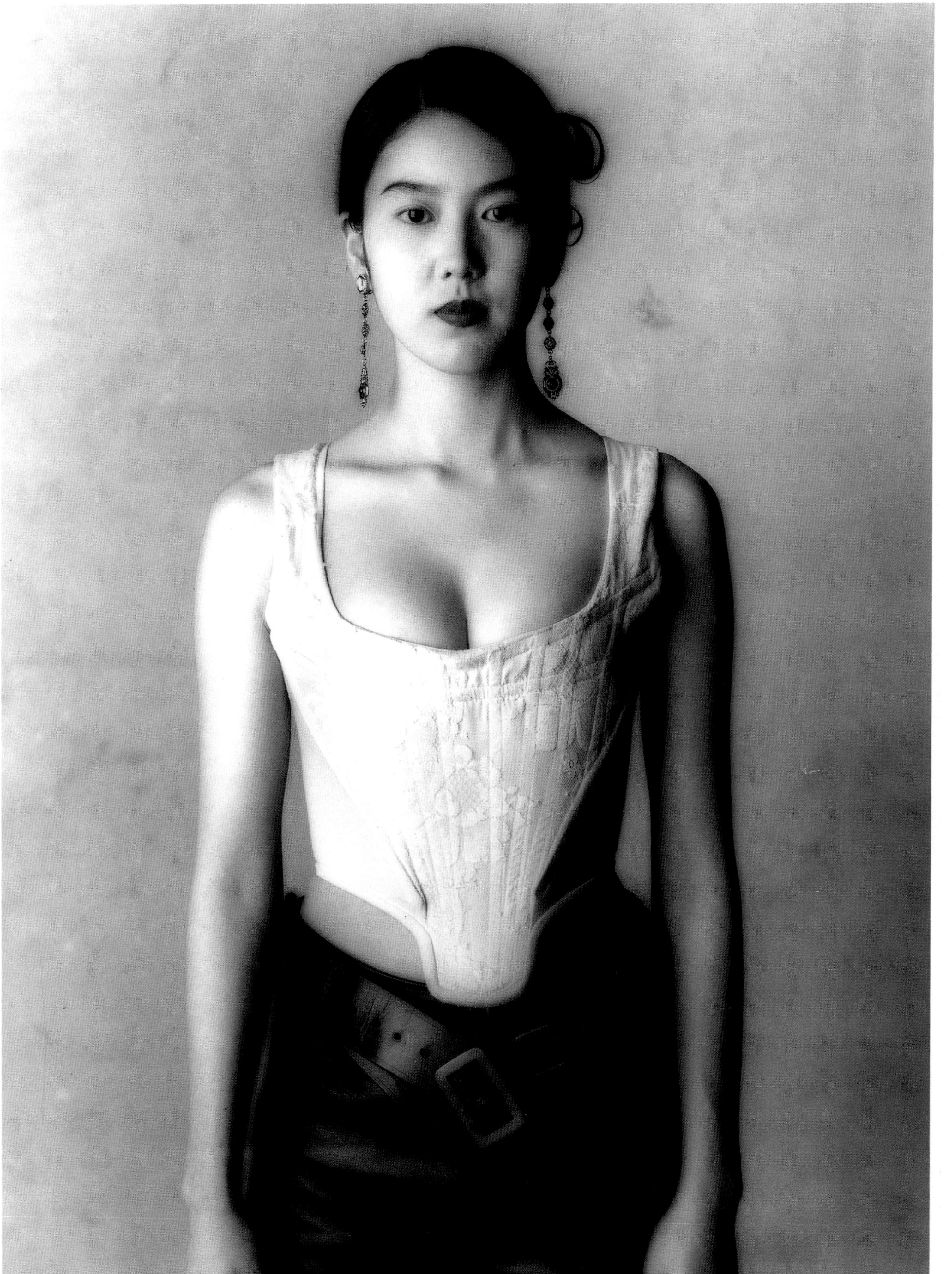

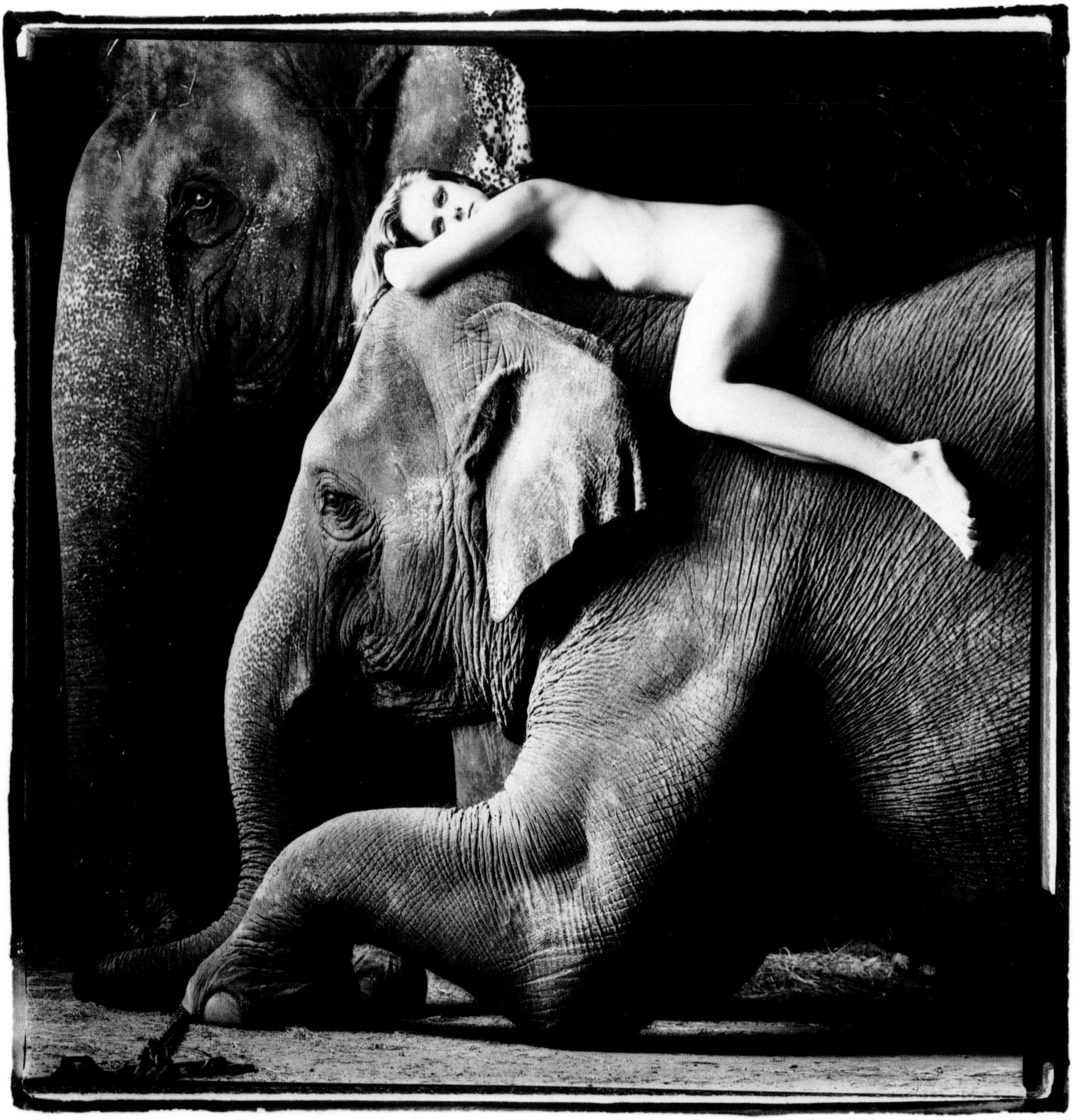

Lee Crum

Self-promotion by photographer Lee Crum.

Eigenwerbung des Fotografen Lee Crum.

Autopromotion du photographe Lee Crum.

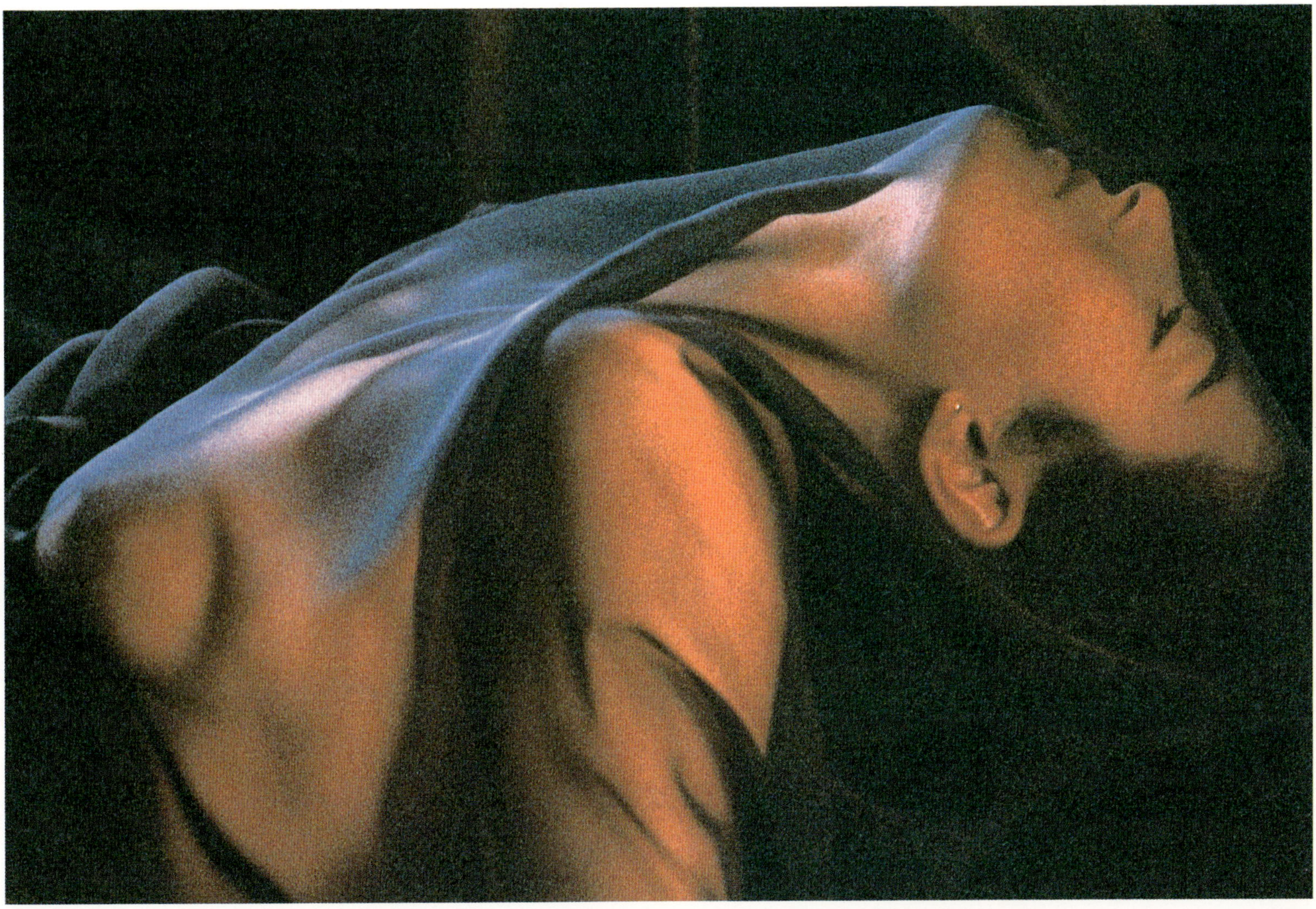

Jody Dole

»Odalisque« is the title of this personal study by photographer Jody Dole.

»Odaliske« ist der Titel dieser persönlichen Studie des Fotografen Jody Dole.

Cette «Odalisque» est une étude personnelle du photographe Jody Dole.

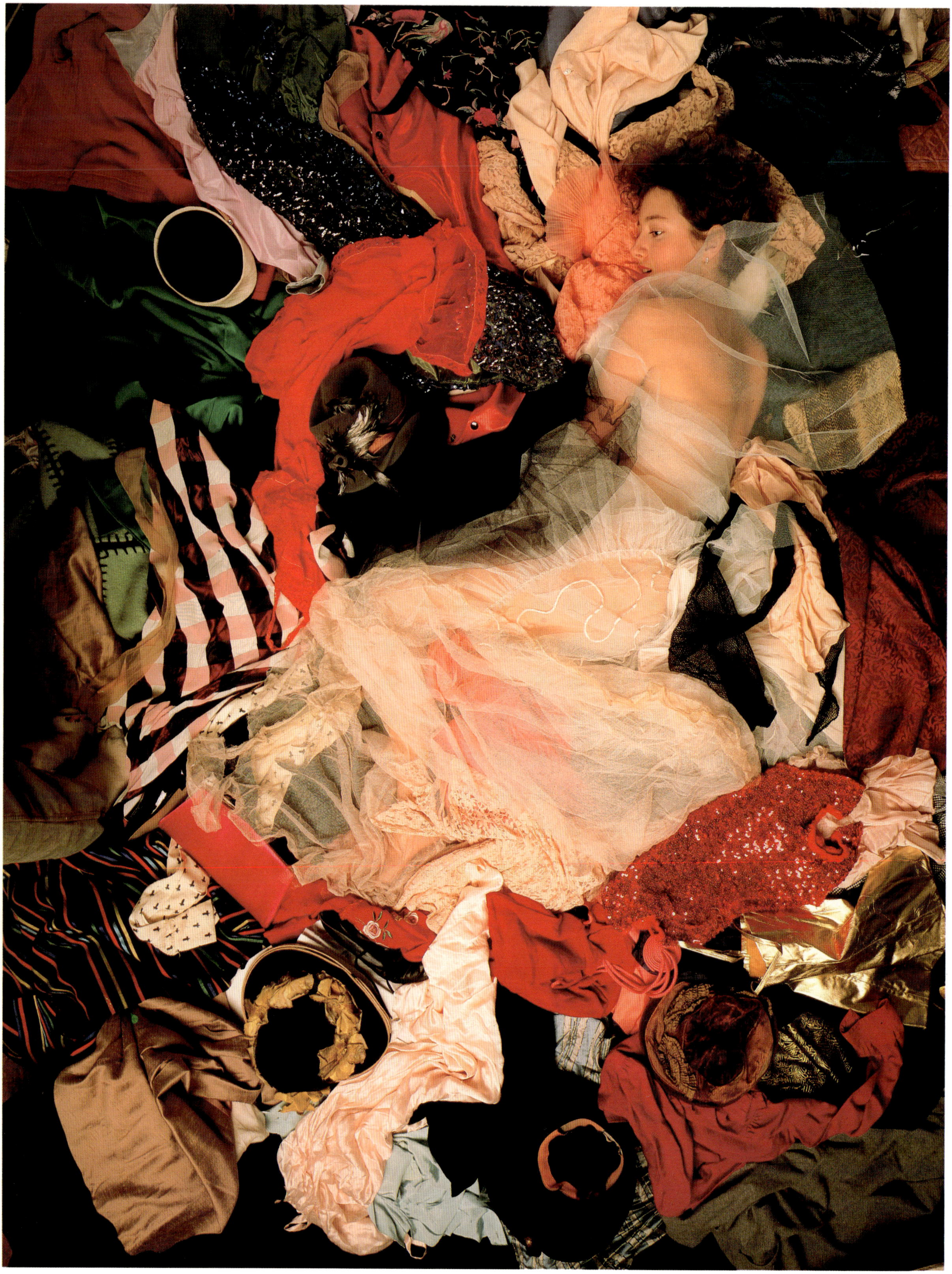

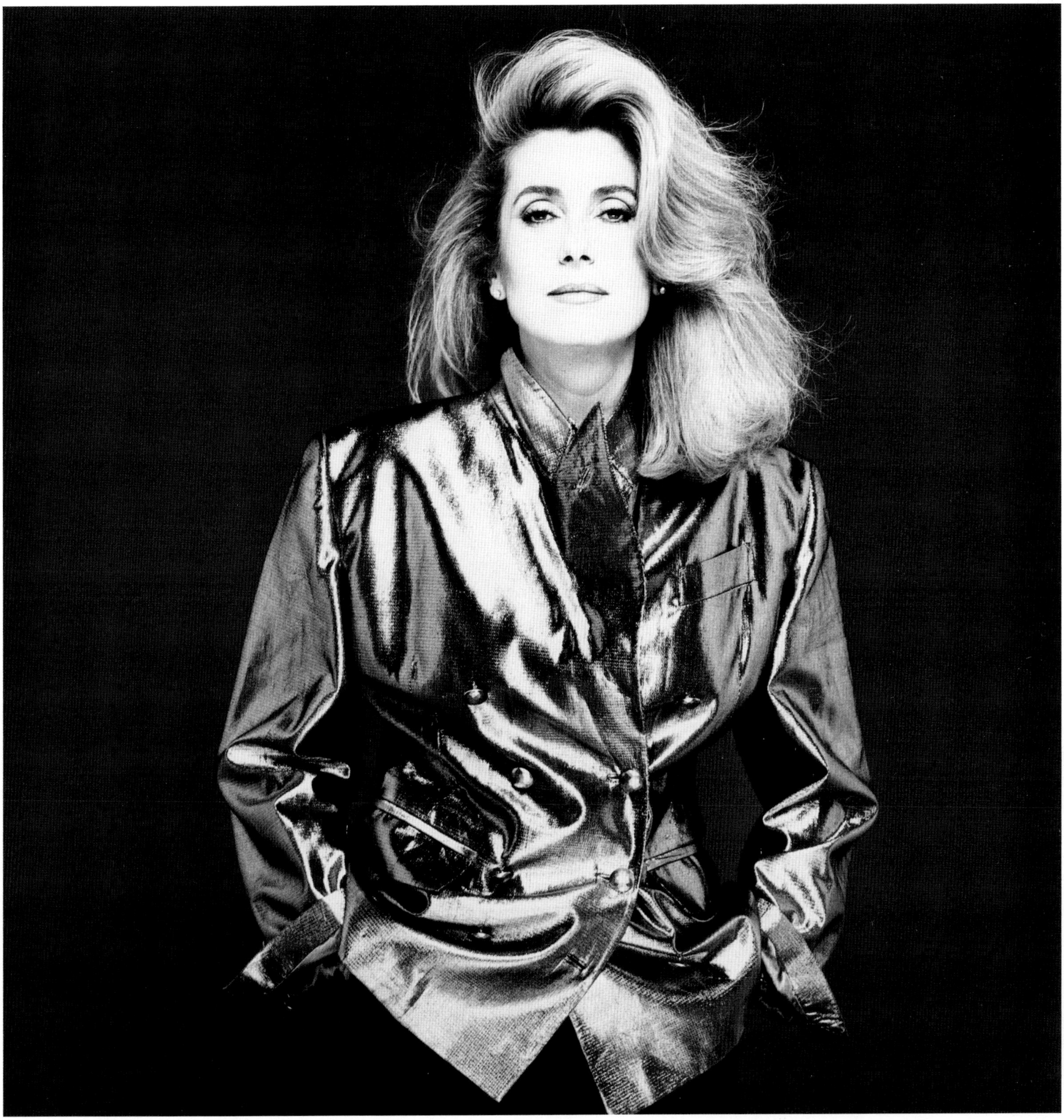

Bettina Rheims

»Catherine Deneuve in a golden jacket, Paris 1988«

»Catherine Deneuve in goldener Jacke, Paris 1988«

«Catherine Deneuve en veste dorée, Paris 1988»

Bruce Peterson

Personal study by photographer Bruce Peterson, Boston.

Persönliche Studie des Fotografen Bruce Peterson, Boston.

Etude personnelle du photographe Bruce Peterson, Boston.

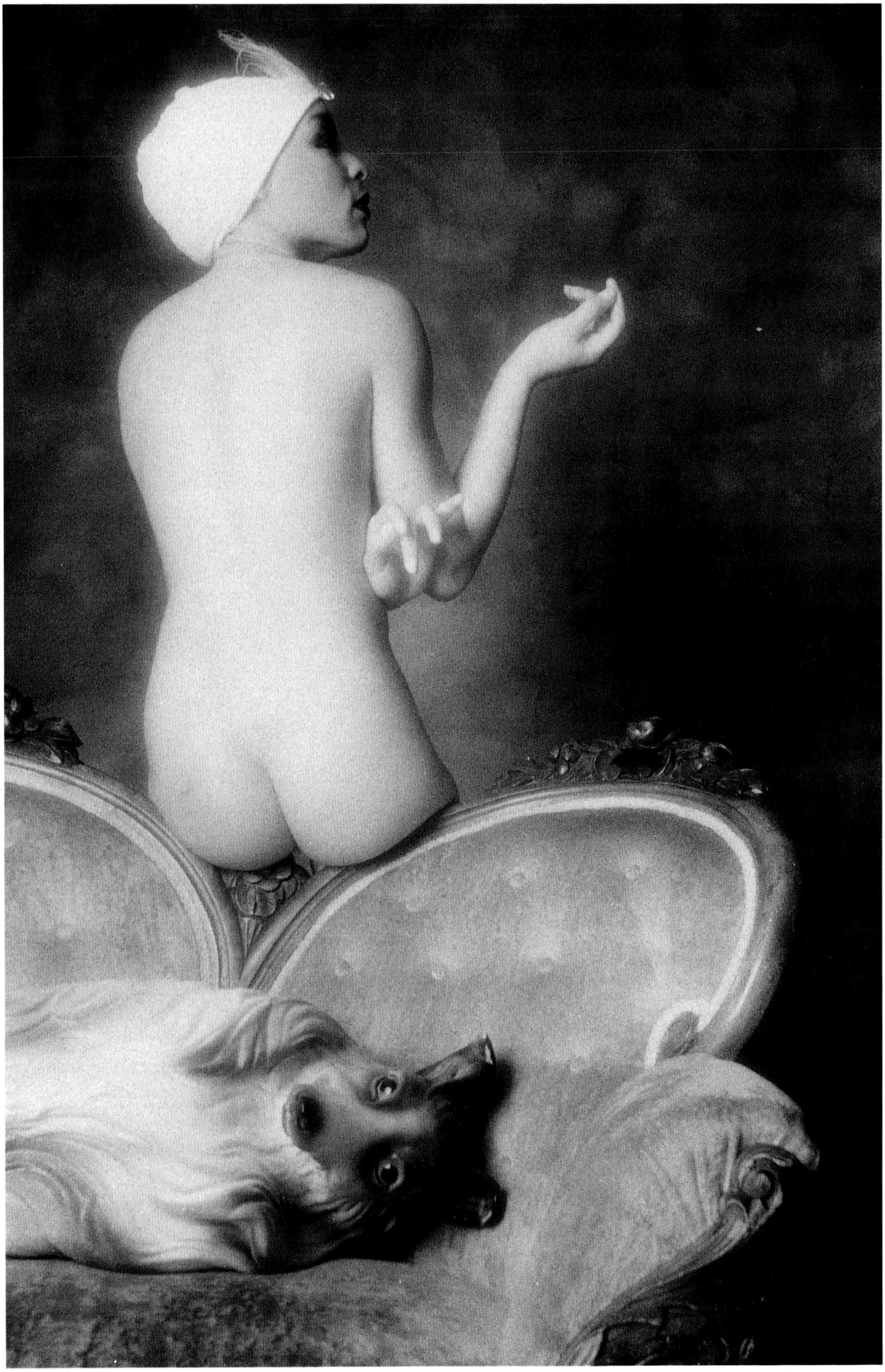

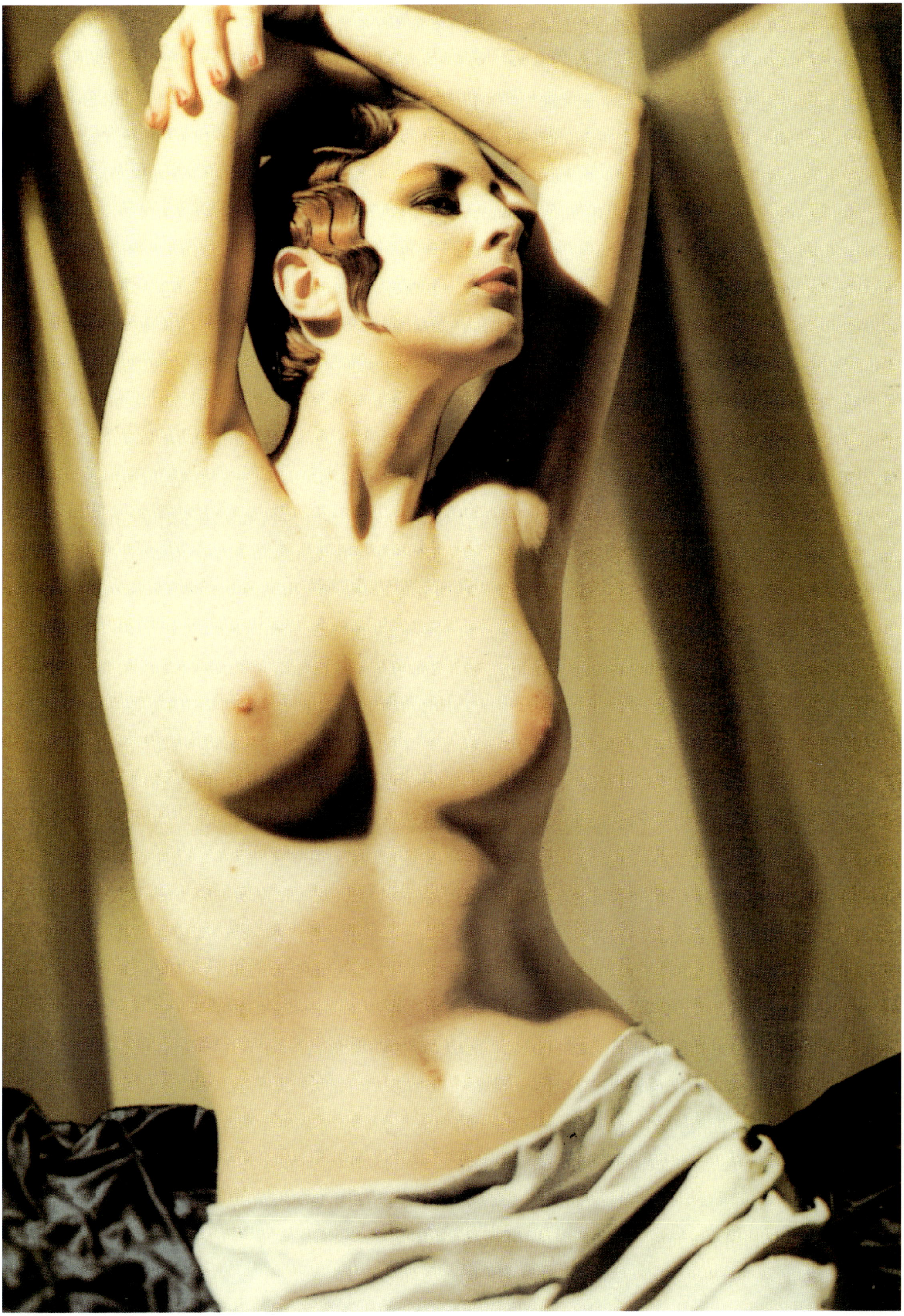

◁◁ Yuri Dojc

This studio photograph on Kodak infra-red-film is part of a series of nudes for a book. The collie is made of plaster.

Diese Studioaufnahme gehört zu einer Reihe von Aktaufnahmen für ein Buch. Der Collie ist aus Gips.

Série de photos de nus pour un livre. Cette photographie fut réalisé en studio. Le colley est en plâtre.

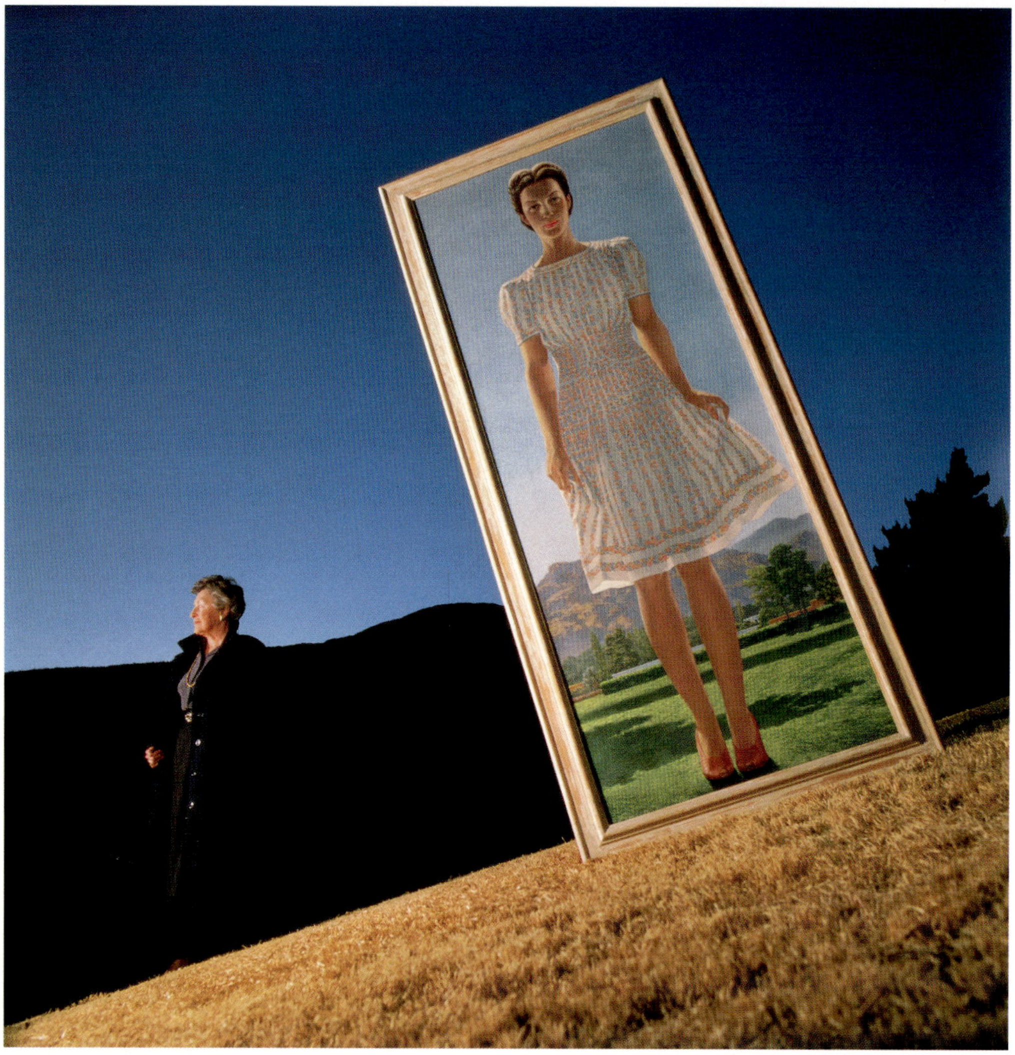

Danny Turner

In this photograph, part of a *Texas Monthly* series on portrait paintings and their subjects, Sarah Lea is shown with a portrait of herself, painted by her husband, the famous mural painter, Tom Lea, in 1947.

Für einen Foto-Essay in *Texas Monthly* über gemalte Porträts und die dargestellten Personen. Sarah Lea ist hier mit dem Porträt gezeigt, das ihr Mann, Tom Lea, ein berühmter Wandmaler, 1947 malte.

Pour un article du *Texas Monthly* présentant des portraits peints et leurs modèles. Sarah Lea pose à côté du portrait que son mari, Tom Lea, célèbre peintre de fresques américain, fit d'elle en 1947.

◁ Marcel van der Vlugt

A photographic interpretation of the picture »L'heure bleue«, painted in 1935 by Tamara de Lempicka (1900–1980).

Eine fotografische Interpretation des Bildes »L'heure bleue«, 1935, von Tamara de Lempicka (1900–1980).

Interprétation photographique du tableau «L'heure bleue», réalisé en 1935 par Tamara de Lempicka (1900–1980).

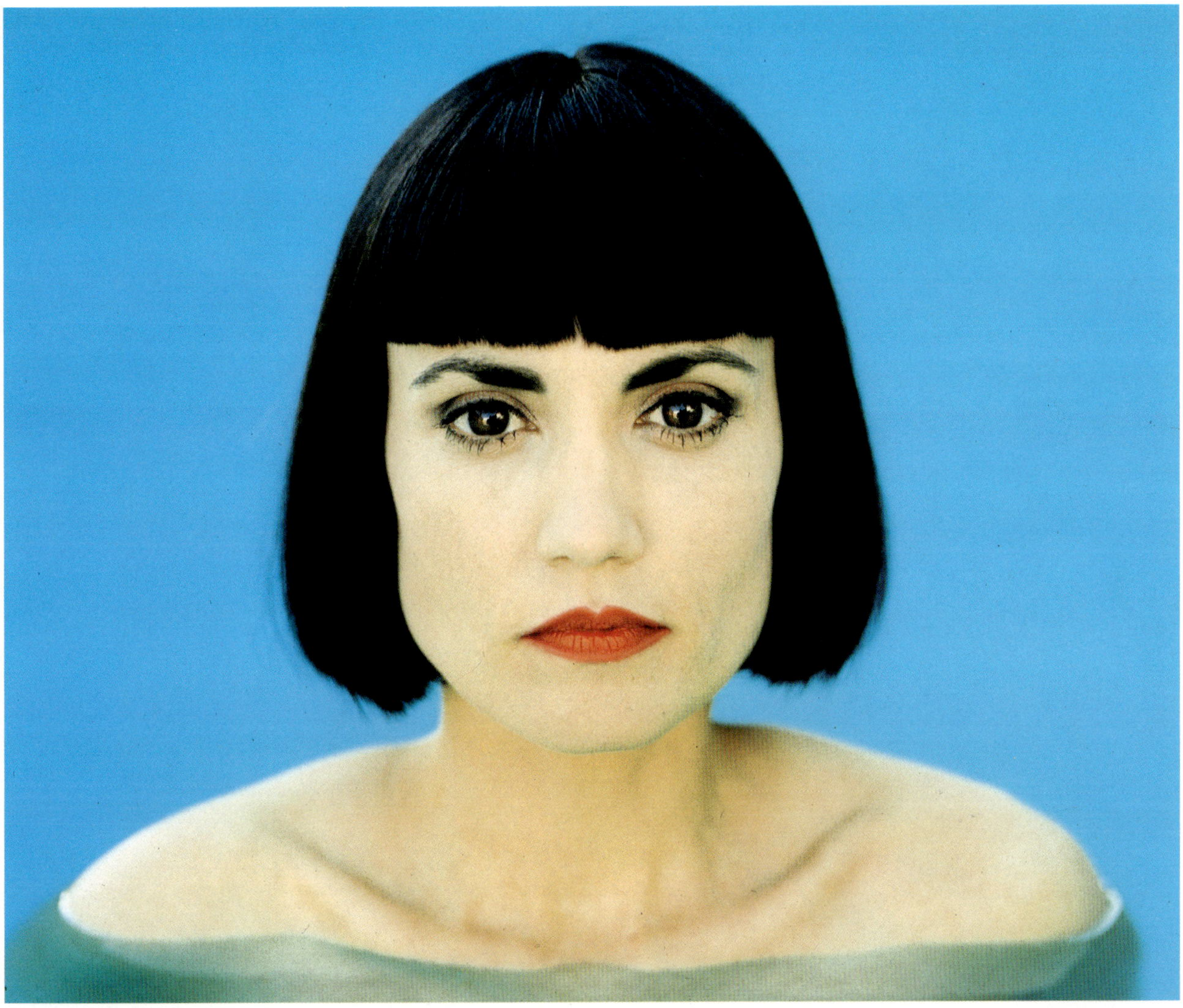

Roland Fischer

Concentrated but absent, close and yet far away – Roland Fischer photographs his models in swimming pools. Normally they stand in the water for an hour, clad in divers' suits, held down by weights, their arms crossed on their backs. He is interested in the model's look, the personality of the model is immaterial; some did not even recognize themselves afterwards.

Konzentriert sollen sie sein, aber ohne Anteilnahme, ganz nah und doch entrückt. Roland Fischer fotografiert seine Modelle im Swimmingpool. Meistens stehen sie eine Stunde im Wasser, eingezwängt in Taucheranzüge, mit Gewichten nach unten gezogen, die Arme auf dem Rücken verschränkt. Der Blick seiner Modelle interessiert ihn, die Persönlichkeit ist ihm gleichgültig. Manche haben sich nicht einmal wiedererkannt.

Totalement concentrée, à la fois proche et lointaine, la femme vue par Roland Fischer. Il fait poser ses modèles dans une piscine. La plupart du temps, elles sont obligées de rester une heure entière dans l'eau, le corps emprisonné dans un vêtement de plongée, les mains dans le dos, complètement immobiles. Leur personnalité lui importe peu, seul l'intensité du regard l'intéresse. Certaines ont eu de la peine à se reconnaître lorsqu'elles découvrent leur photo.

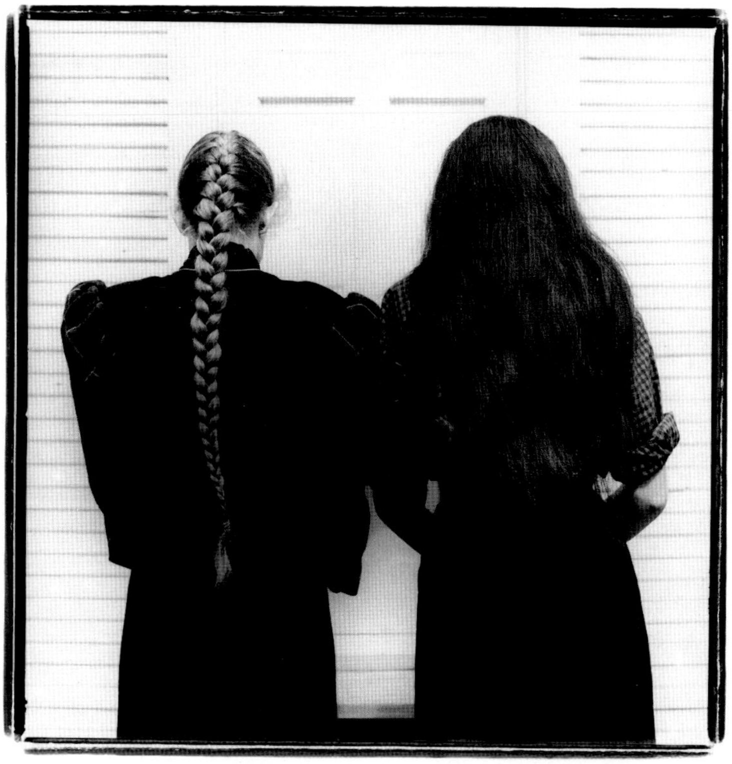

Keith Carter

This photo was made at a small non-denominational church on Little Cow Creek, Newton County in Texas.

Diese Aufnahme entstand in einer nicht konfessionsgebundenen kleinen Kirche in Little Cow Creek, Texas.

Cette photo a été réalisée dans une petite église de Little Cow Creek, dans le Newton County au Texas, qui n'est rattachée à aucune confession.

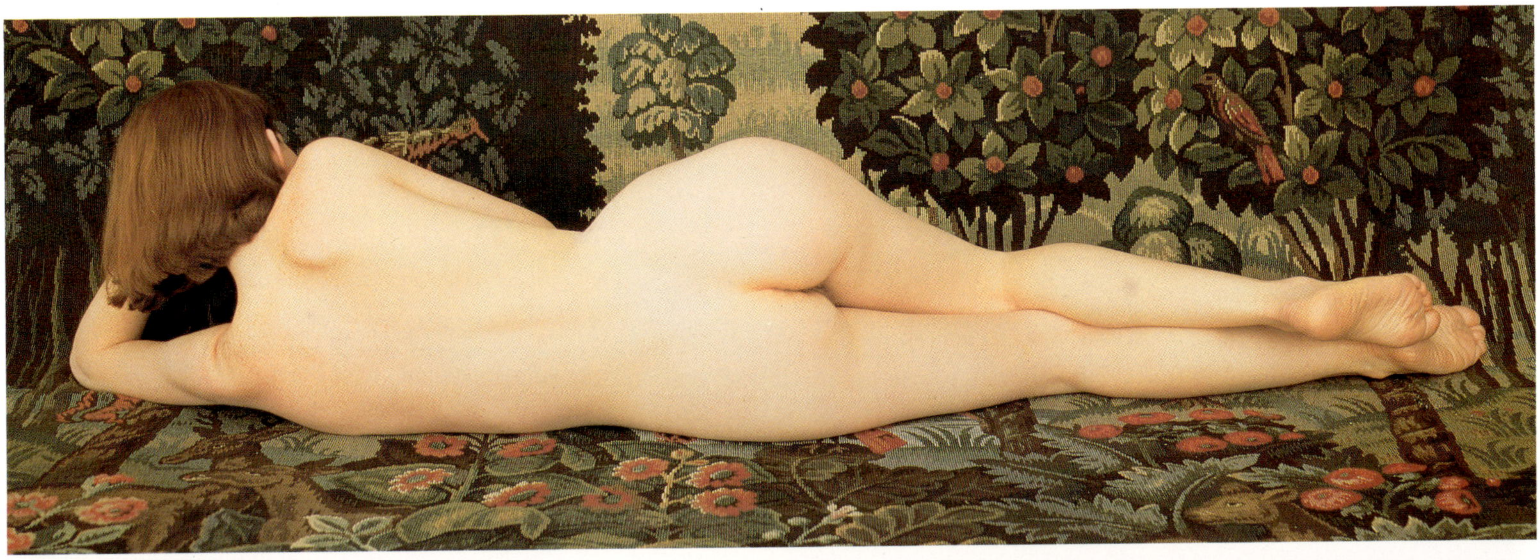

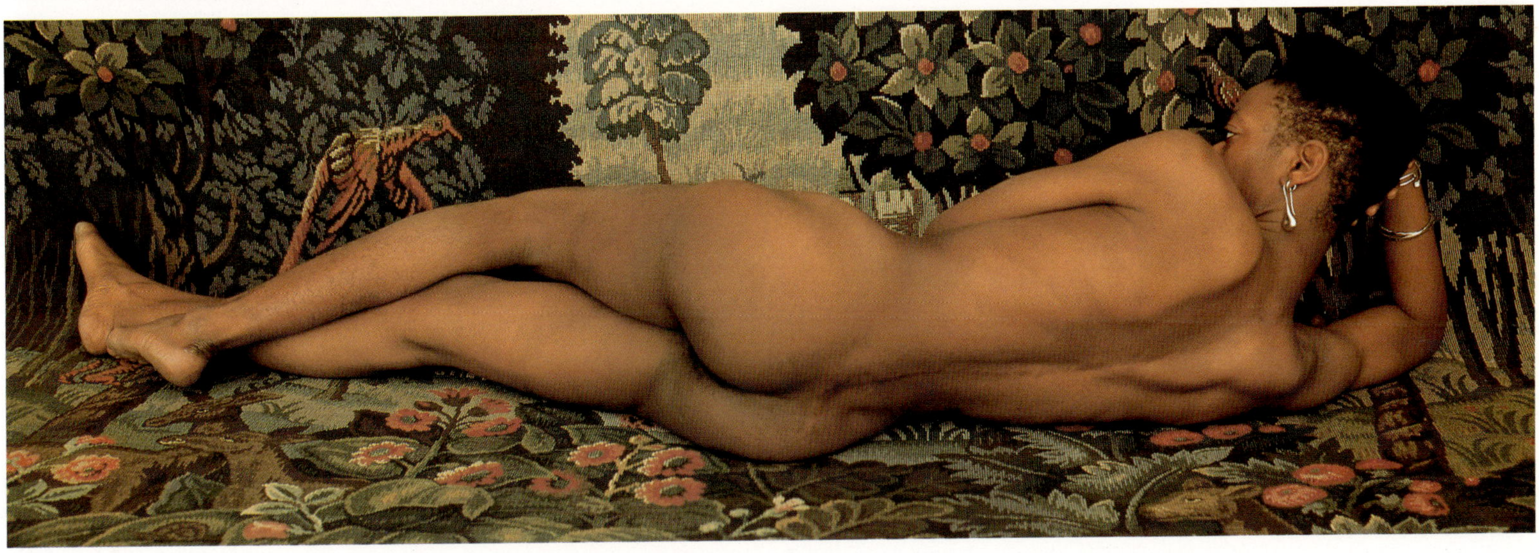

Yoshihiko Ueda

«Heaven» and «Earth» – self-promotional shots for photographer Yoshihiko Ueda.

»Himmel« und „Erde« – als Eigenwerbung verwendete Aufnahmen von Yoshihiko Ueda.

«Ciel» et «Terre» – autopromotion du photographe Yoshihiko Ueda.

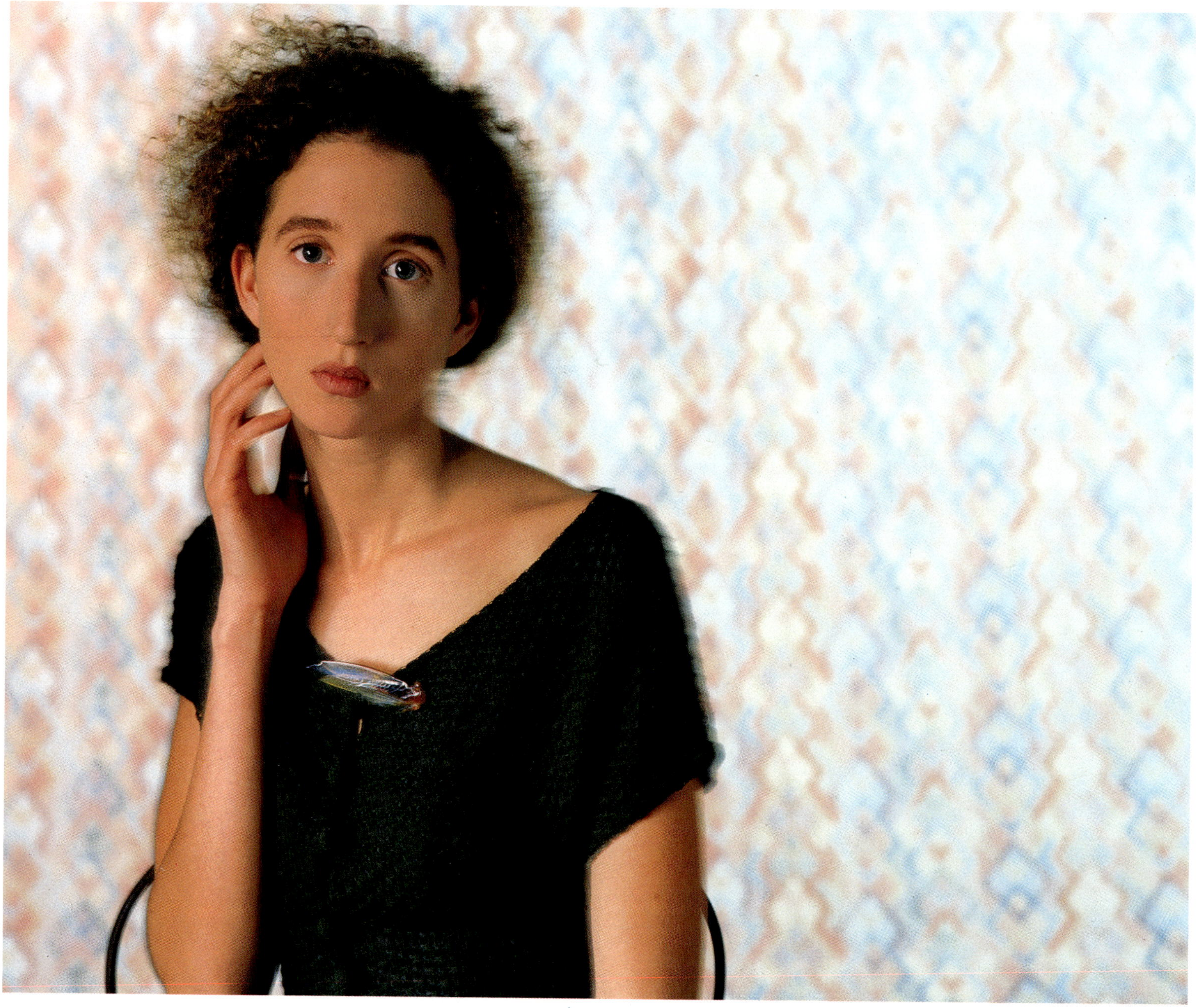

Lillian Birnbaum

It has been said that while Virginia Woolf had a gift for using clothing to describe a person, group or layer of society in her writing, she herself hated buying clothes. The model, who closely resembles the author, wears a dress typical of the style of Ms. Woolf's era: generous yet restrained.

Von Virginia Woolf wird behauptet, daß sie ein sicheres Gefühl für Kleidung hatte, wenn es galt, Menschen zu charakterisieren. Sie selbst aber haßte es einzukaufen. Das Modell, das der Schriftstellerin gleicht, trägt ein Kleid, das auch Virginia Woolf getragen haben könnte: freizügig und zugeknöpft zugleich.

On dit que Virginia Woolf avait un goût très sûr quand il s'agissait de caractériser le vêtement d'une personne ou d'une classe sociale. Elle-même détestait aller dans les magasins. Le modèle, qui ressemble à l'écrivain, porte comme elle un vêtement ample et boutonné, laissant le corps libre.

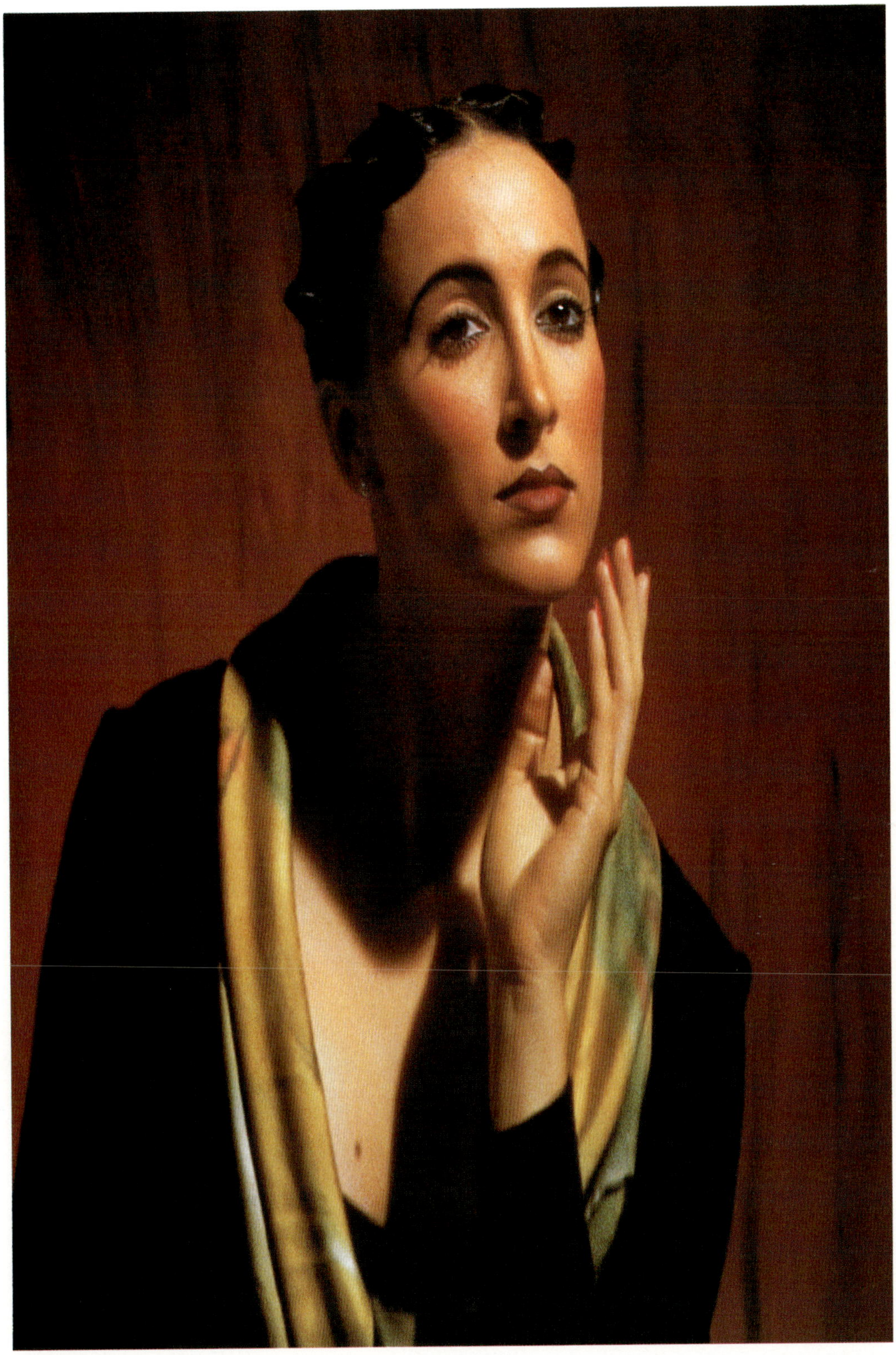

Denis Chapoullié

Portrait of a young woman by Denis Chapoullié.

Porträt einer jungen Frau von Denis Chapoullié.

Portrait d'une jeune femme par Denis Chapoullié.

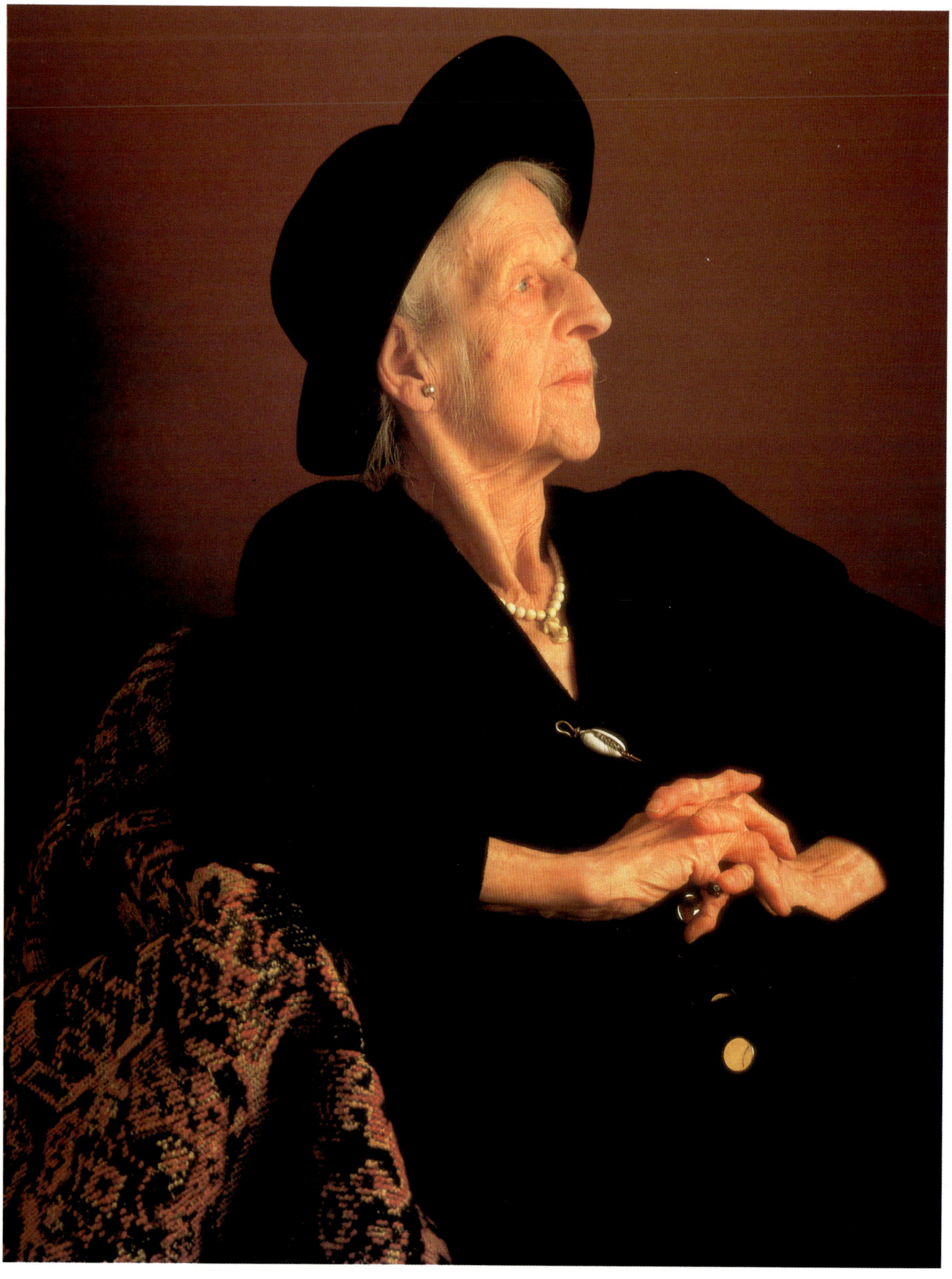

Chris Shorten

»Miss Olive English, born 1902« – portrait of an old lady, from a self-promotional catalogue for the Shorten Winston Studio.

»Miss Olive English, geb. 1902« – Porträt einer alten Dame aus einem Eigenwerbungskatalog des Studios Shorten Winston.

«Miss Olive English, née en 1902» – portrait d'une vieille dame, dans le catalogue autopromotionnel du studio Shorten Winston.

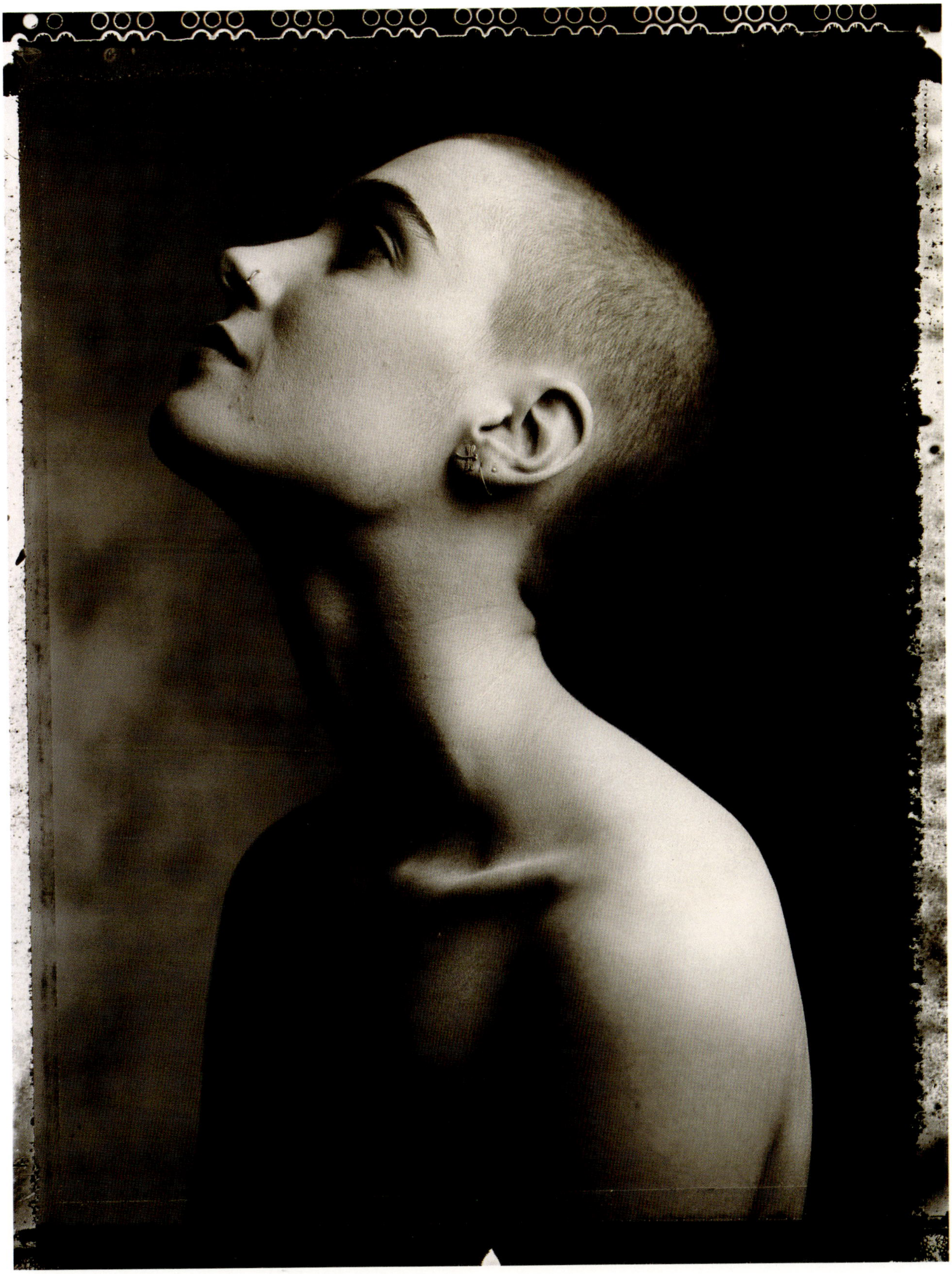

Marc Hauser

This earnest, contemplative face was among those used in a calendar.

Ernste Gesichter, nachdenklich, versonnen. Dieses Porträt wurde für einen Kalender verwendet.

Des visages sérieux, méditatifs, concentrés. Ce portrait a été reproduit dans un calendrier.

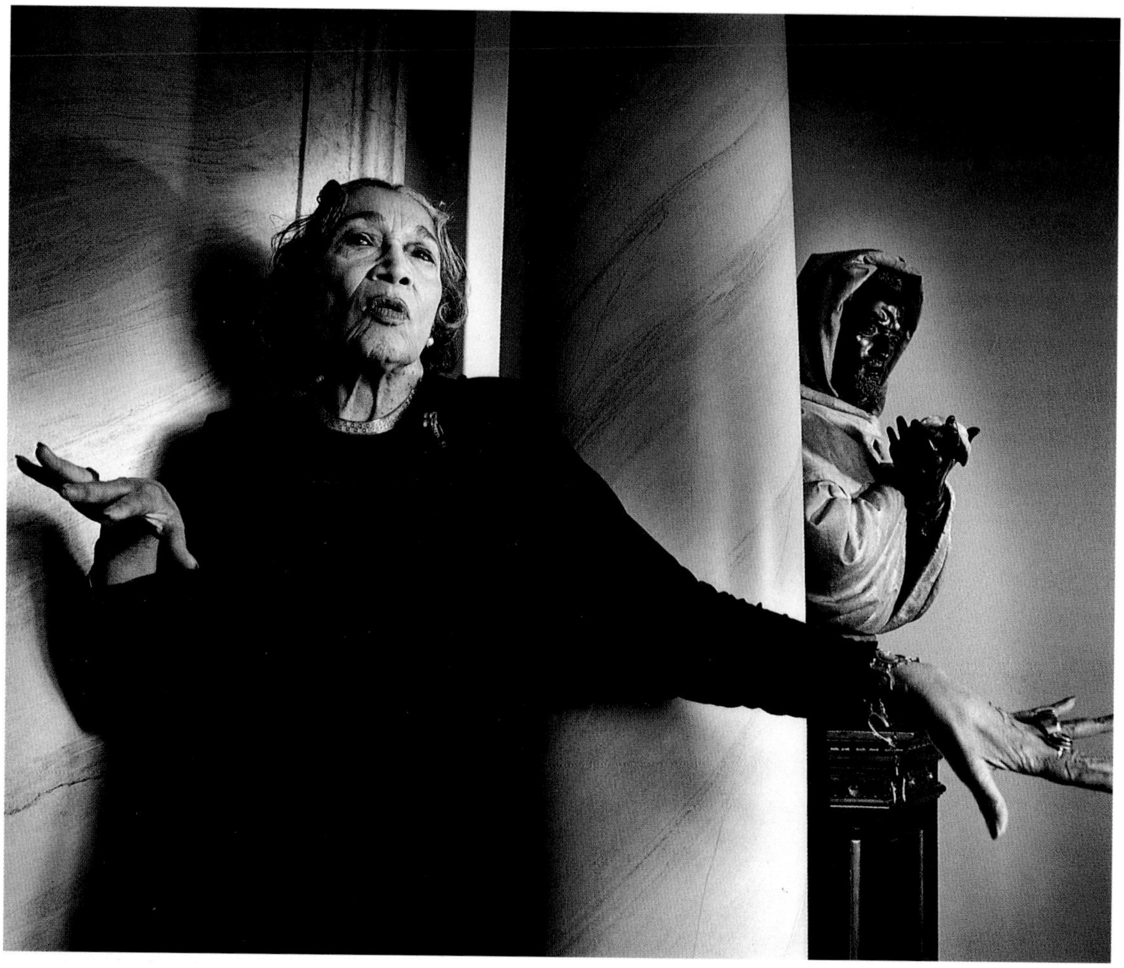

David Gamble

Portrait of American Jazz singer Elizabeth Welch.

Porträt der amerikanischen Jazzsängerin Elizabeth Welch.

La chanteuse de Jazz américaine Elizabeth Welch.

Brian Lanker

From a series featuring portraits of prominent black women: Septima Clark, one of the heroes of the civil rights movement; Ms. Coretta Scott King, President and Chief Executive of the King Center For Non-Violent Social Change; and Eva Jessye, Choral Director for the first Broadway production of »Porgy and Bess«.

Schwarze Frauen, die in der Entwicklung der USA eine große Rolle spielten: Septima Clark, eine der Vertreterinnen der Bürgerrechtsbewegung, Coretta Scott King, Direktorin und Leiterin des King-Zentrums für gewaltlose soziale Veränderungen und Eva Jessye, Chorleiterin der ersten Broadway-Produktion von »Porgy und Bess«.

D'un projet personnel qui montre les femmes de couleur ayant joué un rôle important aux USA: Septima Clark, représentante du mouvement des droits civiques; Coretta Scott King, directrice du King Center, qui s'engage pour des transformations sociales sans violence; la directrice des chœurs de la première production de «Porgy and Bess» à Broadway, Eva Jessye.

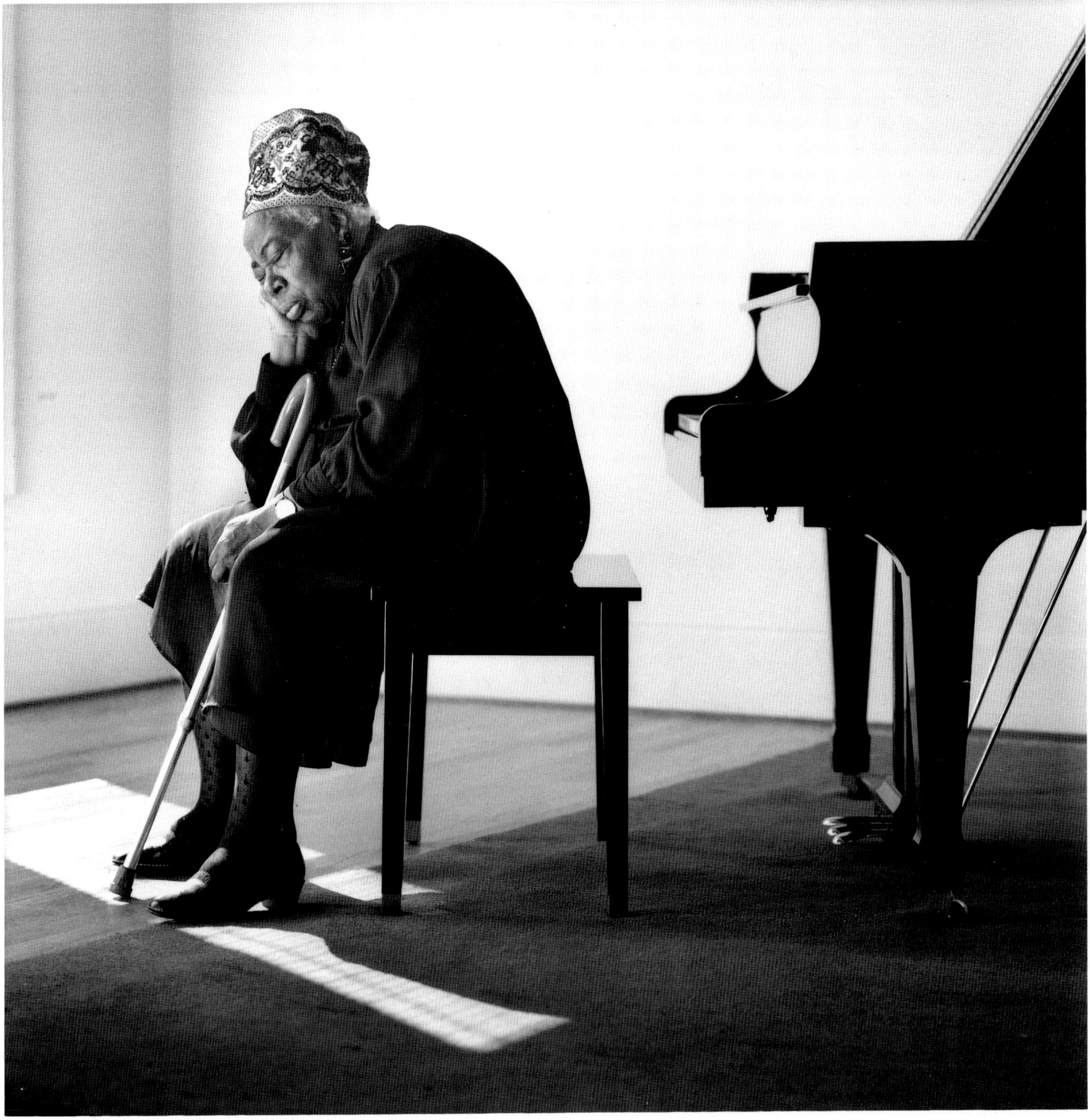

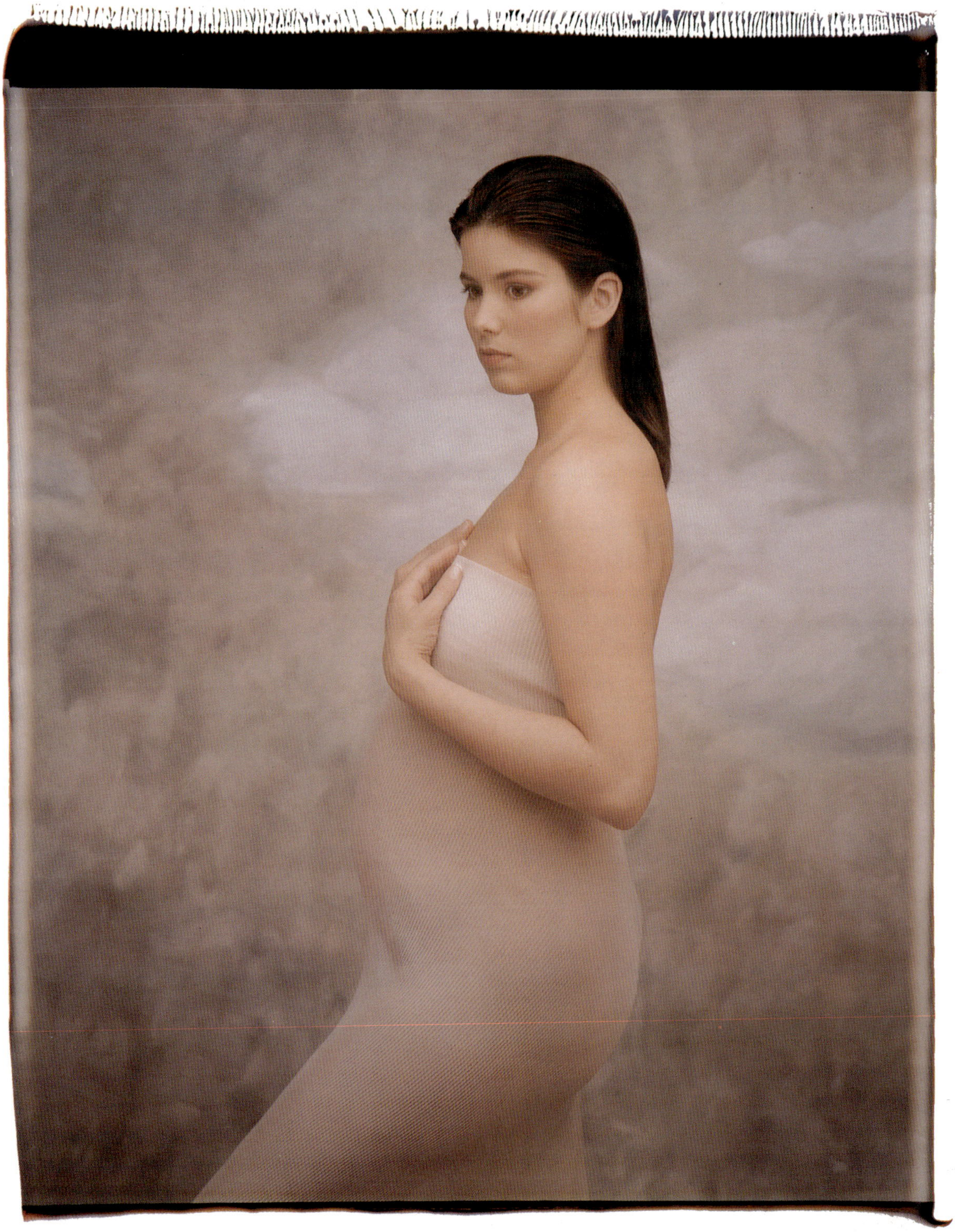

Joyce Tenneson

This photograph illustrated an article in *Parenting* magazine on breast cancer which is being diagnosed in an increasing number of young mothers. A soft box from the ceiling and two on the floor were used to produce even, flat light.

Die Aufnahme illustrierte einen Beitrag im Magazin *Parenting* über Brustkrebs, der in zunehmendem Masse auch bei jungen Müttern festgestellt wird. Eine Softbox an der Decke und zwei auf dem Boden sorgten für gleichmäßiges, gedämpftes Licht.

Cette photo illustrait un article du magazine *Parenting* sur le cancer du sein, qui est de plus en plus diagnostiqué chez les jeunes mères. La lumière régulière a été obtenue à l'aide d'une softbox au plafond et de deux sur le sol.

Michel Sabah

»Sensible, efficient, and enchanting« – this was the headline for an advertisement for Konica camera, for which this photograph was assigned.

»Sensibel, effizient und zauberhaft« – so die Headline einer Anzeige für Konica-Kameras, für die diese Aufnahme gemacht wurde.

«Sensible, efficace et magique» – tel était le gros titre de l'annonce de l'appareil-photo Konica, pour laquelle cette photographie a été réalisée.

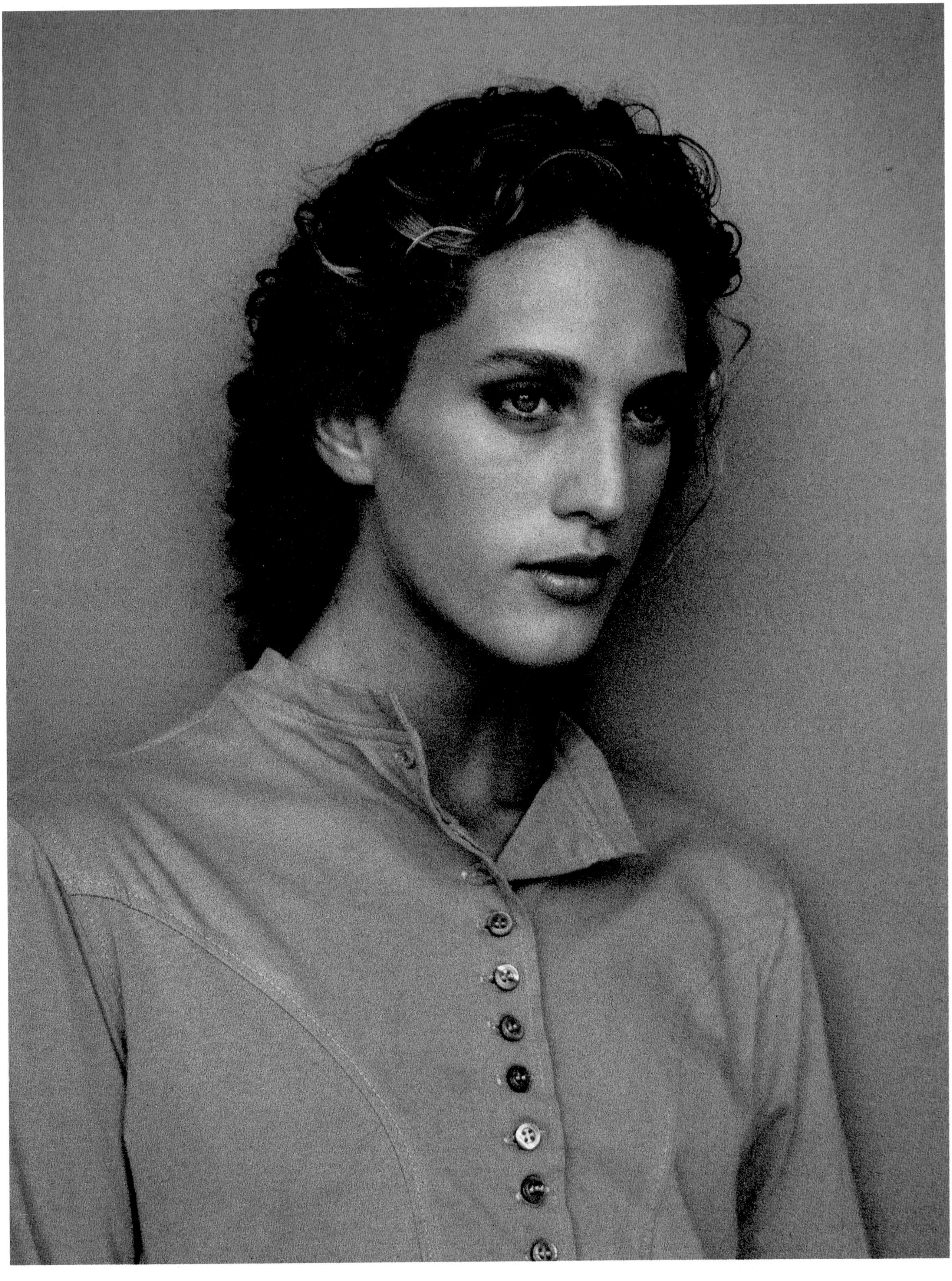

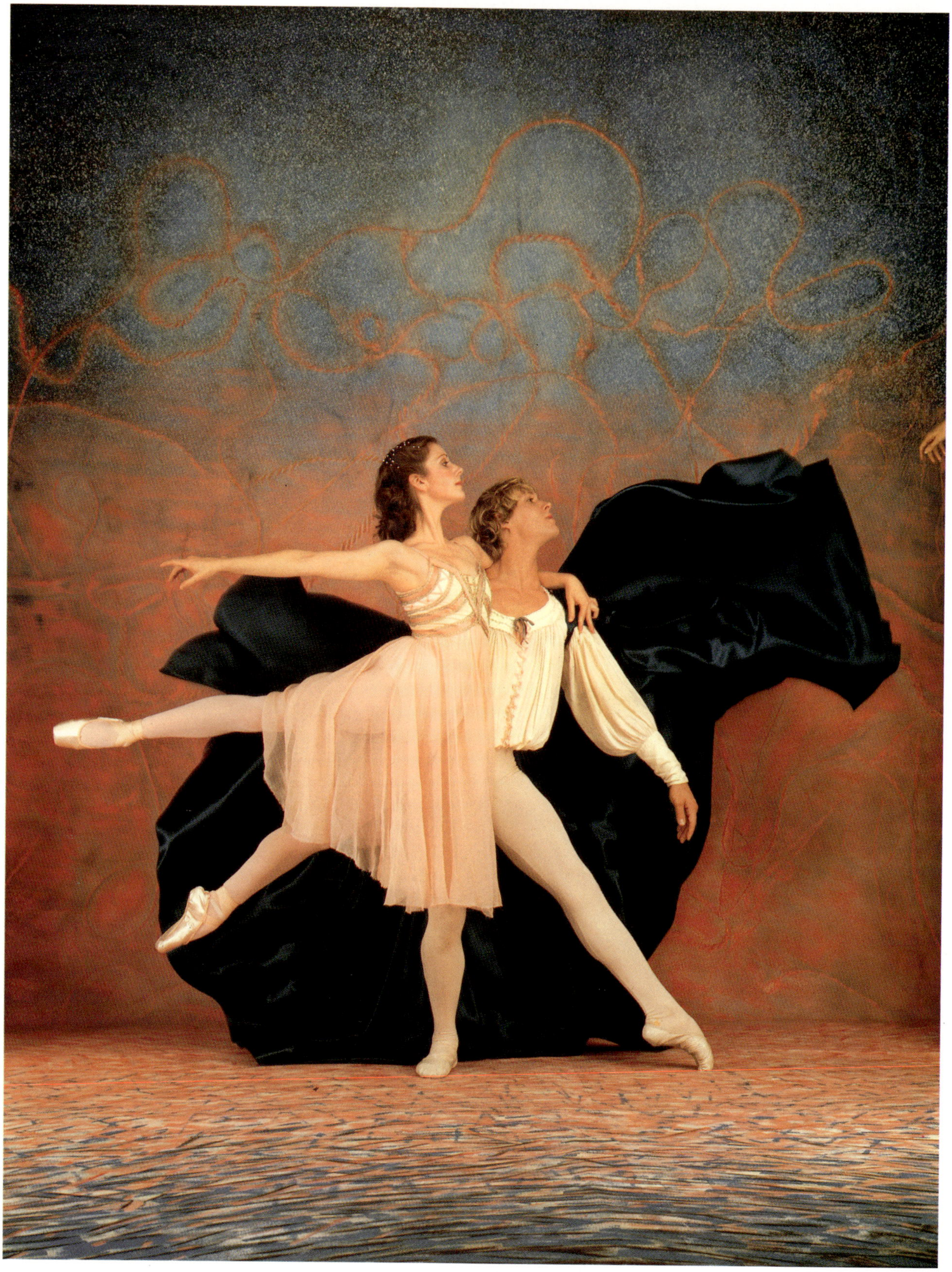

Gilles Larrain

Romeo and Juliet: As the picture was to be used for a life-size poster, Gilles Larrain took the action photograph with a large-format camera. The satin cloth was used as an additional element to add motion. The falling cloth, expression and movement of the dancers, had to be exactly planned and timed.

Romeo und Julia. Gilles Larrain benutzte eine Großformat-Kamera, weil die Aufnahme für ein lebensgroßes Plakat verwendet werden sollte. Das Satintuch sorgt für mehr Bewegung im Bild.

Roméo et Juliette. Gilles Larrain a utilisé un appareil grand format, car les clichés devaient être utilisés pour une affiche grandeur nature. L'étoffe de satin devait donner une certaine dynamique à l'image.

Marc Hauser

A Polaroid portrait simply entitled »Pat« serves as a self-promotional piece for photographer Marc Hauser.

»Pat«. Ein Polaroid-Porträt, das der Fotograf Marc Hauser als Eigenwerbung verwendet.

«Pat». Un portrait au Polaroïd, utilisé comme autopromotion par le photographe Marc Hauser.

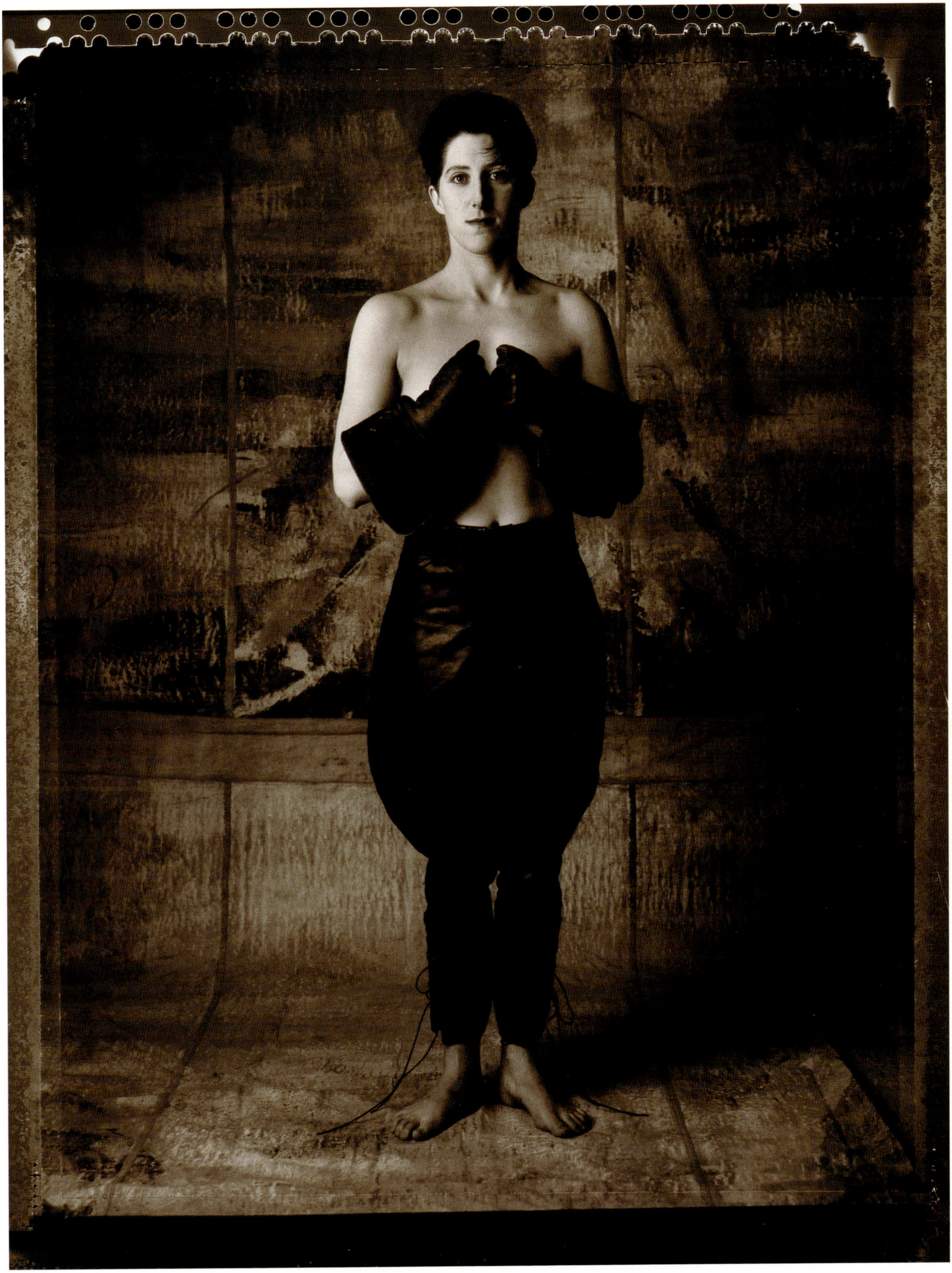

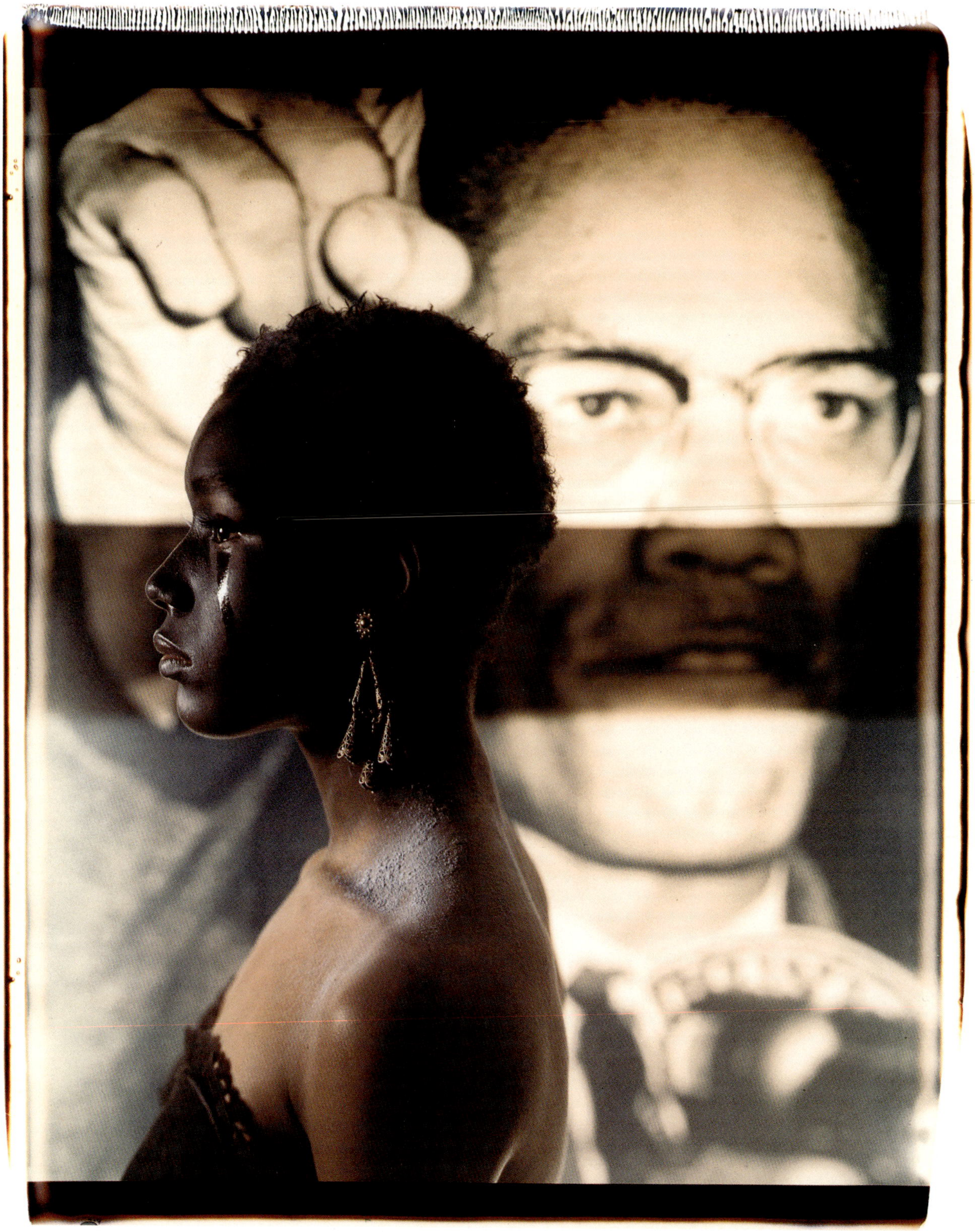

Ron Baxter Smith

Black impressions of America: The images are meant as a protest against the generalizations and stereotypes of African-Americans in the media. The late Malcolm X, American civil rights leader appears with raised arm in the background.

Schwarze Impressionen aus Amerika. Diese Fotografien sind ein Protest gegen die stereotype Darstellung der Amerikaner afrikanischer Herkunft in den Medien. Die Faust gehört Malcolm X.

Impressions d'Amérique. Ces photos sont une protestation contre l'image stéréotypée des Américains d'origine africaine dans les médias.

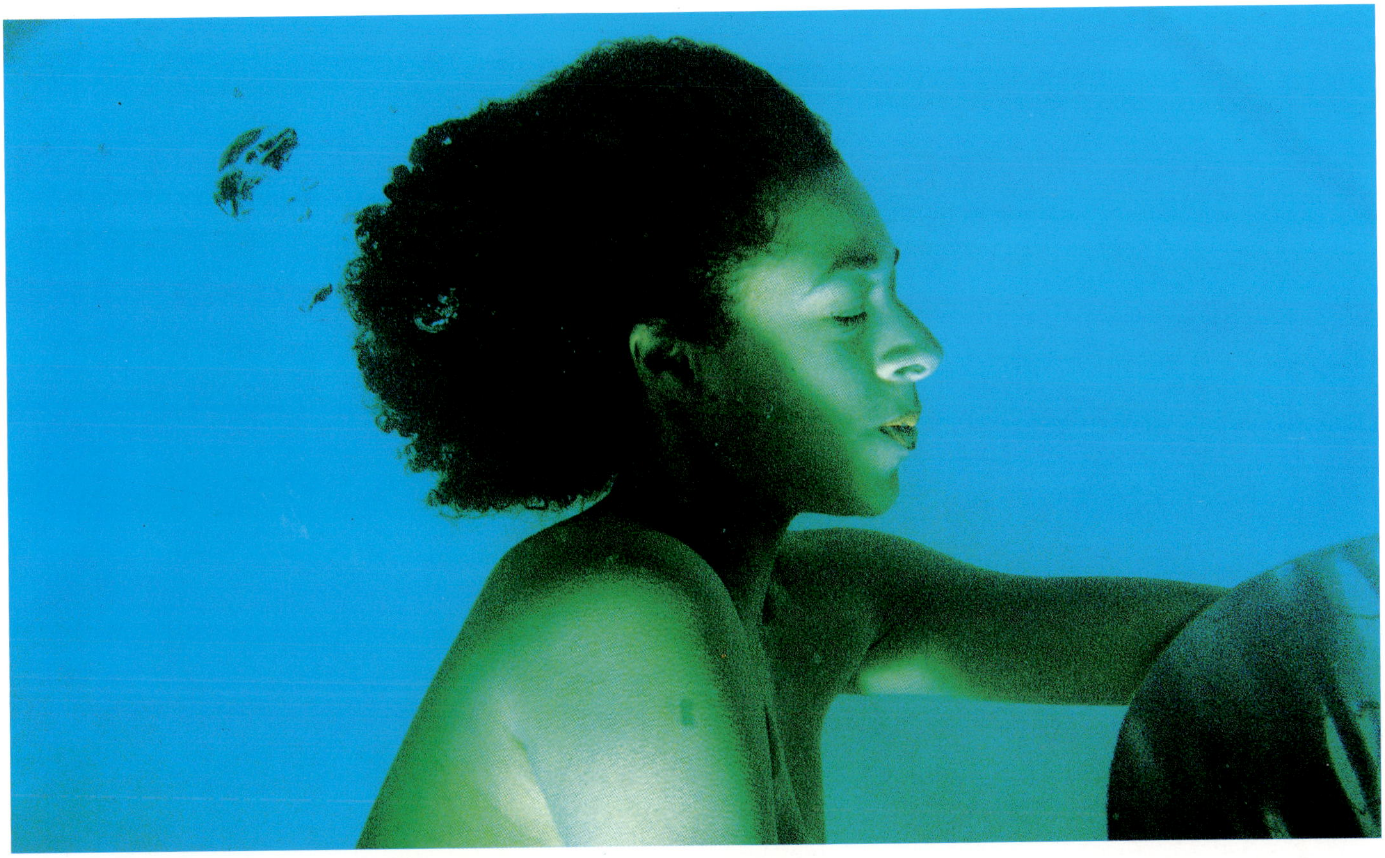

Walter Fogel

Under water, man loses his shyness of the camera and moves freely, weightlessly. The photographer used coloured gel sheets, positive film developed as negative film, and a self-devised flash in combination with his camera.

Unter Wasser verliert der Mensch die Scheu vor der Kamera, er bewegt sich schwerelos und frei. Der Fotograf benutzte farbige Lackfolien, einen Diafilm, der als Negativfilm entwickelt wurde, und eine von ihm konstruierte Blitzanlage.

Sous l'eau, l'individu perd toute inhibition devant l'appareil photo; il se meut en apesanteur, librement. Walter Fogel a utilisé ici de la toile cirée, un film positif développé comme un négatif et un flash qu'il a construit lui-même.

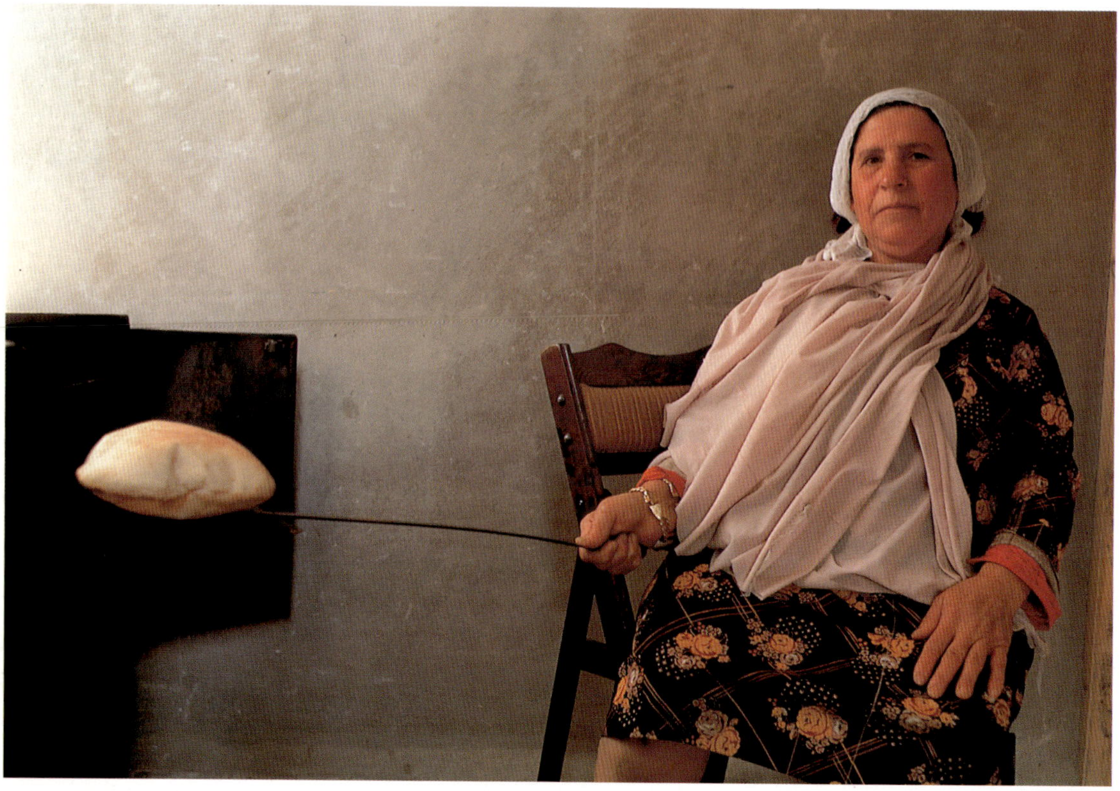

John Running

»Making Bread«, photographed at Al Hussein Camp, Jordan, and published in a book.

»Brotbacken«, in einem Buch veröffentlichte Aufnahme, die im Lager Al Hussein, Jordanien, entstand.

«La Cuisson du Pain». Photo prise dans le Camp d'Al Hussein, en Jordanie, et publiée dans un livre.

Herb Ritts

Portrait of Madonna which appeared with photos from her banned clip in a special issue on rock stars of French magazine *Photo*.

Porträt von Madonna, das zusammen mit Aufnahmen ihres verbotenen Clips in einer Nummer des Magazins *Photo* über Rockstars veröffentlicht wurde.

Portrait de Madonna paru dans un numéro spécial du magazine français *Photo*, dans lequel furent publiées les photos du clip interdit de la chanteuse.

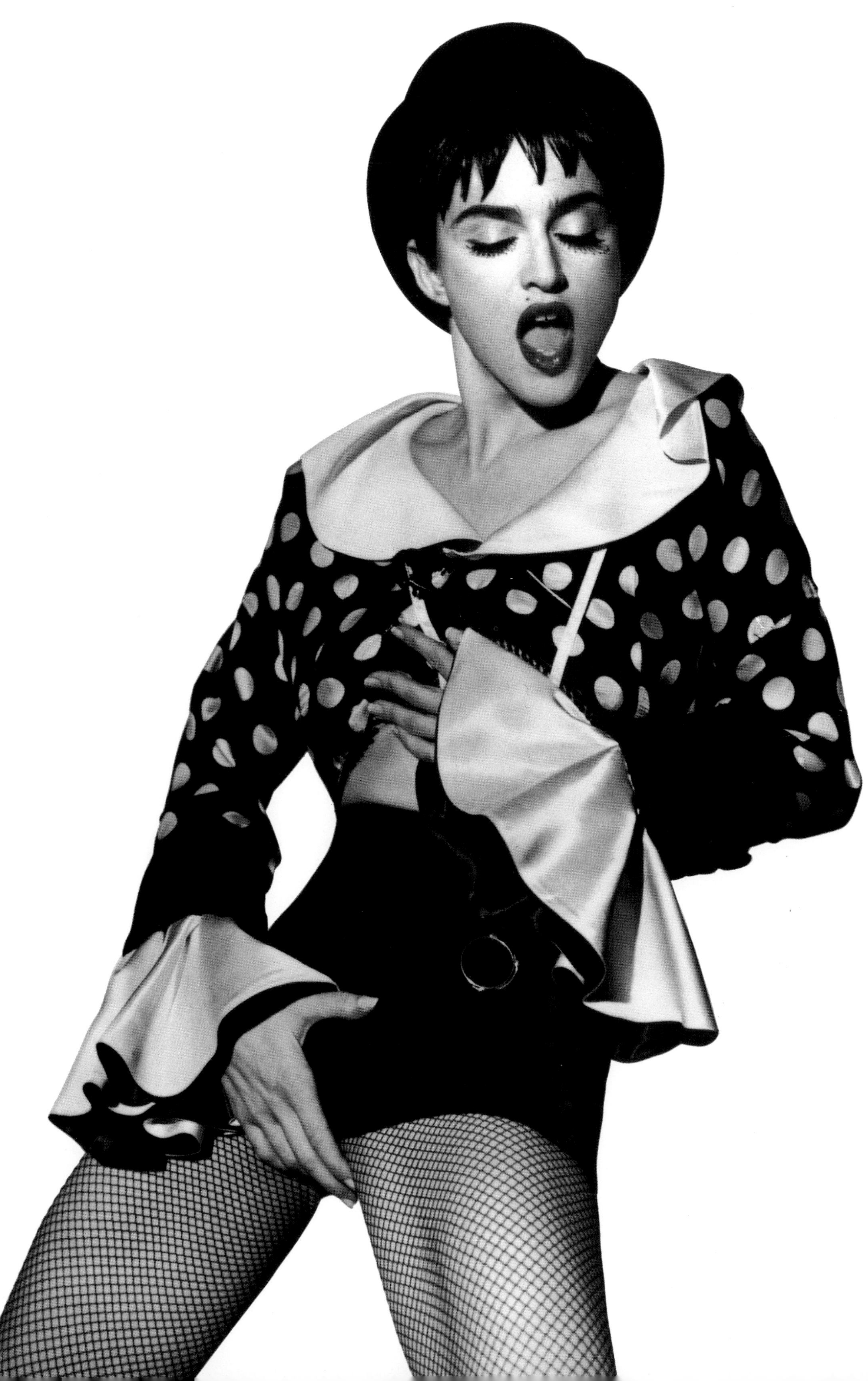

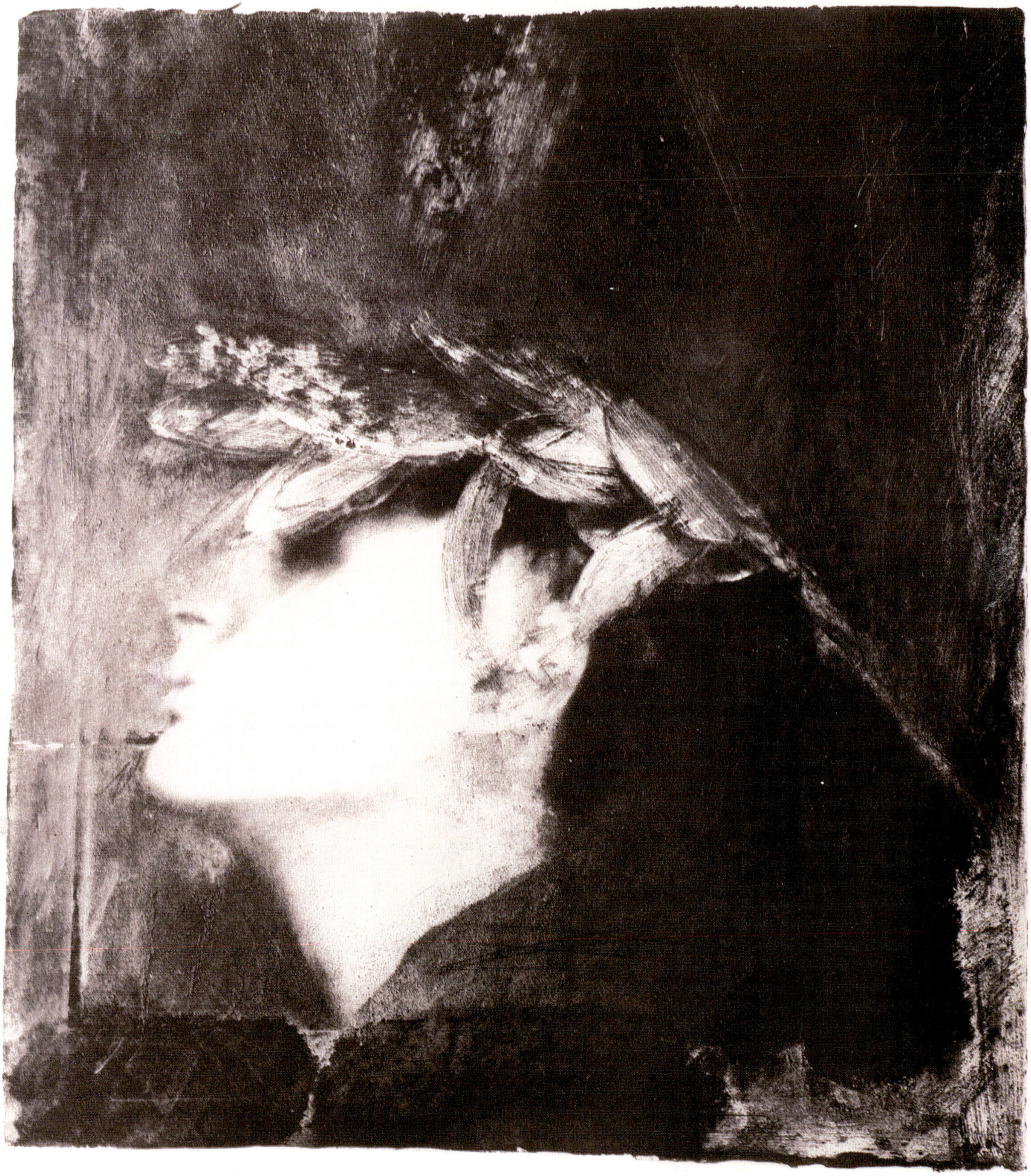

David Hiscock

His photographs are not only exhibited in large fashion stores but also at Madame Tussaud's.

Seine Bilder sind nicht nur in großen Modehäusern ausgestellt, sondern auch bei Madame Tussaud.

Ses photos sont non seulement exposées dans les grands magasins de mode, mais aussi chez Madame Tussaud.

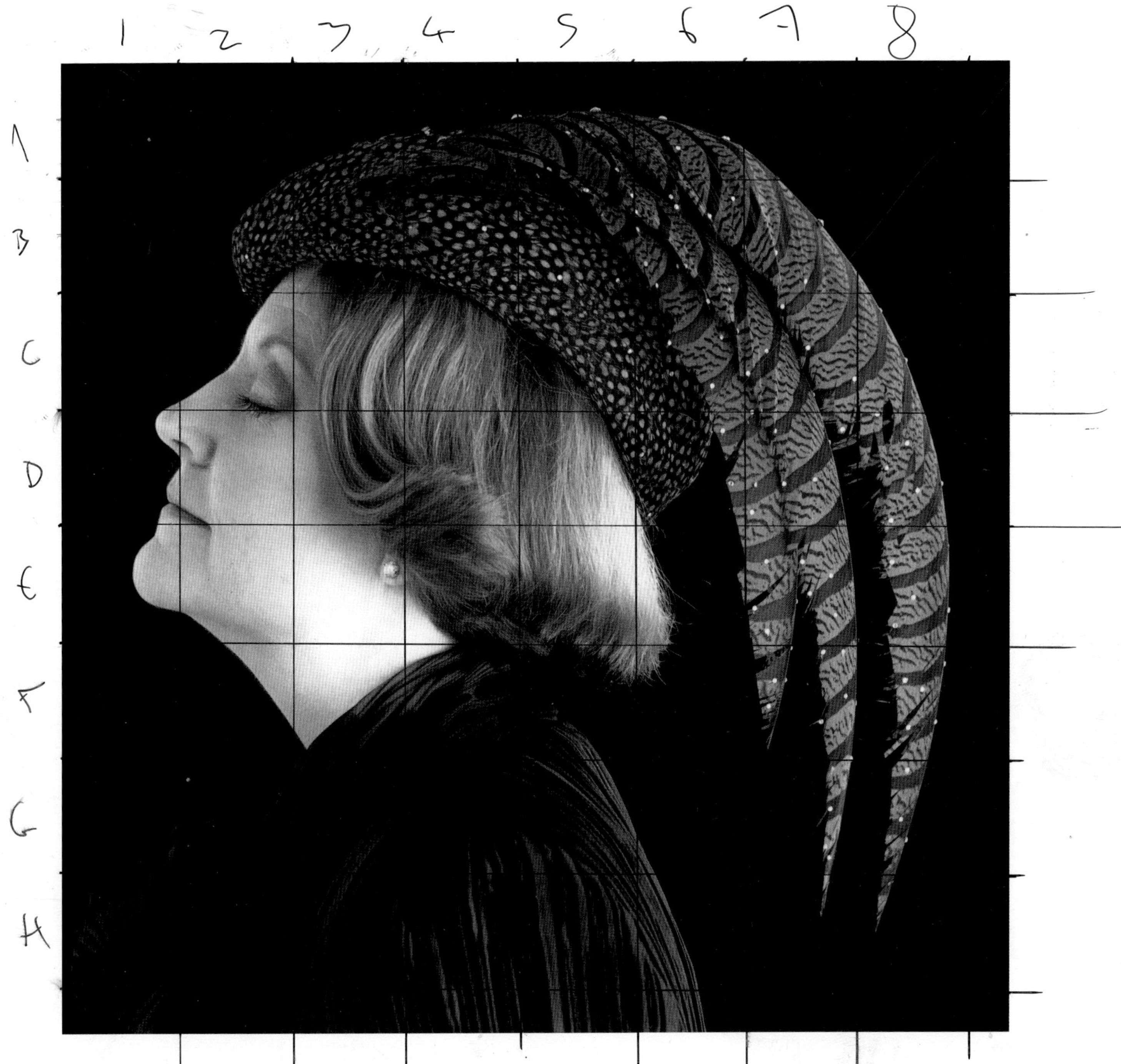

Howard Schatz

Gifted Women is the title of a book that celebrates talented, successful women from the San Francisco Bay area.

Gifted Women ist der Titel eines Buches, das begabten, erfolgreichen Frauen aus der Gegend von San Francisco gewidmet ist.

Gifted Women est un livre qui rassemble des portraits de femmes de la région de San Francisco qui ont réussi.

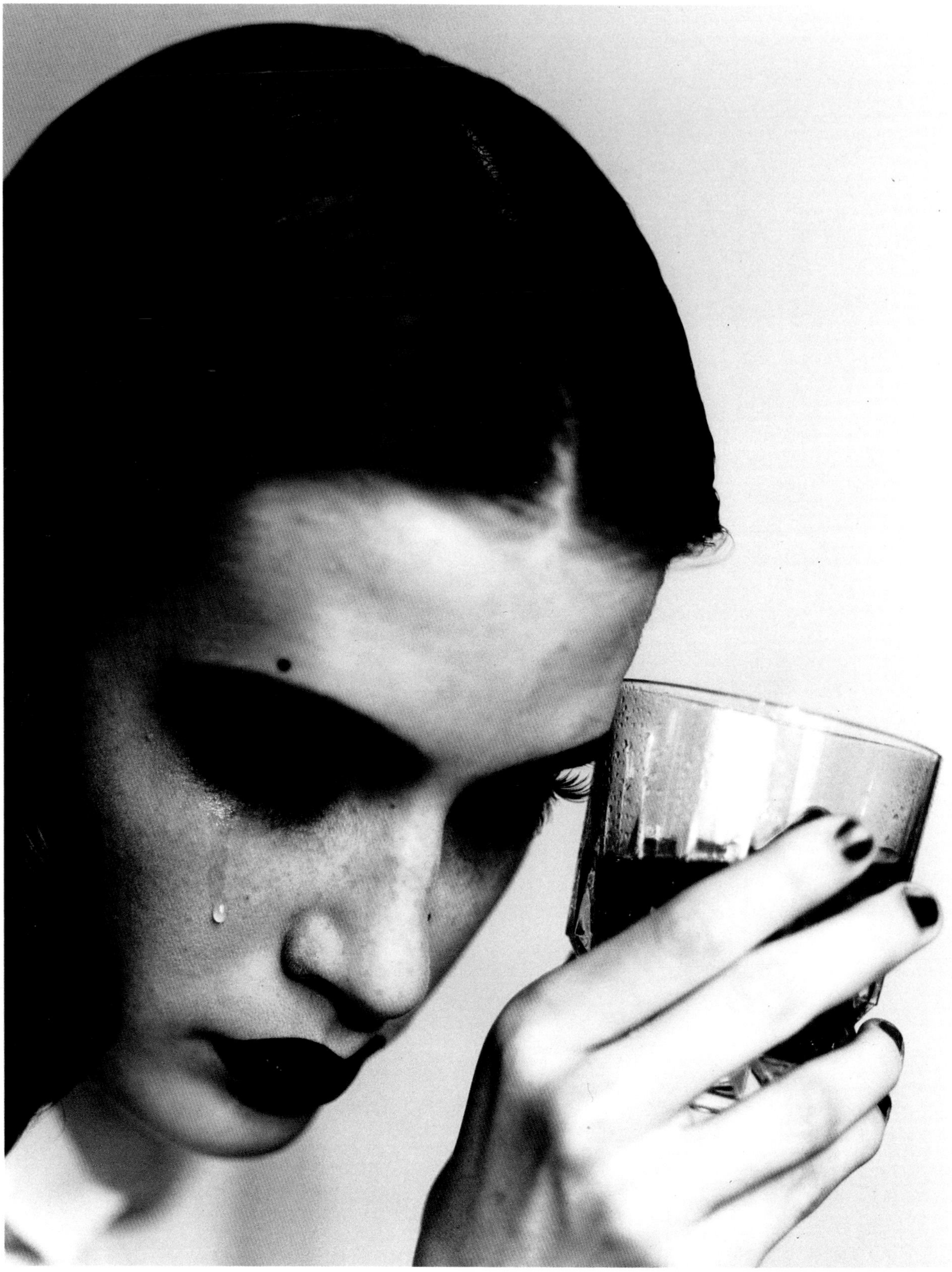

Michel Dubois

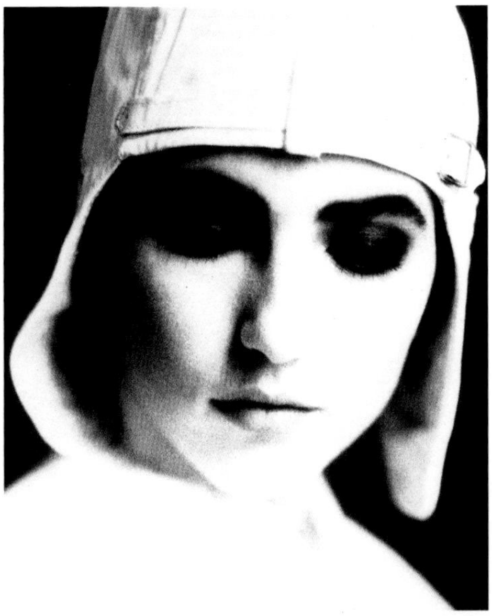

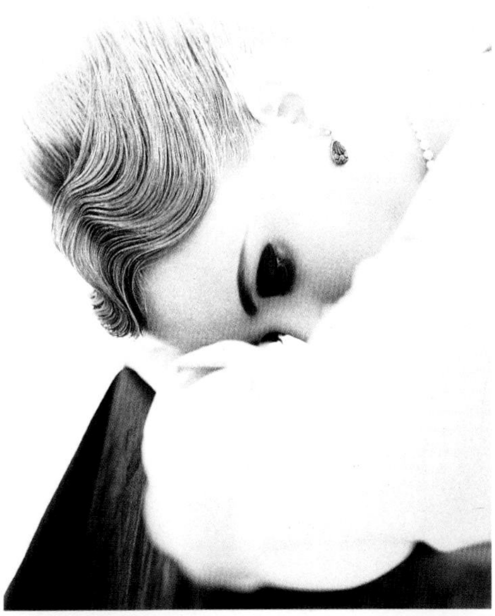

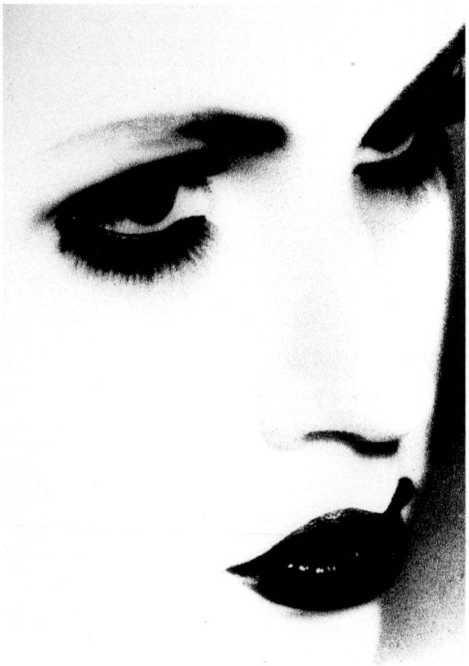

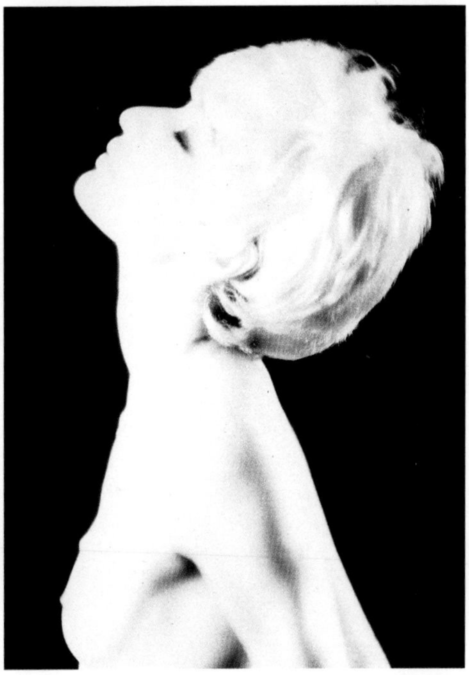

Michel Dubois

Mnemosyne is the title Michel Dubois gave to his book of images of women with poetic texts by Jean-David Jumeau-Lafond. Mnemosyne is the goddess of memory, mother of the nine Muses, and this work concerns itself with unreal memories, with which the observer feels acquainted.

Mnemosyne nennt Michel Dubois seinen Fotoband mit Frauenbildern und Texten von Jean-David Jumeau-Lafond. Mnemosyne ist die Göttin des Gedächtnisses, Mutter der neun Musen, und in diesem Band geht es um Erinnerungen, nicht real aber möglich.

Ces photos de Michel Dubois figurent dans un livre au titre évocateur de *Mnemosyne*, personnification de la Mémoire dans la mythologie grecque et la mère des neuf Muses. Les images de femmes sont accompagnées d'un texte de Jean-David Jumeau-Lafond. L'ouvrage met en scène des souvenirs imaginaires, qui peuvent toutefois paraître familiers au spectateur.

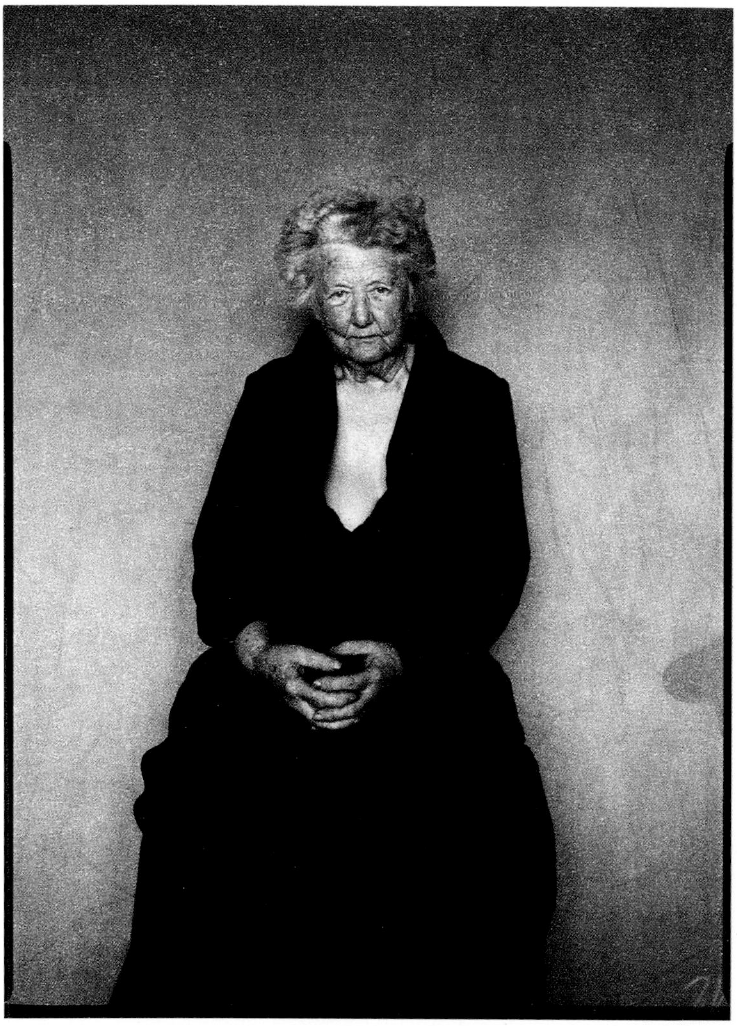

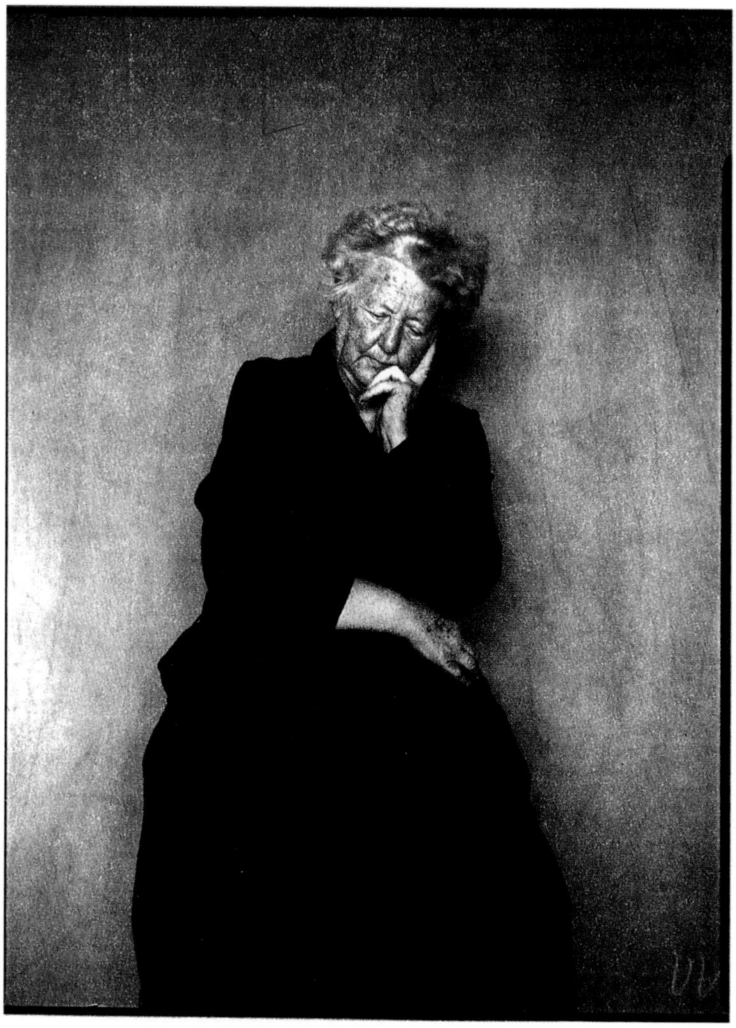

Chrysantha

These two photographs entitled »Portrait of Charlotte« are part of a portrait series for an exhibition. The photographer produced the negative material herself; Print: Gelatine Silver 25 x 33.5 cm.

Die beiden Aufnahmen mit dem Titel »Porträt Charlotte« entstanden innerhalb eines Porträt-Zyklus für eine Ausstellung der Fotografin. Das Negativmaterial stellte sie selbst her. Abzug: Gelatine Silber 25 x 33,5 cm.

Les photos intitulées «Portrait de Charlotte» font partie d'un cycle de portraits, réalisés pour une exposition. La photographe a préparé elle-même son négatif. Tirage: Gelatine Argent 25 x 33,5 cm.

Albert Watson

Sharon Stone, a popular American actress was photographed for the cover of *Rolling Stone*.

Sharon Stone, der heißeste Filmstar des Jahres 1992, für einen Umschlag von *Rolling Stone* fotografiert.

Sharon Stone, l'actrice la plus torride de l'année 92, photographiée pour une couverture du magazine *Rolling Stone*.

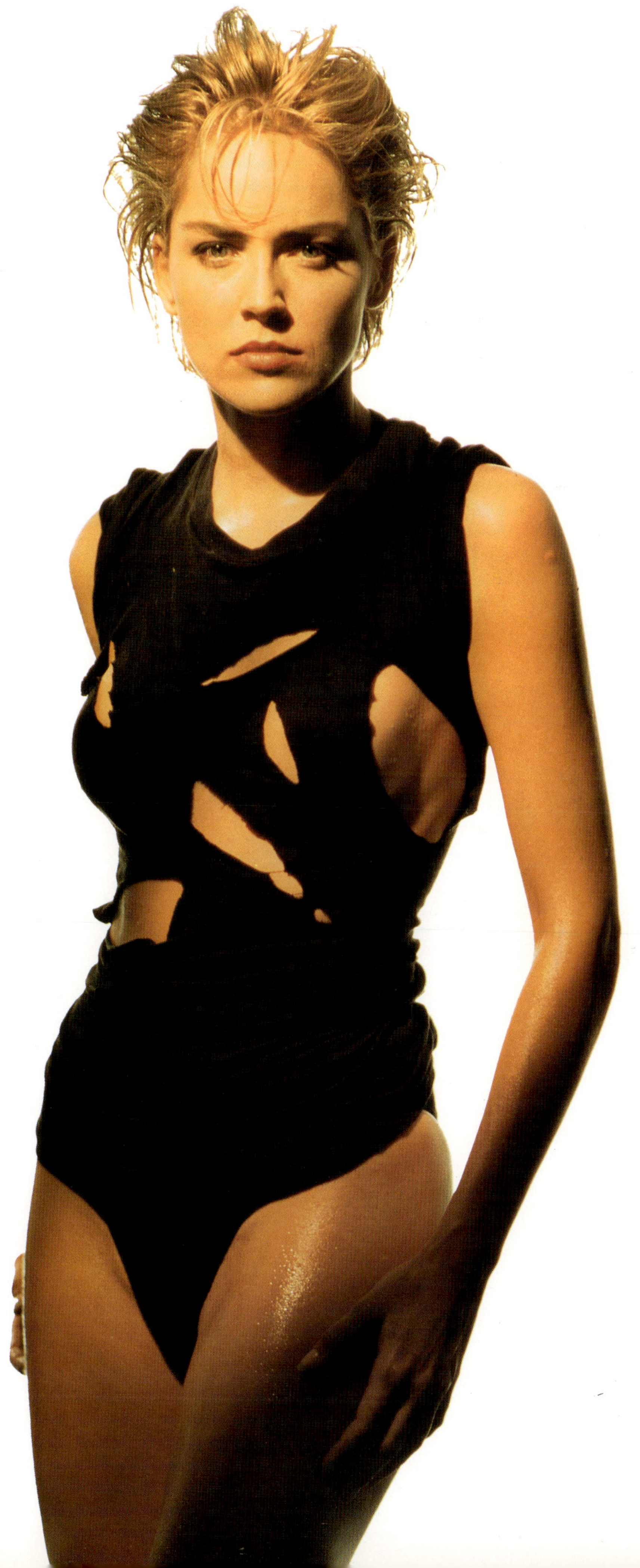

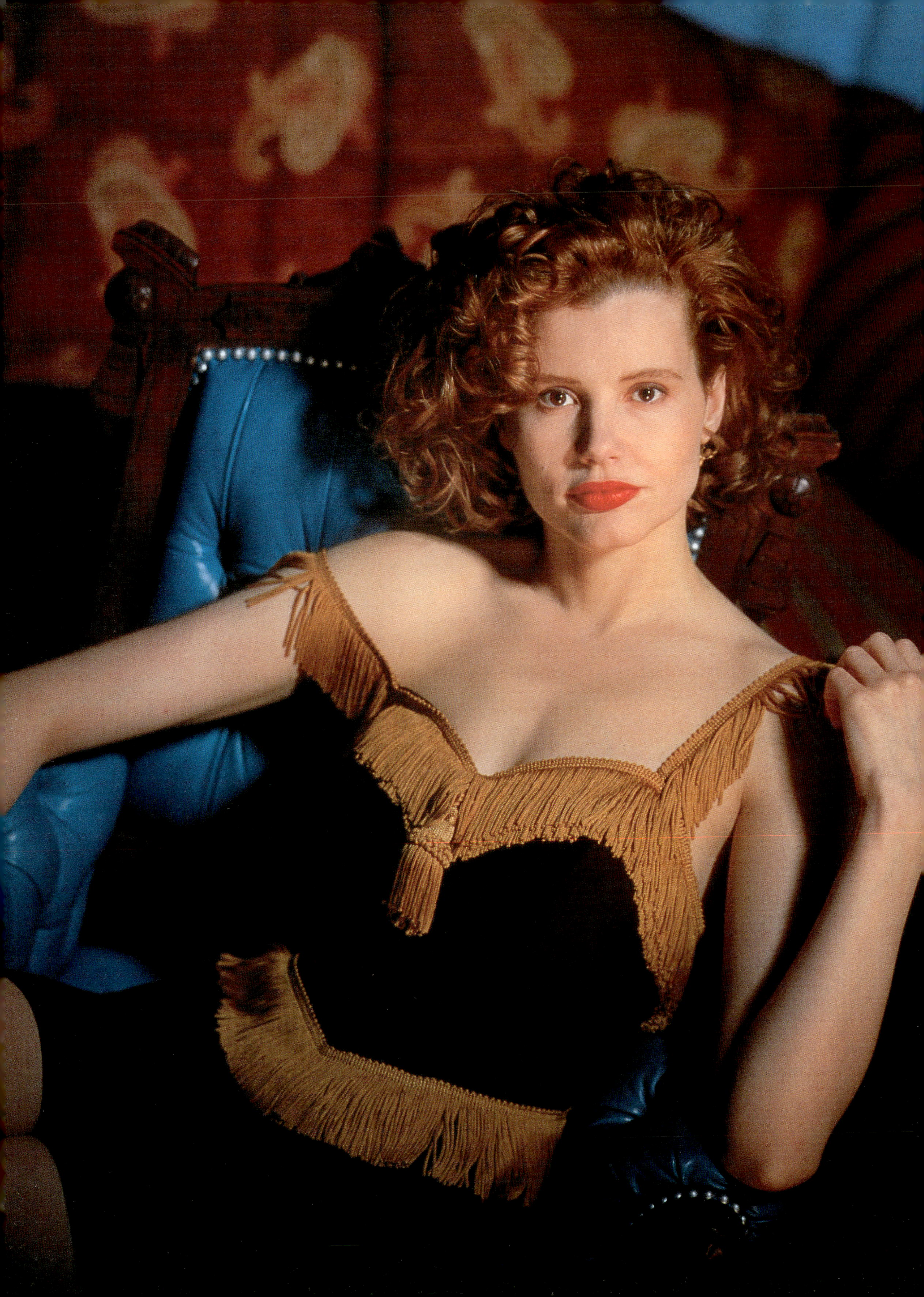

◁ Gregory Heisler

Portrait of Geena Davis, from a cover story for the men's magazine *Esquire* entitled »Women we love«, in which the editors took an affectionate look at their favourite personalities.

Portrait de l'actrice de cinéma Geena Davis. Cette photographie a été réalisée pour un projet du magazine *Esquire* intitulé «Les femmes que nous aimons».

Porträt der Filmschauspielerin Geena Davis. Die Aufnahme entstand für ein Projekt der Zeitschrift *Esquire* unter dem Titel »Frauen, die wir lieben«.

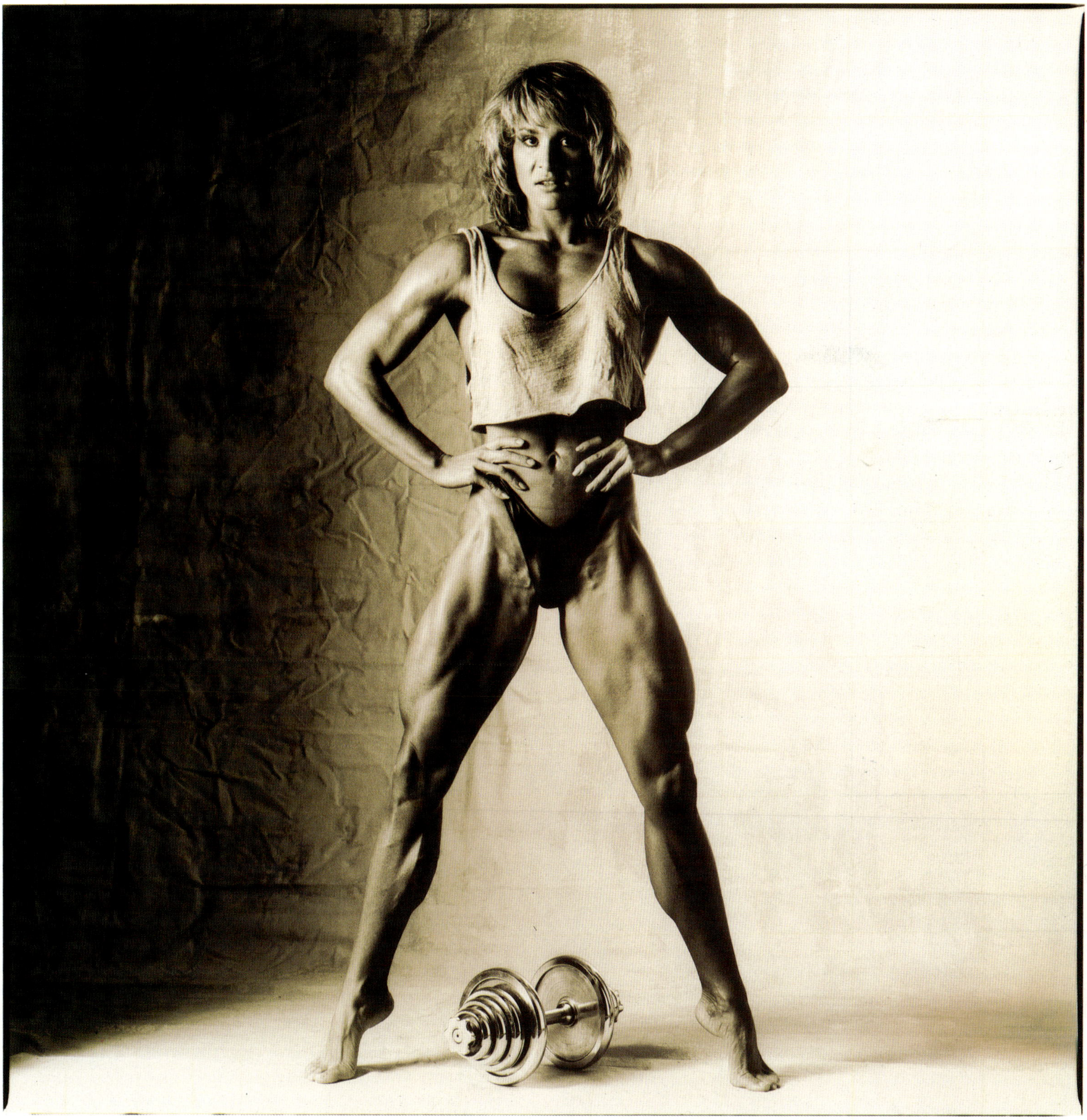

Darrell Peterson

Poster on general sale, showing Cory Everson, bodybuilder: »Miss Olympia«.

Im Handel erhältliches Plakat mit Bodybuilderin Cory Everson: »Miss Olympia«.

Affiche «Miss Olympia» avec la culturiste Cory Everson, en vente libre.

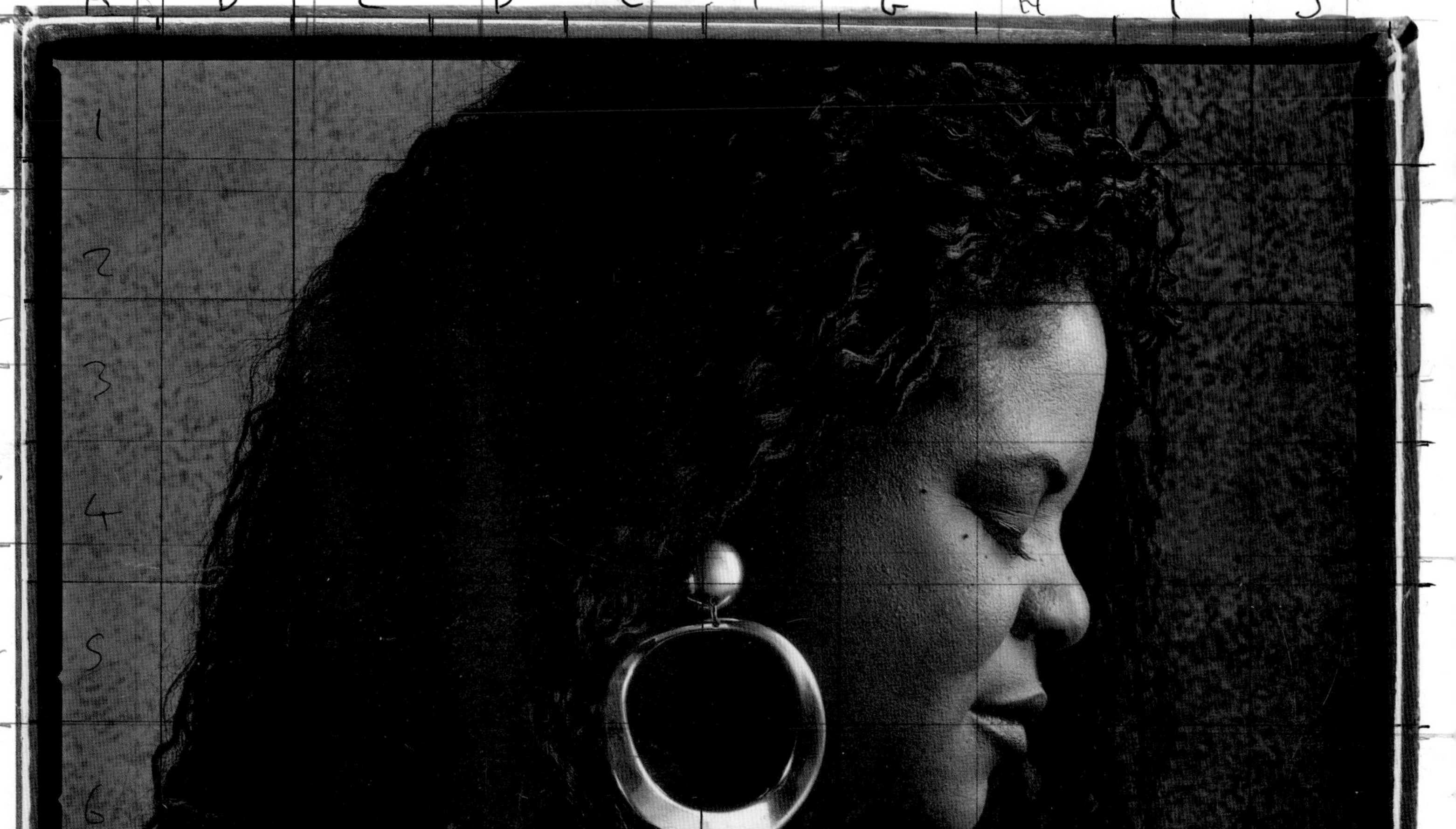

Marc Norberg

Lady Bianca from an ongoing series of portraits of Blues and Jazz musicians. A personal project by the photographer for the Blues Heaven Archives.

Lady Bianca, aus einer Porträt-Reihe von Jazz- und Blues-Musikern, die der Fotograf auf eigene Rechnung für das »Blues Heaven«-Archiv fotografierte.

Lady Bianca dans une série de portraits de musiciens de Jazz et de Blues que le photographe a réalisée à son propre compte pour les archives de la fondation Blues Heaven.

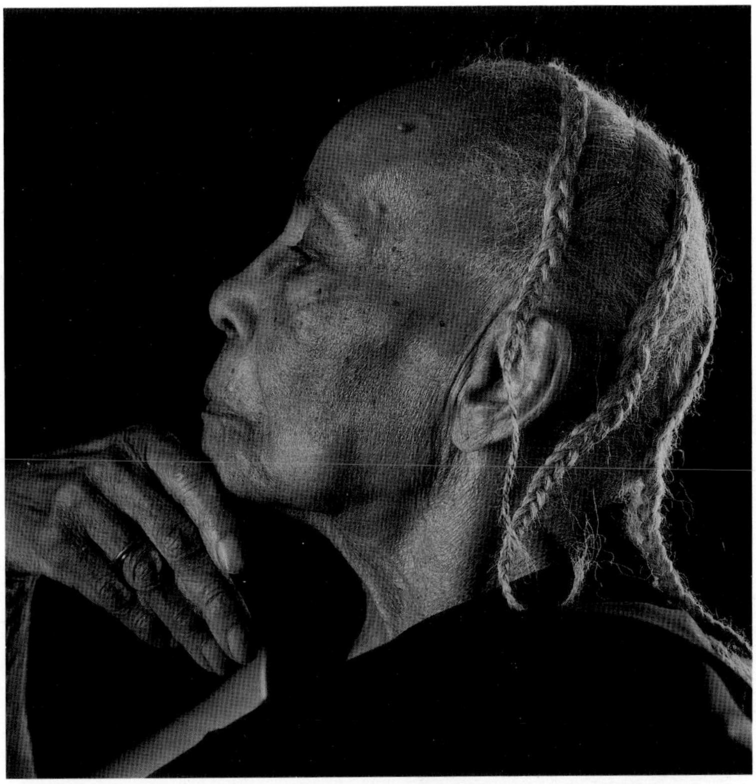

Brian Lanker

From a series featuring portraits of prominent black women: Septima Clark. One of the heroes of the civil rights movement.

Schwarze Frauen, die in der Entwicklung der USA eine große Rolle spielten: Septima Clark, eine der Vertreterinnen der Bürgerrechtsbewegung.

D'un projet personnel qui montre les femmes de couleur ayant joué un rôle important aux USA: Septima Clark, représentante du mouvement des droits civiques.

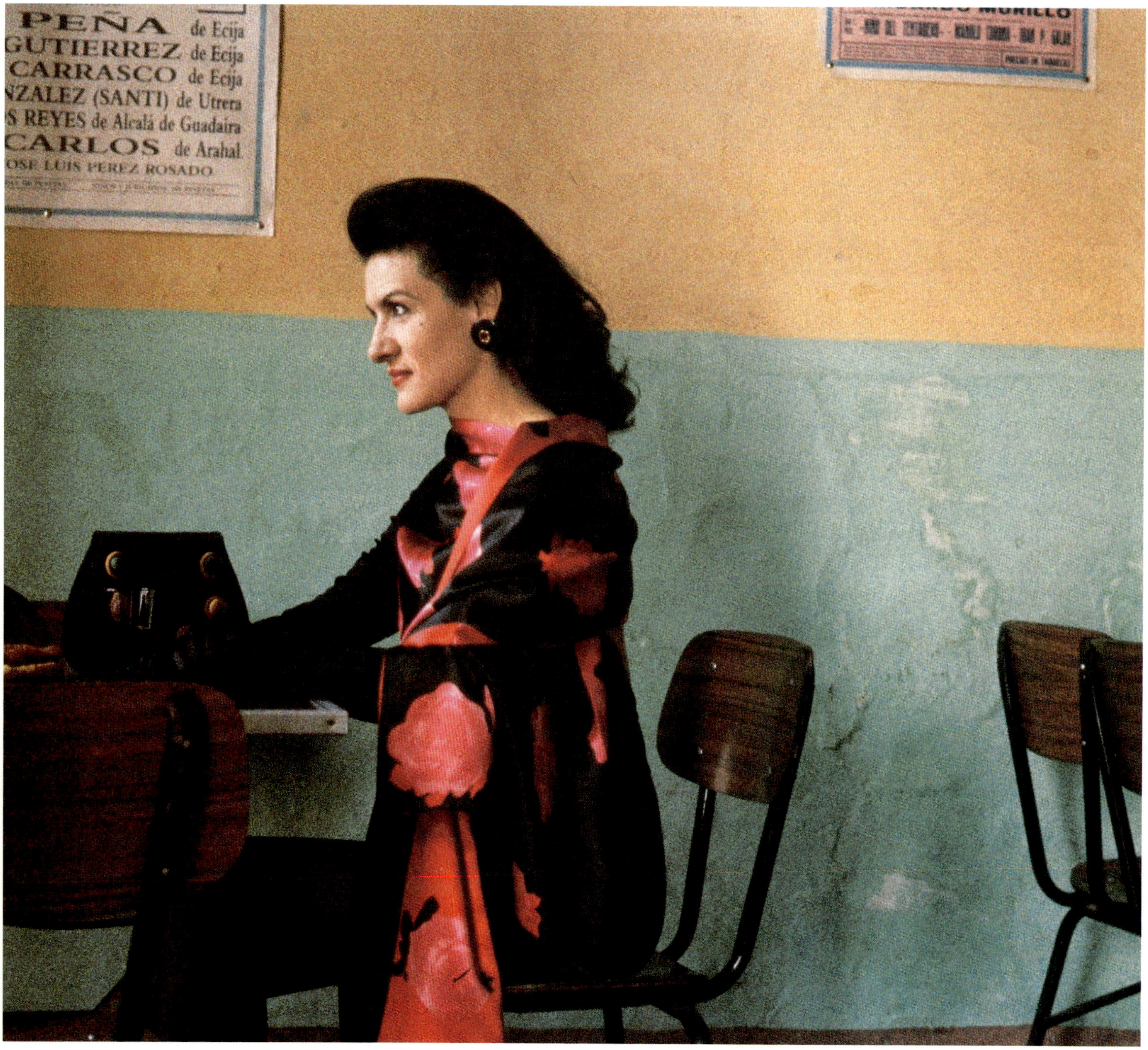

Deborah Turbeville

Paloma Picasso, as seen by Deborah Turbeville. For a portrait of this successful woman by authors Fruttero and Lucentini, published in *Vogue Paris*.

Paloma Picasso, gesehen von Deborah Turbeville. Für ein Porträt dieser erfolgreichen Frau von den Autoren Fruttero und Lucentini in *Vogue Paris*.

Paloma Picasso vue par Deborah Turbeville. Pour illustrer le portrait de cette femme exceptionnelle que les auteurs Fruttero et Lucentini dressent dans *Vogue Paris*.

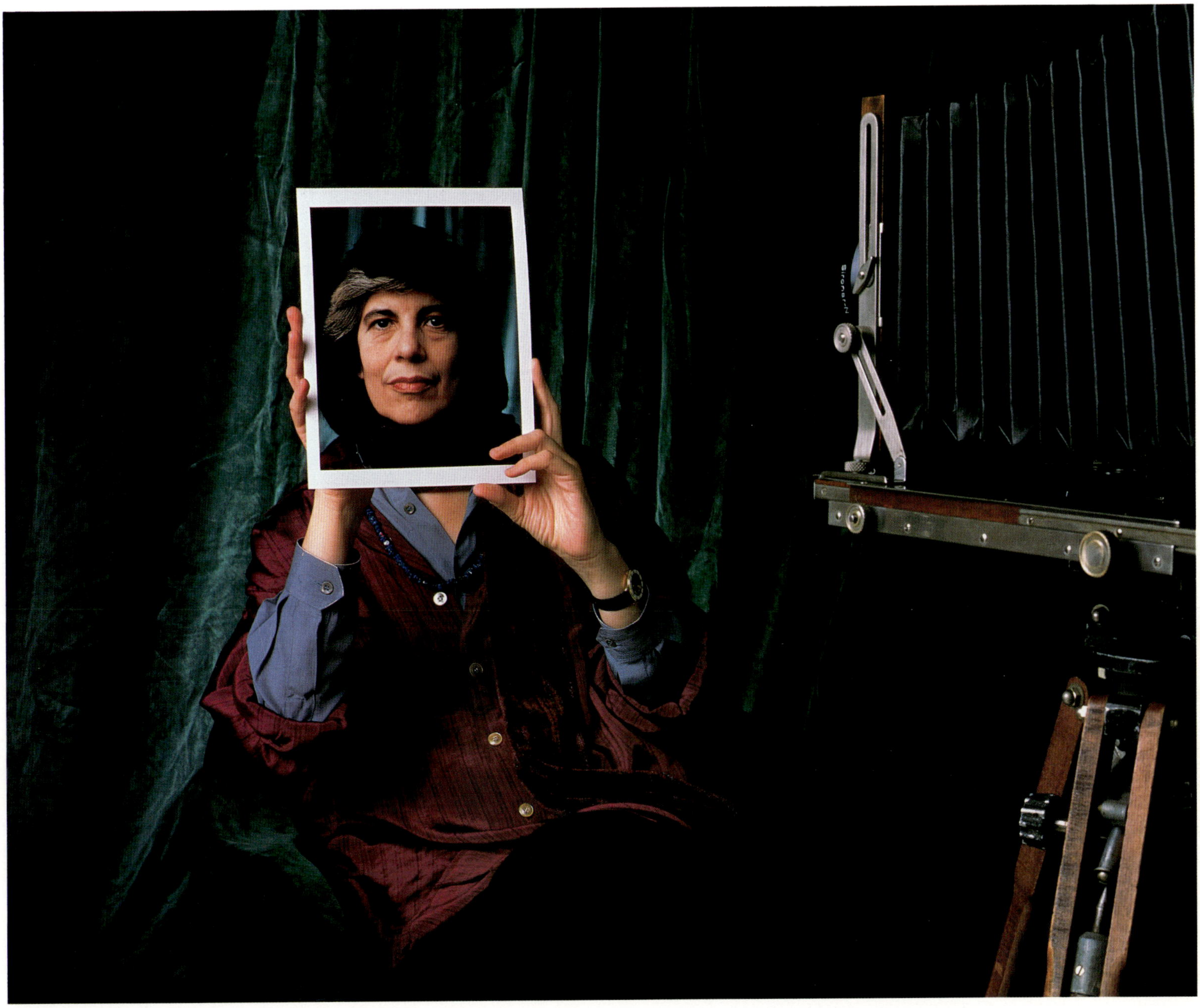

Wolfgang Wesener

Photography and image is the subject of Susan Sontag's essay »About Photography«. Portrait for an article in the *Frankfurter Allgemeine Magazin* about this famous American author.

Das Bild und das Abbild ist das Thema von Susan Sontags Essay »Über Fotografie«. Porträt für einen Artikel über die berühmte amerikanische Schriftstellerin im *Frankfurter Allgemeine Magazin.*

L'image et son reflet, voici le thème de l'étude que Susan Sontag a consacrée à la photographie. Ce portrait illustre un article du *Frankfurter Allgemeine Magazin* au sujet du célèbre écrivain américain.

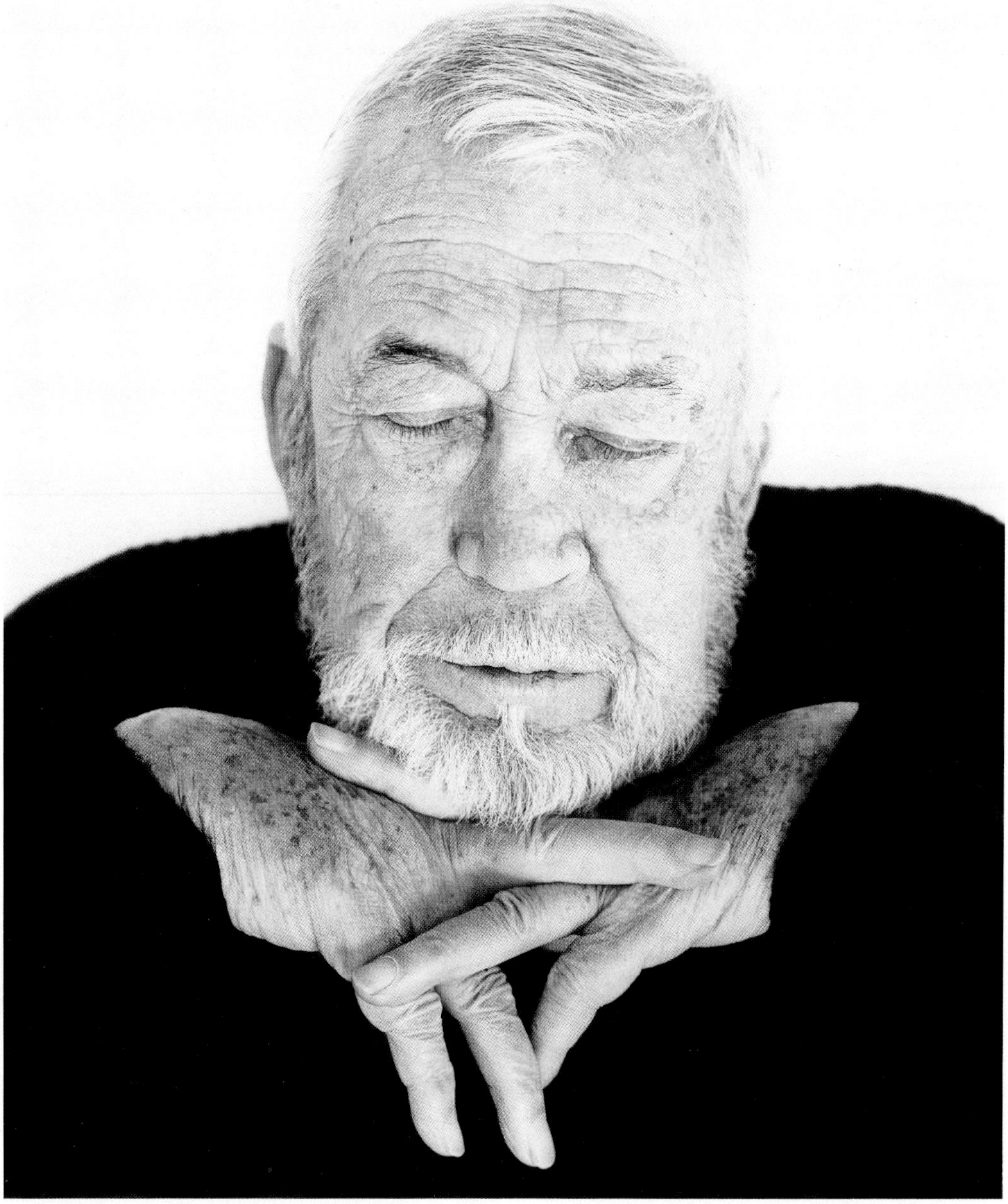

Herb Ritts

Portrait of film director John Huston who died in 1987, published in *Rolling Stone* magazine.

Im Gedenken an den 1987 verstorbenen Filmregisseur John Huston veröffentlichtes Porträt in *Rolling Stone*.

Portrait du cinéaste John Huston, décédé en 1987, publié dans *Rolling Stone*.

Herb Ritts

Photograph from a series of portraits of Djimon by Herb Ritts.

Djimons Porträt aus einer Serie von Herb Ritts.

Portrait de Djimon, extrait d'une série réalisée par le photographe Herb Ritts.

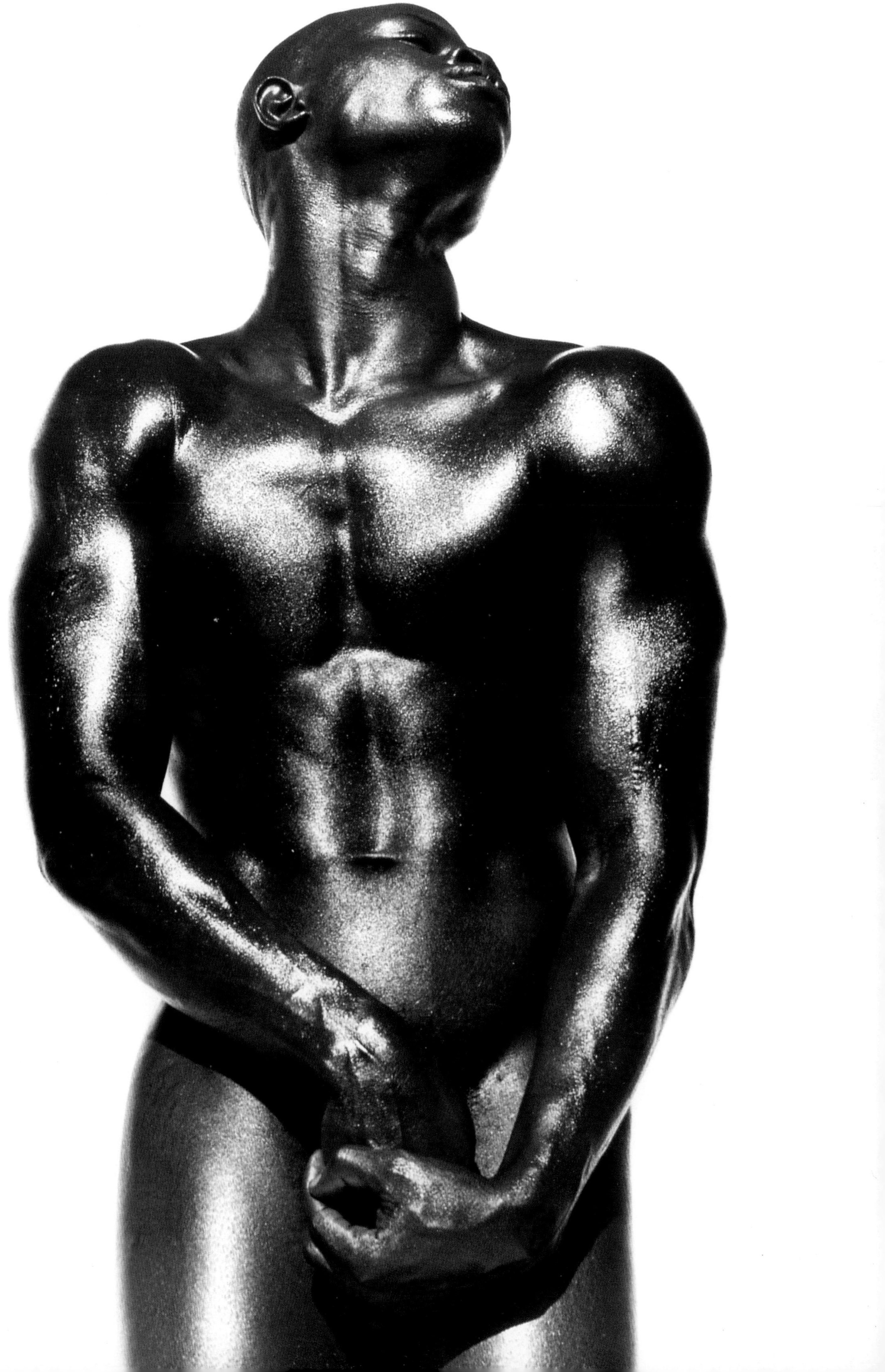

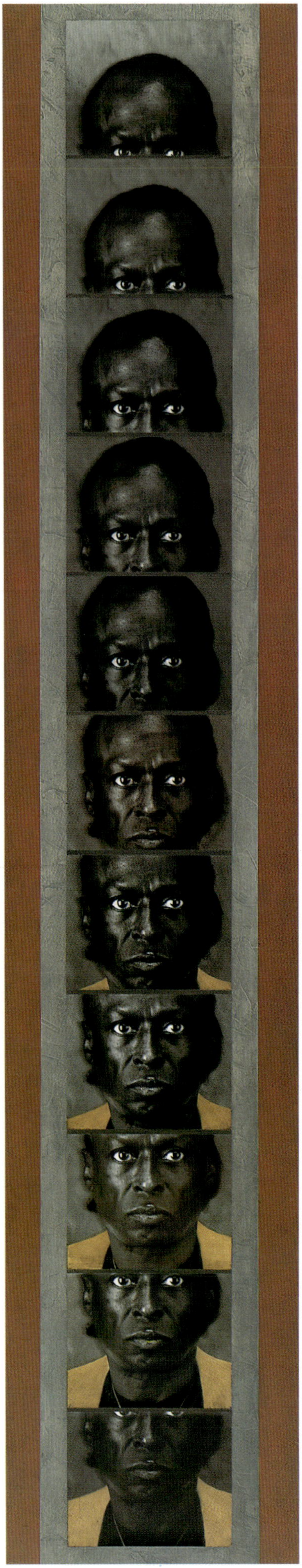

Gilles Larrain

»Sunset and Dawn« and »The Uses of Enchantment«

»Von Sonnenaufgang bis Sonnenuntergang« und »Anwendungen der Verzauberung«

«De l'Aube au Crépuscule» et «Les Usages de la Magie».

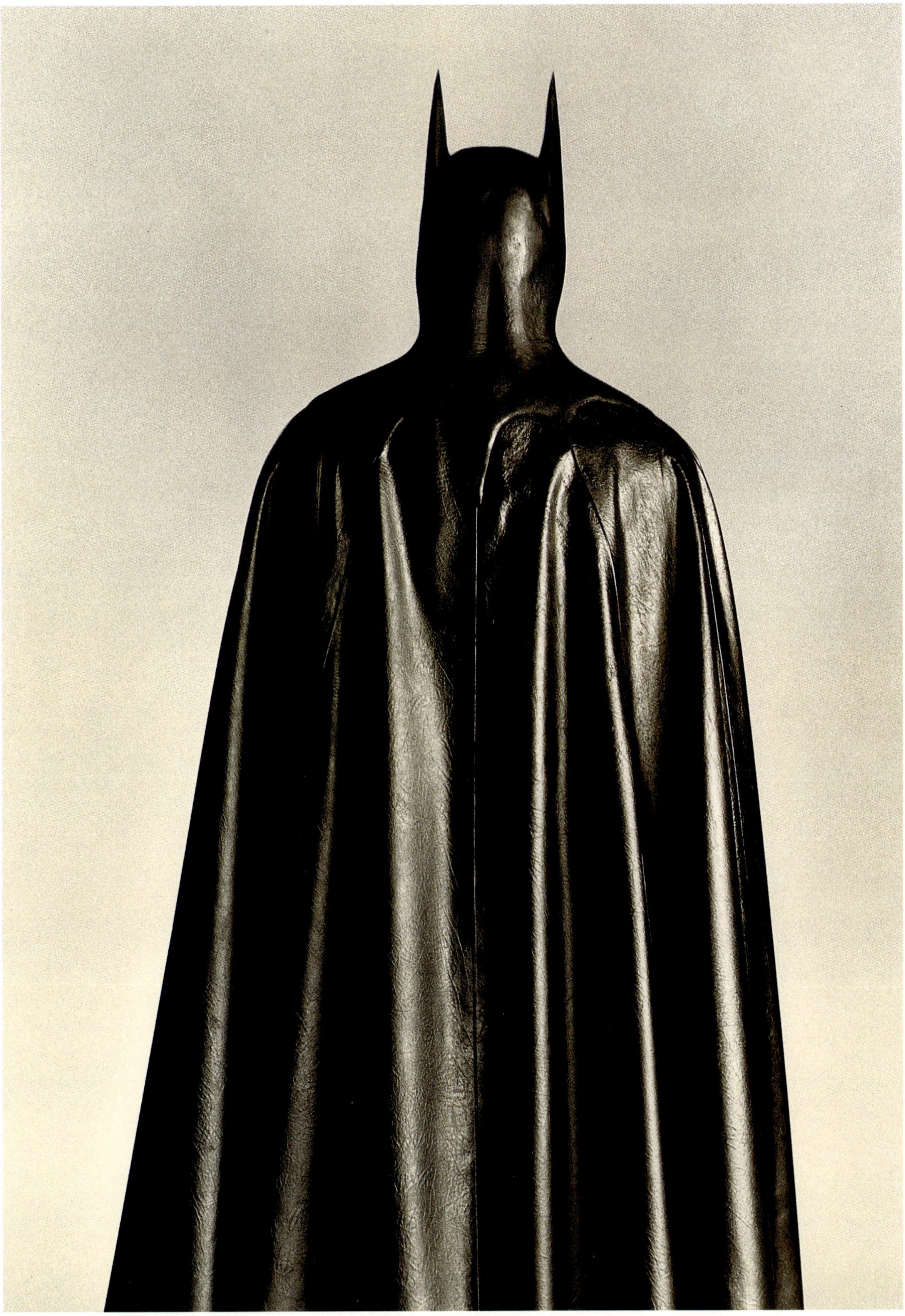

◁ Herb Ritts

Rolling Stone used this photo on the cover of an issue featuring an interview with Tim Burton, the director of *Batman*. As Michael Keaton, who played Batman, would not pose in the costume, the cowl alone had to be used. It was then possible to treat it simply as a sculpture, lit accordingly and photographed.

Rolling Stone brachte diese Aufnahme als Titel, um auf ein Interview mit dem Regisseur des Filmes *Batman* hinzuweisen. Der Hauptdarsteller Michael Keaton wollte nicht im Kostüm fotografiert werden. So wurde das Batman-Thema nur durch das Kostüm dargestellt, das wie eine Skulptur beleuchtet wurde.

Cette photo a été publiée en couverture de *Rolling Stone*, afin d'attirer l'attention sur une interview du metteur en scène du film *Batman*. L'acteur principal, Michael Keaton, n'avait pas voulu endosser le costume de Batman pour la photo. C'est pourquoi le héros du film est uniquement symbolisé par son déguisement, qui est éclairé comme une sculpture.

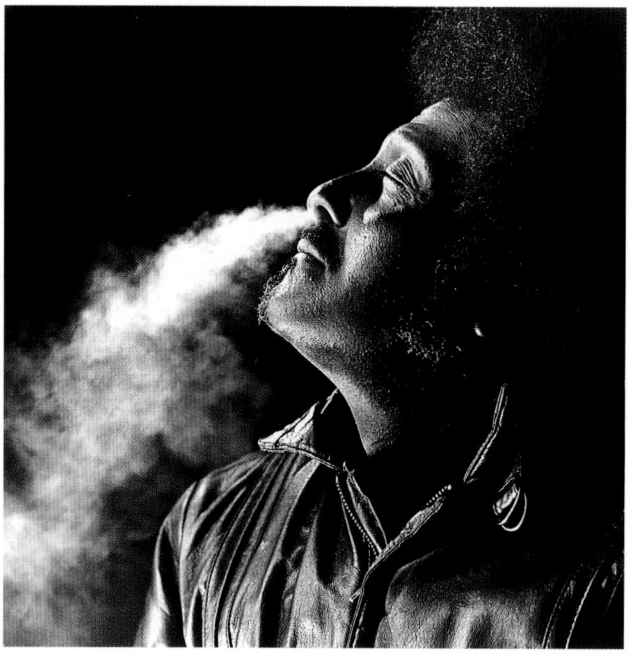

Marc Norberg

The portrait of musician Albert Collins for a limited edition portfolio to benefit the Blues Heaven Foundation, a non-profit organization.

Porträt des Musikers Albert Collins für eine Fotomappe in limitierter Auflage zugunsten der Stiftung Blues Heaven.

Le musicien Albert Collins. Série de photos réalisées pour la Blues Heaven Foundation, une organisation à but non lucratif.

Albert Watson

Portrait of Keith Richards for an article in *Rolling Stone* magazine.

Porträtaufnahme von Keith Richards aus der Zeitschrift *Rolling Stone*.

Portrait de Keith Richards pour un article paru dans le magazine *Rolling Stone*.

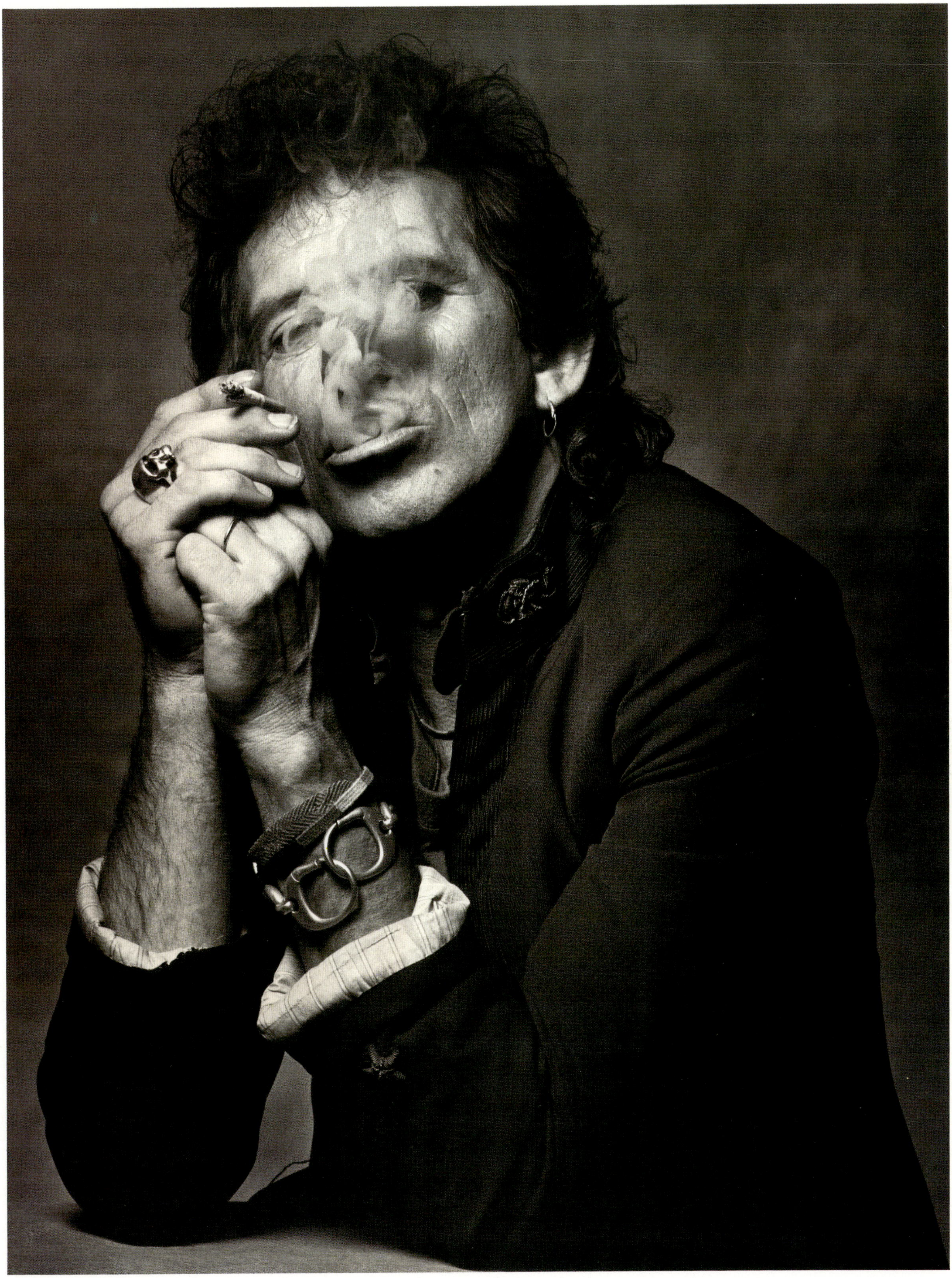

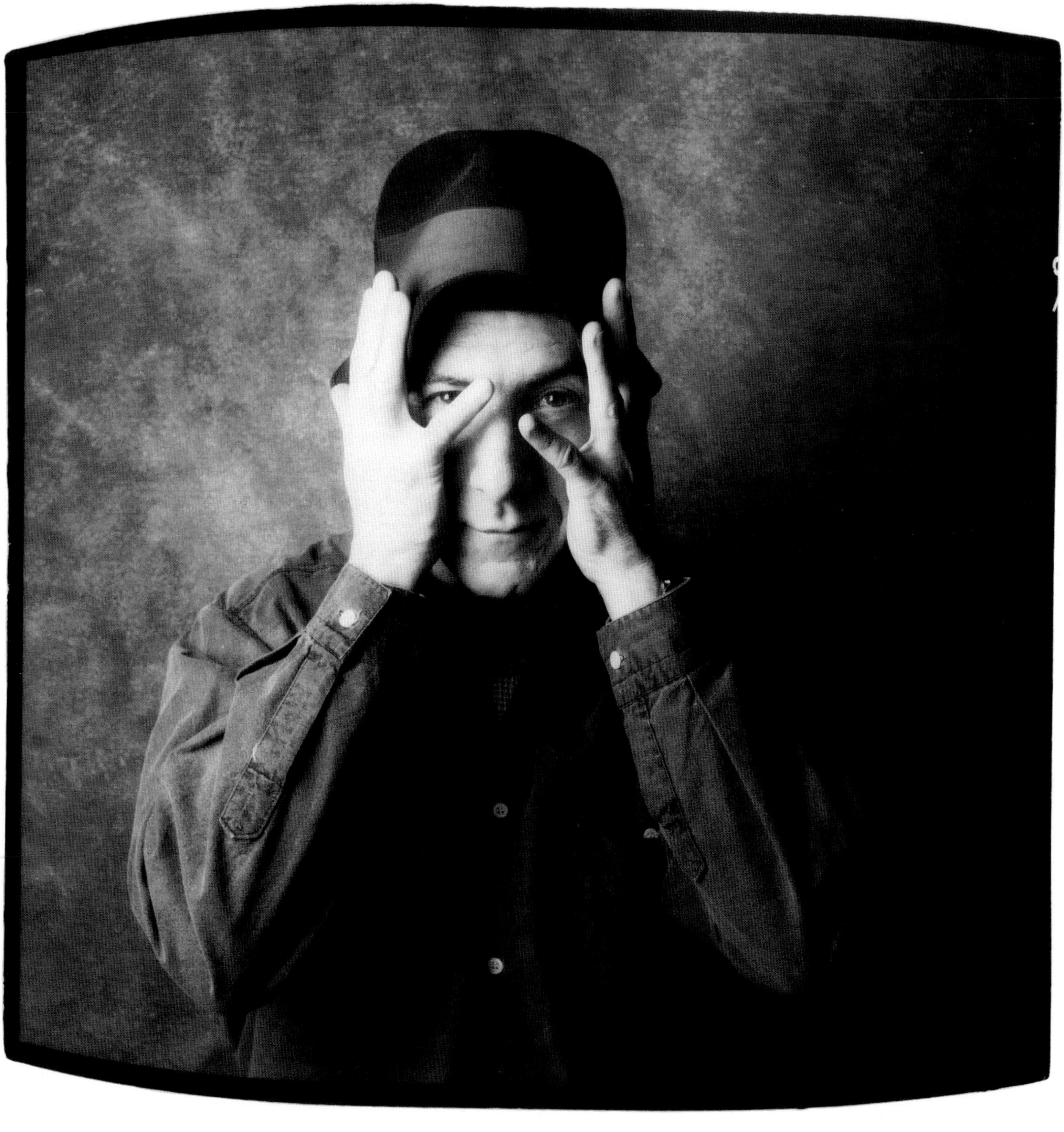

William Coupon

When Dustin Hoffman was to be photographed for the *New York Times Sunday Magazine*, he could not figure out what he wanted and finally tried out some faces in the mirror.

Als Dustin Hoffman für das *New York Times Sunday Magazine* fotografiert werden sollte, war er unschlüssig und probierte schließlich vor dem Spiegel verschiedene Gesichter aus.

La vedette hollywoodienne Dustin Hoffman se montra indécis lorsqu'il fallut faire des photos pour le *New York Times Sunday Magazine*; finalement, il essaya plusieurs poses devant le miroir.

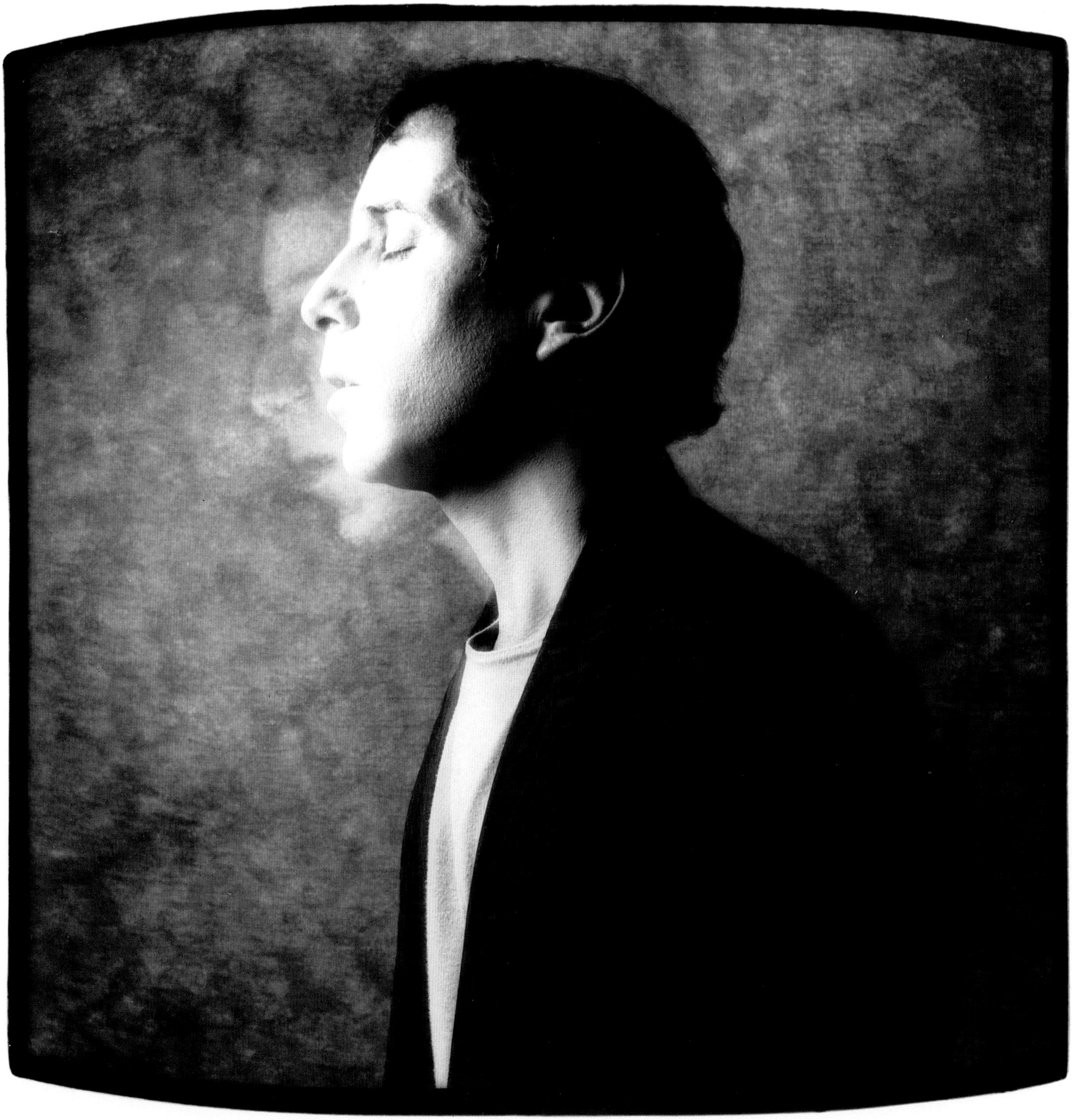

William Coupon

Portrait of rock/pop singer Paul Simon (formerly of Simon & Garfunkel) for an article in *Vogue Italia.*

Porträt des Rock-Sängers Paul Simon (früher »Simon & Garfunkel«) für einen Beitrag in *Vogue Italia.*

Portrait du chanteur de pop rock Paul Simon, autrefois associé à Garfunkel, pour un article de *Vogue Italia.*

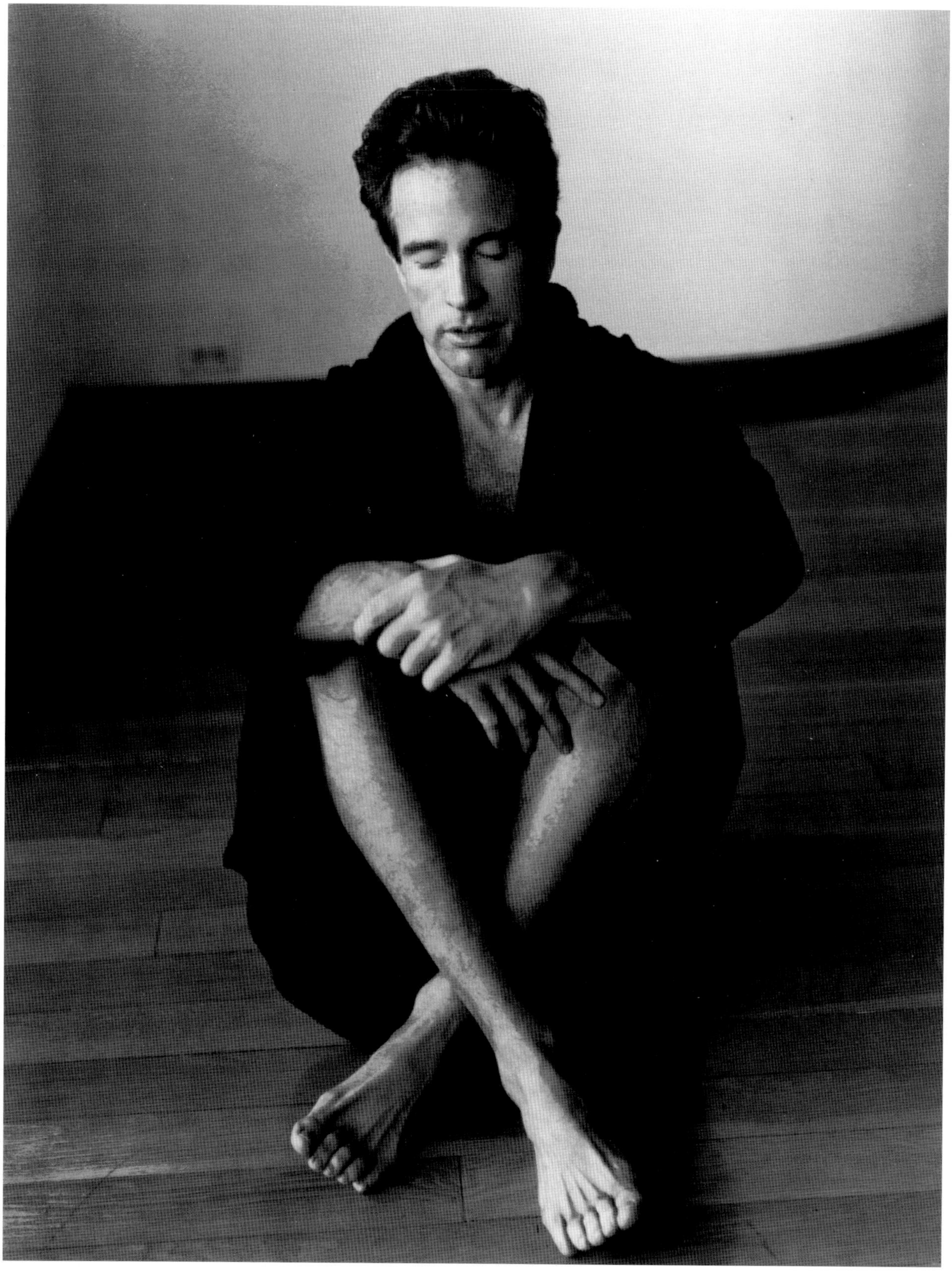

Herb Ritts

Here we see the often-reclusive actor Warren Beatty in a relaxed moment, as captured by Ritts for the pages of *Rolling Stone* magazine.

Dieses spezielle Porträt des Filmschauspielers Warren Beatty beim Entspannen erschien in einem Artikel in der Zeitschrift *Rolling Stone*.

Ce portrait de l'acteur de film Warren Beatty en train de se relaxer a été publié dans le magazine *Rolling Stone*.

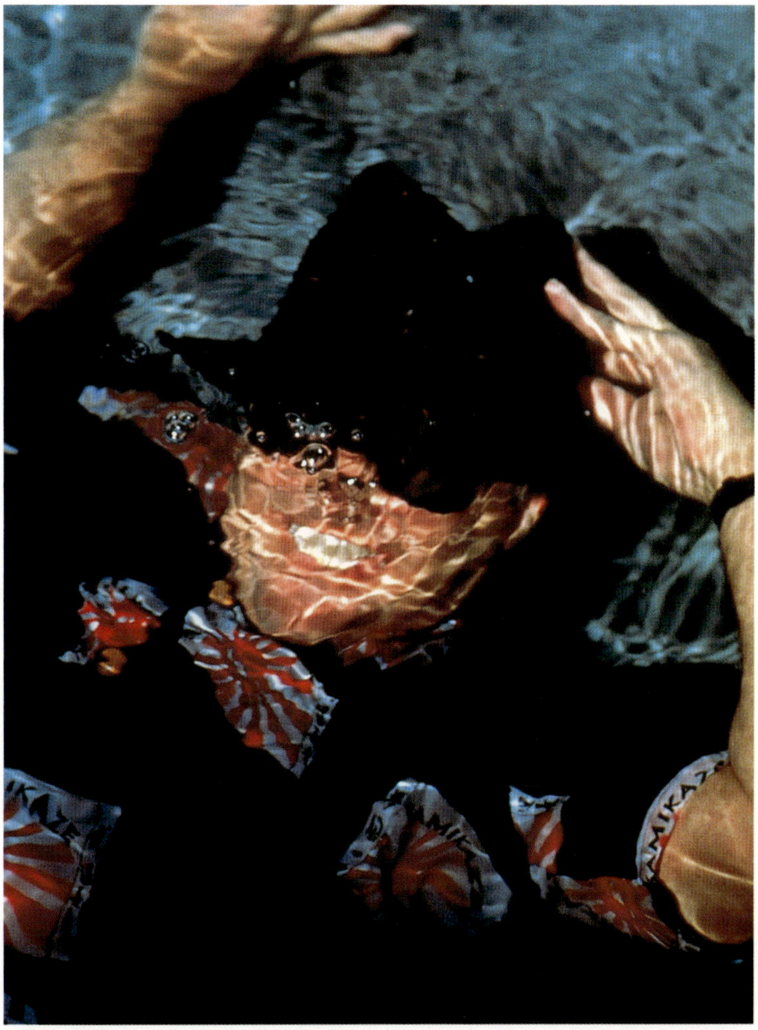

Herb Ritts

Unusual portrait of American film star Jack Nicholson, taken by Herb Ritts.

Ungewöhnliches Porträt des amerikanischen Filmschauspielers Jack Nicholson von Herb Ritts.

Portrait insolite de l'acteur de cinéma américain Jack Nicholson par Herb Ritts.

Mark Seliger

Portrait of Slash for a cover story in *Rolling Stone* magazine. The photograph was taken in the backyard of Slash's home.

Porträt des Sängers Slash, Mitglied der Gruppe Guns n' Roses, für einen Beitrag in der amerikanischen Zeitschrift *Rolling Stone*.

Portrait de Slash, membre du groupe rock Guns n' Roses, publié en couverture d'un numéro de *Rolling Stone*.

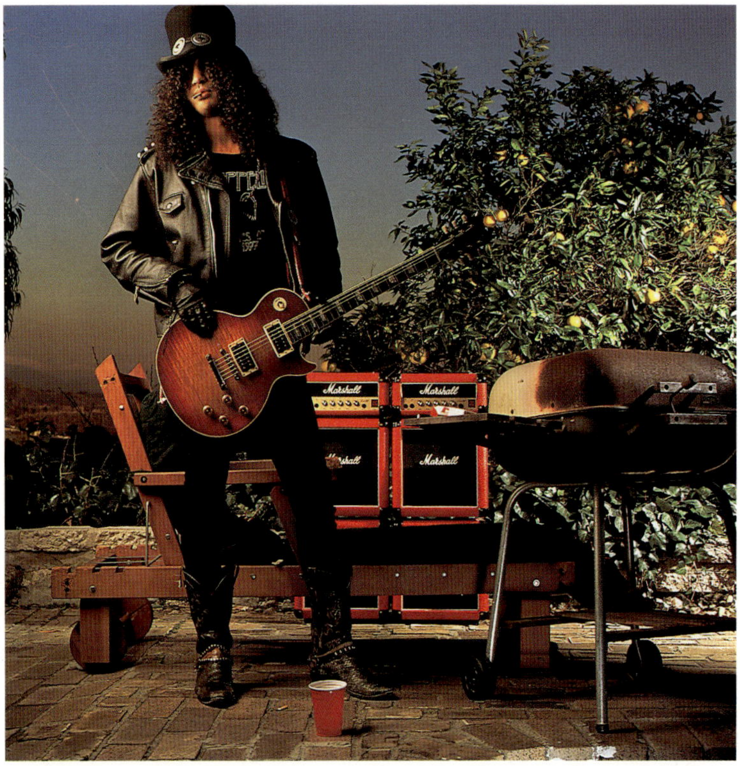

Mark Seliger

From an unpublished series of portraits of blues musician John Lee Hooker. The photographer wanted these portraits to be serious, straightforward and respectful, showing his appreciation of musicians.

Aus einer Reihe unveröffentlichter Porträts des Blues-Musikers John Lee Hooker. Der Fotograf wollte ernste, ehrliche und respektvolle Porträts der Musiker, um seine Achtung vor ihnen auszudrücken.

Un exemple d'une série de portraits inédits représentant le musicien de blues, John Lee Hooker. Le photographe voulait faire des portraits sérieux, authentiques et respectables des musiciens, exprimant son admiration pour eux.

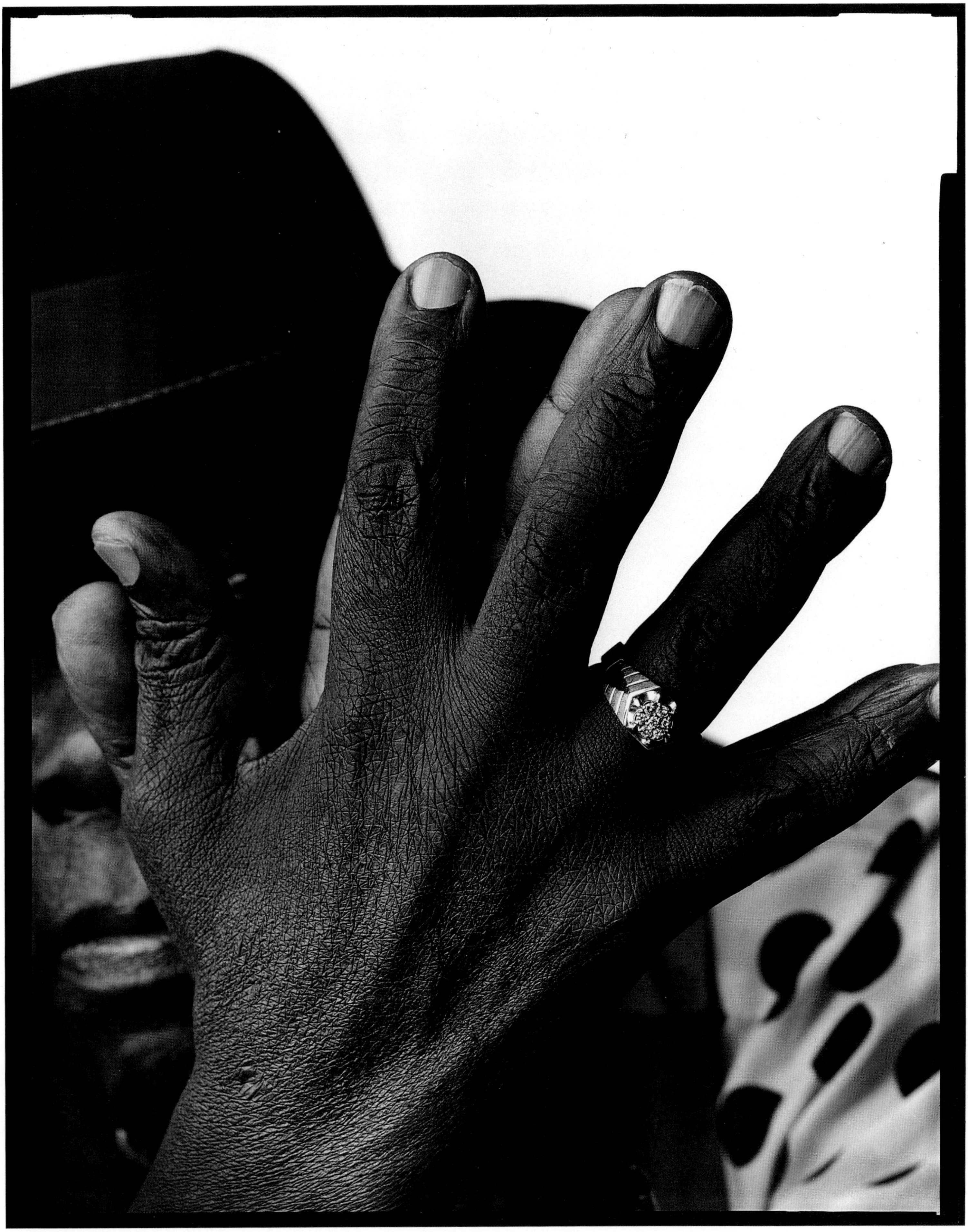

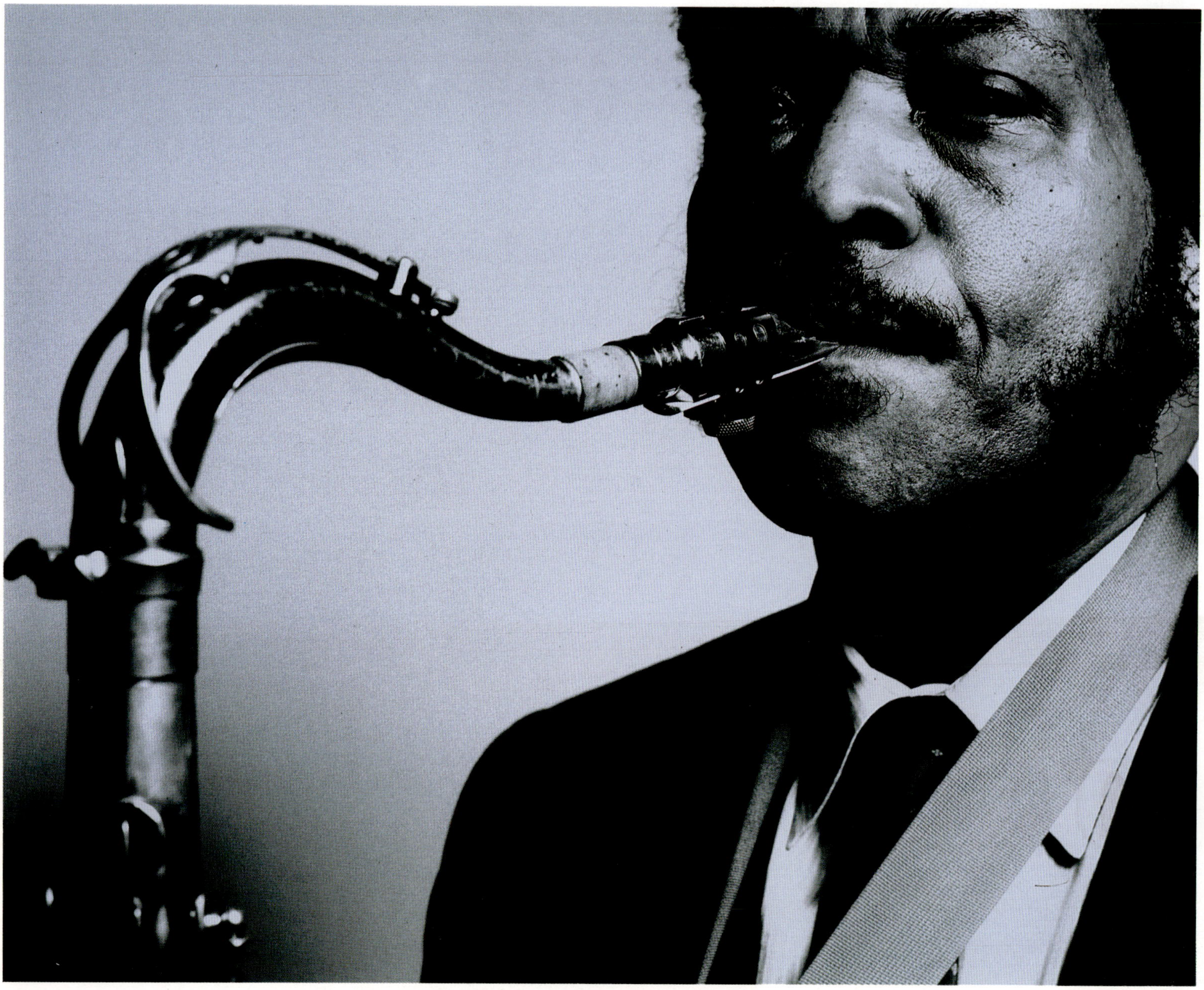

John Claridge

Black-and-white portraits from the book *One Hundred Photographs* by John Claridge. Shown are George Coleman, jazz musician, 1986; banjo-player, Tennessee, 1986; Chet Baker, jazz musician, 1986.

Schwarzweiß-Porträts aus dem Fotoband *One Hundred Photographs* des Fotografen John Claridge. Hier George Coleman, Jazz-Musiker,1986; Banjo-Spieler, Tennessee, 1986, und Chet Baker, Jazz-Musiker, 1986.

Portraits en noir et blanc illustrant l'album photo *One Hundred Photographs* de John Claridge. On voit ici George Coleman, musicien de jazz, 1986; un banjoïste du Tennessee, 1986; Chet Baker, musicien de jazz, 1986.

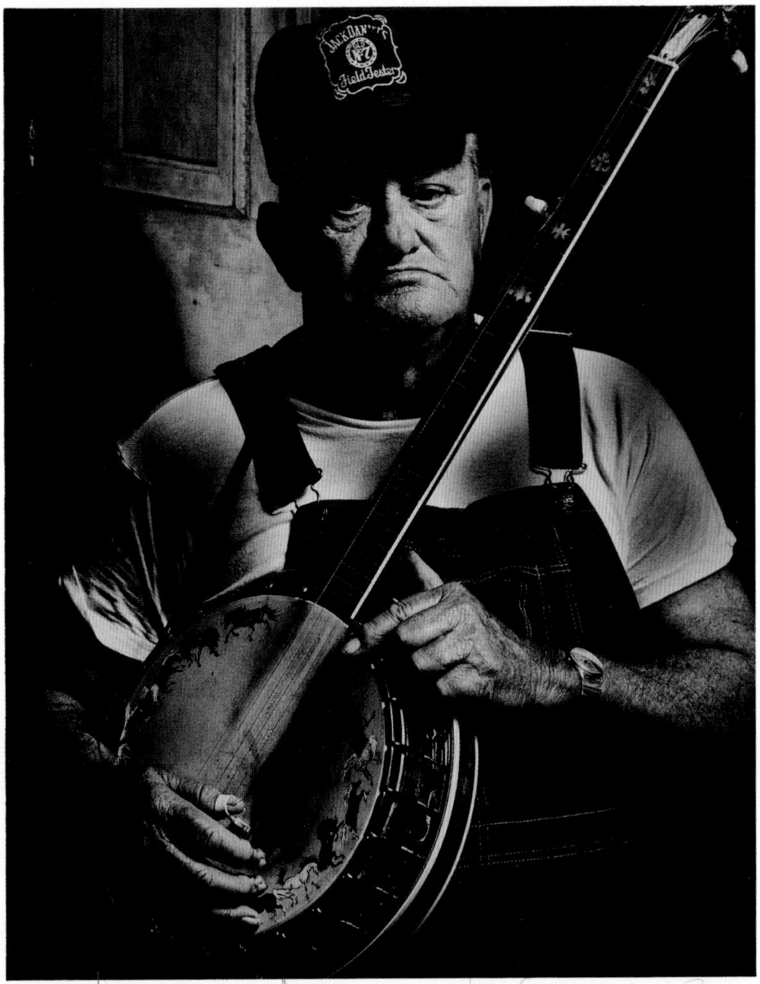

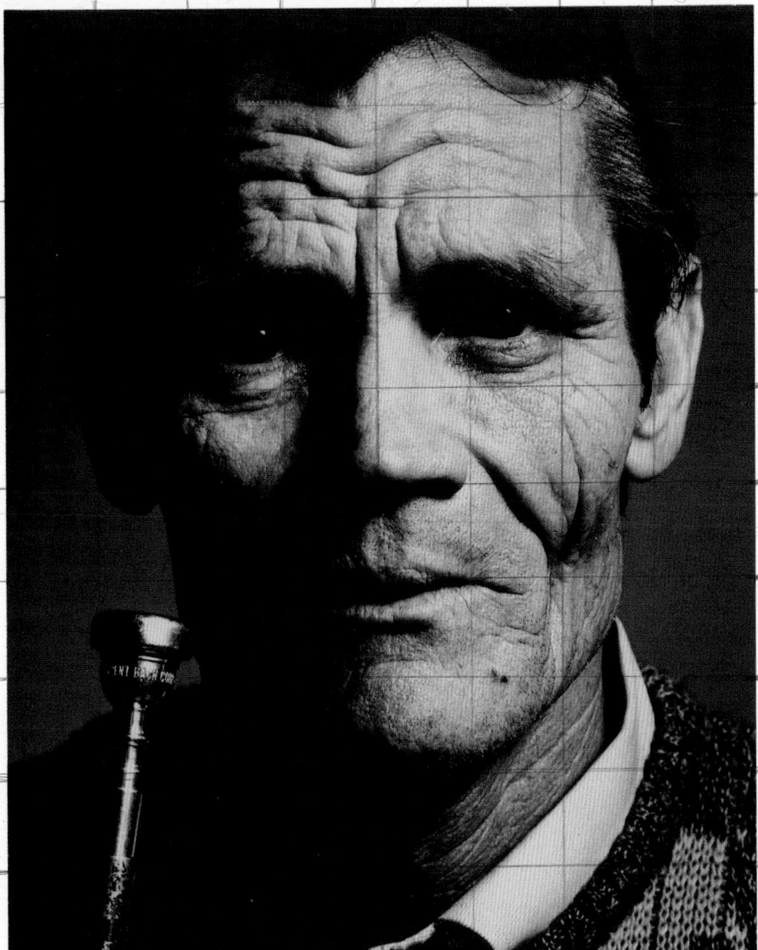

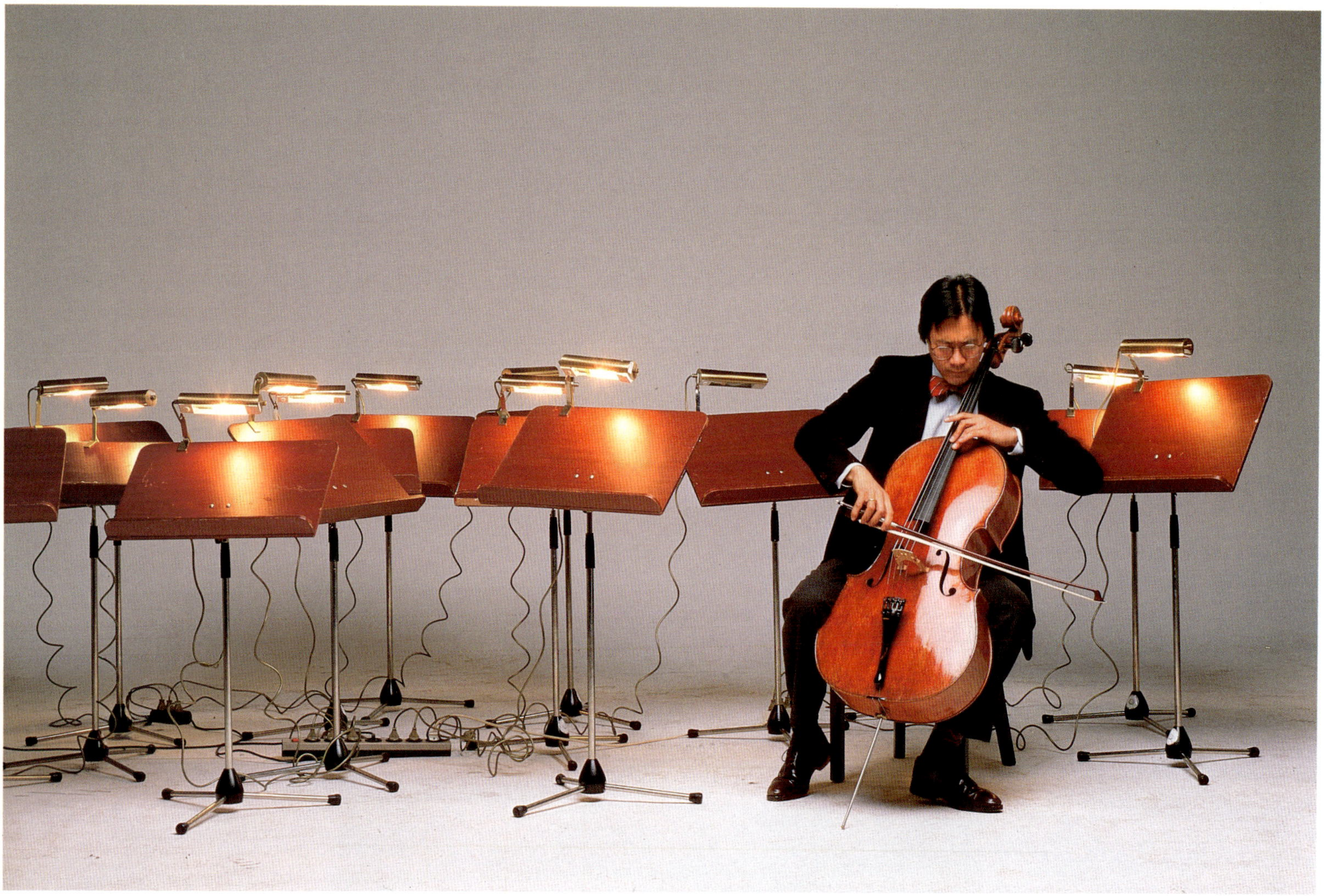

Jürgen Röhrscheid

Yo-Yo Ma – the cello soloist who enjoys playing with other musicians.

Der Cellist Yo-Yo Ma, ein Solist, der das Zusammenspiel mit vielen Musikern liebt.

Le violoncelliste Yo-Yo Ma, un soliste qui aime s'associer à de nombreux autres musiciens.

Tom Zimberoff

Herbert von Karajan, a shot by Tom Zimberoff.

Herbert von Karajan, gesehen von Tom Zimberoff.

Herbert von Karajan vu par Tom Zimberoff.

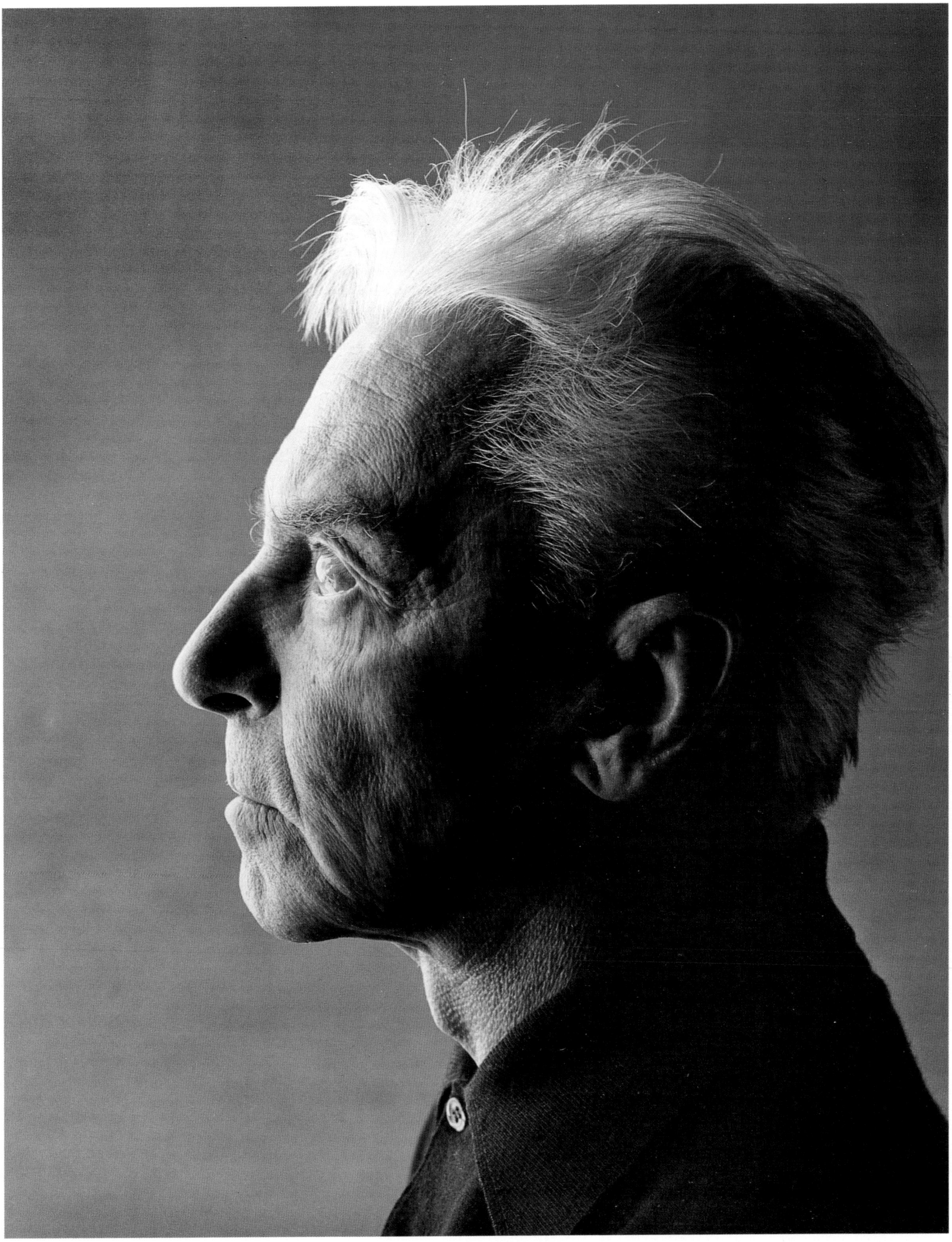

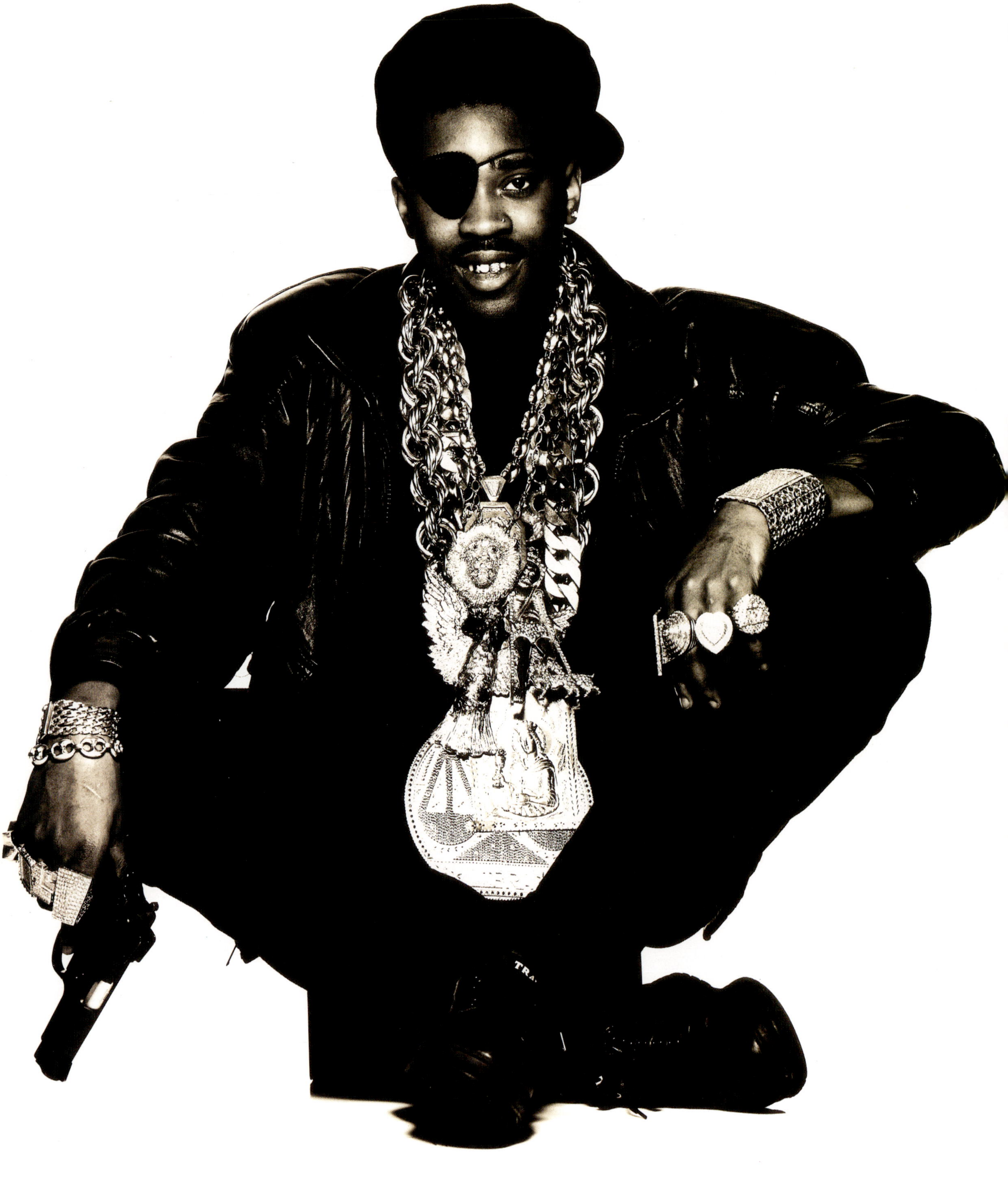

◁ Albert Watson

Rap Artist Slick Rick

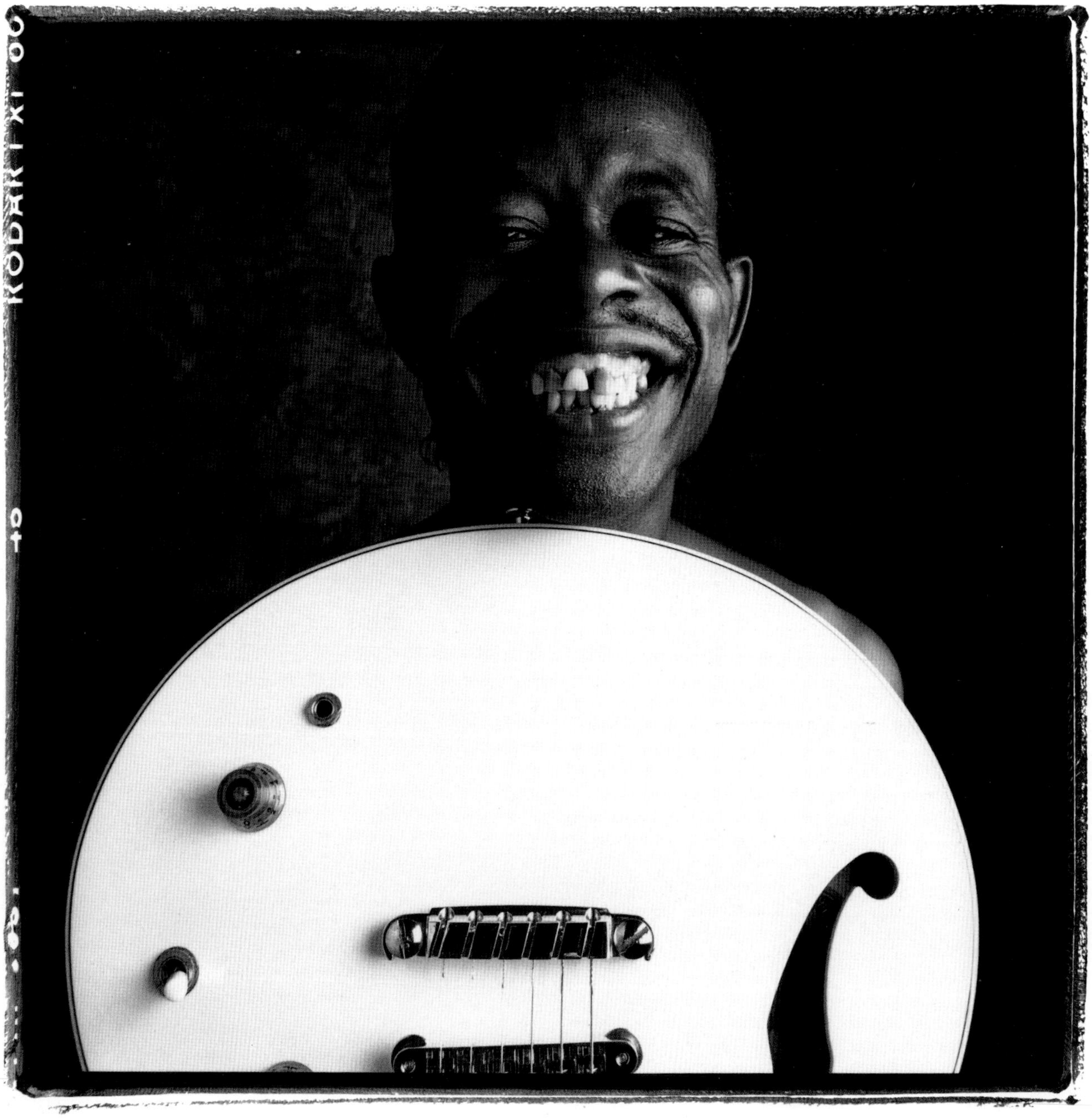

Marc Norberg

In an ongoing assignment, Marc Norberg portrays blues and jazz musicians for the archives of the Blues Heaven Foundation.

Für das Archiv der Blues-Heaven-Stiftung porträtiert Marc Norberg Blues- und Jazz-Musiker.

Marc Norberg fait les portraits des musiciens de blues pour les archives de la Fondation Blues Heaven.

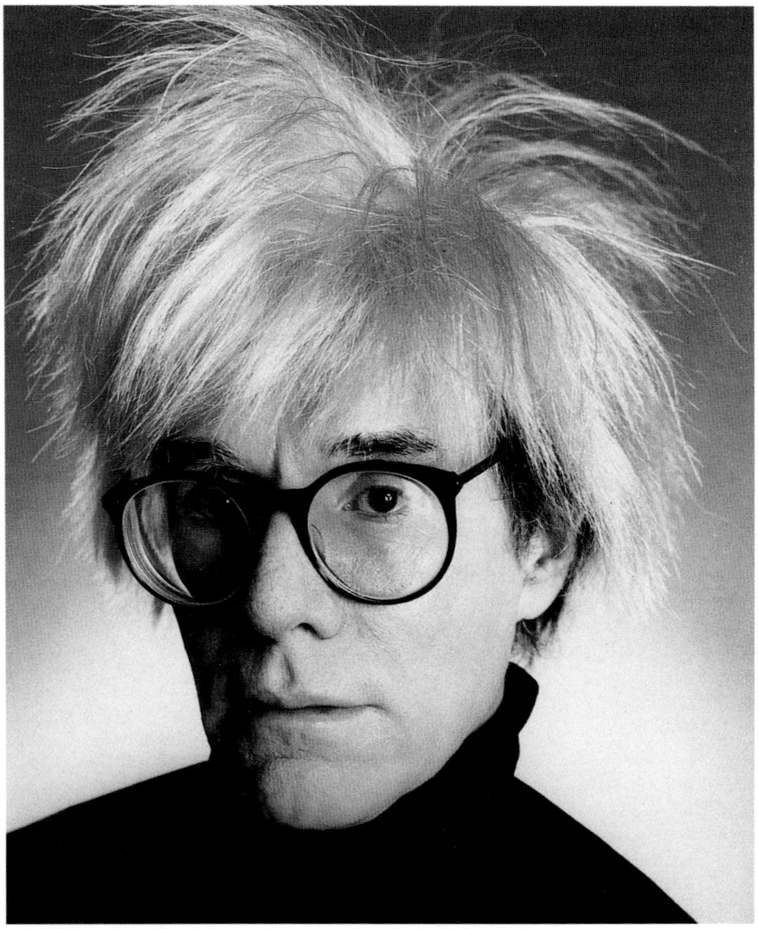

Christopher Makos

Photograph for the cover of the photo book *Warhol – Makos*, a photographic biography in black and white. Photographer Christopher Makos was one of the closest friends of this famous artist.

Aufnahme für den Umschlag des Bildbandes *Warhol – Makos*, eine Fotografie in Schwarzweiß. Der Fotograf Christopher Makos war einer der engsten Freunde des berühmten Künstlers.

Photo de couverture utilisée pour l'album *Warhol – Makos*, photobiographie en noir et blanc. Le photographe Christopher Makos était un ami intime du célèbre artiste.

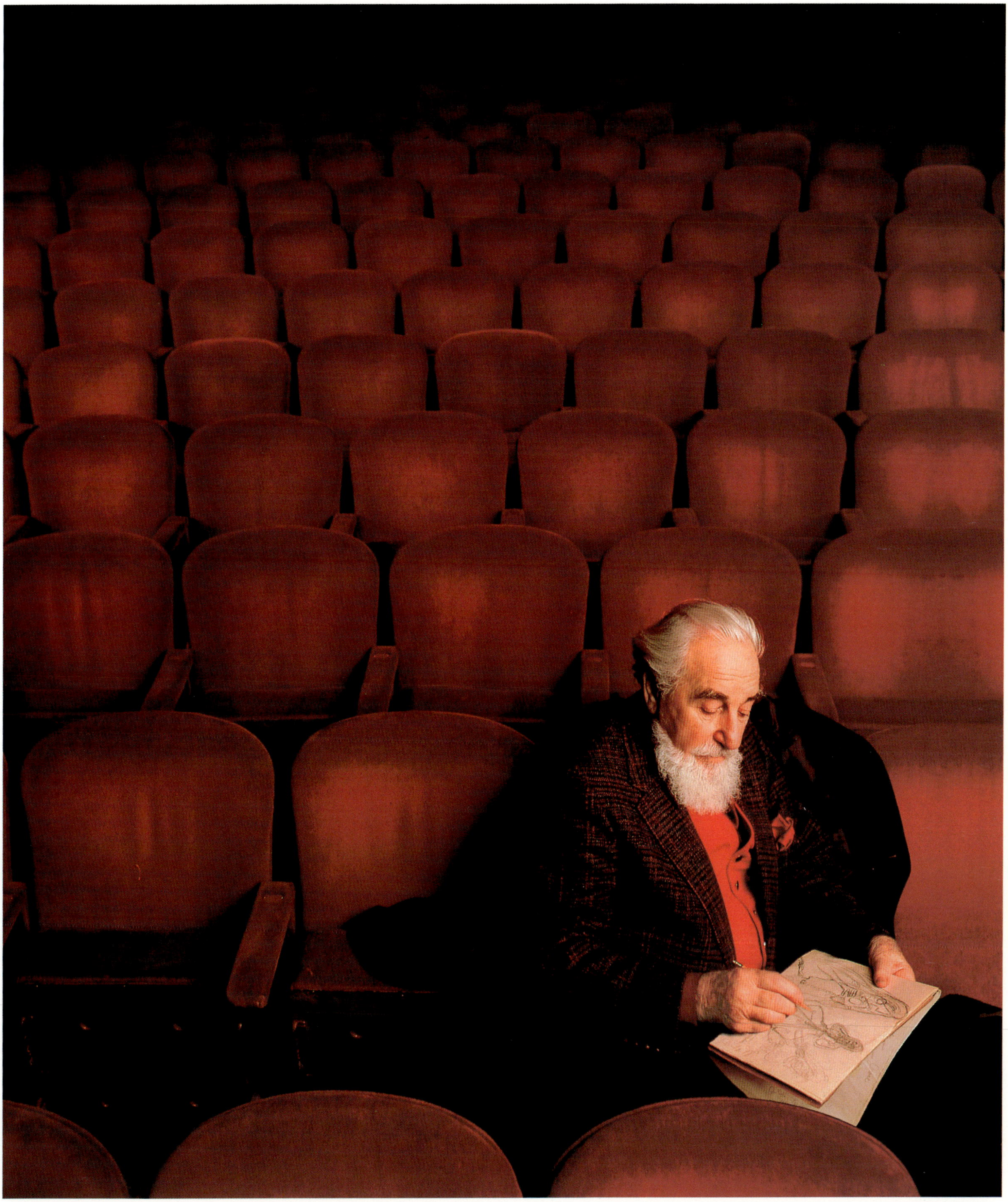

Annie Leibovitz

Al Hirschfeld, chronicler of the New York City theater and entertainment scene.

Al Hirschfeld, Chronist der New Yorker Theater- und Unterhaltungsszene.

Al Hirschfeld, chroniqueur du monde new-yorkais des spectacles (théâtre et autres).

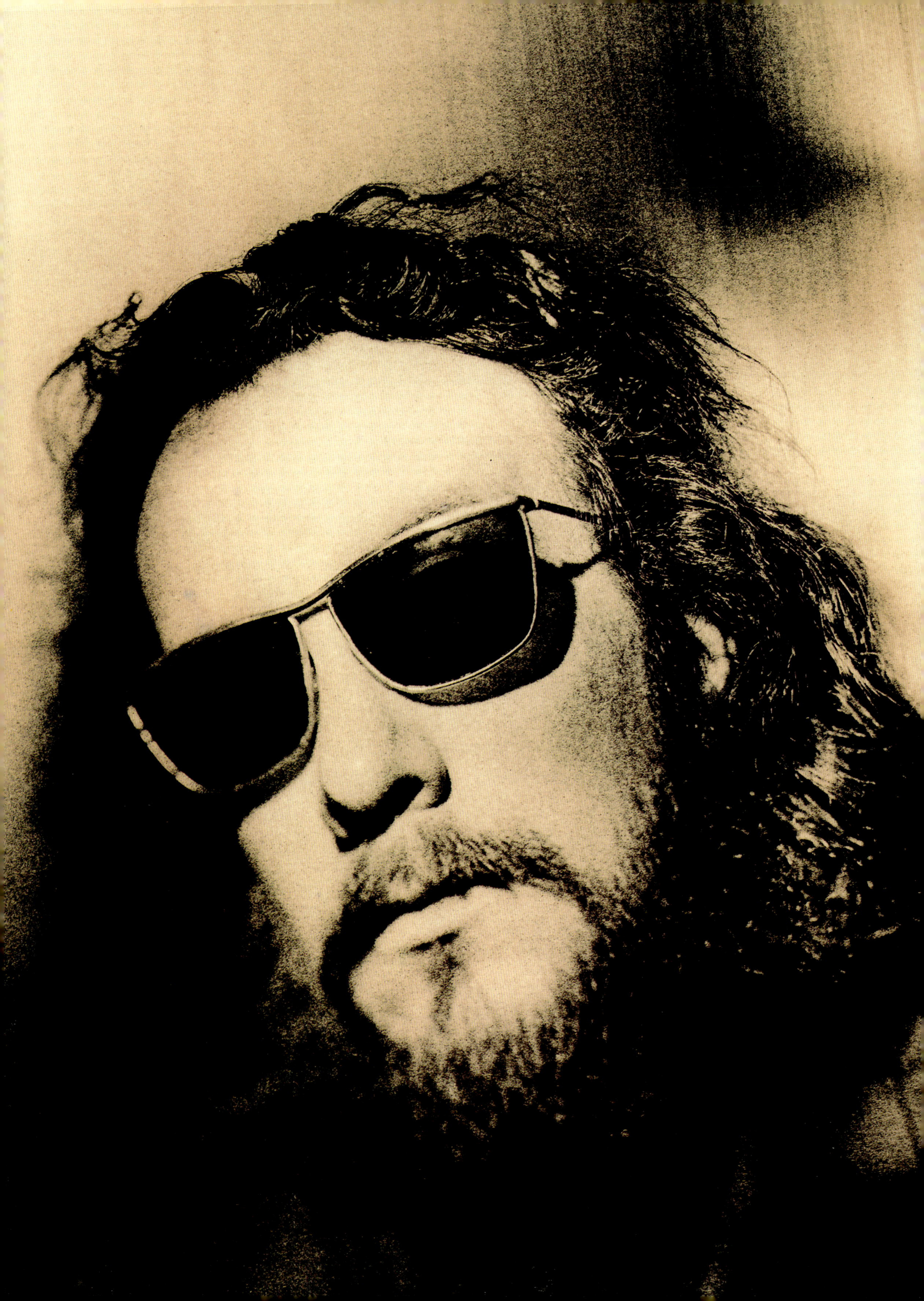

Chris Callis

Ray Charles and Peter Martins, photograph published in the magazine *Esquire*.

Ray Charles und Peter Martins, Aufnahme für die Zeitschrift *Esquire*.

Ray Charles et Peter Martins, photo publiée dans le magazine *Esquire*.

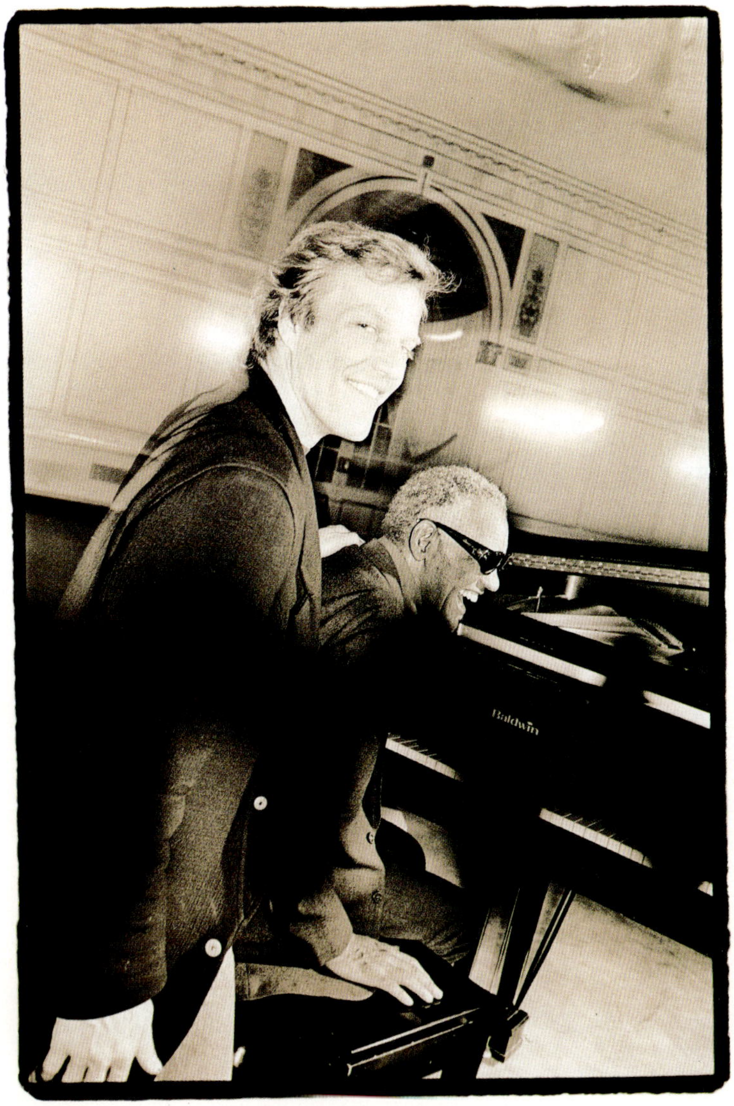

◁ Frank W. Ockenfels 3

A portrait of Elvis Costello for *Creem* Magazine. Most of the shooting took place in a park near Elvis' home in London, but this picture was taken in the photographer's hotel room.

Porträt von Elvis Costello für ein Interview in *Creem*. Wegen schlechter Wetterbedingungen wurde die Aufnahme im Hotelzimmer des Fotografen statt wie vorgesehen in einem Londoner Park gemacht.

Portrait du musicien de rock Elvis Costello pour un reportage publié dans le magazine *Creem*. En raison du mauvais temps, celle-ci fut réalisée dans la chambre d'hôtel du photographe.

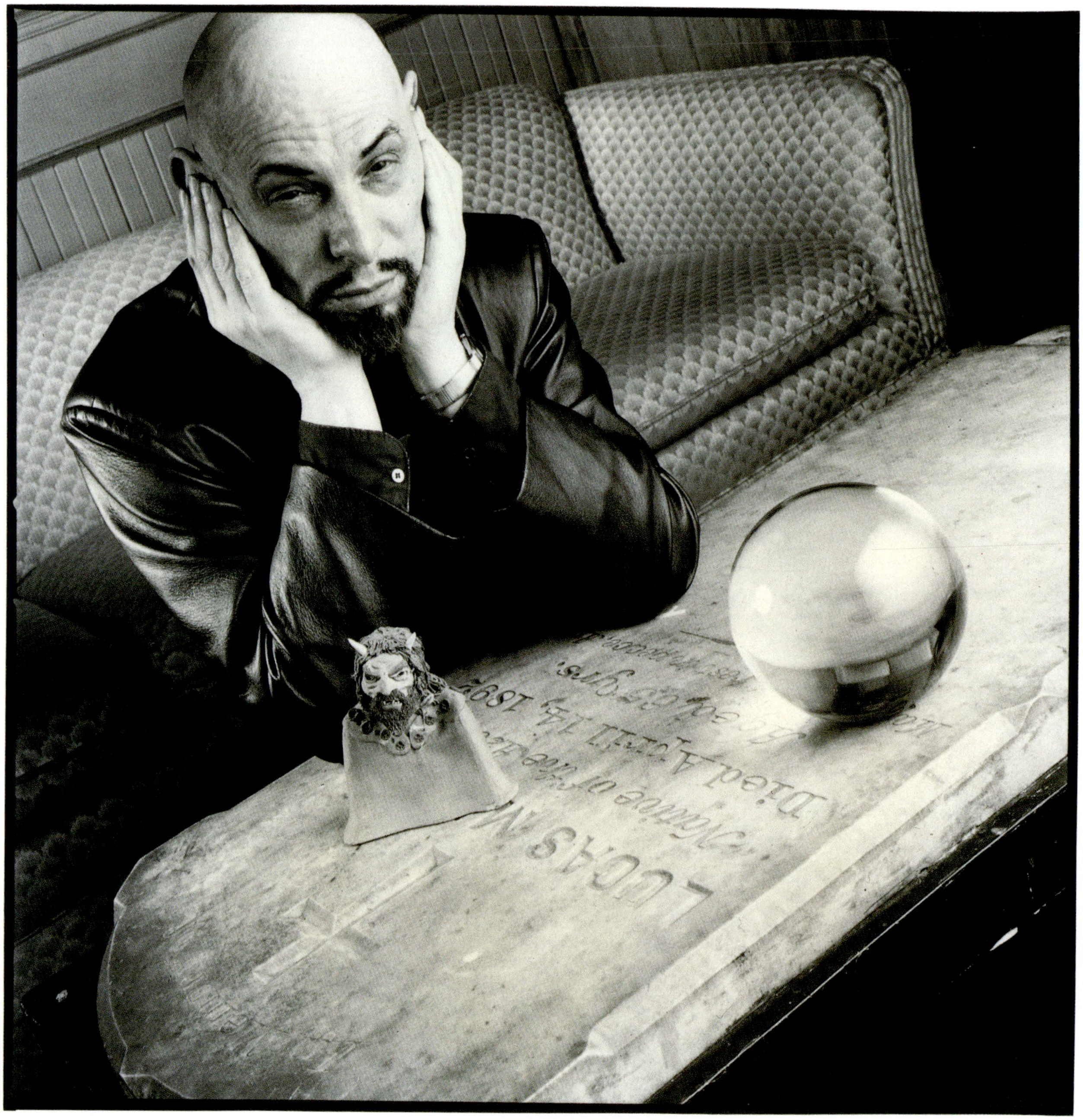

Mary Ellen Mark

»It's not easy being evil in a world that's gone to hell« was the headline of an article about Anton La Vey, who earned a reputation as the Devil incarnate by establishing the Church of Satan in San Francisco, and through his writings, notably *The Satanic Bible*.

»In einer Welt, die zum Teufel gegangen ist, ist es nicht leicht, teuflisch zu sein«, so lautete die Headline zu einem Artikel in der Zeitschrift *Rolling Stone* über Anton La Vey, der sich als Inkarnation des Teufels einen Namen machte: er gründete in San Francisco die Kirche des Satans und verfaßte u.a. »Die satanische Bibel«.

«Dans un monde qui est devenu infernal, il n'est pas facile d'être diabolique», tel était le titre d'un article du *Rolling Stone* consacré à Anton La Vey, personnage qui s'est fait un nom en se faisant passer pour l'incarnation du diable. Il a fondé l'Eglise de Satan à San Francisco et il a rédigé notamment «La Bible satanique».

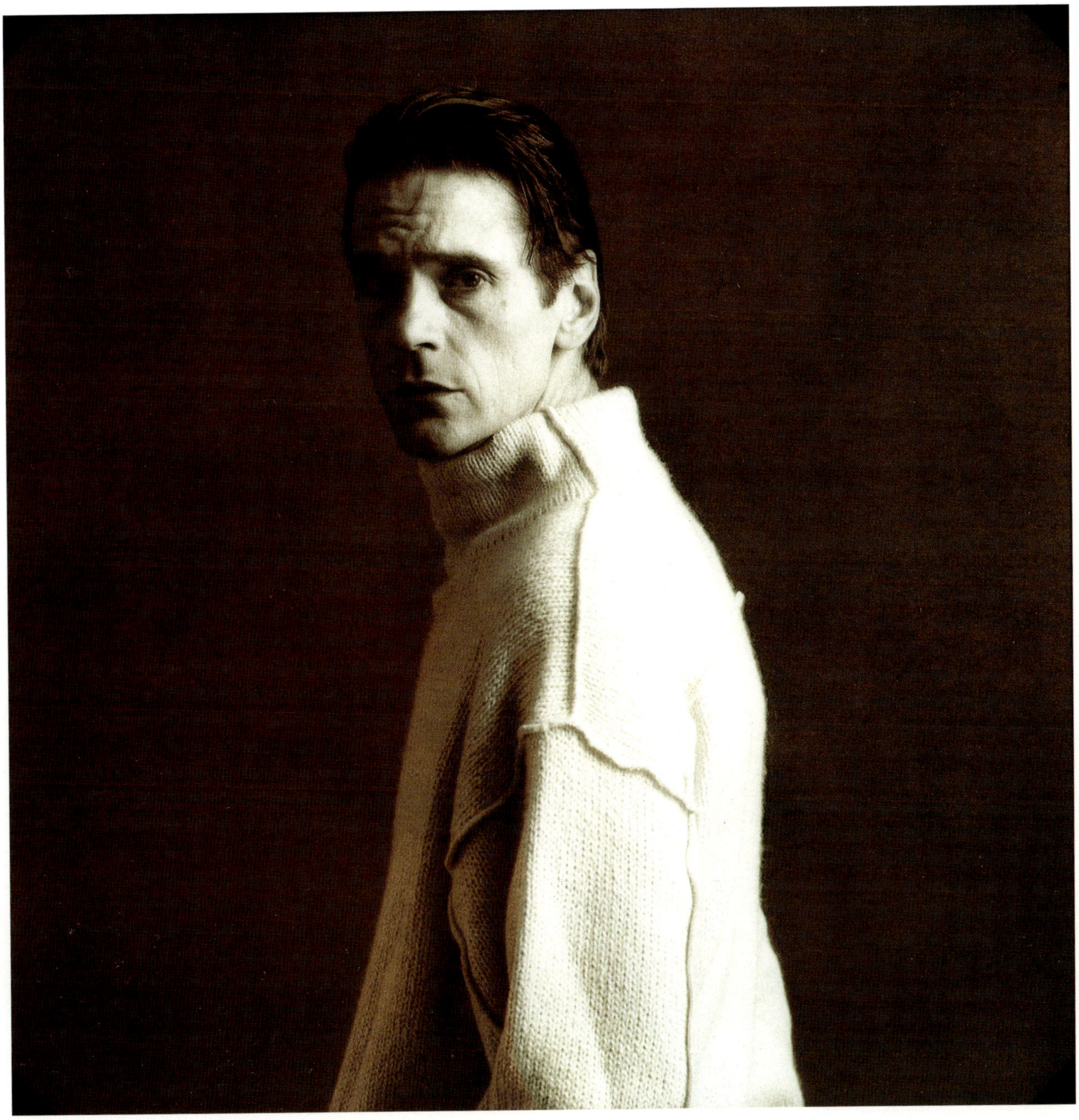

Timothy White

Portrait of the actor Jeremy Irons.

Porträt des Schauspielers Jeremy Irons.

Portrait de l'acteur Jeremy Irons.

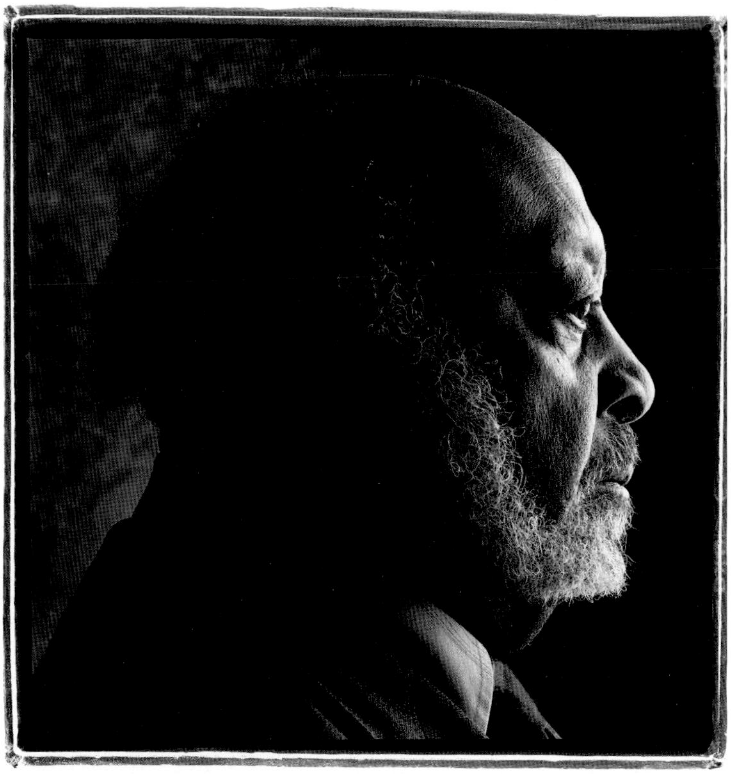

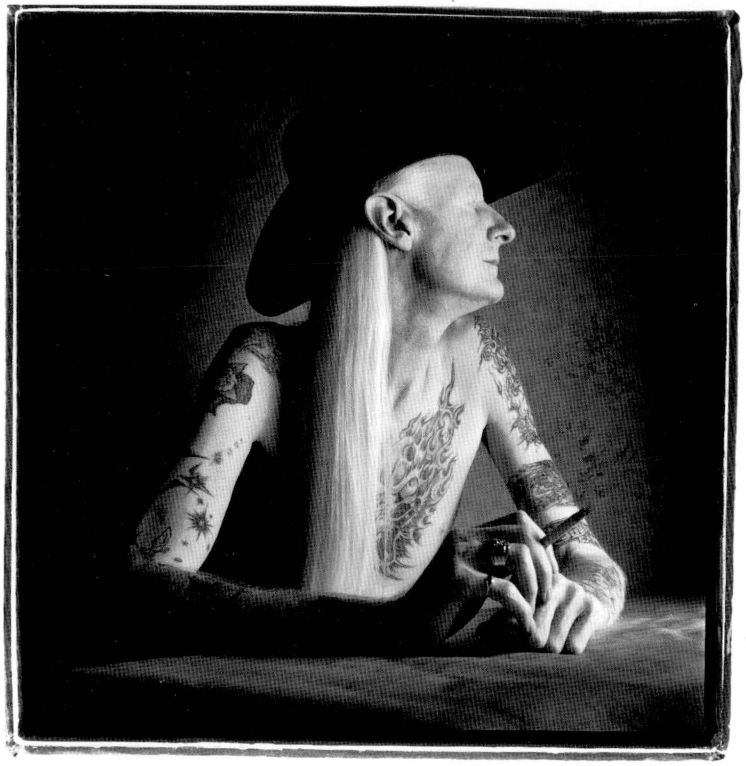

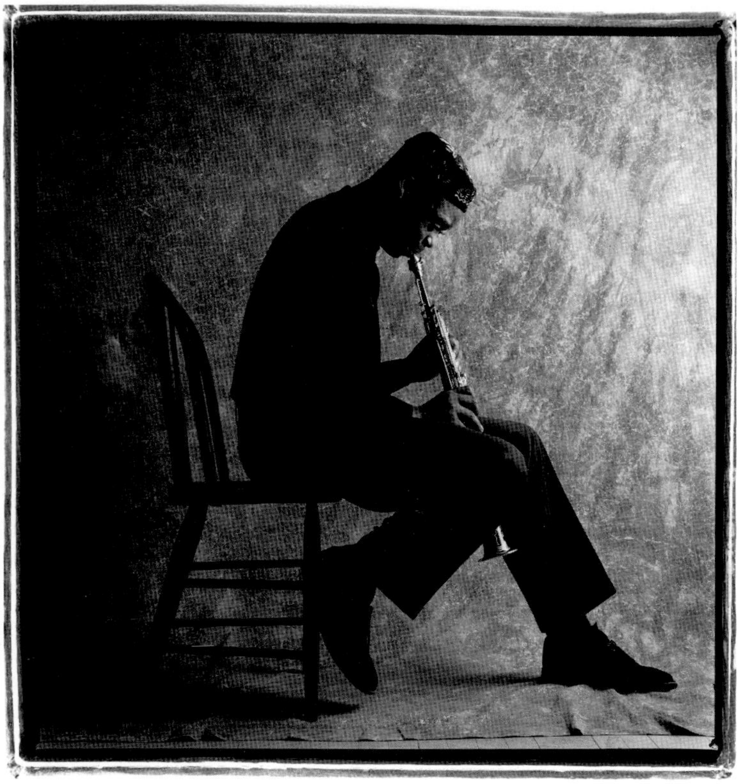

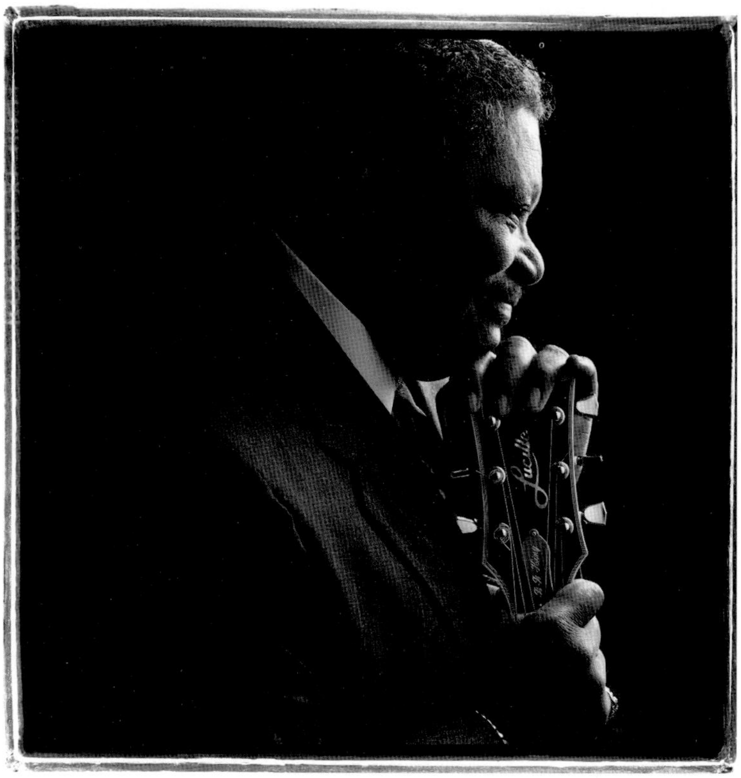

Marc Norberg

Examples from an ongoing series of portraits of blues and jazz musicians. P. 76: Robert Junior Lockwood, Johnny Winter, Courtney Pine, B.B. King; p. 77: Sam Myers, Marlena Shaw, Vanessa Rubin, John Campbel.

Beispiele aus einer Porträt-Reihe von Jazz- und Blues-Musikern. S. 76: Robert Junior Lockwood, Johnny Winter, Courtney Pine, B.B. King; S. 77: Sam Myers, Marlena Shaw, Vanessa Rubin, John Campbel.

Exemples d'une série de portraits de musiciens de jazz et de blues. P. 76: Robert Jr. Lockwood, Johnny Winter, Courtney Pine, B.B. King; p. 77: Sam Myers, Marlena Shaw, Vanessa Rubin, John Campbel.

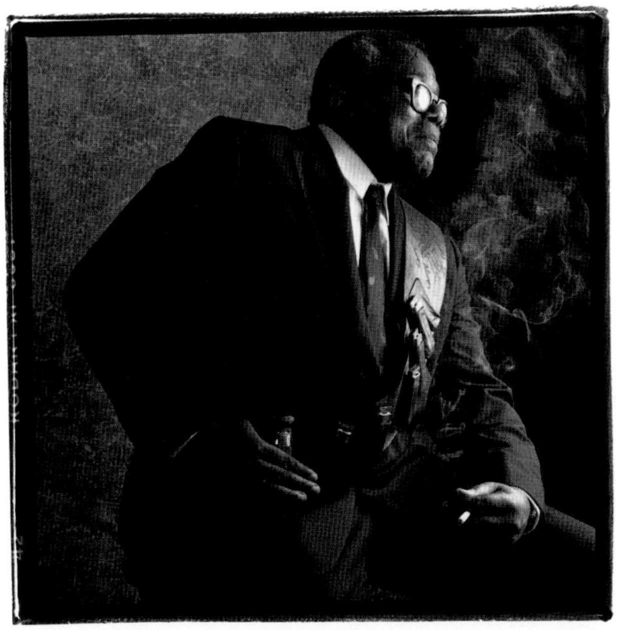

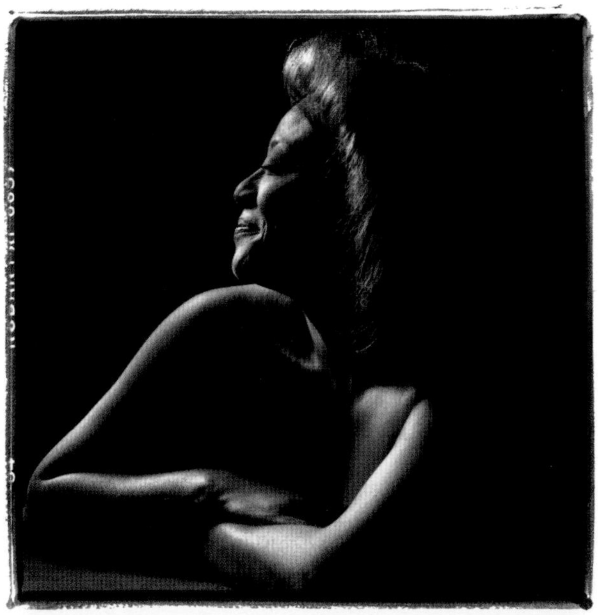

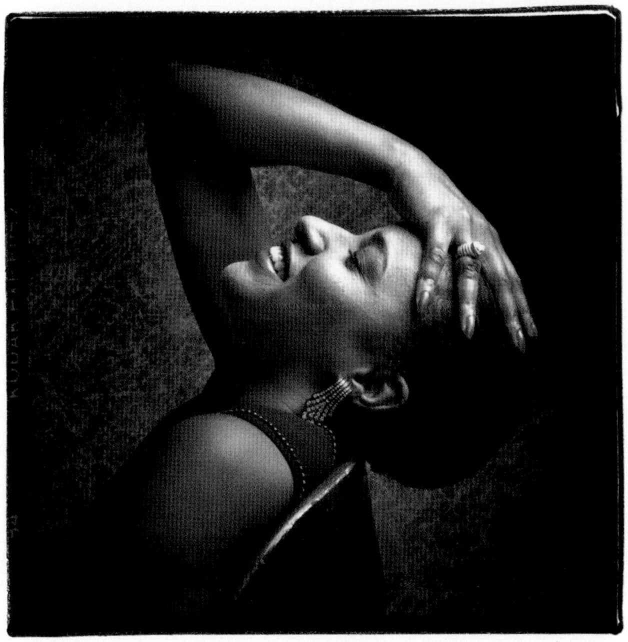

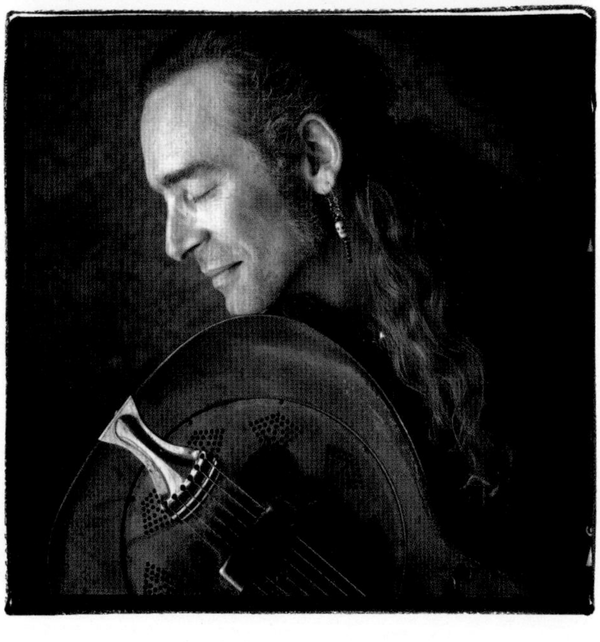

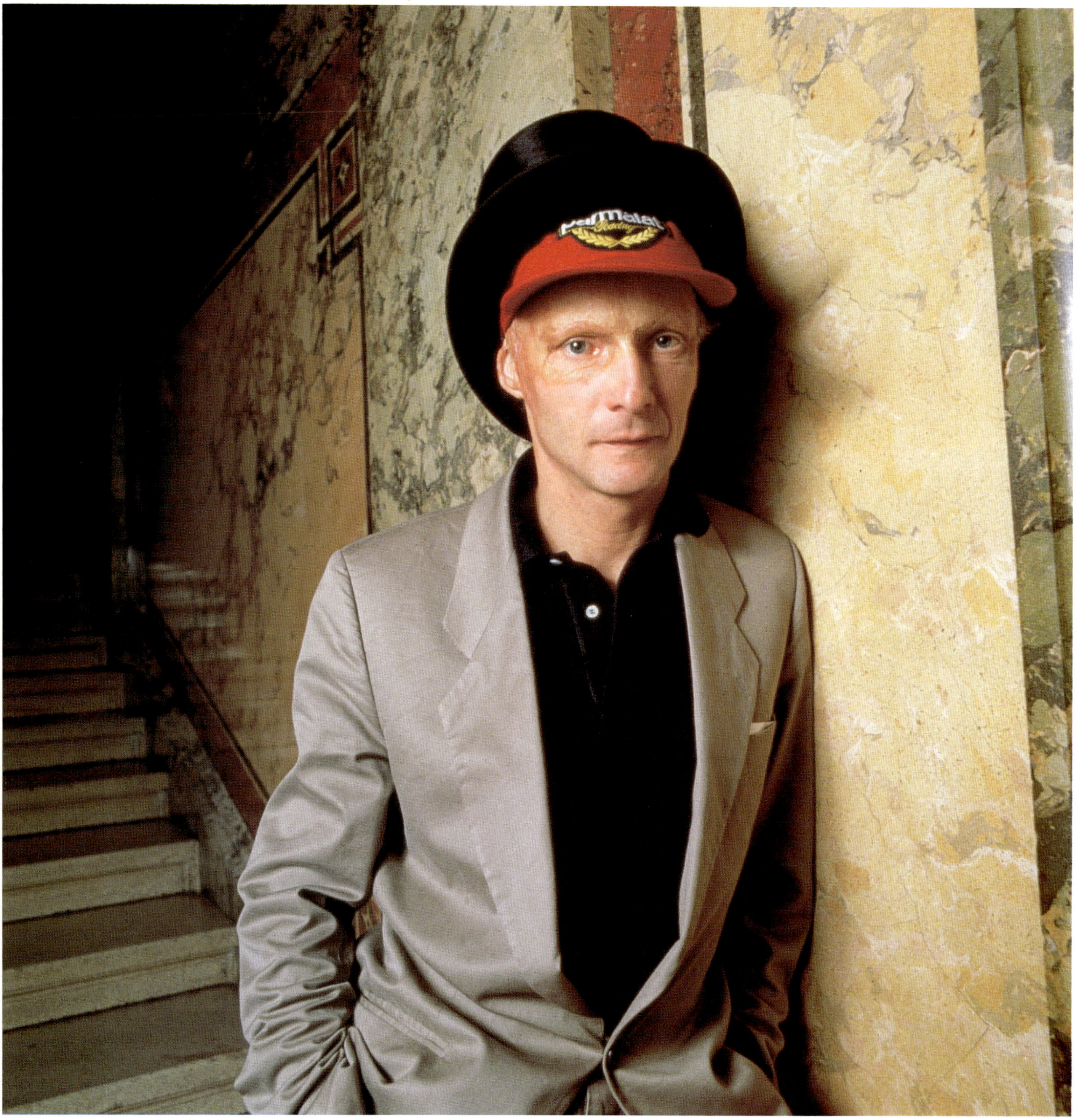

Paul Schirnhofer

Portrait of Niki Lauda, three-times Formula I World Champion – and also proprietor of an airline.

Porträt Niki Laudas, dreifacher Formel-I-Weltmeister und Besitzer einer Fluglinie.

Portrait de Niki Lauda, trois fois champion du monde de formule I et propriétaire d'une compagnie aérienne.

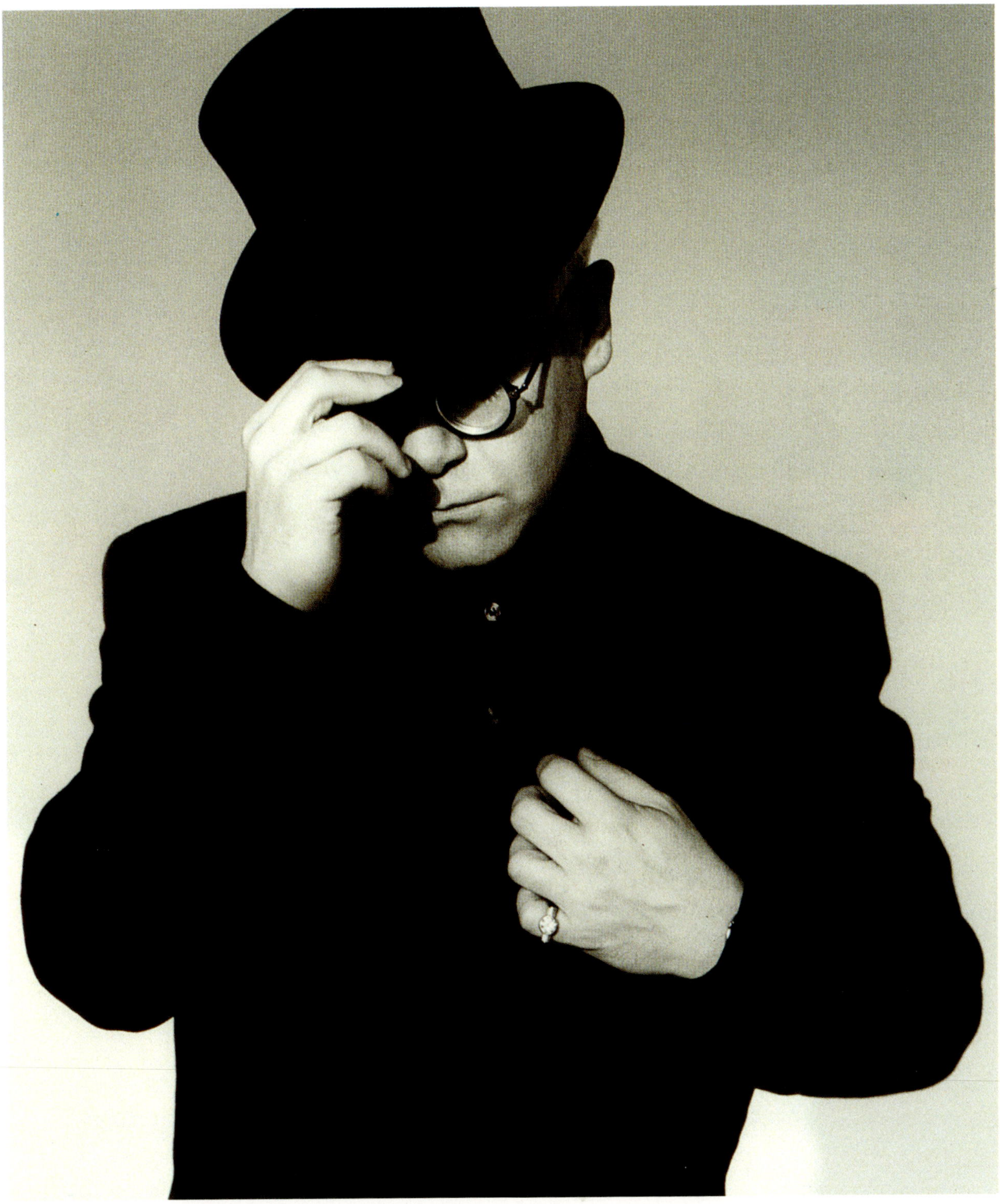

Herb Ritts

»The New Elton John: Clean, Happy and in Love.« *Rolling Stone* magazine used this photo on the cover of an issue containing the story of Elton John's drug and alcohol abuse and subsequent recovery.

»Der neue Elton John: sauber, glücklich und verliebt.« *Rolling Stone* berichtete über den Popstar, der eine Drogen- und Alkoholentziehungskur hinter sich hat.

«Un nouvel Elton John: désintoxiqué, heureux et amoureux.» Ce portrait introduisait un article dans *Rolling Stone* sur le chanteur pop, qui a réussi à se libérer de l'emprise de la drogue et de l'alcool.

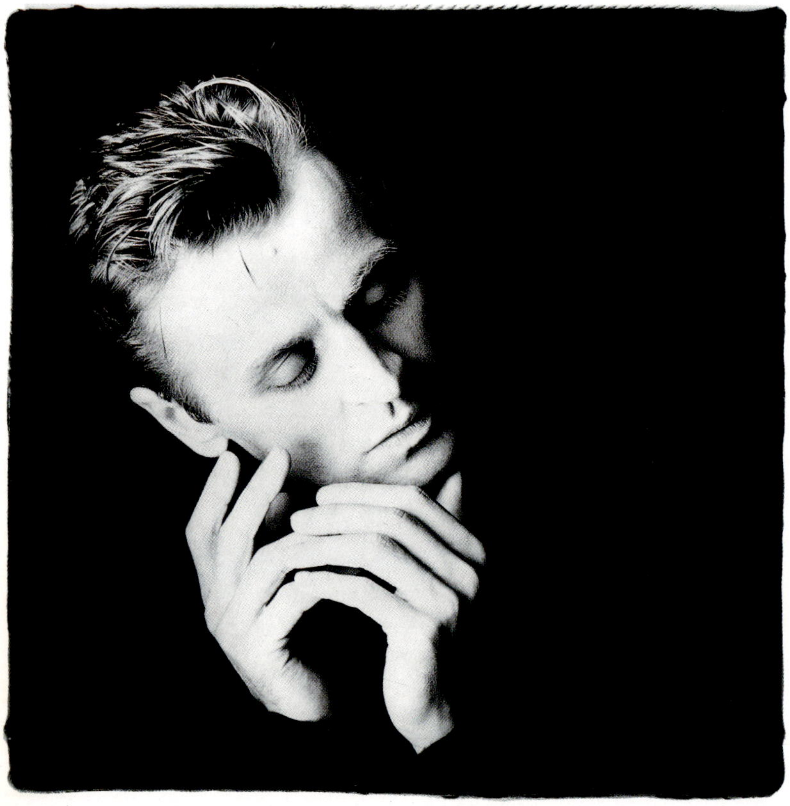

Matthew Rolston

Portrait of dancer Mikhail Baryshnikov from *Rolling Stone* magazine.

Porträtaufnahme des Tänzers Michail Barischnikow aus der Zeitschrift *Rolling Stone*.

Portrait du danseur Mikhaïl Barychnikov du magazine *Rolling Stone*.

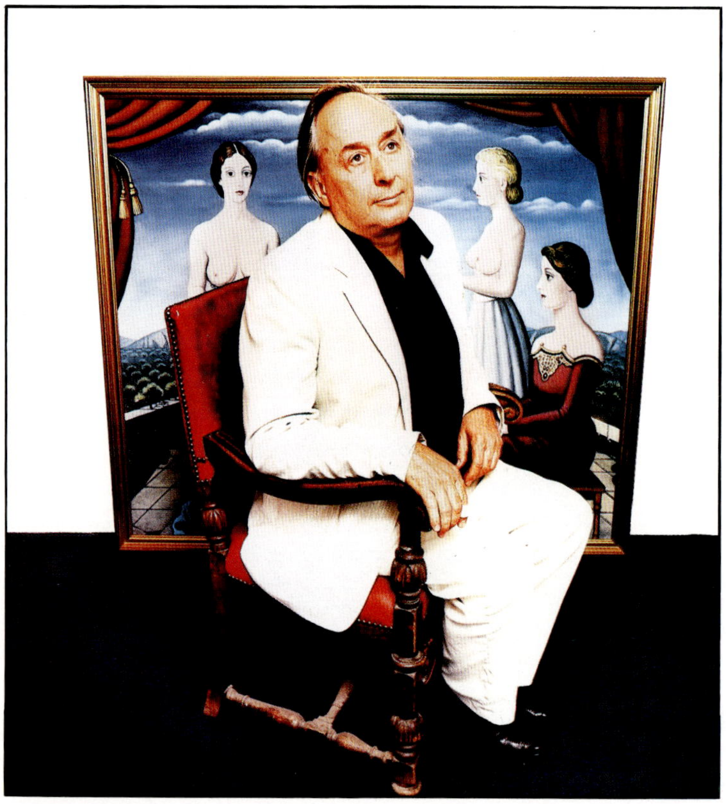

Richard Croft

Portrait of author J. G. Ballard from *Rolling Stone* magazine.

Porträtaufnahme des Autors J. G. Ballard aus der Zeitschrift *Rolling Stone*.

Portrait de l'auteur J. G. Ballard du magazine *Rolling Stone*.

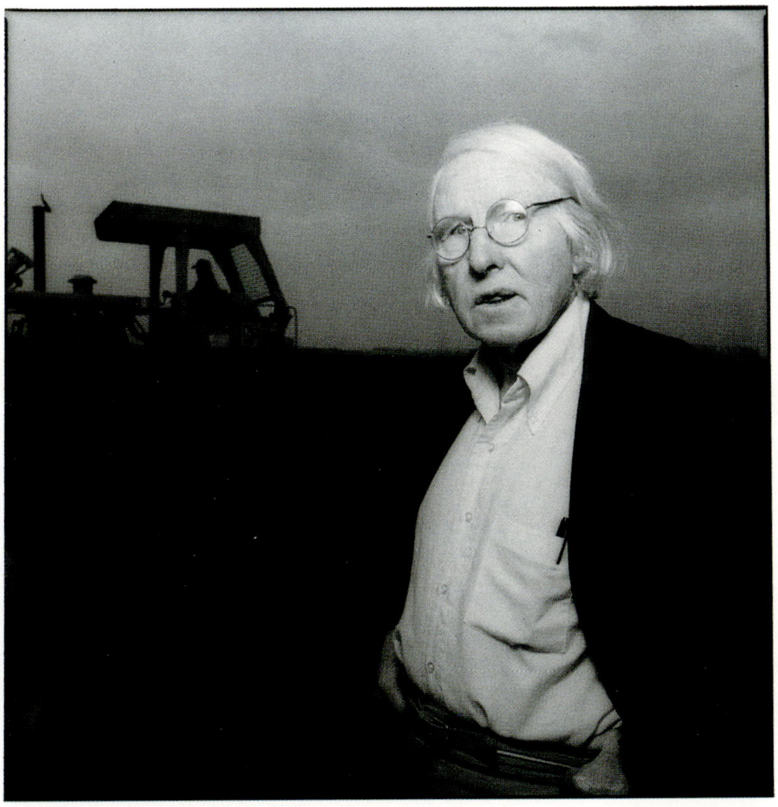

Rick English

Portrait of landscape architect Dan Kilen to accompany an article in *Peninsula Magazine*.

Porträtaufnahme des Landschaftsarchitekten Dan Kilen für einen Artikel im *Peninsula Magazine*.

Portrait de l'architecte-paysagiste Dan Kilen pour un article paru dans le *Peninsula Magazine*.

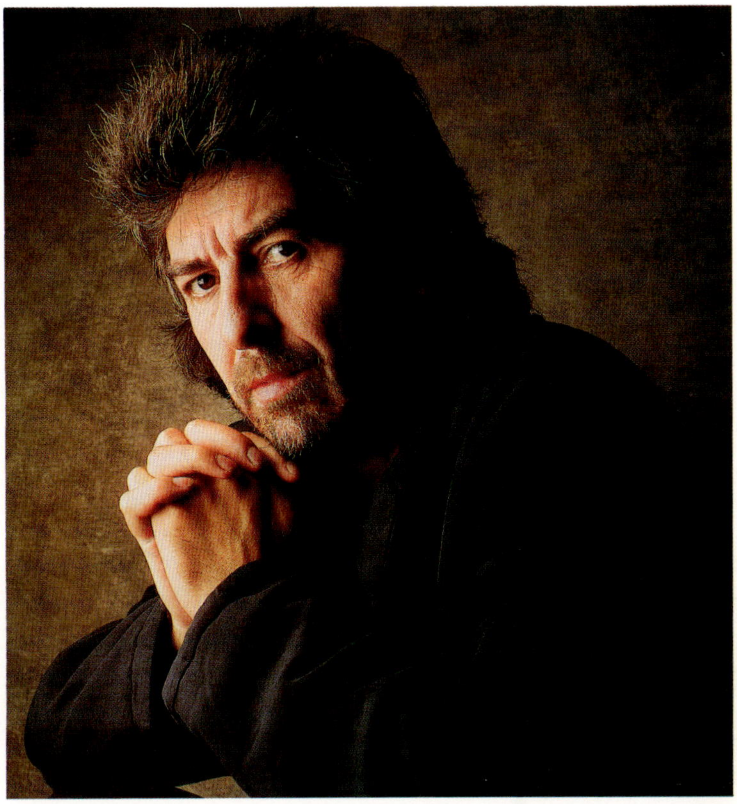

William Coupon

Portrait of former Beatle George Harrison from *Rolling Stone* magazine.

Porträtaufnahme vom Ex-Beatle George Harrison aus der Zeitschrift *Rolling Stone*.

Portrait de l'ancien Beatle George Harrison du magazine *Rolling Stone*.

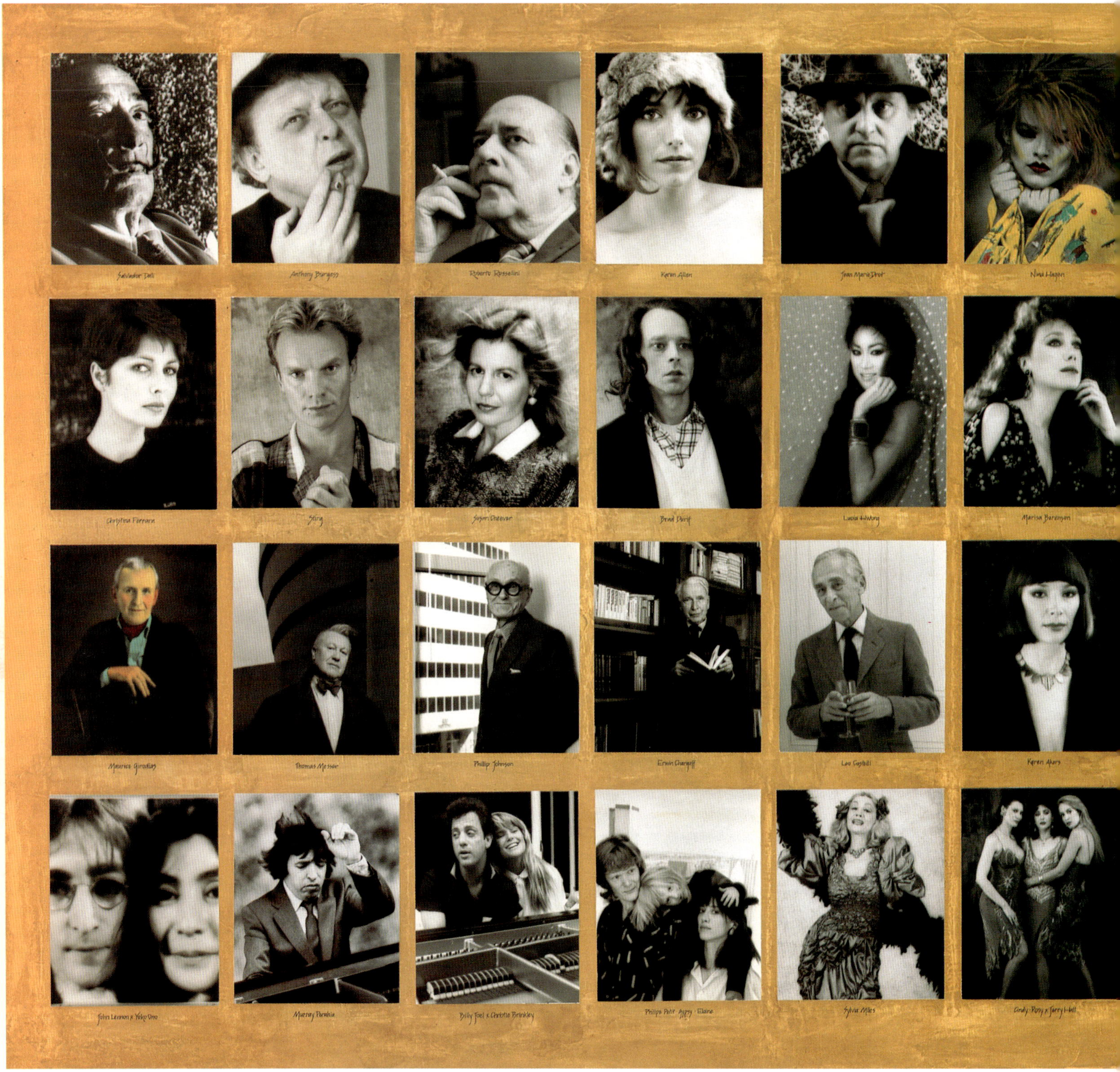

Gilles Larrain

A gallery of portraits of celebrities presented in a catalogue for an exhibition of photographer Gilles Larrain's work at the Meadows Museum. The photos were mounted on a wood panel and fixed with a beeswax composite.

Porträts von berühmten Persönlichkeiten aus dem Katalog für eine Ausstellung des Fotografen Gilles Larrain in Dallas. Die Aufnahmen wurden auf Holz aufgezogen und mit einer Bienenwachsmischung fixiert.

Portraits de célébrités figurant dans le catalogue d'une exposition du photographe Gilles Larrain au Meadows Museum, à Dallas. Les photos étaient montées sur bois et fixées avec un mélange à base de cire d'abeille.

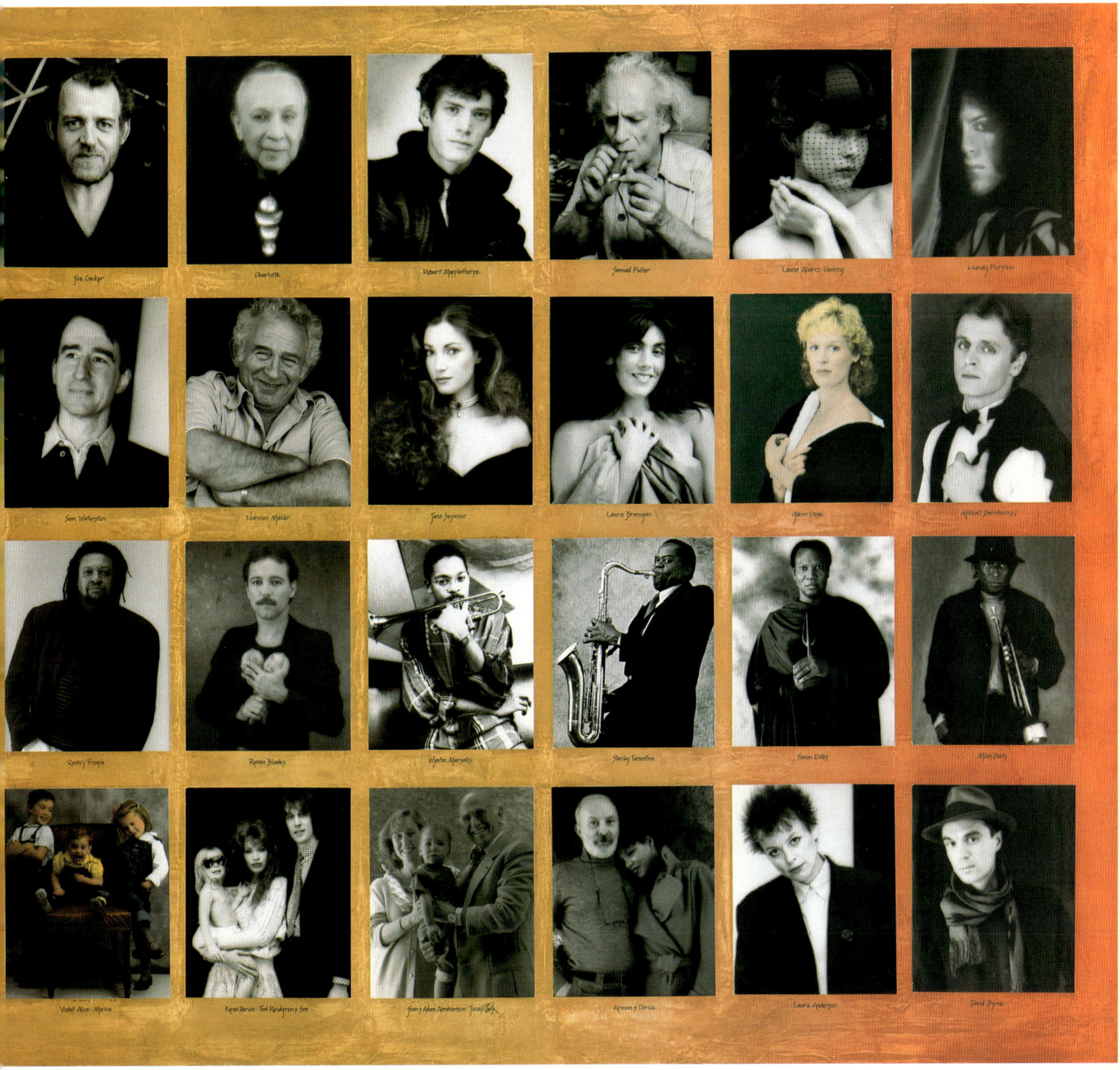

Joe Cocker
Charlotte
Robert Mapplethorpe
Samuel Fuller
Harvey Fierstein
Sam Waterston
Norman Mailer
Jane Seymour
Laura Branigan
Glenn Close
Mikhail Baryshnikov
Quincy Troupe
Ruben Blades
Wynton Marsalis
Stanley Turentine
Simon Estes
Miles Davis
Violet · Alice · Marina
Karen Darvin · Tod Rundgren y Son
Joan y Adam Abrahamson · Jonas Salk
Armon y Corice
Laurie Anderson
David Byrne

Michael O'Brien

»An Eye for Danger« – this portrait of crime- and adventure-story author Robert Stone was taken for the cover of the *New York Times Magazine.*

Robert Stone ist ein amerikanischer Autor, der sich mit Abenteuer- und Kriminalliteratur befaßt. Sein Porträt erschien auf dem Umschlag vom *New York Times Magazine* mit der Headline: »Ein Auge für die Gefahr«.

Robert Stone est un auteur américain, spécialisé dans le livre d'aventures et le roman policier. Ce portrait a été publié en couverture du *New York Times Magazine* sous le titre «Un œil pour le danger».

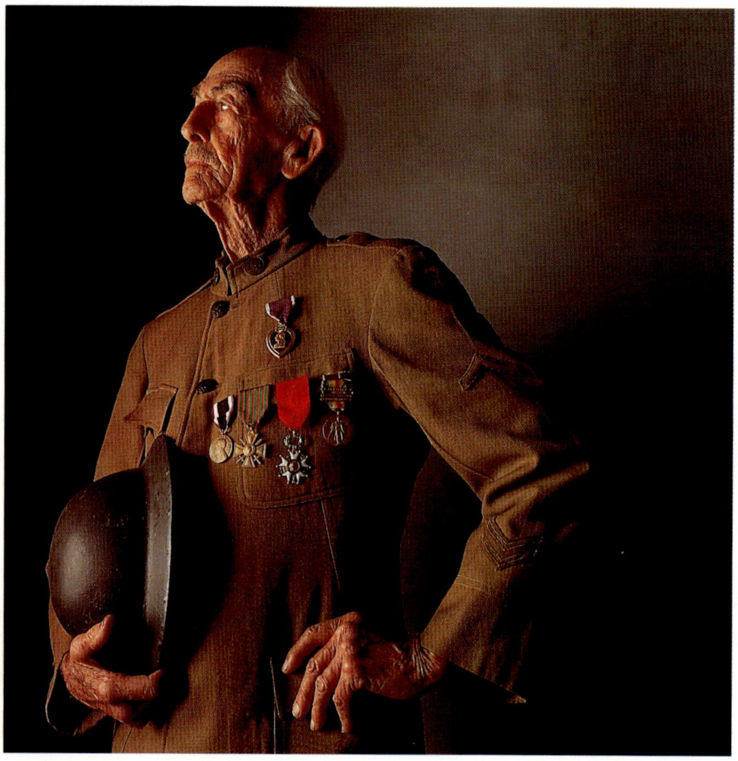

Michael O'Brien

Winston Roche, 92, who served in the US Army during World War I, photographed for a series on war veterans, assigned by *Life* magazine.

Ein 92jähriger Veteran, der als Leutnant für die USA im ersten Weltkrieg kämpfte. Aus einer Porträtreihe von Kriegsveteranen für *Life.*

Série sur les vétérans de l'armée américaine, pour *Life.* Winston Roche, 92 ans, servit sous les drapeaux pendant la première guerre mondiale.

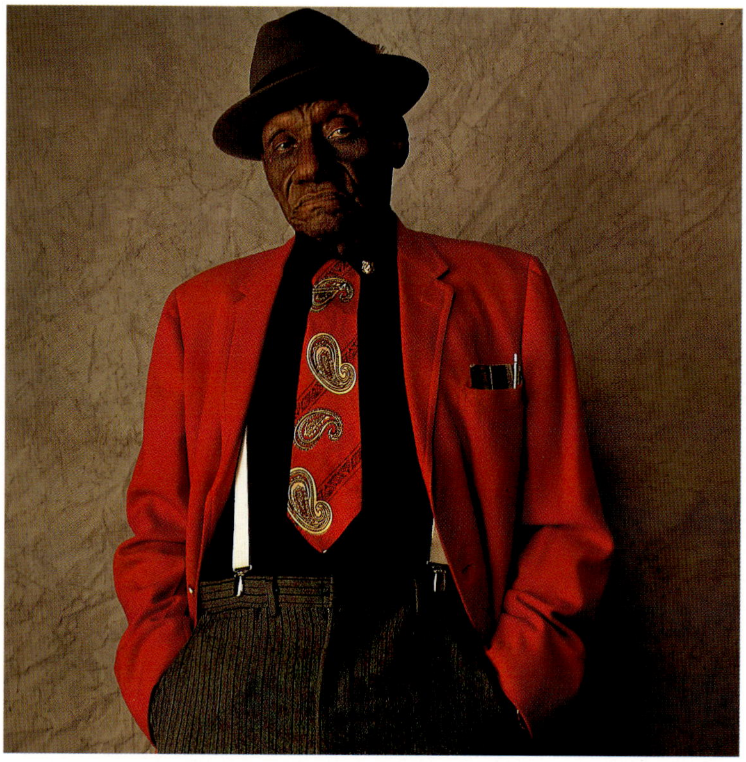

Michael O'Brien

Roosevelt Thomas Williams, 87-year-old barrelhouse blues musician, known as the grey ghost, who used to travel by freight train playing from town to town. He was portrayed for a feature in *National Geographic* magazine who wanted a cross-section of the citizens of Austin, Texas.

Roosevelt Thomas Williams, 87 Jahre alt und Blues-Musiker. Früher reiste er für seine Auftritte mit Güterzügen von Stadt zu Stadt. Das Magazin *National Geographic* hatte den Fotografen beauftragt, Porträts eines Querschnitts der Bürger von Austin, Texas, zu machen.

Série sur les habitants de la ville d'Austin, réalisée pour le magazine *National Geographic.* Ici, Roosevelt Thomas Williams, 87 ans, le musicien de blues qui se déplaçait de ville en ville dans des wagons de marchandises, apparaissant et disparaissant «Tel le Fantôme».

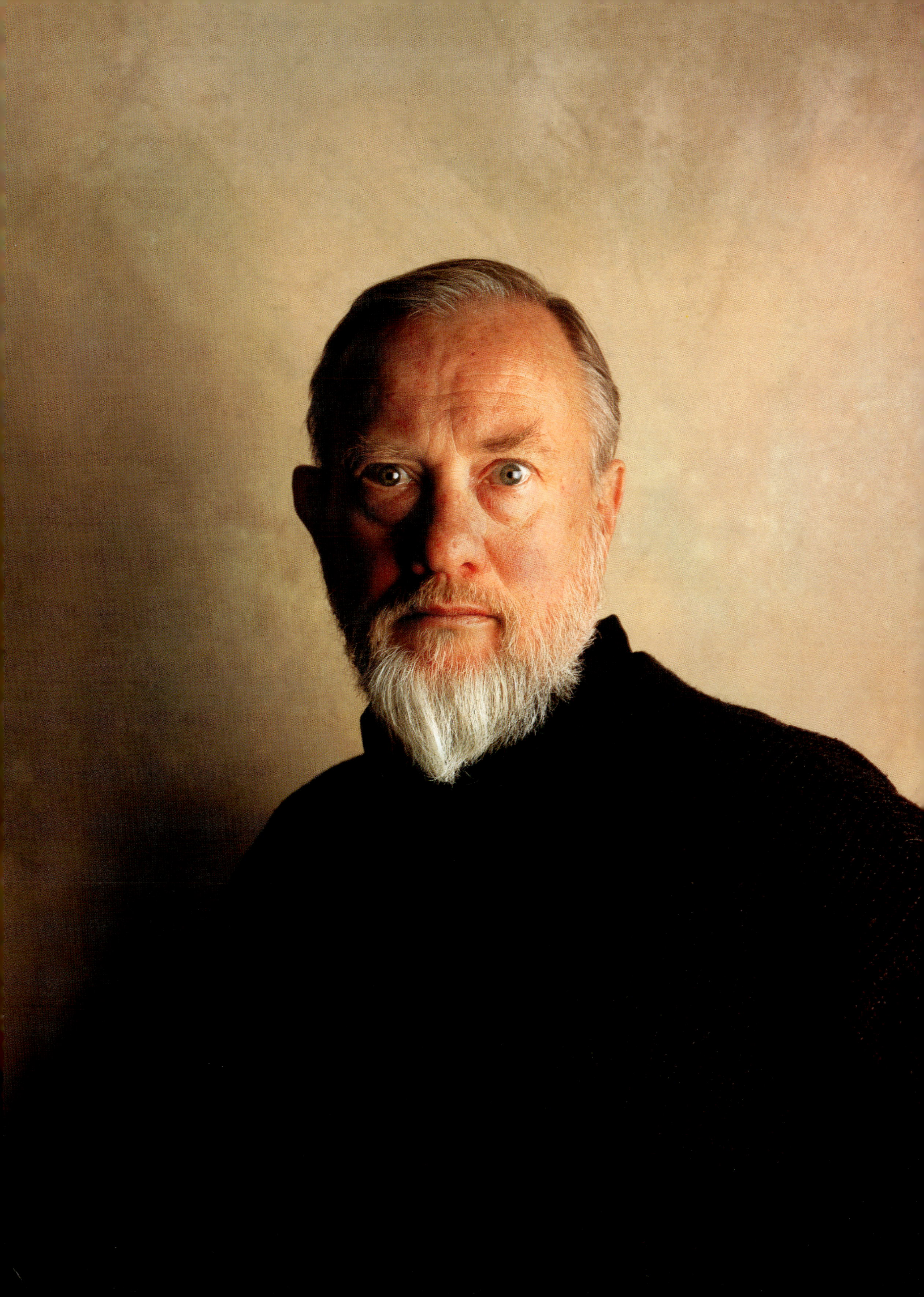

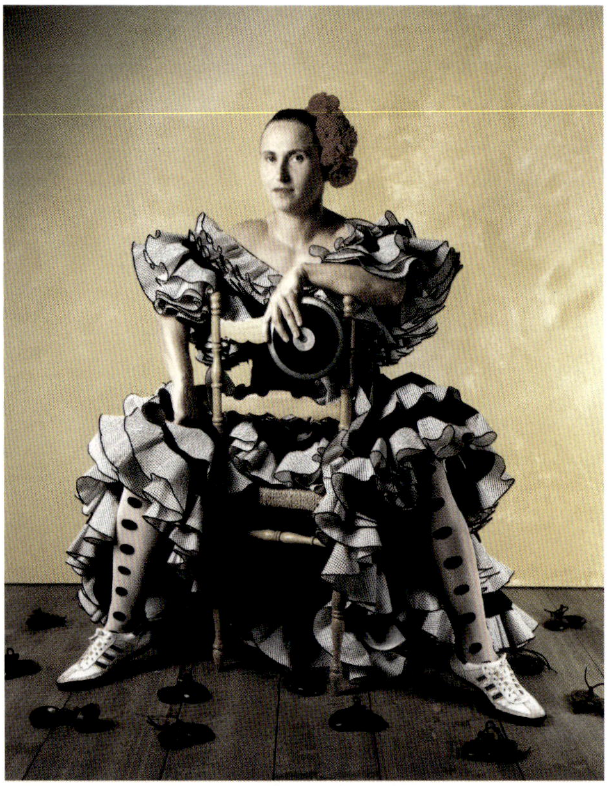

Claudio Alessandri

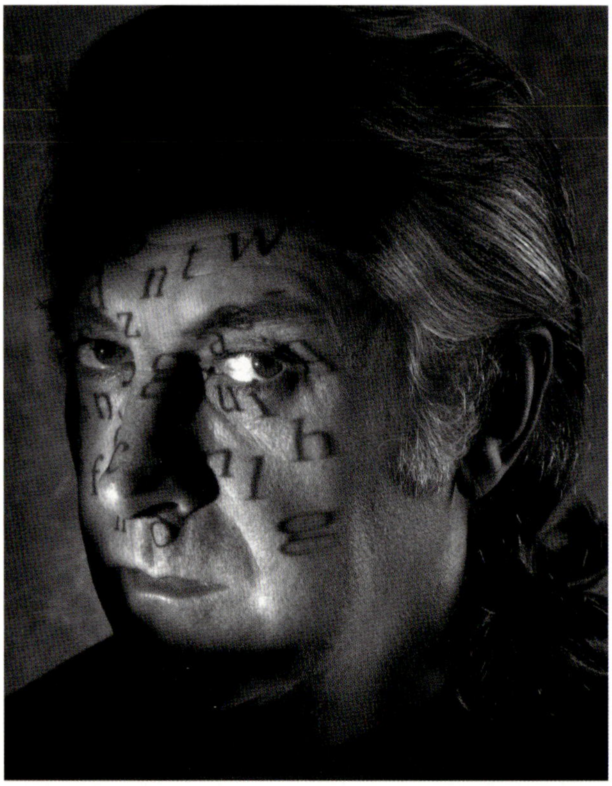

Steve Marsel

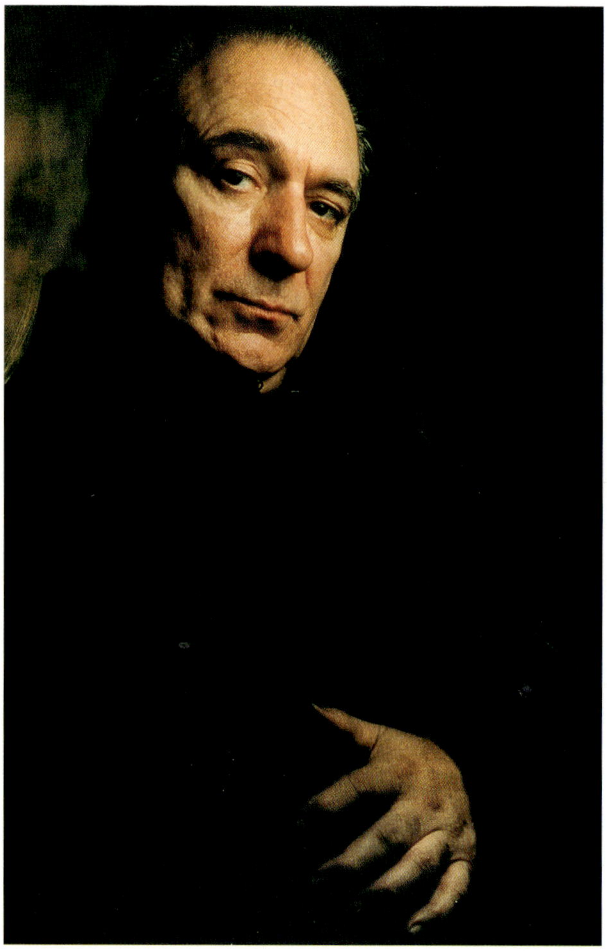

Peter Liepke

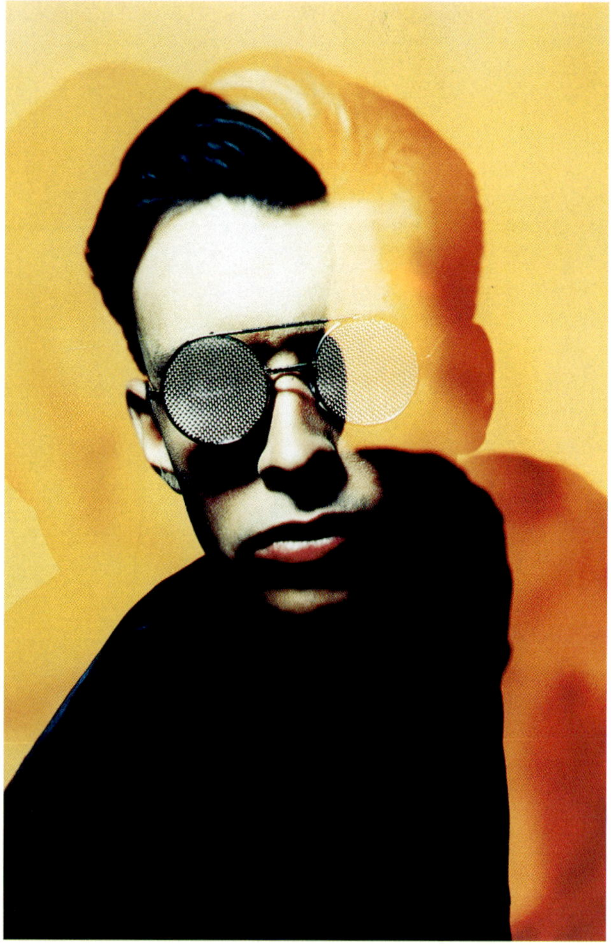

Christiane Marek

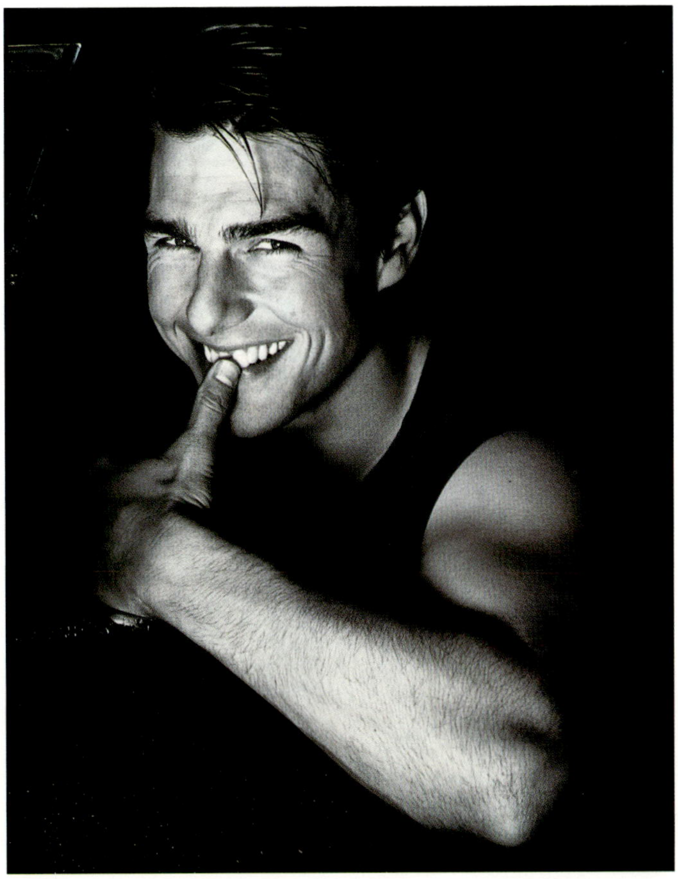

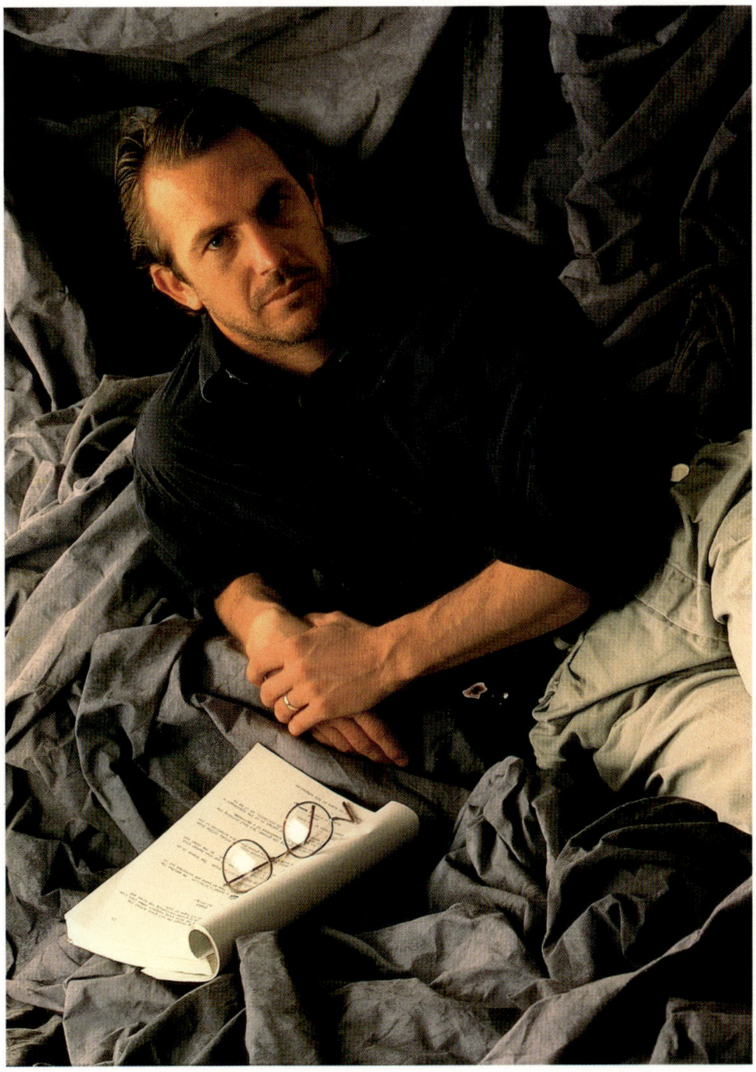

◁ Albert Watson

American actor Tom Cruise, who is hard to pin down for an interview and ferociously protective of his private life.

Der amerikanische Schauspieler Tom Cruise, der schwer für ein Interview zu haben ist und sein Privatleben konsequent abschirmt.

L'acteur américain Tom Cruise: qui se laisse difficilement interviewer et protège farouchement sa vie privée.

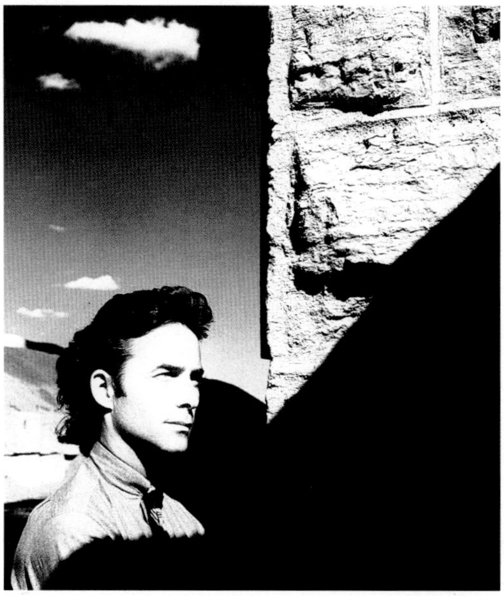

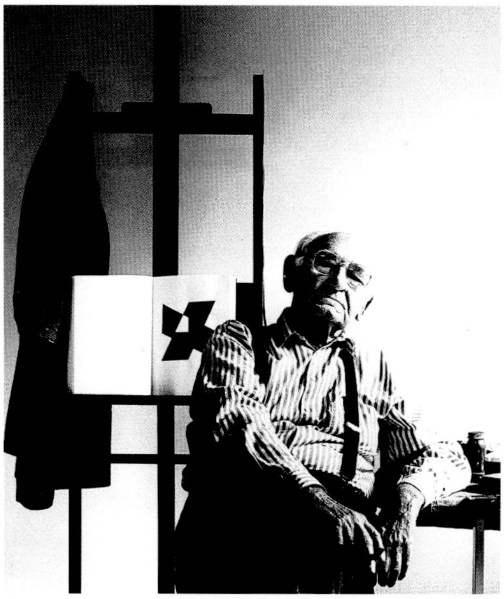

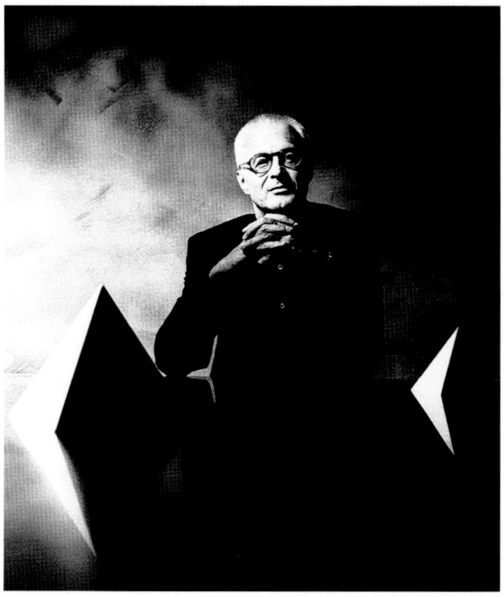

Günter Pfannmüller

An advertising campaign promotes the image of Berthold typefaces by associating the company with an international array of famous designers. Shown here from left to right are: Joe Duffy (Duffy Design Group), Anton Stankowski (Graphic Designer), Peter Schmidt (Designer); Massimo Vignelli (Vignelli Associates), Karl Gerstner (The first G of GGK), Dr. Florian Langenscheidt (Langenscheidt Publishers).

Porträts berühmter Leute der Design- und Werbeindustrie, die in einer Image-Kampagne für Berthold-Schriften verwendet wurden. Von links nach rechts: Joe Duffy (Duffy Design Group), Anton Stankowski (Designer), Peter Schmidt (Designer), Massimo Vignelli (Architekt und Designer, Vignelli Associates), Karl Gerstner (Das Erste G von GGK), Dr. Florian Langenscheidt (Langenscheidt Verlag).

Ces portraits des célébrités du monde du design et de la publicité illustraient une campagne de prestige pour Berthold, entreprise spécialisée dans la typographie. De gauche à droite: Joe Duffy (Duffy Design Group), Anton Stankowski (Graphiste), Peter Schmidt (Designer), Massimo Vignelli (Vignelli Assoc.), Karl Gerstner (Le Premier G de GGK), Dr. Florian Langenscheidt (Editeur).

◁ Brian Lanker

On assignment for *New York Times Sunday Magazine* the photographer was granted 20 minutes and a vacant office for this portrait of actor Kevin Costner.

Dieses Porträt des Schauspielers Kevin Kostner entstand für das *New York Times Sunday Magazine*. Dem Fotografen standen nur 20 Minuten in einem leeren Büro zur Verfügung.

Ce portrait de l'acteur américain Kevin Kostner a été réalisé pour le *New York Times Sunday Magazine*. Le photographe ne disposait que de 20 minutes dans un bureau vide.

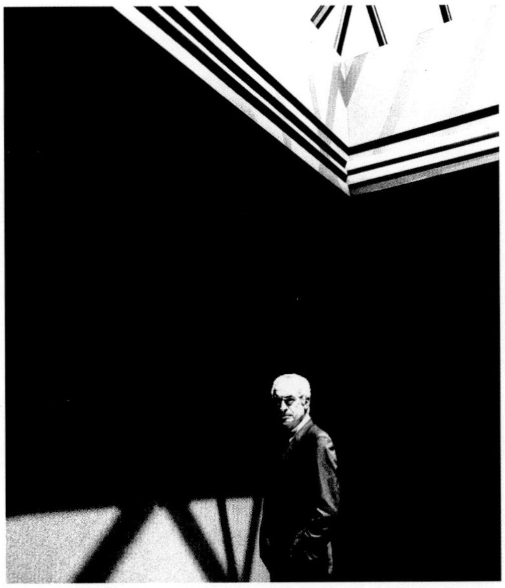

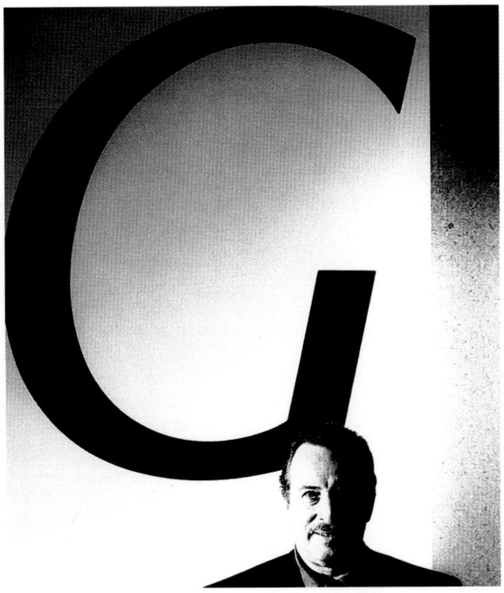

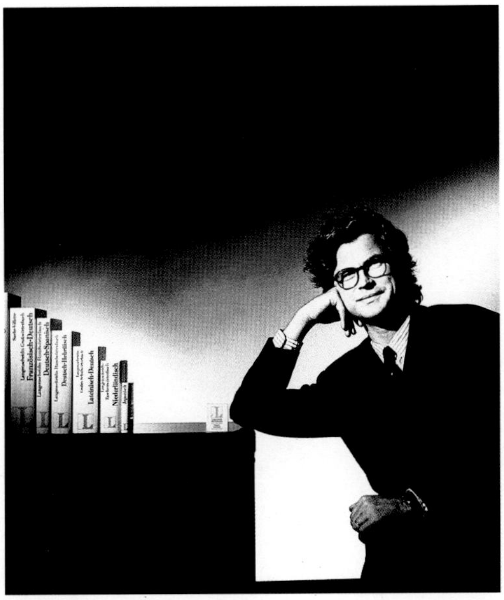

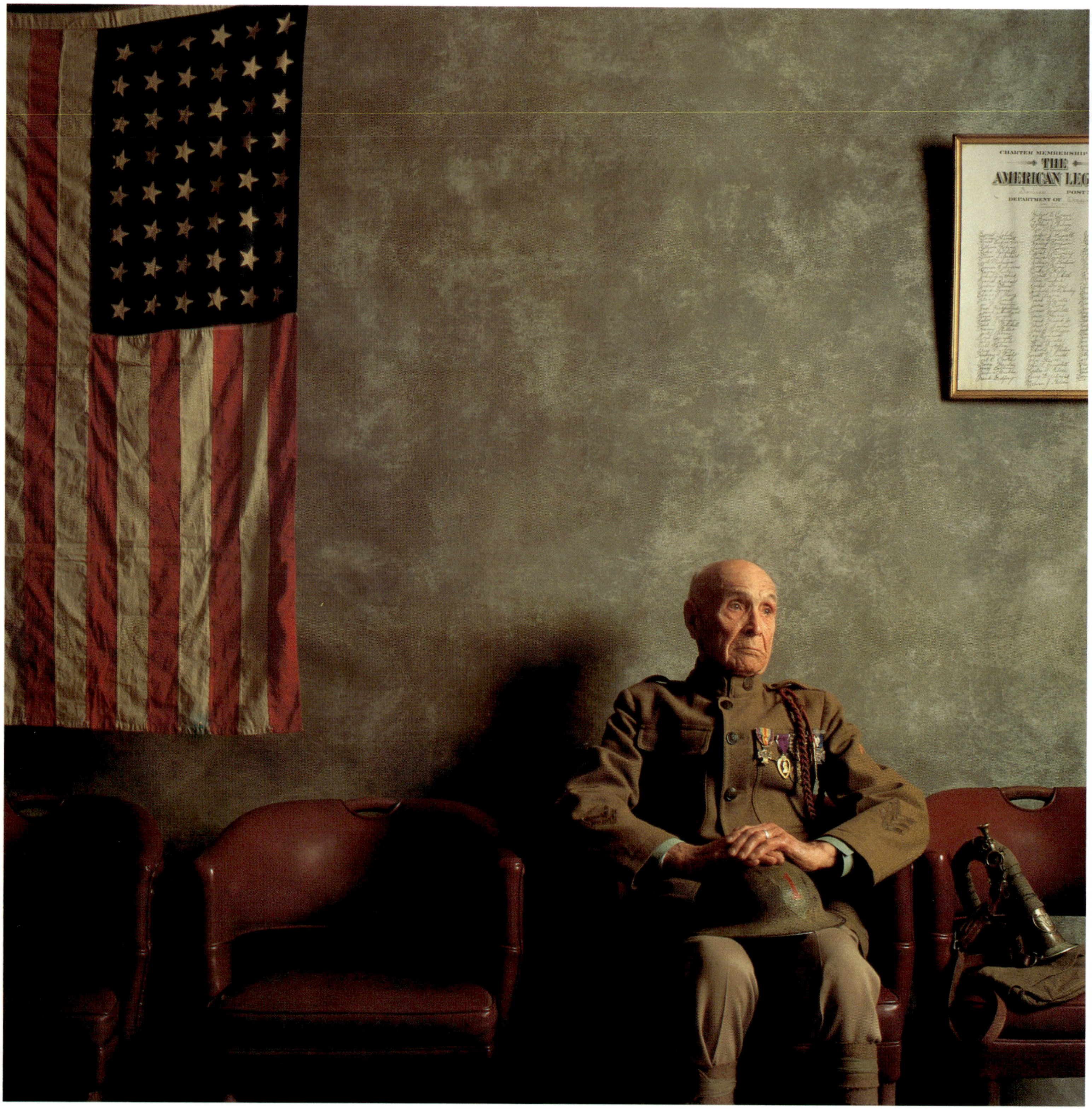

Pete Stone

Portrait of a 92-year-old veteran of World War I. It was used as a self-promotional poster for the photographer Pete Stone.

Porträt eines 92jährigen Veteranen aus dem 1. Weltkrieg. Es wird als Eigenwerbungsplakat des Fotografen Pete Stone verwendet.

Portrait d'un vétéran de la première guerre mondiale âgé de 92 ans, utilisé sur une affiche autopromotionnelle du photographe Pete Stone.

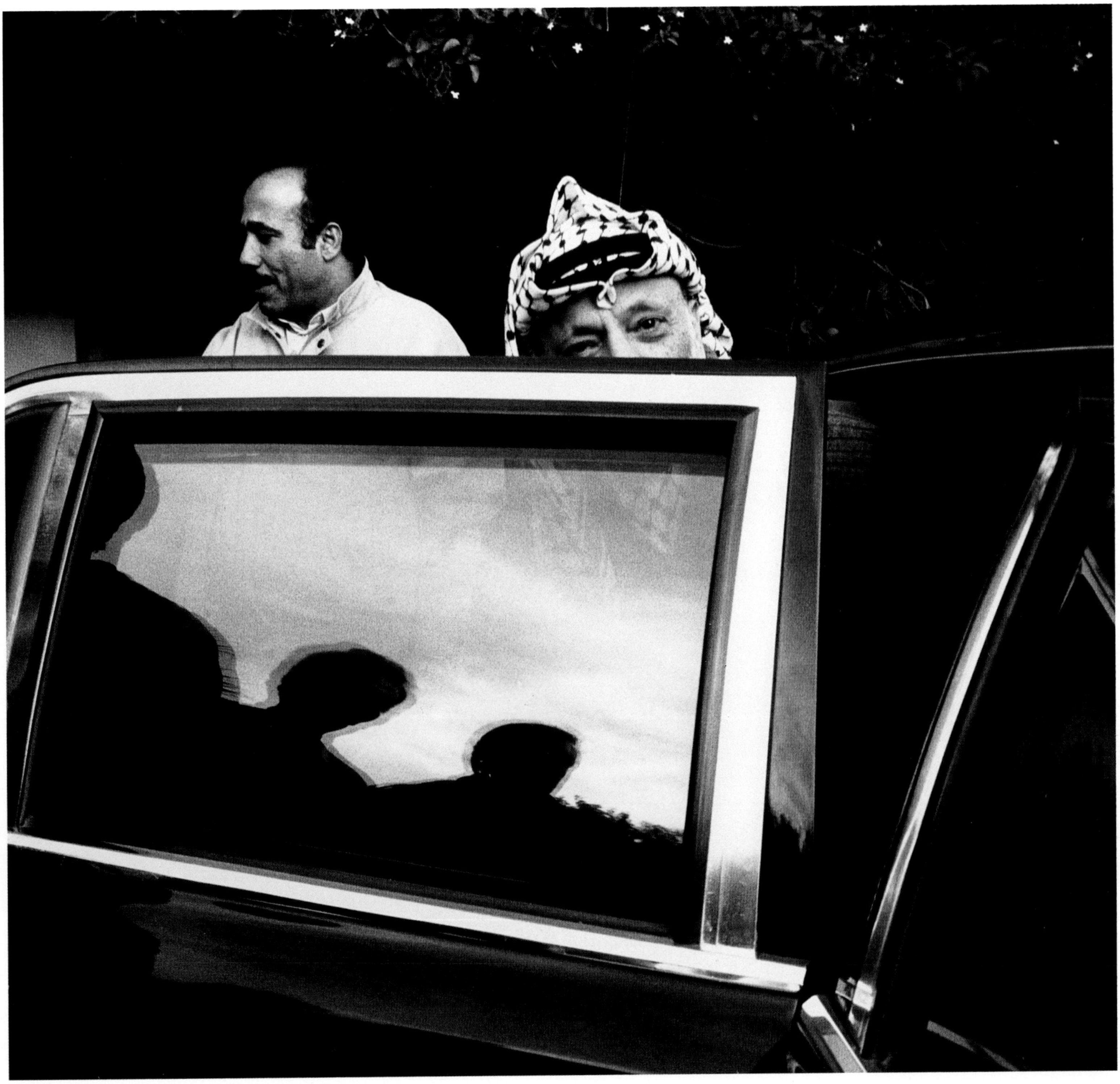

Abbas/Magnum

Yasser Arafat on a promotional tour. Photograph from an article in the magazine *Tempo*. The author, T.D. Allman, accompanied the PLO leader on a 40-hour trip across four countries.

Jassir Arafat auf Promotiontour – Aufnahme aus einem Artikel in der Zeitschrift *Tempo*. Der Autor T.D. Allman begleitete den PLO-Führer auf einem 40-Stunden-Trip durch vier Länder.

Yasser Arafat en tournée de prospection. Photo pour un article du magazine *Tempo*. Son auteur, T.D. Allman, a accompagné le leader de l'OLP durant son voyage de 40 heures dans 4 pays différents.

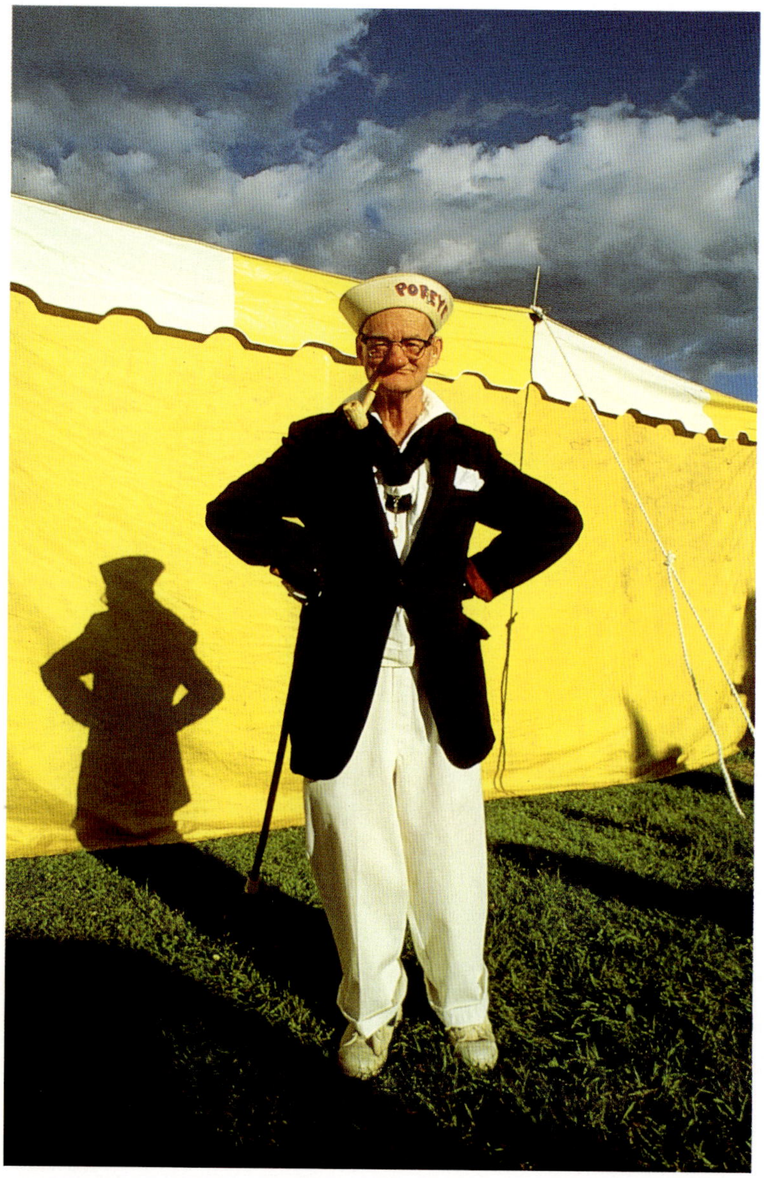

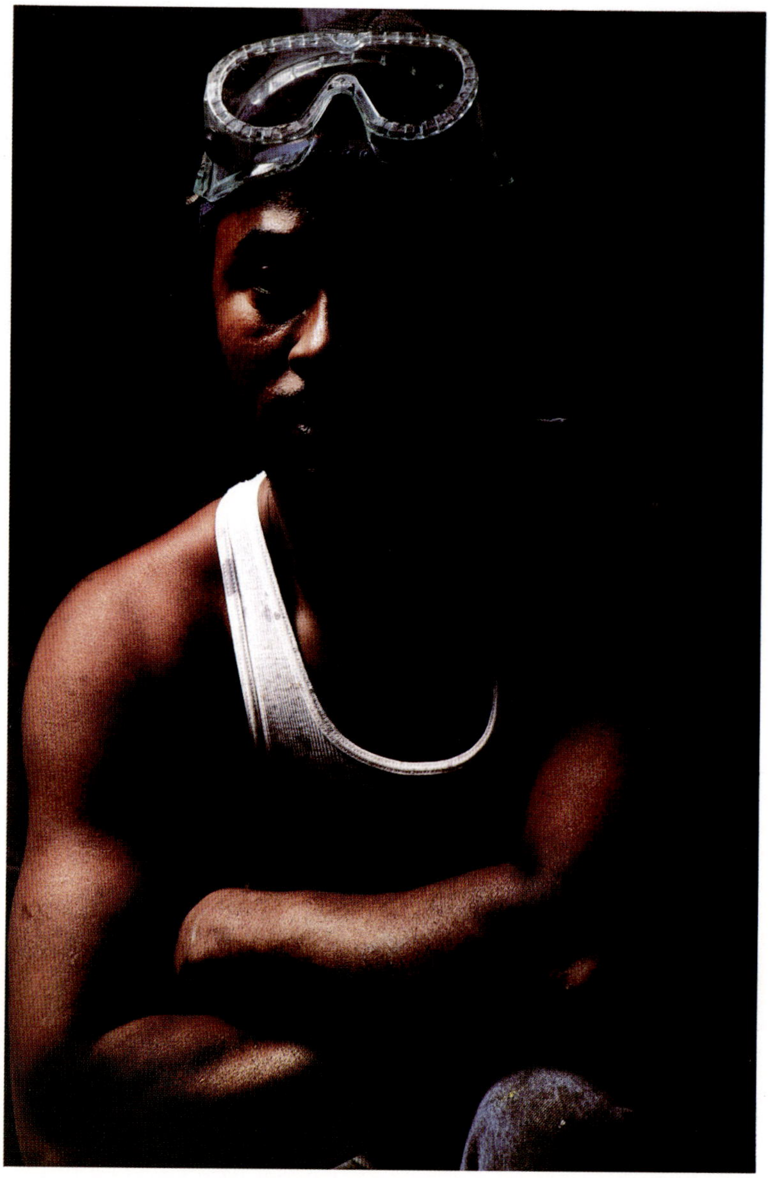

Joe Baraban

With this photo of a man in »Popeye« costume the photographer wants to demonstrate the influence of light. It is used by him for teaching purposes.

Mit dieser Aufnahme eines Mannes im »Popeye«-Kostüm will der Fotograf den Einfluß des Lichtes demonstrieren. Er verwendet sie für Unterrichtszwecke.

Par le biais de cette photo d'un homme en costume de «Popeye», le photographe veut démontrer l'influence de la lumière. Il se sert de cette photo à des fins didactiques.

Jim Krantz

Photograph used as advertising for a printing company.

Aufnahme als Werbung für eine Druckerei.

Photo utilisée pour la publicité d'un imprimeur.

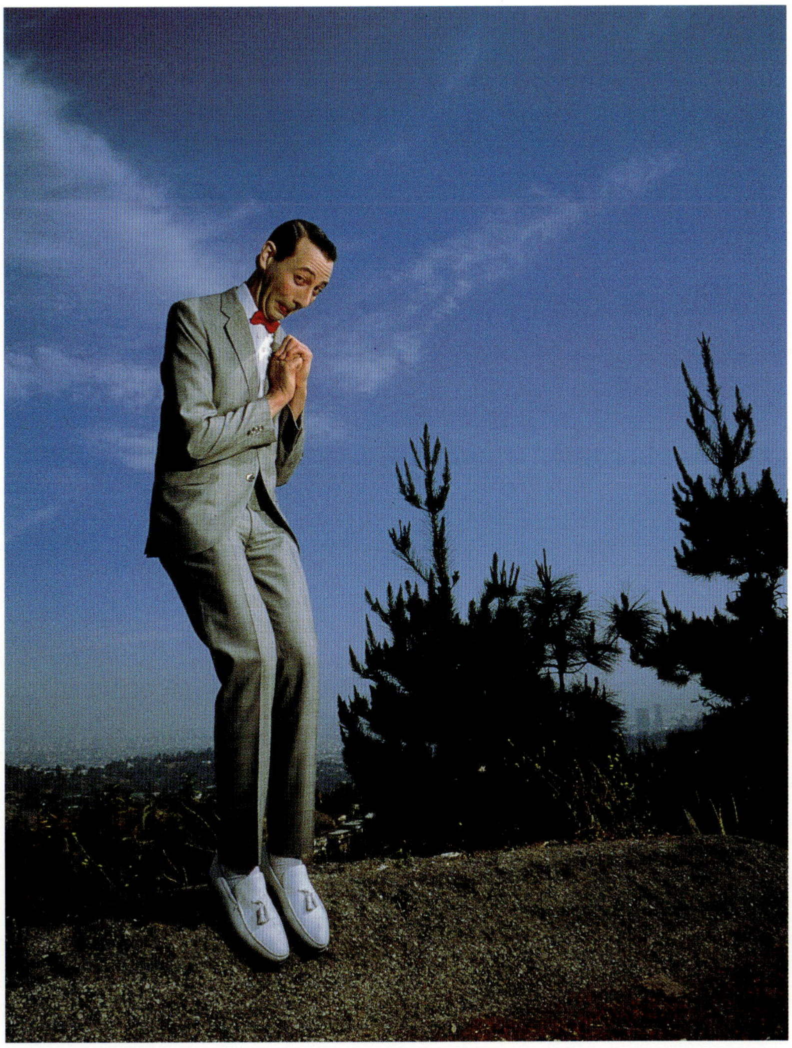

Xavier Lambours/Métis

Pee Wee Herman, Hollywood's latest comedian – portrait from the magazine *Tempo.*

Pee Wee Herman, Hollywoods neuster Komiker-Star – Porträt aus der Zeitschrift *Tempo*

Pee Wee Herman, la nouvelle vedette hollywoodienne du répertoire comique. Portrait dans *Tempo.*

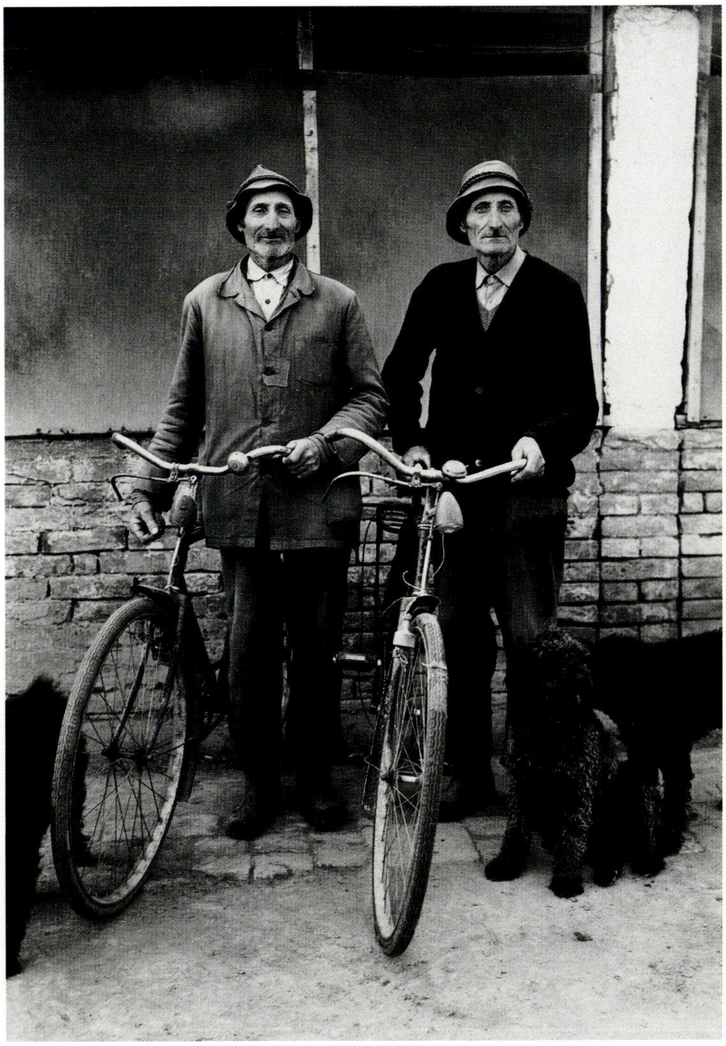

Janos Stekovics

The twin brothers Lukacs – photograph from a portfolio about isolated farmers in Hungary.

Die Zwillingsbrüder Lukacs – Aufnahme aus einem Portfolio über ungarische Einödbauern.

Les frères jumeaux Lukacs – portrait figurant dans un album de photos de paysans hongrois solitaires.

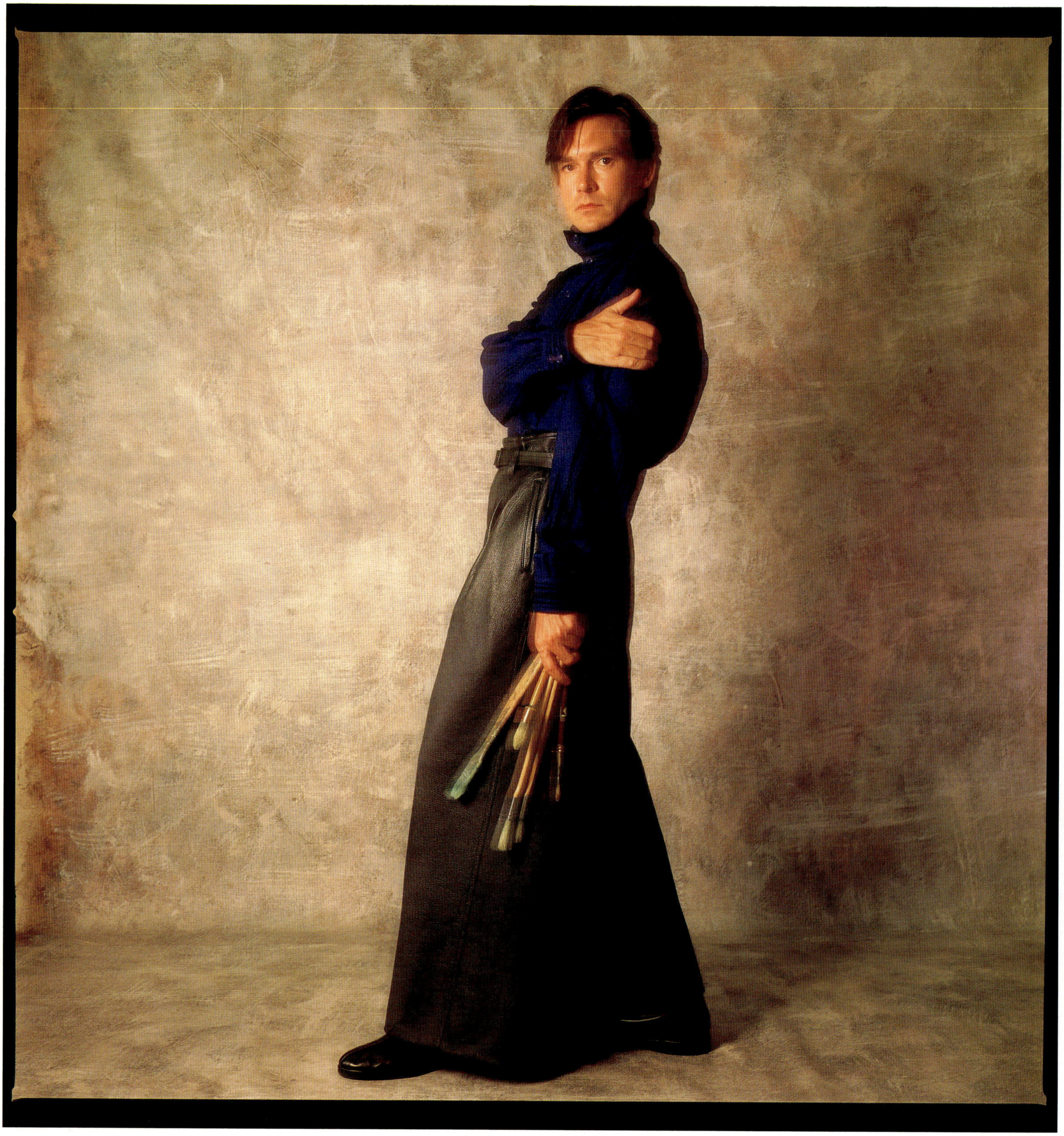

William Coupon

Duncan Hannah – from a series of five portraits in »Motion« for an Issey Miyake campaign published in *Dansen Magazine*.

»Dan und Pat Moore, 18«, Aufnahme aus einer Serie des Fotografen Kent Barker, die Radfahrern gewidmet ist und in der Zeitschrift *Regardie's* veröffentlicht wurde.

«Dan et Pat Moore, 18» – photo réalisée par Kent Barker pour une série vouée au cyclisme et publiée dans le magazine *Regardie's*.

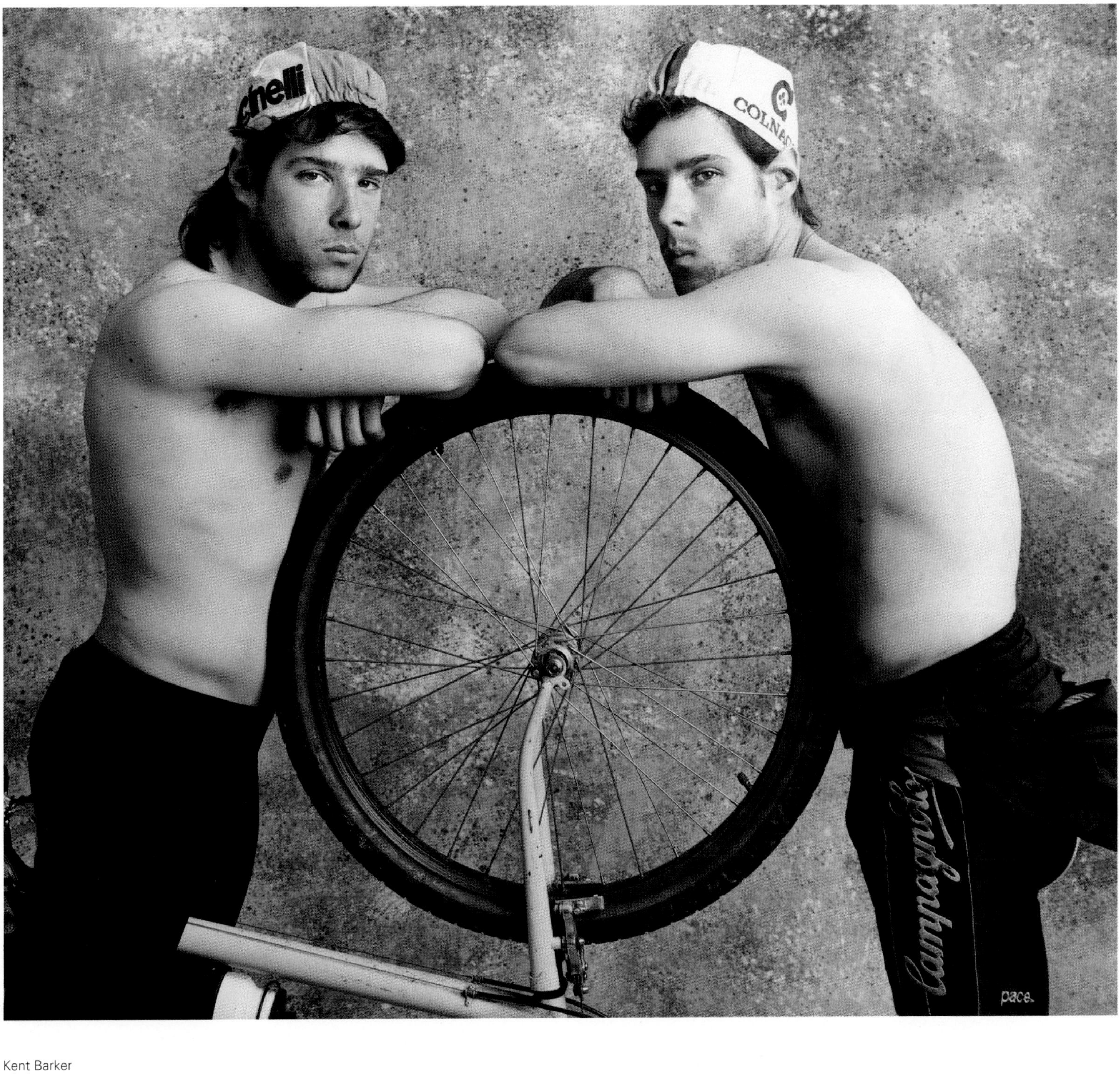

Kent Barker

»Dan and Pat Moore, 18«. Shot from a series devoted to cyclists, taken by photographer Kent Barker and published in *Regardie's* magazine.

Duncan Hannah – aus einer Reihe von fünf Porträts für eine Issey-Miyake-Kampagne in der japanischen Zeitschrift *Dansen Magazine*.

Duncan Hannah – portrait figurant dans une série de cinq pour une campagne publicitaire Issey Miyake dans *Dansen Magazine*.

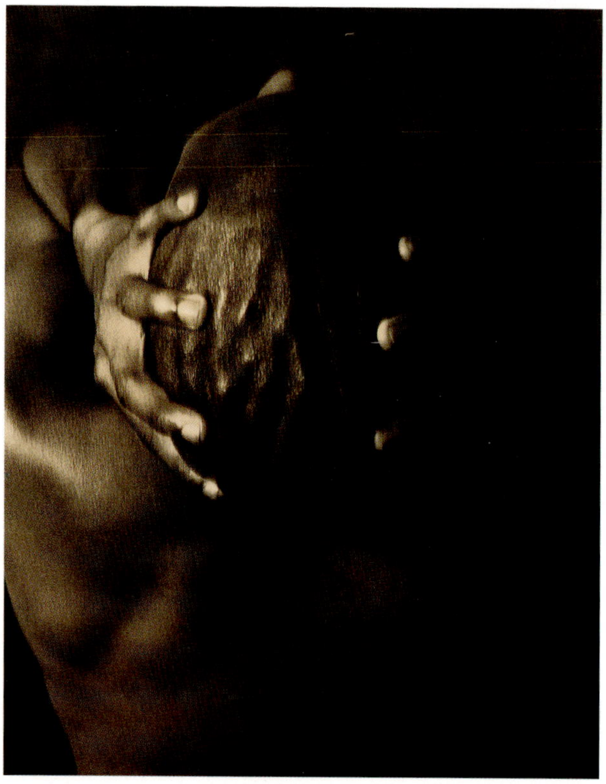

Jeff Sowards

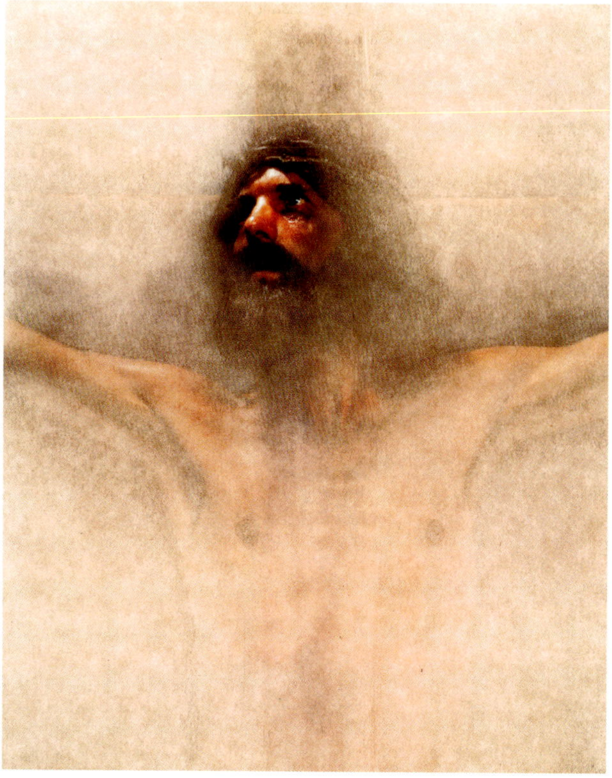

David Holt

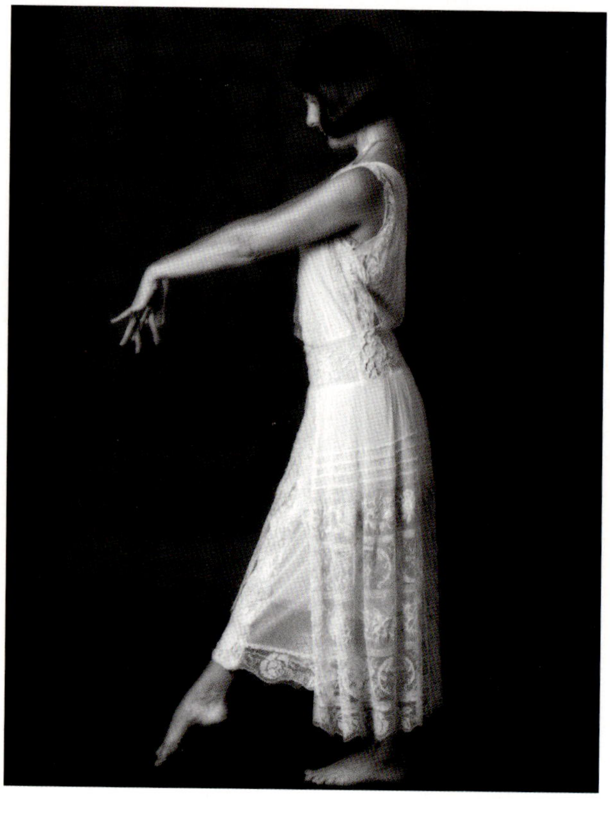

Howard Schatz

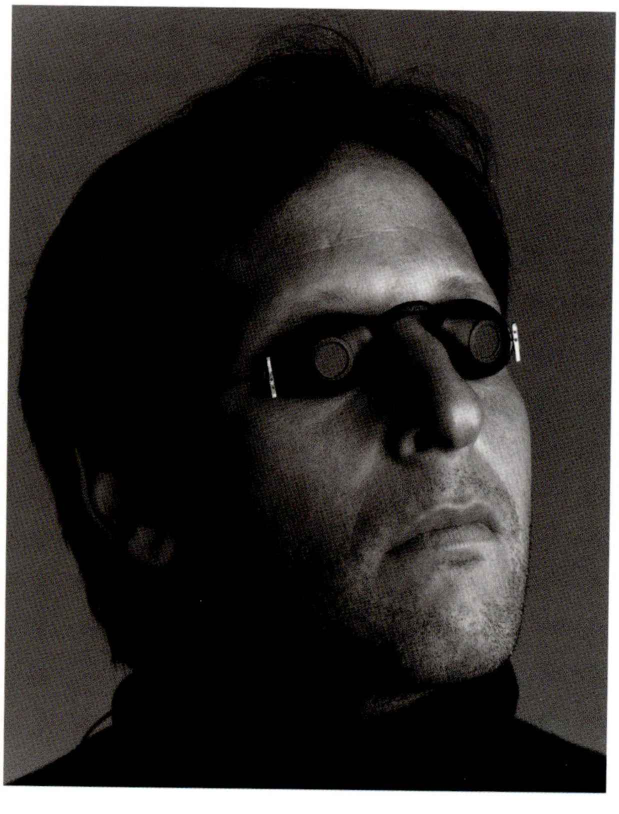

Steve Marsel

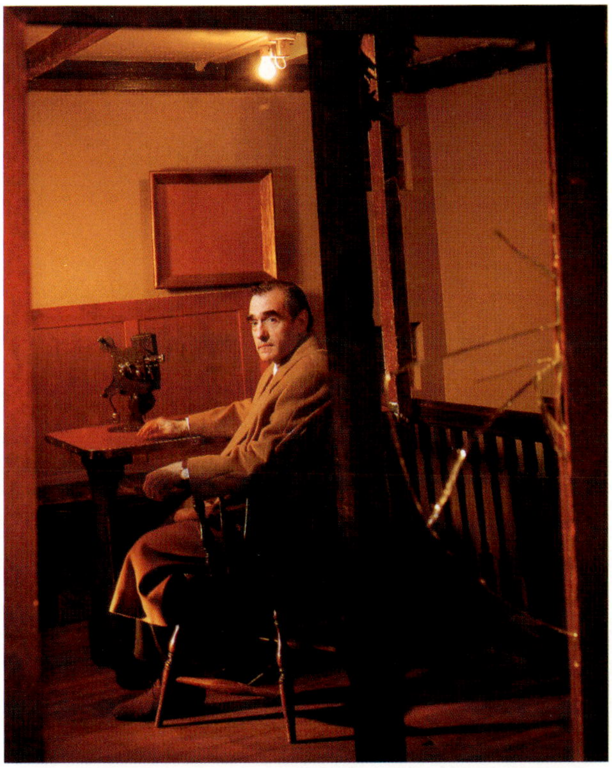

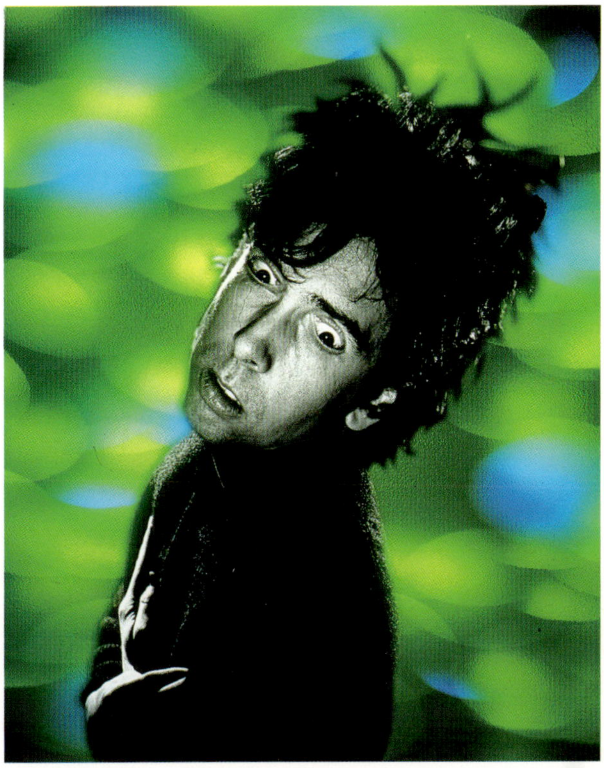

Max Aguilera-Hellweg

Michael Llewellyn

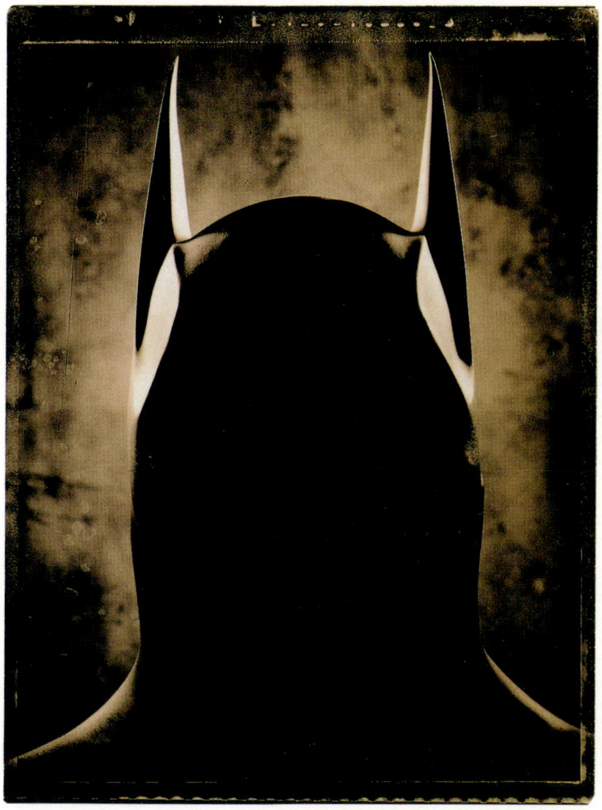

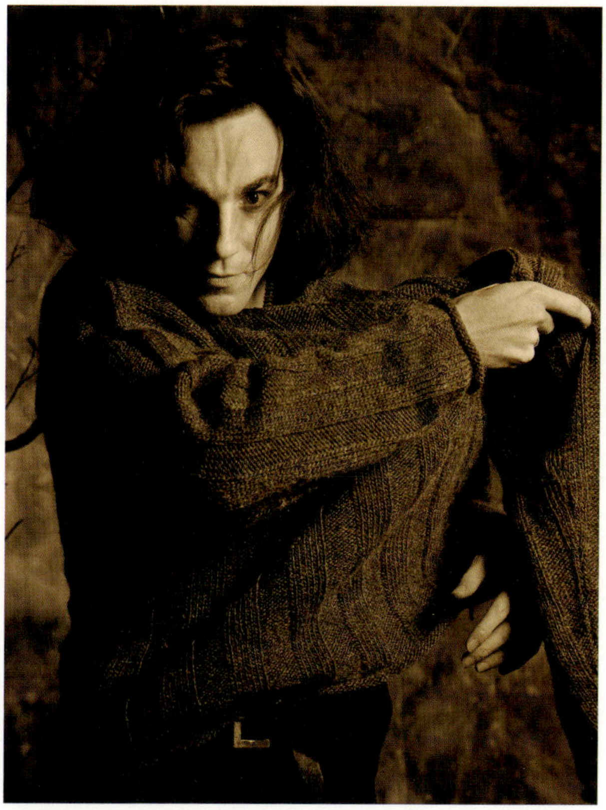

Mark Hanauer

Michele Clement

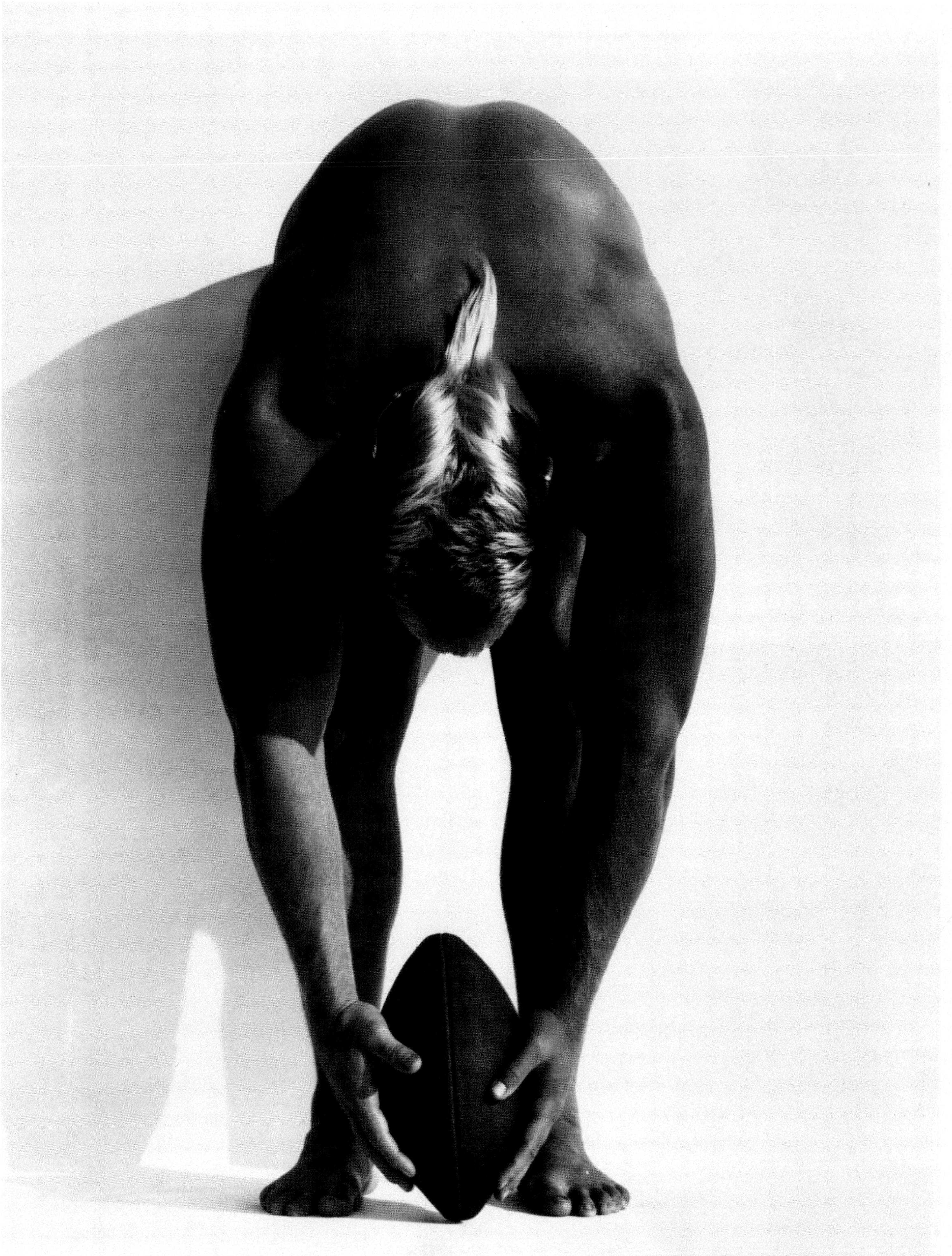

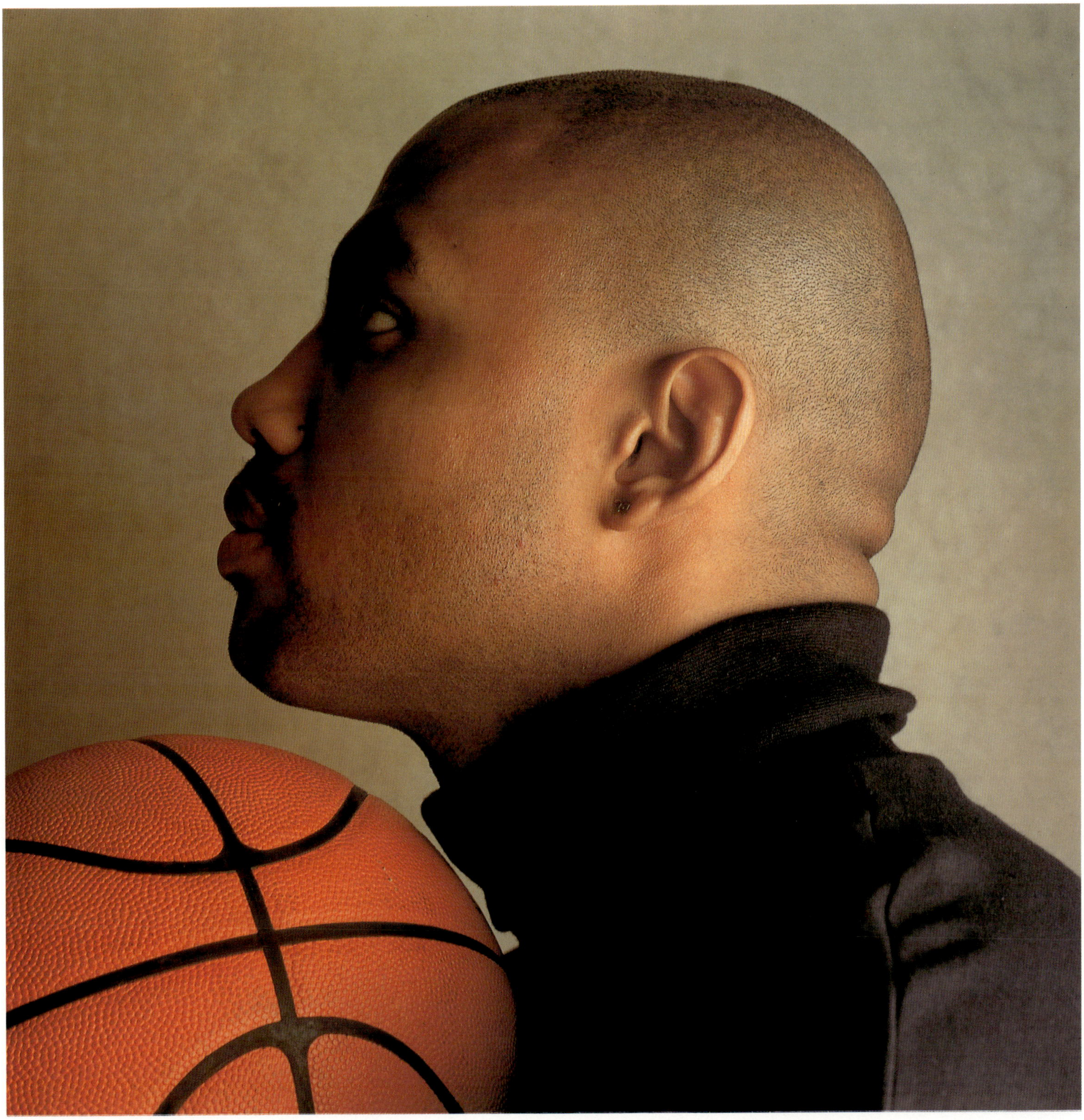

Herb Ritts

Brian Bosworth, the American football star – a spectator attraction, not only because of his Mohican haircut.

Brian Bosworth, amerikanischer Football-Star und nicht nur wegen seines Mohawk-Haarschnitts *die* Zuschauerattraktion.

Brian Bosworth, vedette de football qui se fait remarquer par sa coupe de cheveux digne d'un Mohawk.

Michael O'Brien

»Headstrong« was the headline on the cover of the *New York Times Magazine* which assigned this portrait of basketball star Charles Barkley of the Philadelphia 76ers.

»Kopfstark« war die Schlagzeile auf dem Umschlag des *New York Times Magazine* mit diesem Porträt des Basketball-Star Charles Barkley von den Philadelphia 76ers.

Le célèbre joueur de basket-ball de l'équipe américaine des Philadelphia 76ers, Charles Barkley; photo publiée en couverture du *New York Times Magazine* sous le titre «Tête dure».

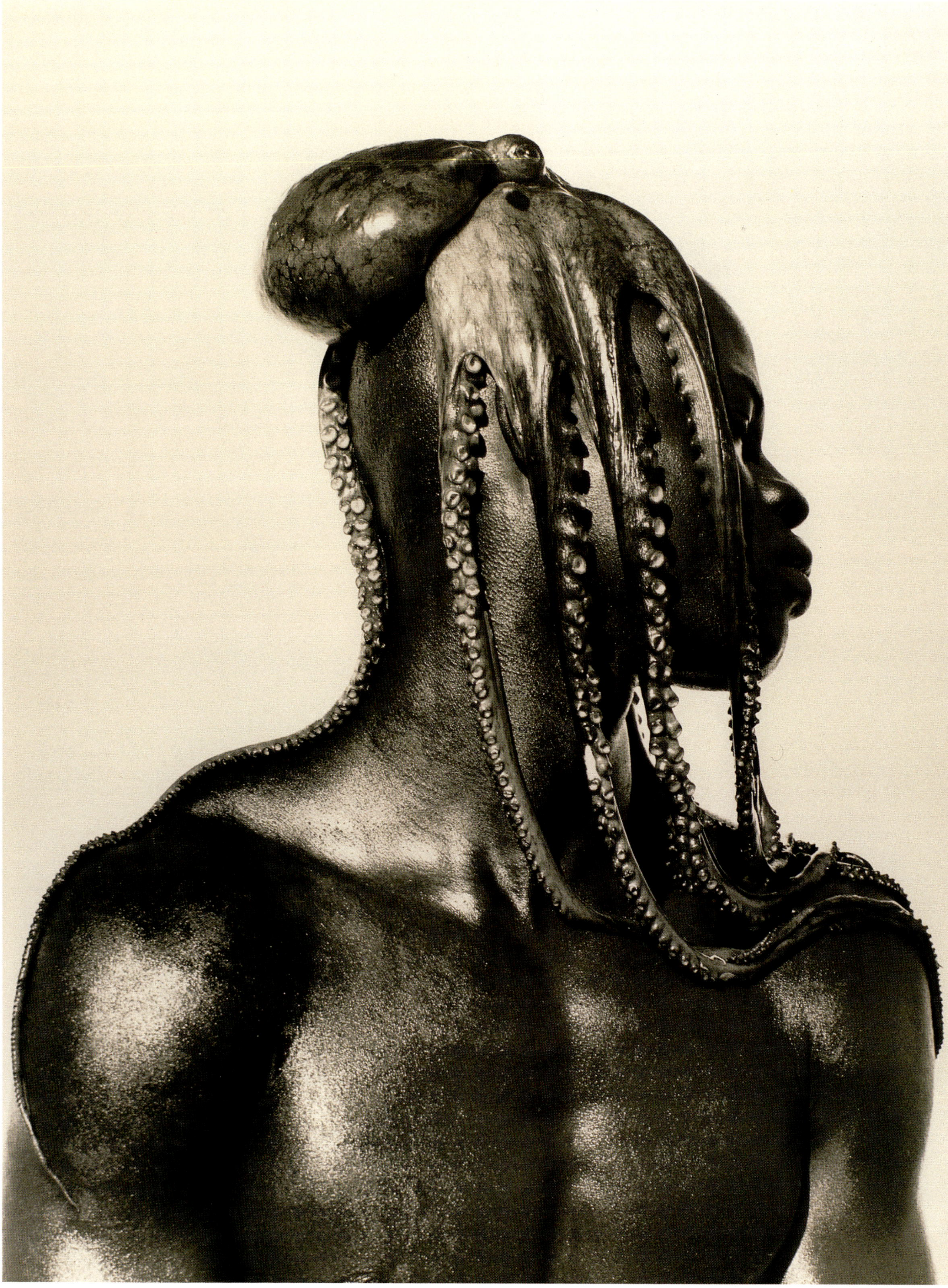

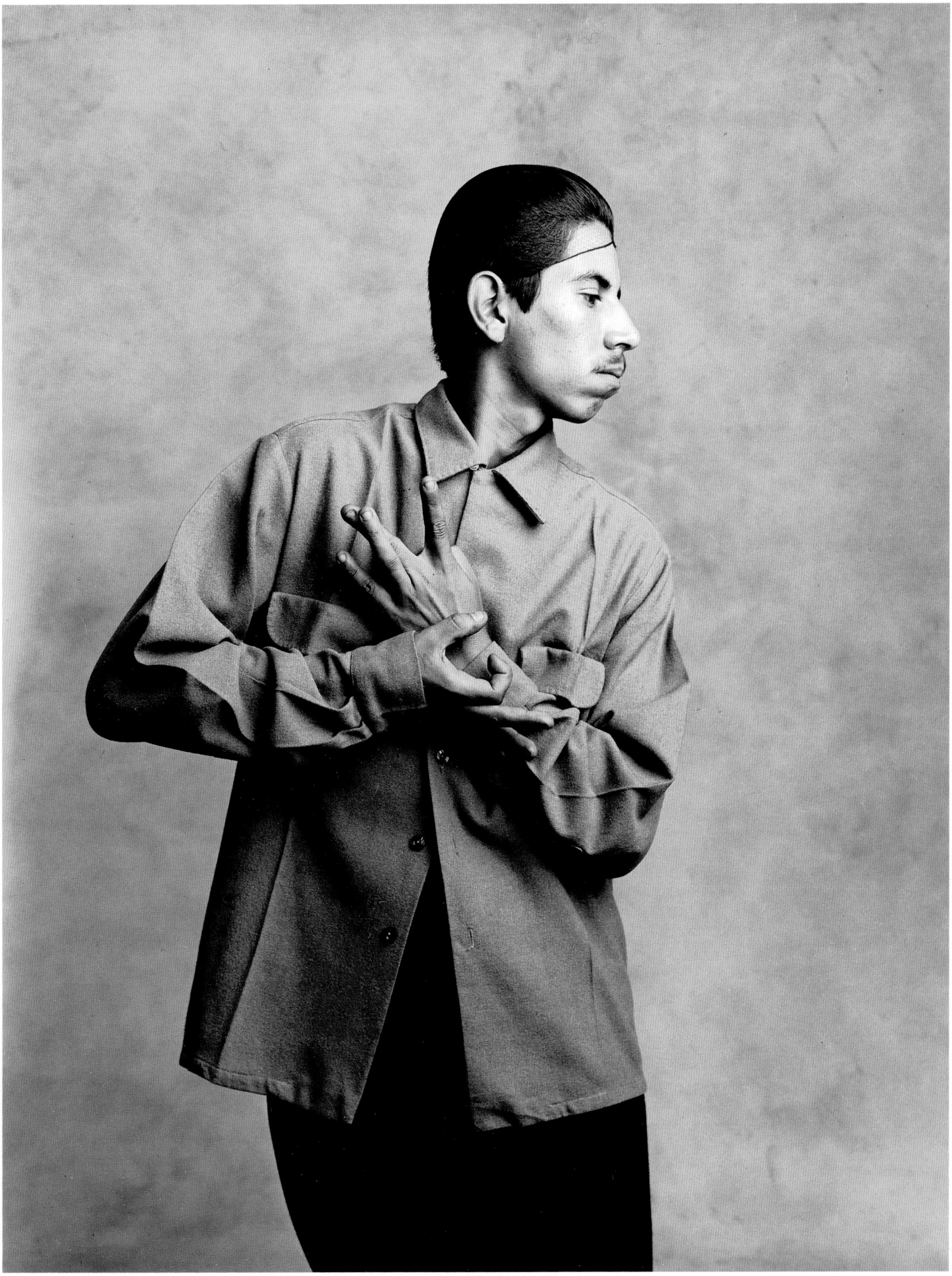

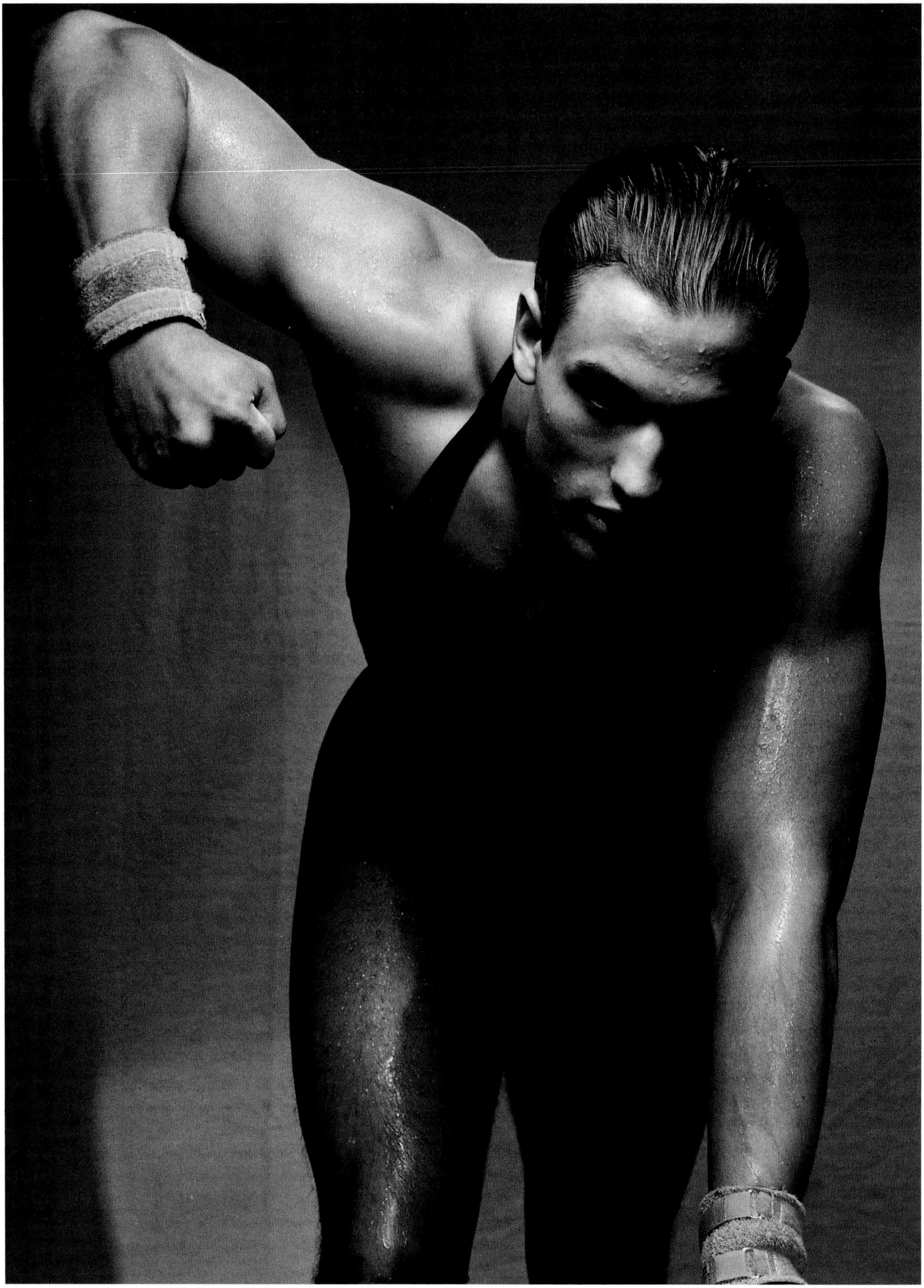

◁ Volkmann

This photograph was part of an editorial on men's fitness and grooming for the Spanish *Vogue*. It was taken in the studio with calumet spot strobe rigged for speedotron power packs.

Diese Aufnahme erschien in einem Artikel in der spanischen *Vogue* über Fitness und Körperpflege der Männer. Sie entstand im Studio mit Stroboskop-Blitzlicht.

Photo illustrant un article sur la mise en forme et l'entraînement sportif masculin, paru dans l'édition espagnole de *Vogue*. Elle a été prise en studio avec lumière stroboscopique.

◁ ◁ ◁ Herb Ritts

Djimon with Octopus, from the collection of Herb Ritts photographs entitled *Men / Women*. Eroticism is a constant presence in Ritts' photography, whether the purpose is celebrity reportage, fashion, or his own personal work. This photograph, exhibiting a more androgynous sensuality, was actually taken on the roof of his Hollywood home.

»Djimon mit Tintenfisch«, eine Aufnahme aus Herb Ritts Fotoband *Men / Women*. Erotik spielt in seinen Fotografien eine große Rolle. Ob es sich um Aufnahmen von Berühmtheiten, um Modefotos oder um freie Arbeiten handelt. Diese Aufnahme, eher ein Zwitter, was die Erotik angeht, machte Herb Ritts auf dem Dach seines Hauses in Hollywood.

»Djimon et le poulpe», photographie tirée du livre de Herb Ritts *Men / Women*. L'érotisme joue un rôle essentiel chez Ritts, qu'il s'agisse de portraits de stars, de photos de mode ou d'études personnelles. Cette image d'une extrême sensualité présente un caractère androgyne. Elle a été prise sur le toit de la maison du photographe.

◁ ◁ Tom Zimberoff

Portrait of a young man from the Mexican-American district of Los Angeles. He wears whatever the barrio gang dictates – whether it be a black hairnet or a pink tutu. »Be cool or be through« is the motto.

Porträt eines jungen Mannes aus dem mexikanischen Quartier in Los Angeles. Er ist ganz dem Modediktat seiner Quartier-Gang unterworfen: Schwarzes Haarnetz oder was immer »in« ist.

Portrait d'un jeune homme du quartier mexicain de Los Angeles coiffé d'un filet à cheveux noir et habillé à la mode dictée par les mouvements de jeunes de son quartier.

Ania Walisiewicz

The brother of the photographer posing as roach.

Der Bruder der Fotografin, eine Küchenschabe darstellend.

Le frère de la photographe imite ici un cancrelat.

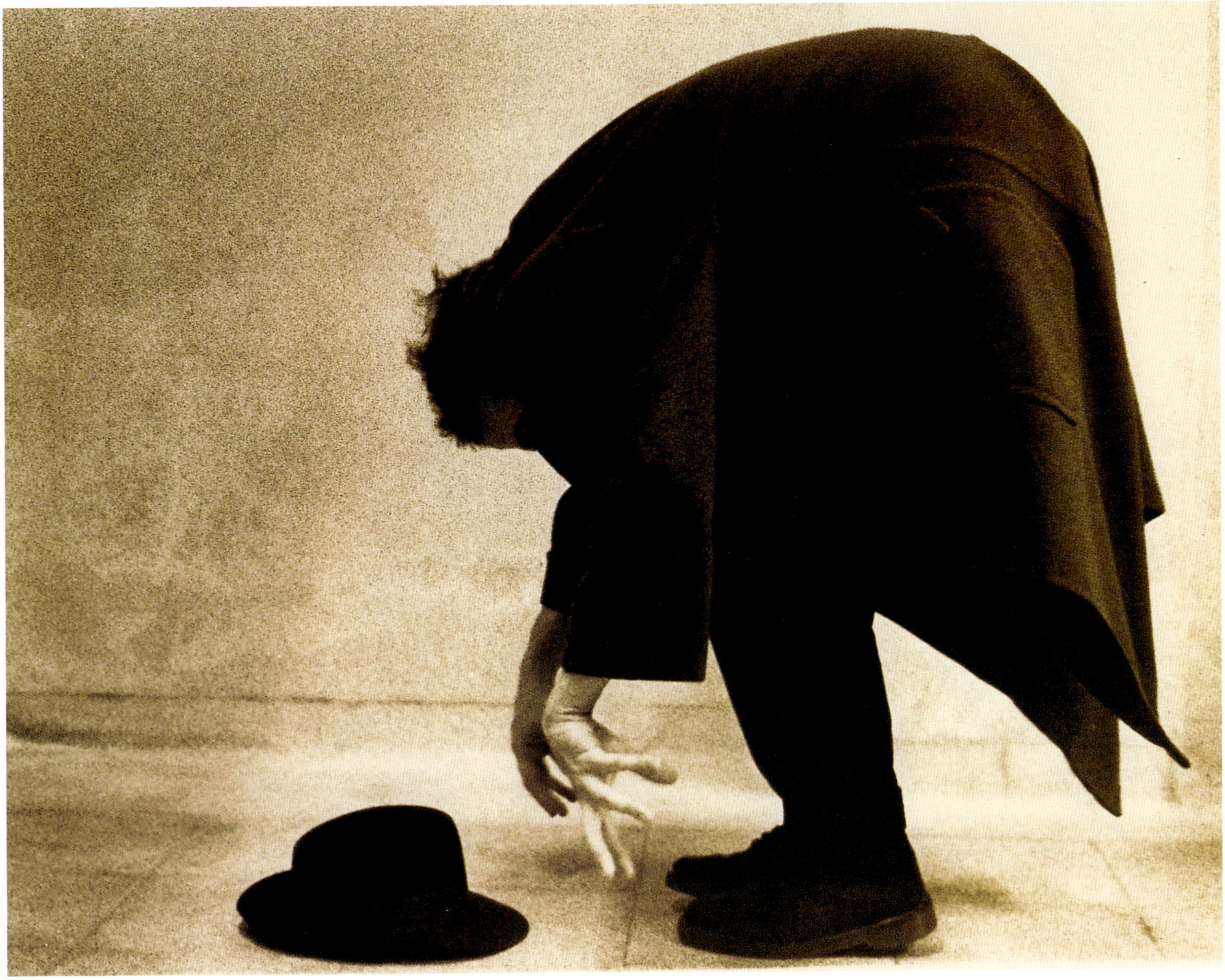

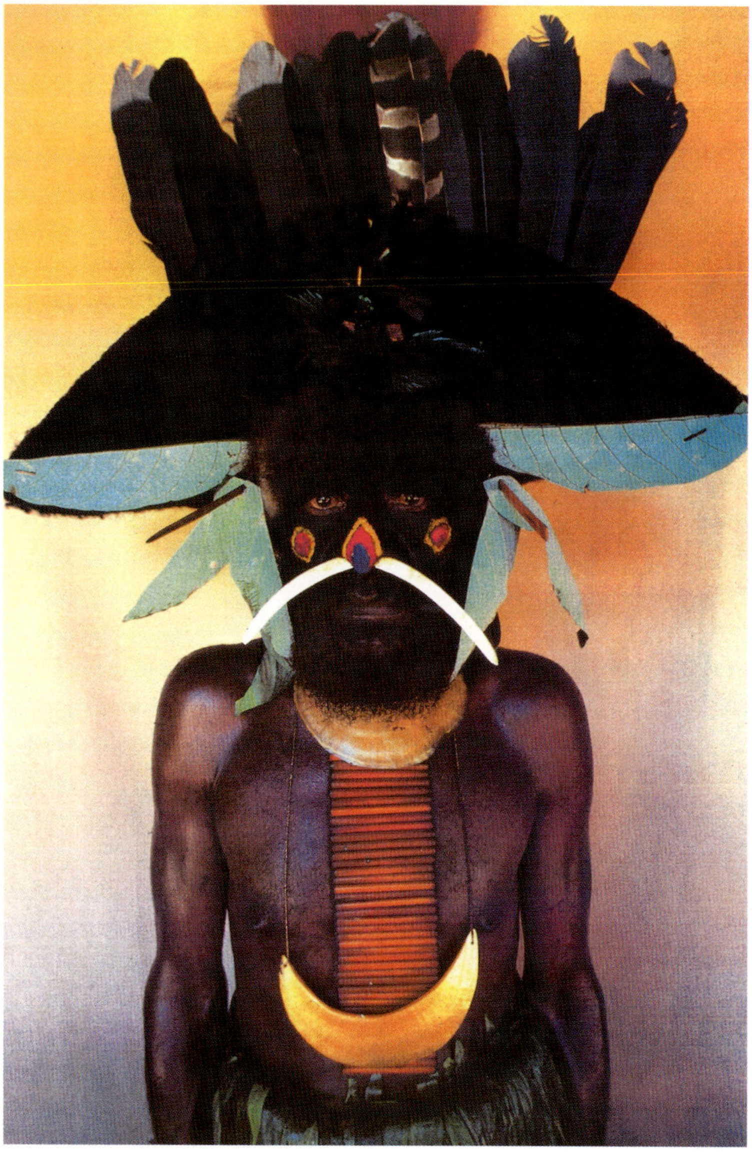

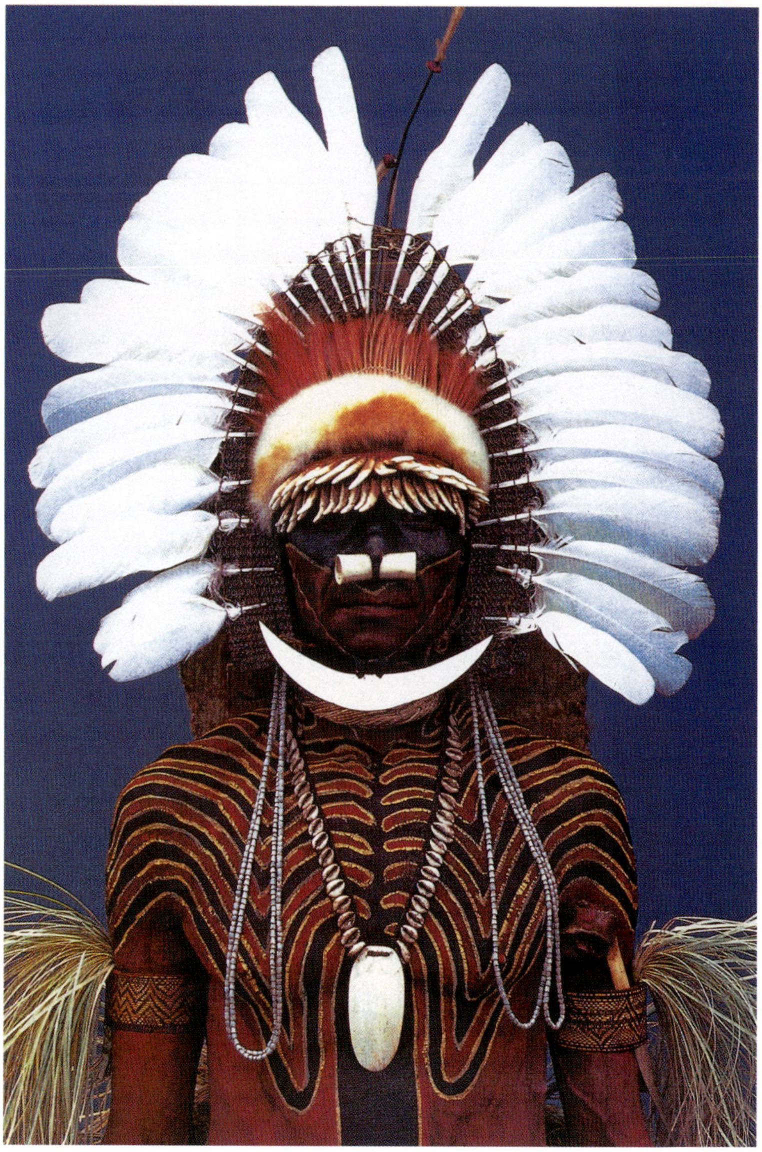

Malcolm Kirk

Portraits of inhabitants of Papua, New Guinea, from left to right: one of the Melpa tribe (the single striped feather comes from the plumage of the long-tailed buzzard), a Samo man from the region of the Nomad River in the West Province (the nosepeg is made of a cassowary bone), a Huli tribesman from the Southern Highland Province (everyday wig made of coloured human hair), Mendi tribesman from the Southern Highland Province (his headdress borrowed from bird-catchers). The photographs are taken from the book *People and Masks* by New York photographer Malcolm Kirk, and were also used for a Sandoz Calendar.

Menschen aus Papua Neuguinea, von links nach rechts: ein Angehöriger des Melpa-Stammes (die einzelne gestreifte Feder stammt aus dem Gefieder des Langschwänzigen Bussards), ein Samo-Mann aus dem Gebiet des Nomad-River in der Westprovinz (der Nasenpflock besteht aus einem Kasuar-Knochen), ein Huli-Stammesangehöriger aus der Südlichen Hochland-Provinz (Alltags-Perücke aus gefärbtem menschlichem Haar), ein Mendi-Stammesangehöriger aus der Südlichen Hochland-Provinz (seinen Kopfschmuck hat er von Vogelfängern ausgeliehen). Die Aufnahmen stammen aus dem Buch »Menschen und Masken« und wurden auch für einen Sandoz-Kalender verwendet.

Papous de Nouvelle-Guinée. De gauche à droite: un membre da la tribu des Melpa (la grande plume rayée provient du plumage d'un busard à longue queue), un Samo de la région de la Nomad River, à L'ouest de l'île (l'ornement nasal est constitué d'un os de casoar); un indigène de la tribu Huli, qui vit dans les Massifs Montagneux de la Province Sud (il porte une perruque ordinaire de cheveux teints); un membre de la tribu des Mendi, qui habite lui aussi dans les Massifs Méridionaux (il a emprunté sa coiffure à un oiseleur). Ces photographies sont tirées du livre «Des hommes et des Masques» et ont été publieés sous forme de calendrier.

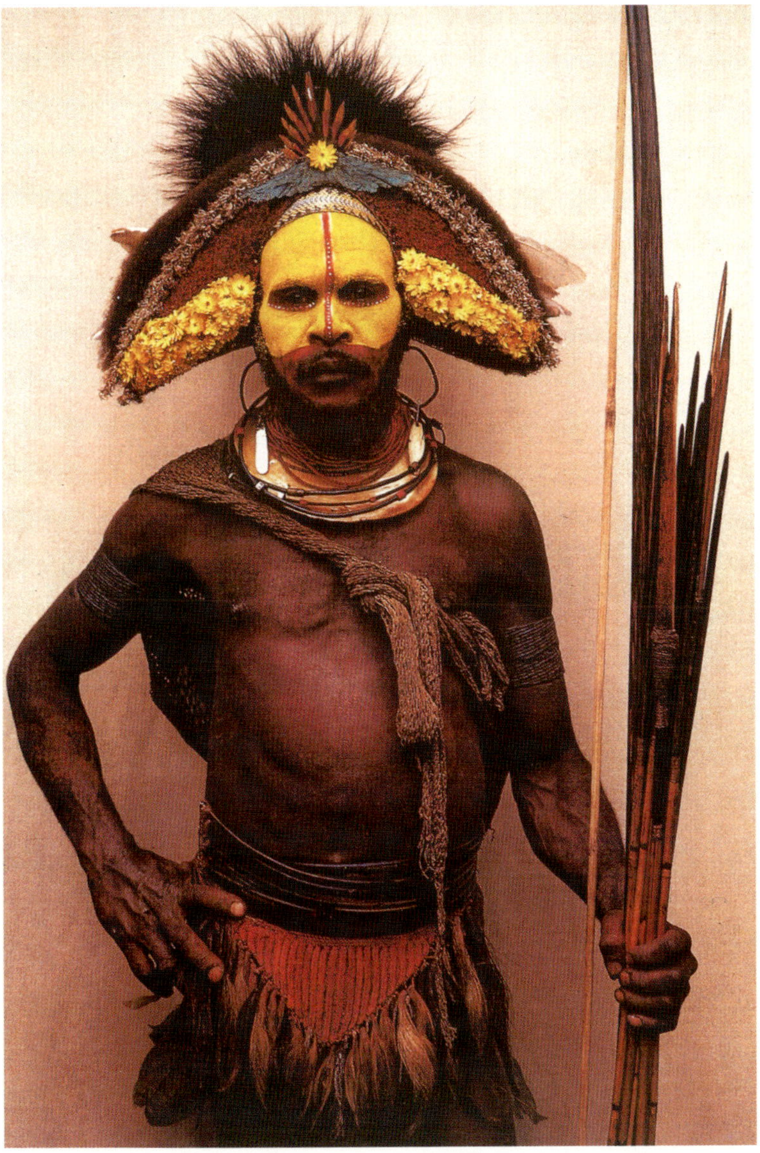

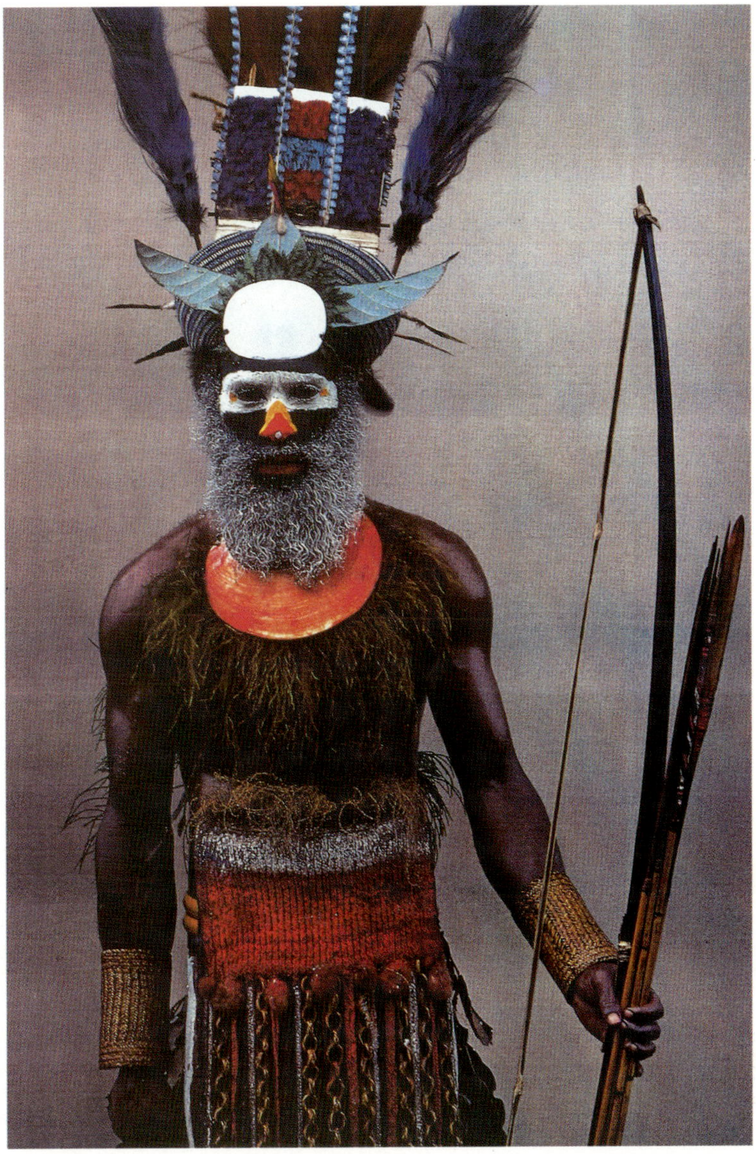

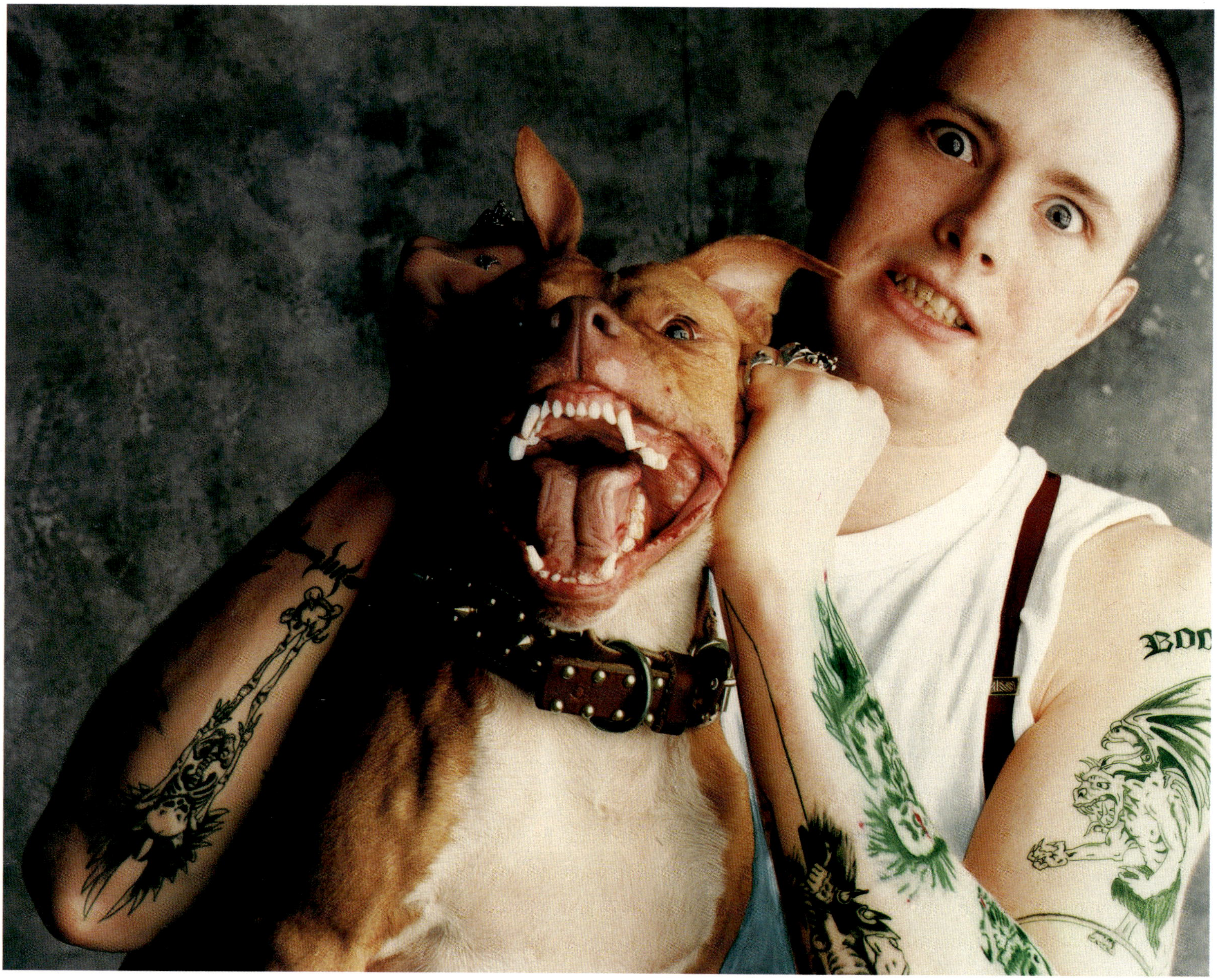

Chris Santuci

Freelance work by photographer Chris Santuci of Buffalo, New York.

Freie Arbeit des Fotografen Chris Santuci aus Buffalo, New York.

Etude libre du photographe Chris Santuci de Buffalo, dans l'Etat de New York.

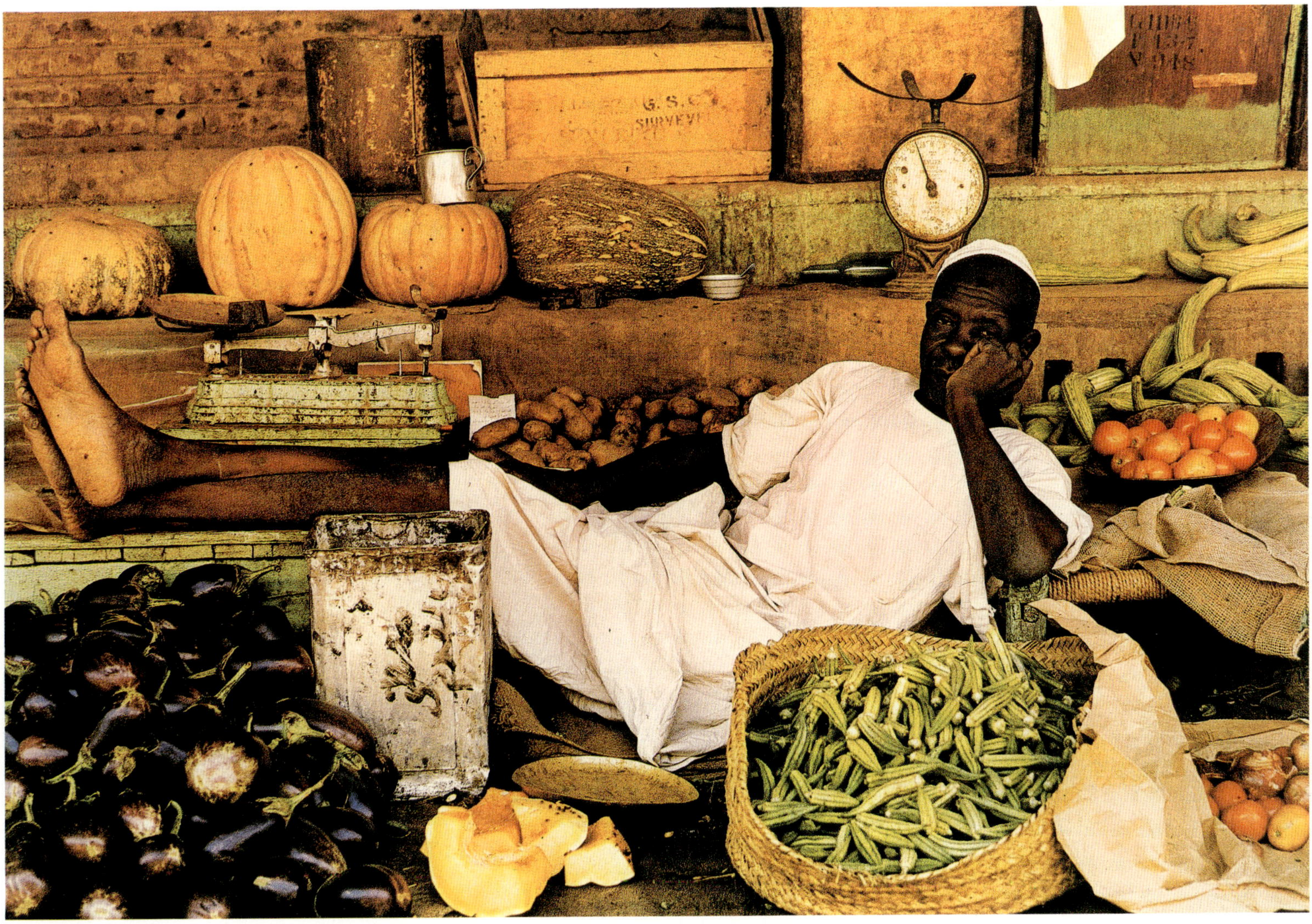

Jay Maisel

A photograph used for the announcement of a lecture by photographer Jay Maisel.

Für die Ankündigung eines Vortrages des Fotografen Jay Maisel verwendete Aufnahme.

Photo utilisée pour l'annonce d'une conférence du photographe Jay Maisel.

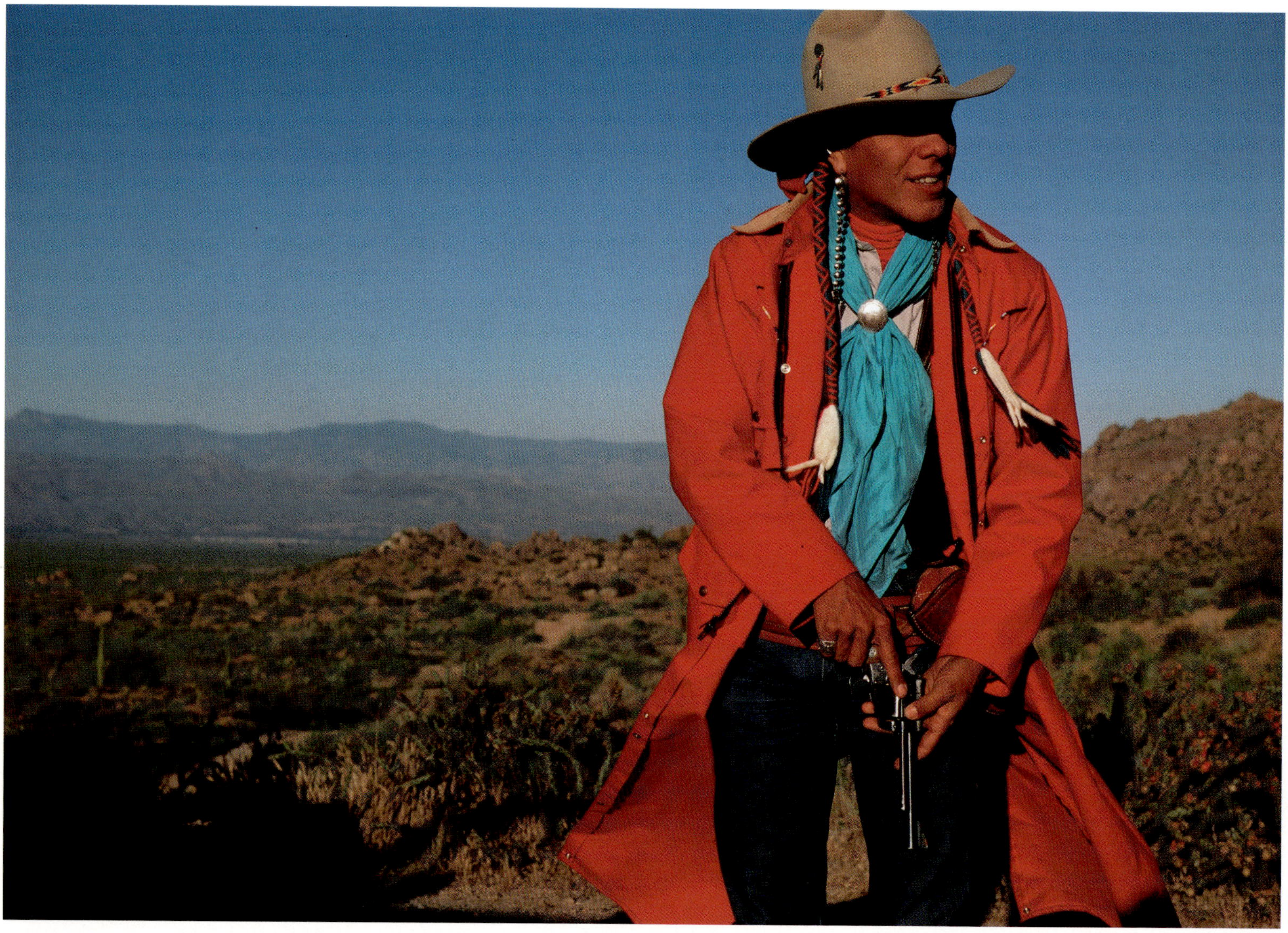

Russ Schleipman

An Arizona resort hotel assigned photographer Russ Schleipman to depict activities available for guests. This image refers to back country tours with an Indian guide.

Ein Ferienhotel in Arizona beauftragte den Fotografen, die Freizeitmöglichkeiten für die Gäste zu dokumentieren. Diese Aufnahme bezieht sich auf Ausflüge ins Hinterland mit einem indianischen Führer.

Un hôtel de vacances en Arizona demanda au photographe de documenter toutes les distractions à la disposition des clients. Cette photo a trait aux excursions dans l'arrière pays en compagnie d'un guide indien.

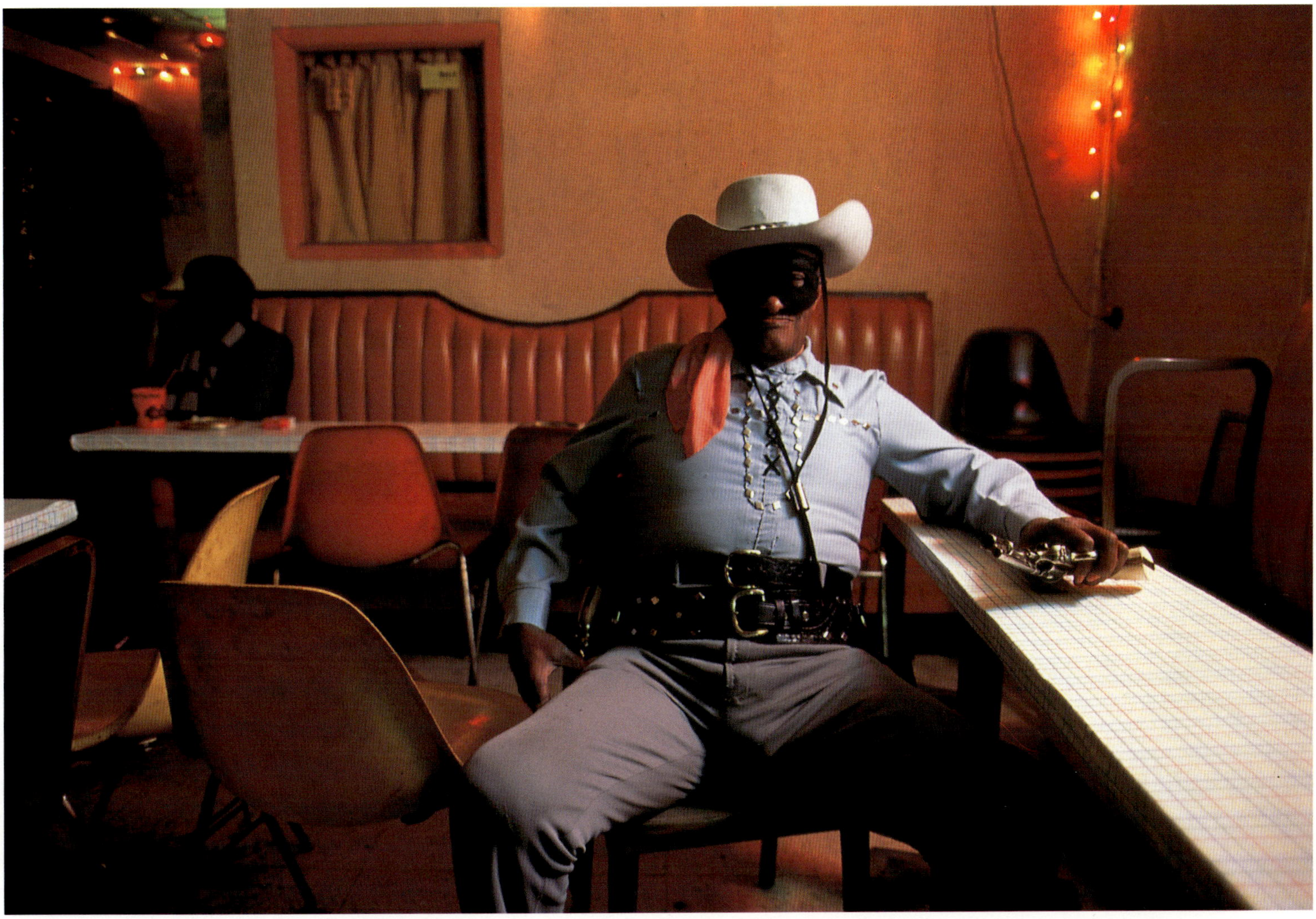

Tim Bieber

The »Black Lone Ranger«, from a series on Chicago night-clubs. The lone ranger is a regular character in Checkerboard Lounge, a blues club.

Der »Black Lone Ranger« ist regelmäßiger Gast in der Checkerboard Lounge, einem Blues Club in Chicago. Aufnahme für ein Touristikbüro.

«Black Lone Ranger», image d'une série sur les night-clubs à Chicago. Portrait d'un habitué du Checkerboard Lounge, un club de blues.

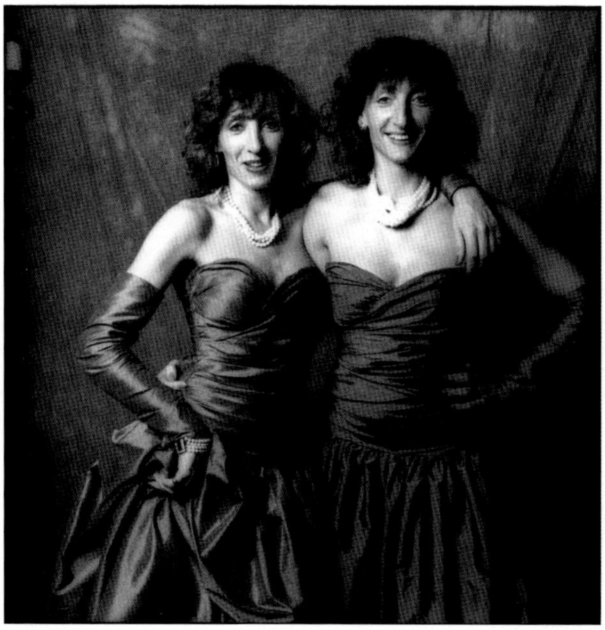

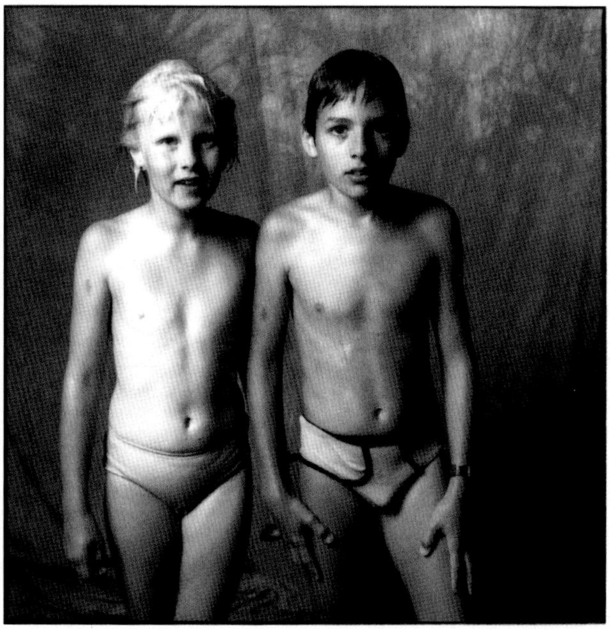

Wulf-Eike

The images are part of the series on parties and guests. The photographer attempts to bring out the character of his subjects through their way of posing for the camera. Here he focused on (left) the competition between twins and (right) the way a girl and a boy handle their first romantic awareness.

Aus der Serie »Hochzeitsbilder von Festen und Gästen«. Der Fotograf versuchte, durch die Selbstdarstellung seiner Sujets ihren Charakter herauszuarbeiten. Hier spielten Beziehungsmuster eine besondere Rolle: die Konkurrenz der Zwillinge (links) und der Umgang der Kinder mit ersten sexuellen Gefühlen.

Ces images proviennent d'une série intitulée «Photos de fêtes de mariage et d'invités». Le photographe a voulu exprimer le caractère des personnages à travers leur façon de se présenter devant son objectif. Il met l'accent sur les relations entre ses modèles, ici la concurrence entre les jumelles ou le comportements d'enfants qui s'éveillent à la sexualité.

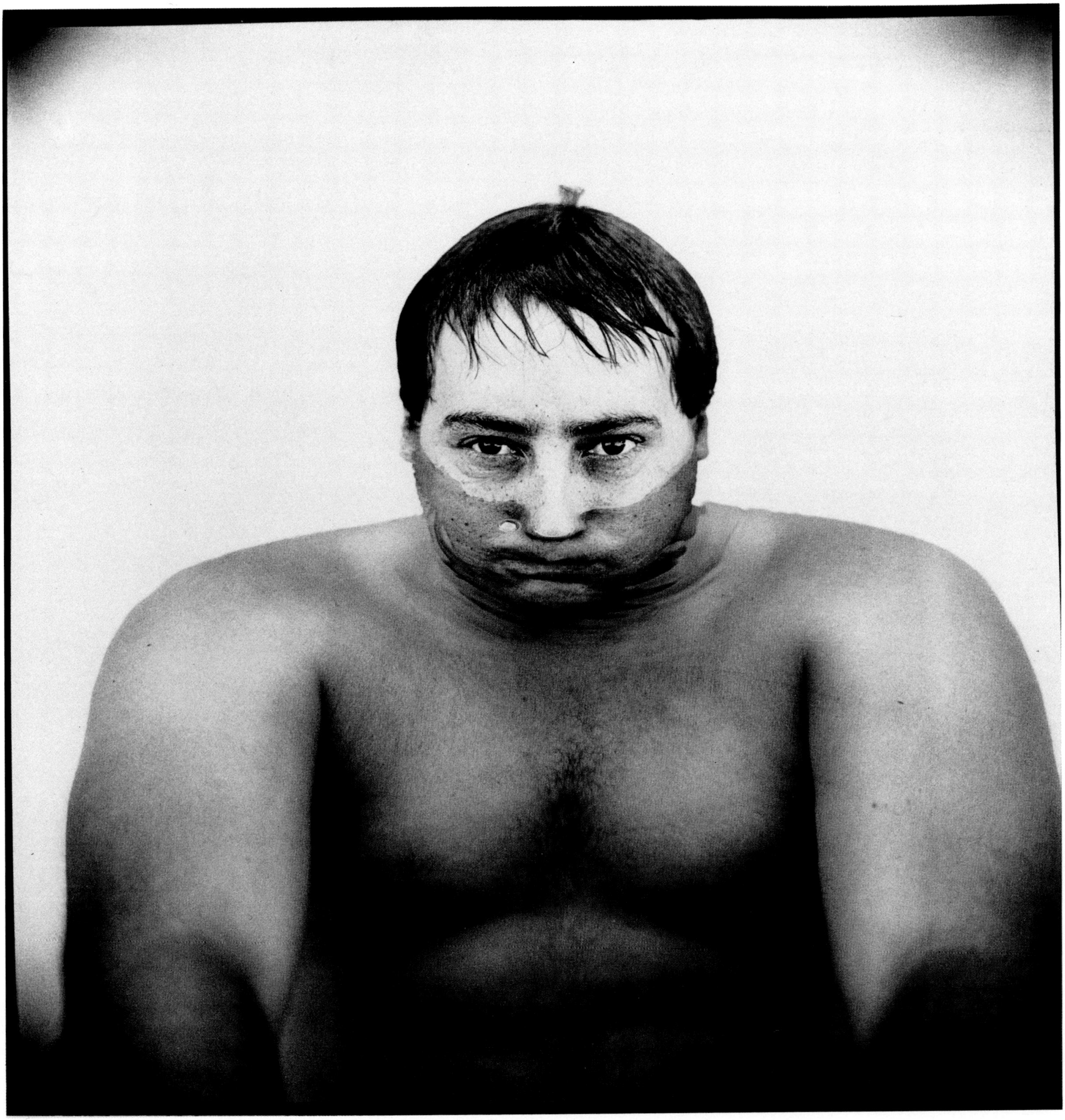

Daniel Winters

Photograph of a man in the swimming pool – taken by photographer Daniel Winters.

Bild eines Mannes im Swimming Pool – Aufnahme des Fotografen Daniel Winters.

Photo d'un homme dans une piscine. Elle est l'œuvre du photographe Daniel Winters.

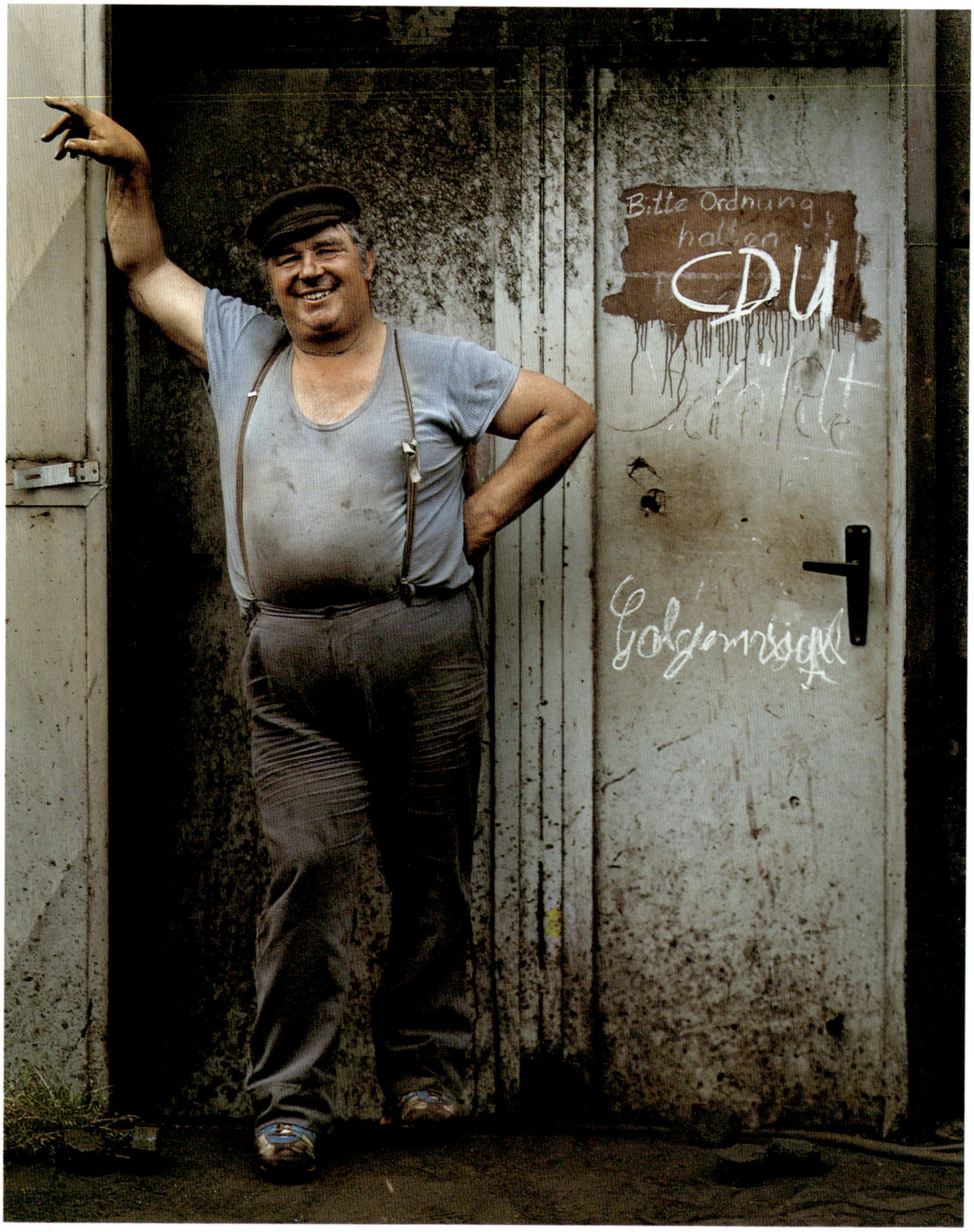

Eberhard Grames

A truck driver from Meissen. This photograph was taken in daylight and is part of a portrait series of labourers, women and children in East Germany after the demolition of the Wall.

Ein Lastwagenfahrer aus Meissen – Porträt aus einer Serie über Menschen im Osten Deutschlands nach Öffnung der Mauer, bei Tageslicht auf Negativmaterial fotografiert.

Un chauffeur de poids lourd de Meissen. Portrait tiré d'une série sur le peuple est-allemand après la réunification. Photo sur négatif prise en lumière naturelle.

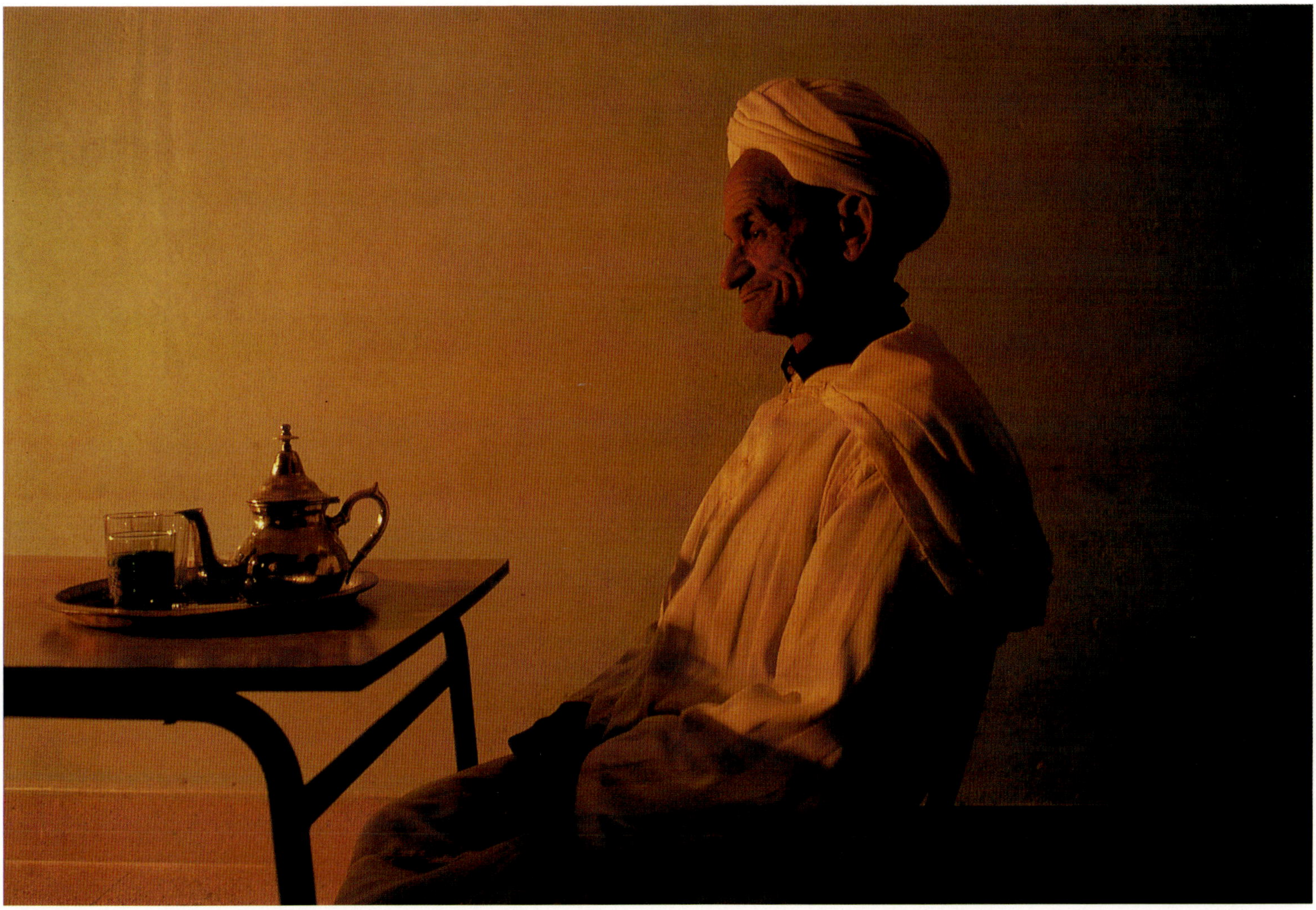

Tim Bieber

Out-take from a cigarette shooting in Southern Morocco. The man was sitting in a dark cafe, illuminated only by the light of an oil lamp.

Das Bild entstand in Marokko bei Aufnahmen für Zigarettenwerbung. Der Mann saß in einem dunklen Café, nur vom Licht der Öllampe beleuchtet.

Cette photo a été réalisée durant des prises de vue pour une publicité de cigarettes. L'éclairage se limitait à une simple lampe à huile.

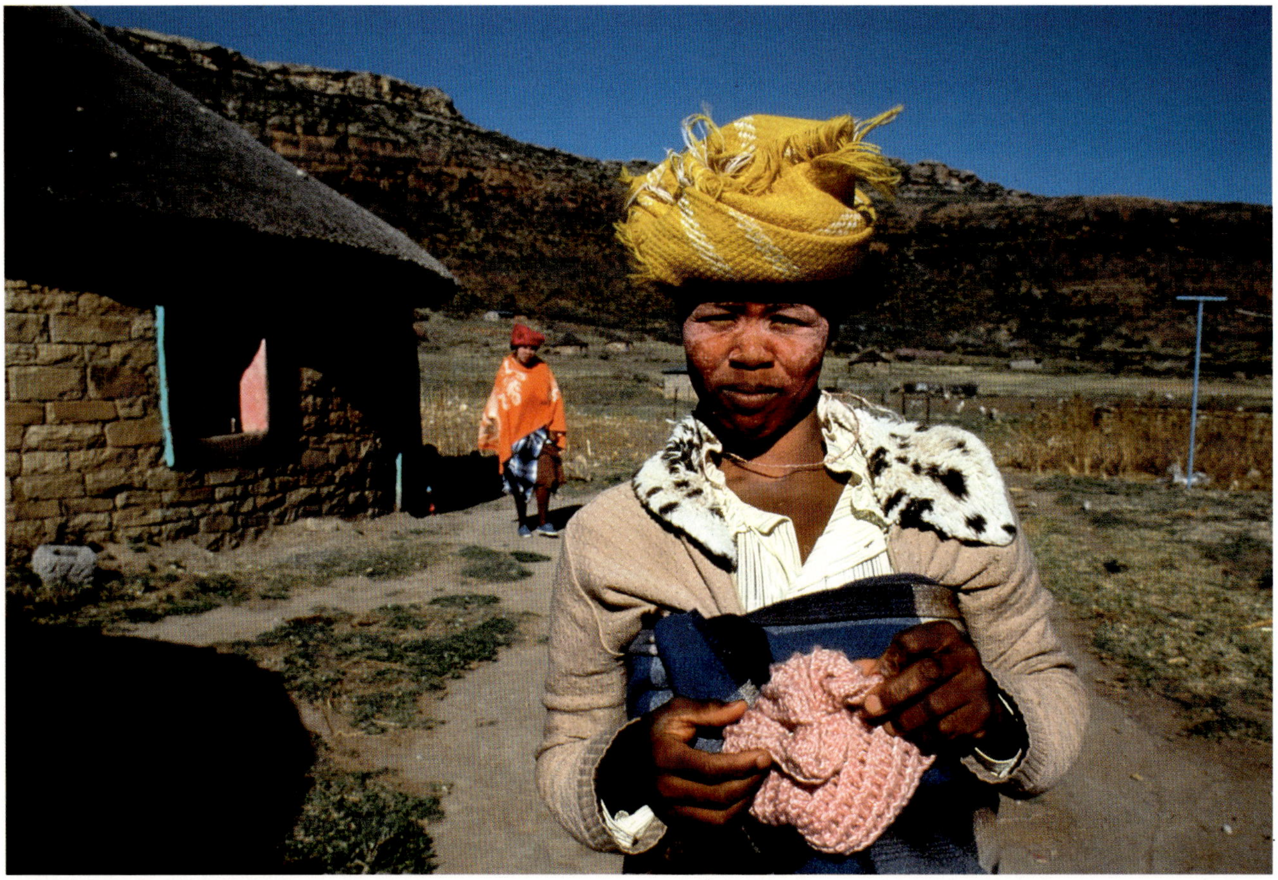

Stephenie Hollyman

Unicef commissioned photojournalist Stephenie Hollyman to document the effects of apartheid on children living in the countries bordering South Africa for a book entitled *Children of the Front Line*. The photographer spent three months in Angola, Mozambique, Lesotho, Namibia, Zimbabwe and Botswana. The subject of this photograph is a woman living in Lesotho, very near the South African border.

Die Unicef beauftragte die Fotojournalistin Stephenie Hollyman, die Auswirkungen der Apartheid auf die Kinder in den angrenzenden Ländern Südafrikas für ein Buch mit dem Titel *Children of the Front Line* zu dokumentieren. Drei Monate lang reiste sie durch Angola, Mozambique, Lesotho, Namibia, Zimbabwe und Botswana. Die Frau auf dem Foto lebt nahe der Grenze zwischen Lesotho und Südafrika.

L'Unicef avait demandé à Stephenie Hollyman, reporter photographe américain, de documenter les effets de l'apartheid sur les enfants vivant dans les pays bordant l'Afrique du Sud pour un livre intitulé *Children of the Front Line*. Pendant trois mois, elle a voyagé en Angola, au Mozambique, au Lesotho, en Namibie, au Zimbabwe et au Botswana. La femme sur cette photo vit au Lesotho, près de la frontière Sud-Africaine.

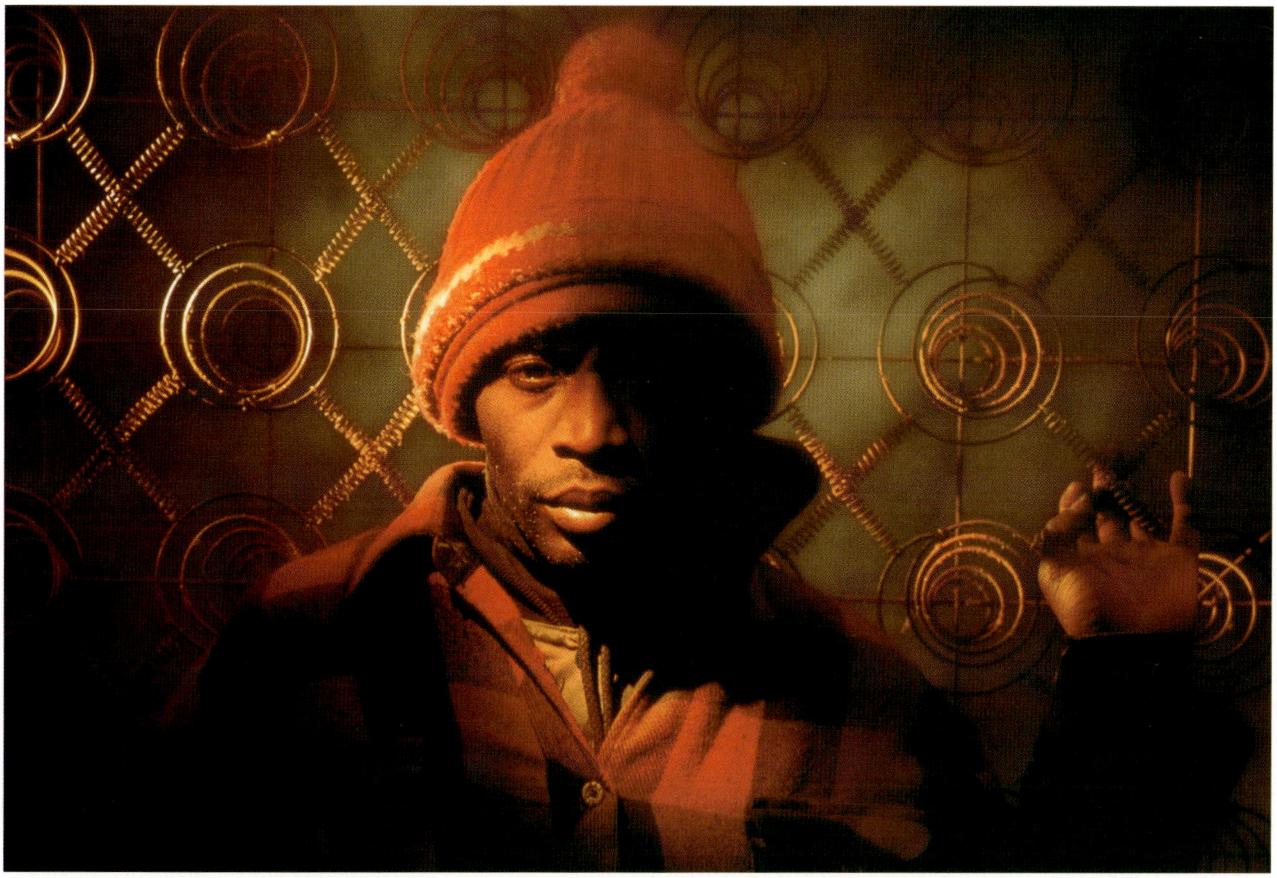

Nick Vedros

The subject of this portrait had been a cook in New Orleans. Now he is unemployed and homeless, living on the streets of Kansas City. In this photograph, part of a series of personal work by the photographer, the bed-springs serve as a metaphor for the imprisonment of the homeless in America.

Der Mann auf diesem Foto war früher Koch in New Orleans und ist heute arbeitslos. Er lebt als Obdachloser in den Straßen von Kansas City. Diese Aufnahme gehört zu einer Serie von freien Studien des Fotografen. Die Sprung-federn auf dem Bild dienen ihm als Metapher für die ge-fängnisähnliche Situation der Obdachlosen.

Portrait d'un cuisinier au chômage et sans-abri à la Nou-velle-Orléans que le photographe a rencontré dans les rues de Kansas City. Cette photo fait partie d'une série d'études personnelles. Les ressorts du matelas sont pour le photo-graphe une métaphore de la situation sans issue dont cet homme est le prisonnier.

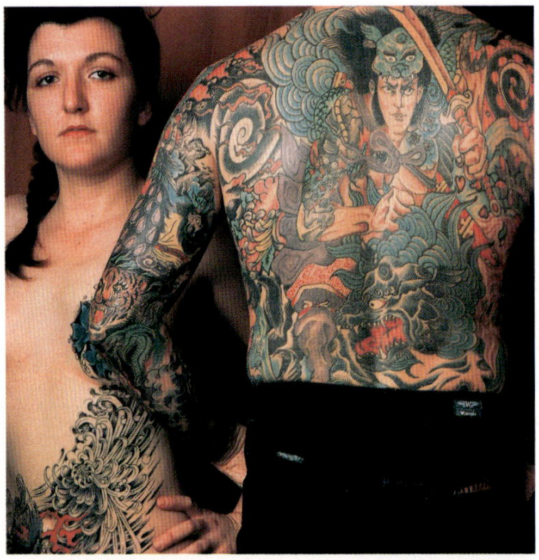
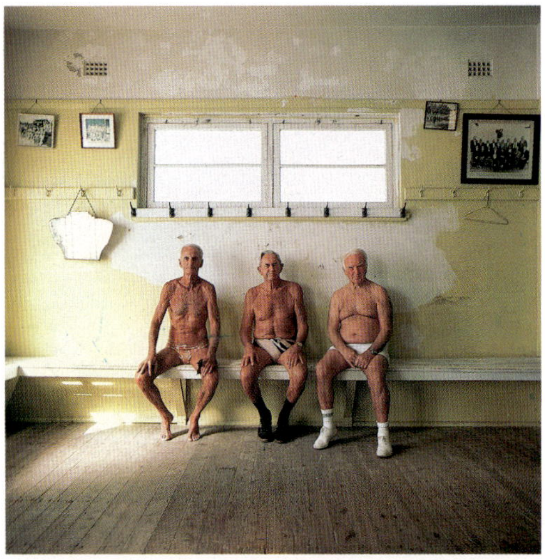
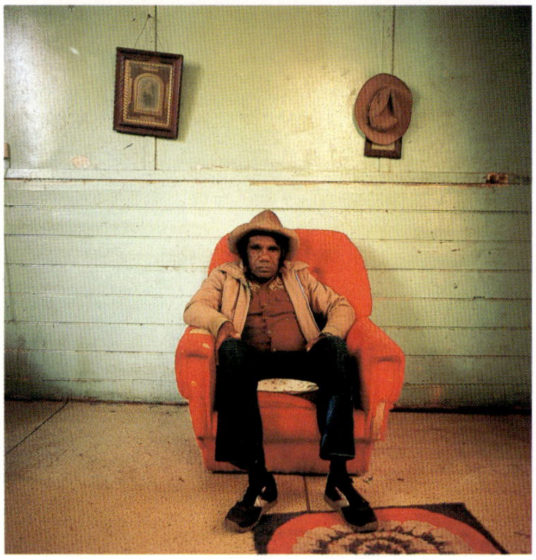
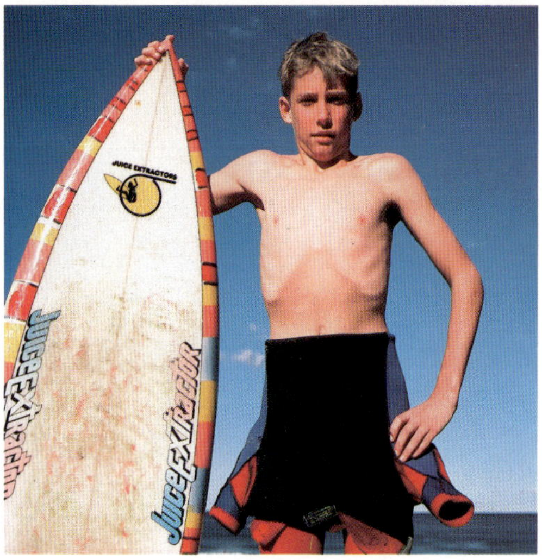

Michael O'Brien

Photographs from an issue of *National Geographic* magazine devoted to Australia.

Aufnahmen aus einer Ausgabe von *National Geographic*, die Australien gewidmet ist.

Photos illustrant un numéro de *National Geographic* consacré à l'Australie.

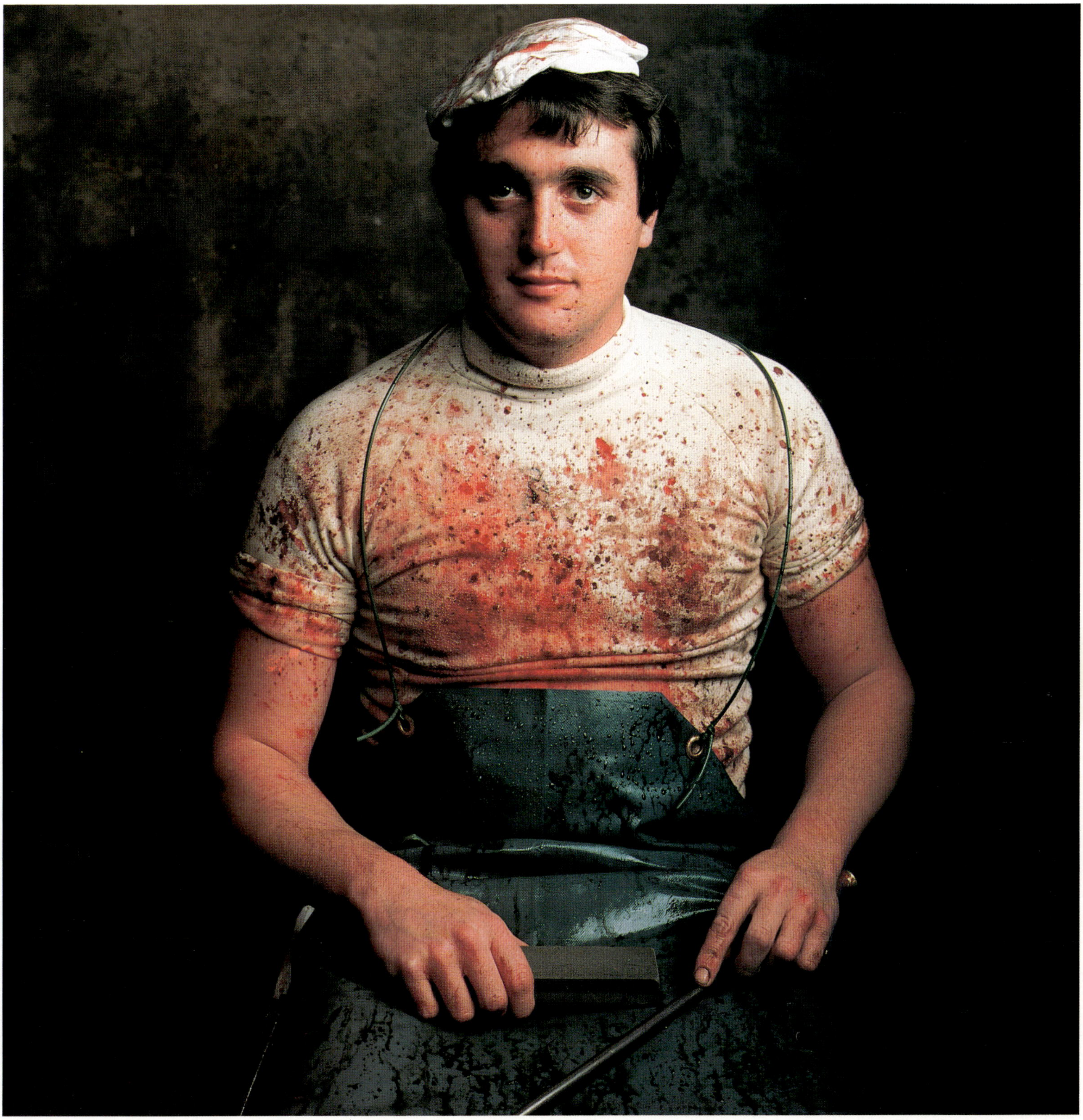

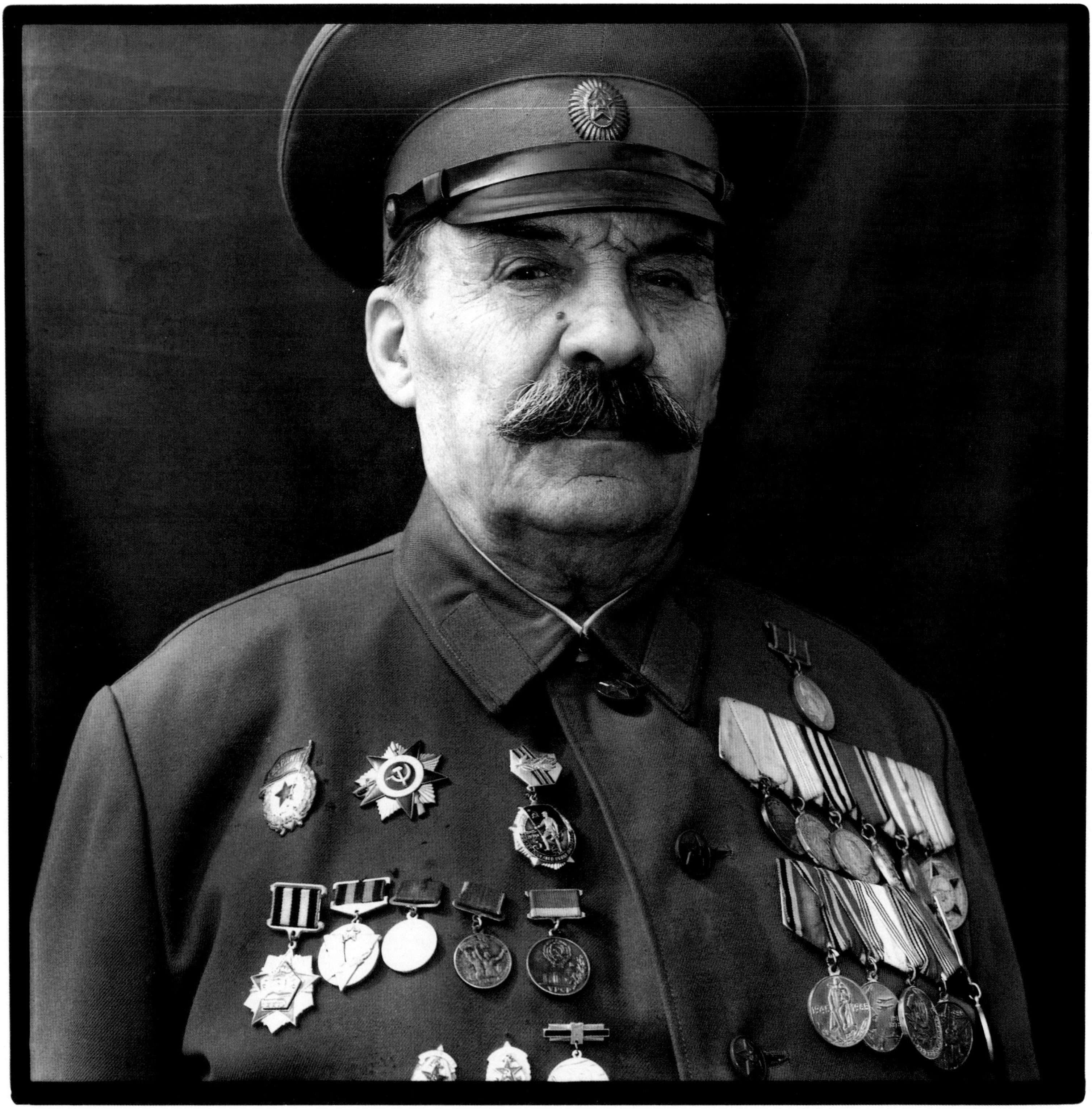

Linkevicius Kazimieras

Richly decorated soviet military veteran: Gordiyevsky Mitrofanovich.

Reich dekorierter Veteran des sowjetischen Militärs: Gordiyevsky Mitrofanovich.

Vétéran de l'armée soviétique, couvert de décorations: Gordiyevsky Mitrofanovich.

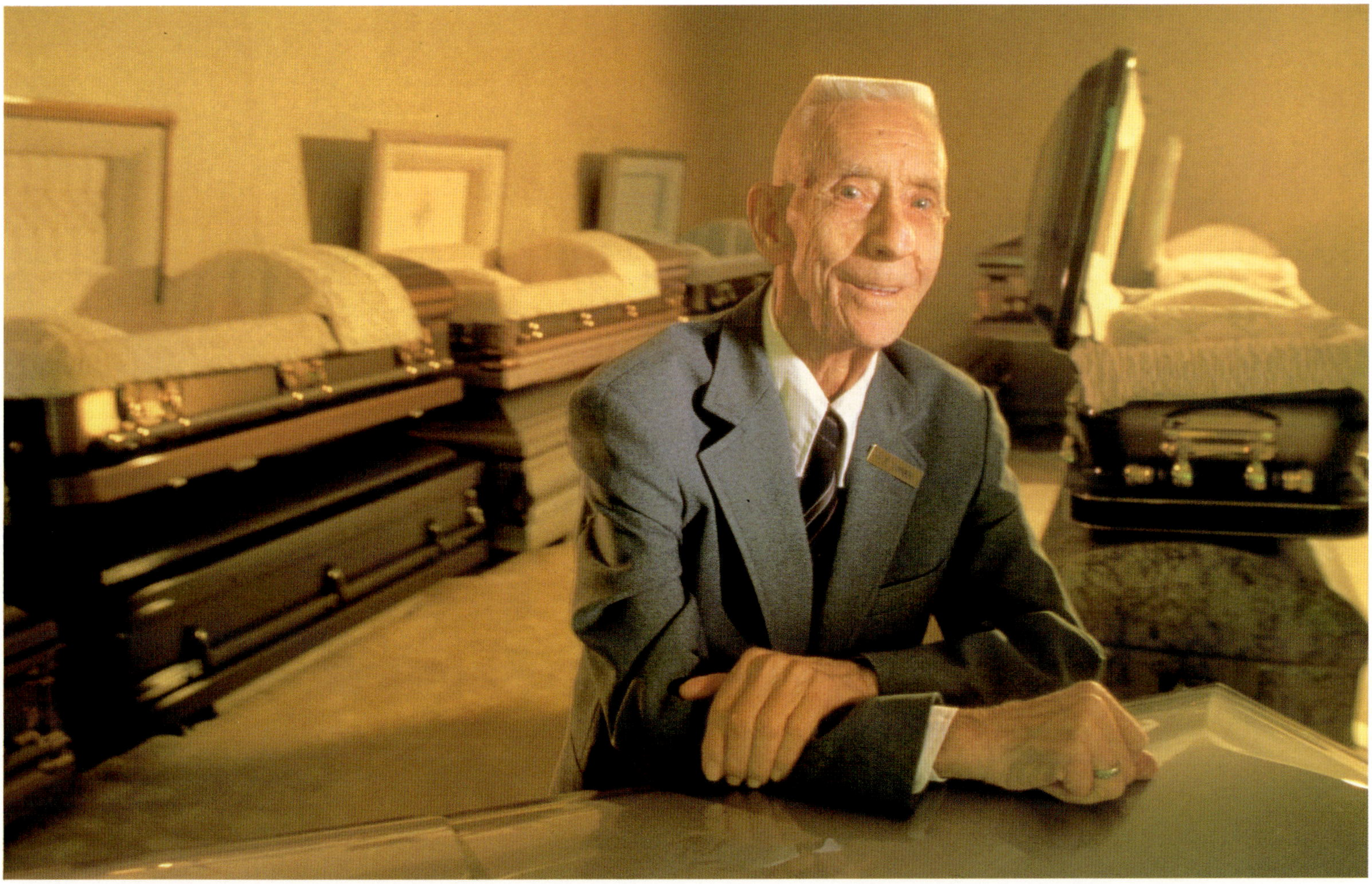

Will van Overbeek

Portrait shot to accompany an article in the *Texas Monthly*: Bert Turner, funeral home greeter.

Porträtaufnahme für einen Beitrag in *Texas Monthly*: Bert Turner, Angestellter eines Beerdigungsinstituts.

Portrait pour un article du *Texas Monthly*: Bert Turner, employé des pompes funèbres.

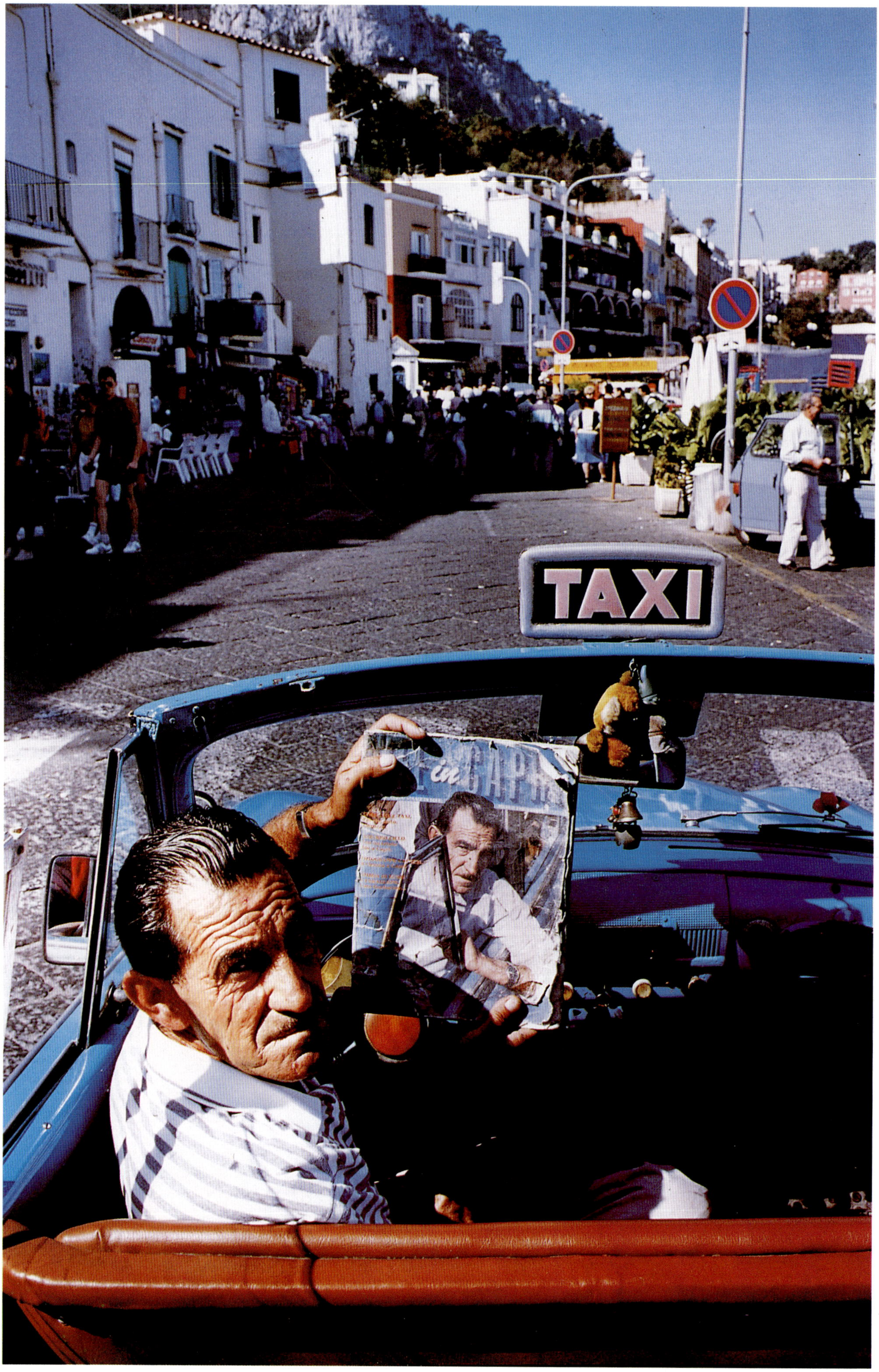
TAXI

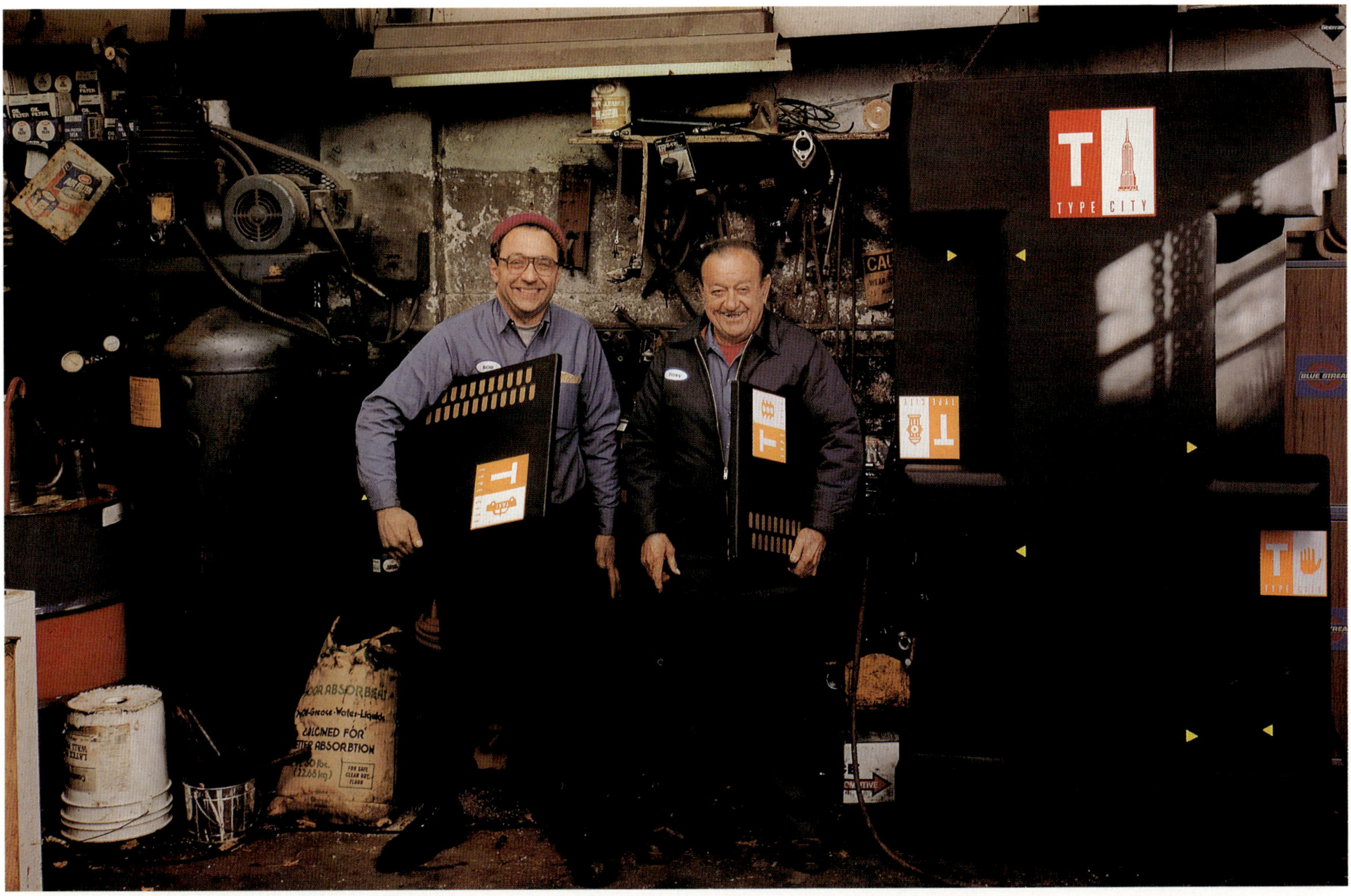

Helmut Newton

A Capri taxi driver in June 1991. Photographed for an article in *Condé Nast Traveler*. He has driven all the stars that came to Nice, photographer Helmut Newton included.

Ein Taxifahrer auf Capri – Aus einem Artikel in der Zeitschrift *Condé Nast Traveler*. Er hat alle Stars, die in Nizza waren, gefahren, einschließlich den Fotografen Helmut Newton.

Photo prise à Capri, pour un article paru dans *Condé Nast Traveler*. Ce chauffeur a conduit toutes les stars qui sont venues à Nice, y compris le photographe Helmut Newton.

Steve Marsel

The idea was to show the expandable font cartridge for laser jet printers with people in provocative environments. This eight foot high model of the cartridge was built out of foam. The primary light was strobe, diffused through a soft box.

Statt einer einfachen Produktaufnahme wurden erweiterbare Schriftkassetten für Laser-Jet-Drucker mit Leuten in spezieller Umgebung gezeigt. Dieses 2,5 Meter hohe Modell besteht aus Schaumstoff. Das Stroboskoplicht wurde mit einer Softbox gestreut.

Les cassettes de caractères pour imprimante à jet laser sont présentées dans un cadre spécial, avec des gens intéressants. La maquette est en mousse. Le photographe a utilisé une lumière de flash stroboscopique, diffusée par une soft box.

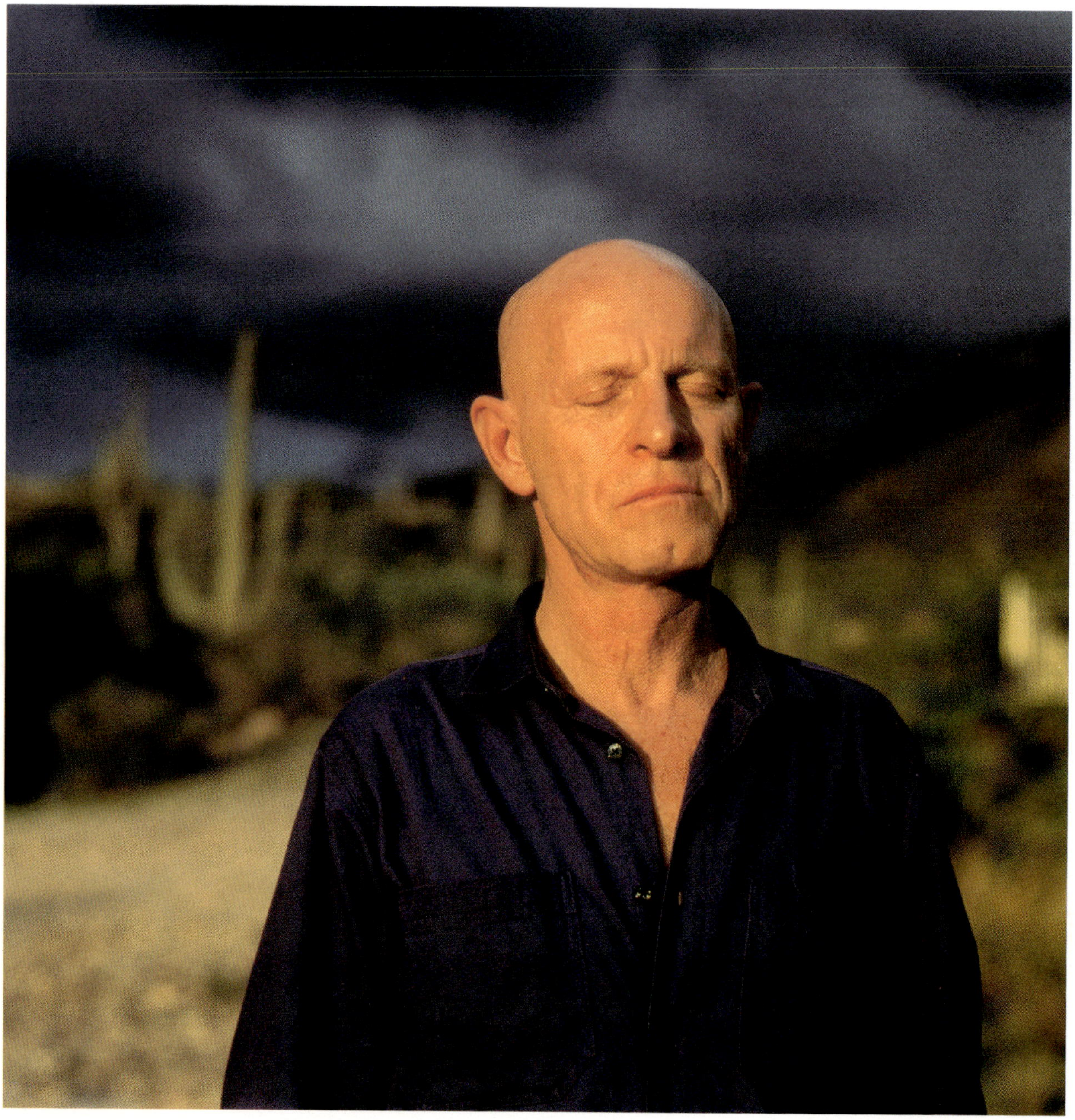

Tom Zimberoff

This photo was selected from a promotional book for Tom Zimberoff.

Porträt aus einem Promotionbuch des Fotografen Tom Zimberoff.

Portrait tiré d'un livre promotionnel du photographe Tom Zimberoff.

David Hiscock

From a series of shots by English photographer David Hiscock, presented in *Zoom* photo magazine.

Aus einer Reihe von Aufnahmen des englischen Fotografen David Hiscock, der in *Zoom* vorgestellt wurde.

Photo figurant dans une série de prises de vues de l'Anglais David Hiscock, que le magazine *Zoom* a présenté à ses lecteurs.

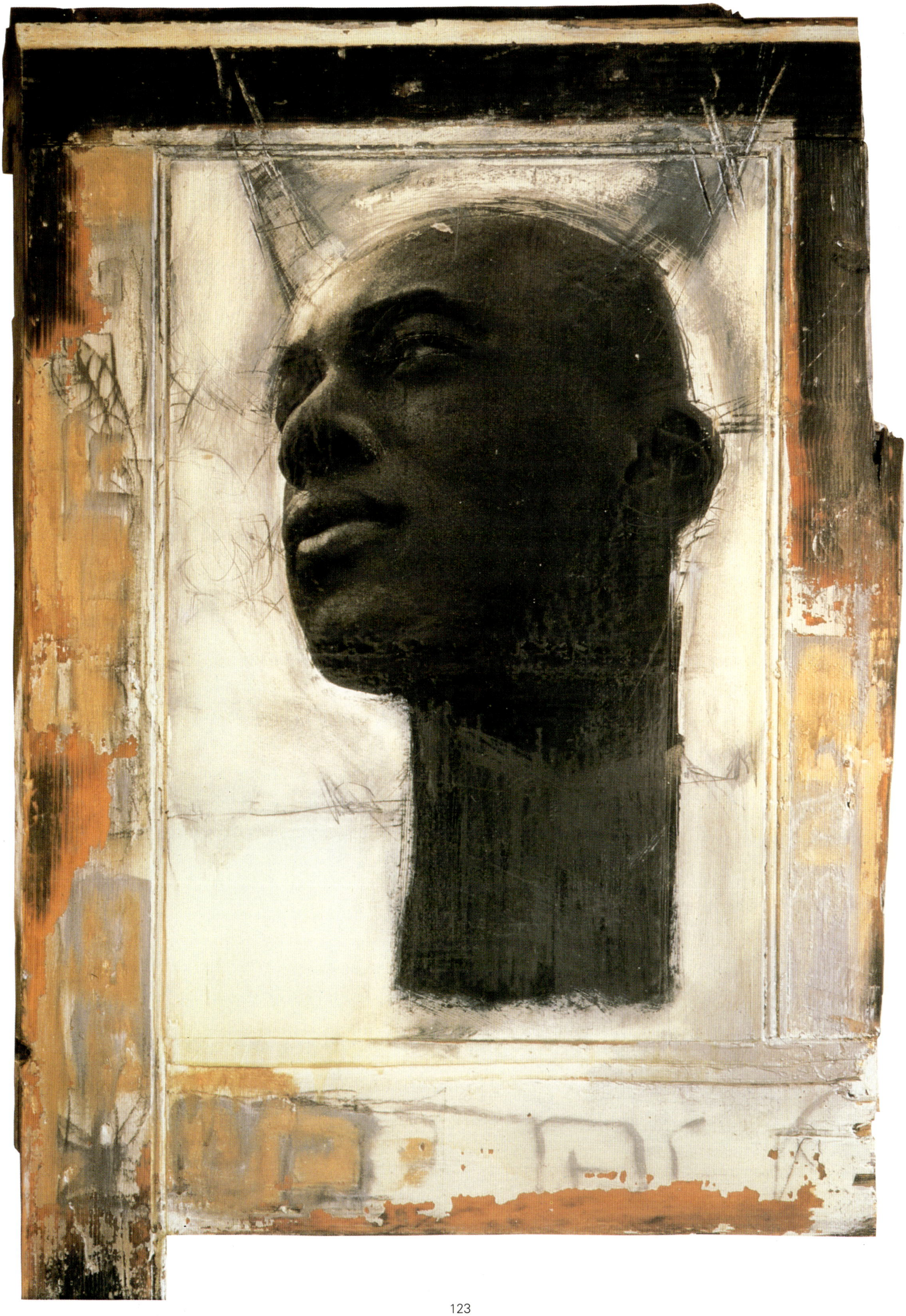

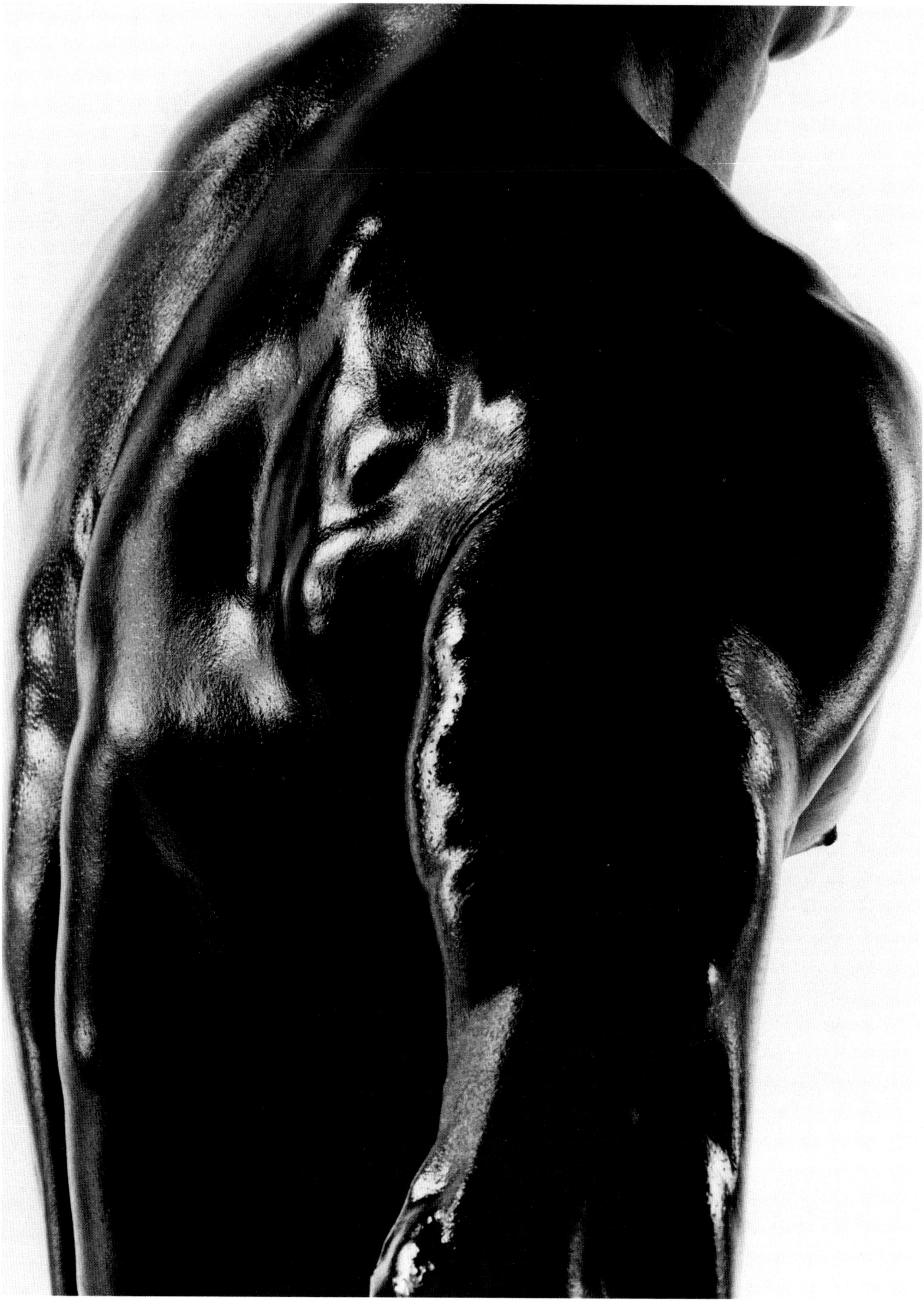

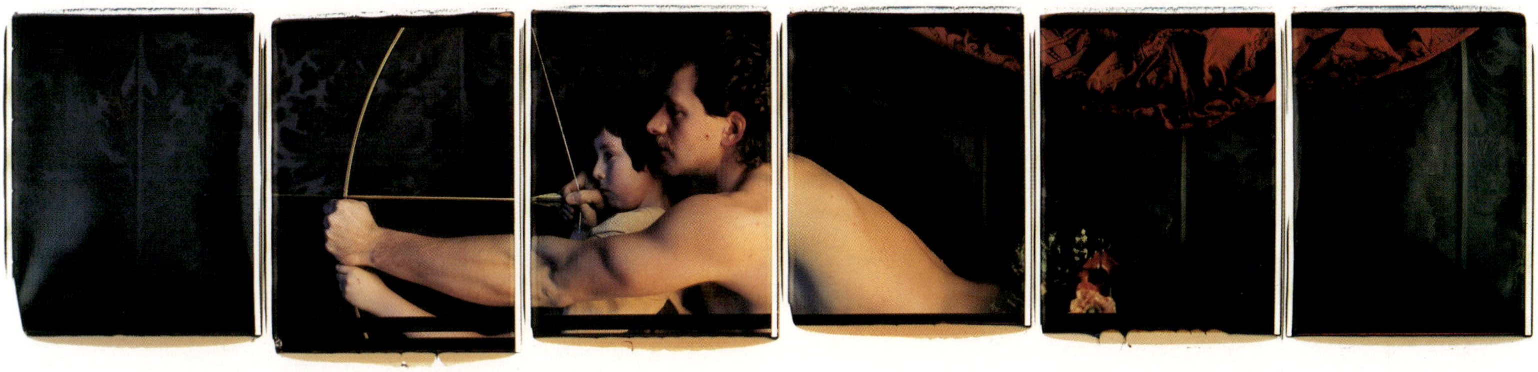

Evergon

»Centaur Teaching the Young Hercules to use the Bow and Arrow« – 6-part Polaroid photograph, 56 x 672 cm

»Zentaur unterrichtet den jungen Herkules im Umgang mit Pfeil und Bogen« – sechsteilige Polaroid-Aufnahme, 56 x 672 cm.

«Centaure apprenant au jeune Héraclès le maniement de l'arc» – Photo originale Polaroid hexapartite, 56 x 672 cm.

Seiichi Kazunaga

Photograph used for a self-promotional catalogue for photographer Seiichi Kazunaga.

Für einen Eigenwerbungskatalog verwendete Aufnahme der Fotografin Seiichi Kazunaga.

Cliché de la photographe Seiichi Kazunaga illustrant un catalogue autopromotionnel de l'artiste.

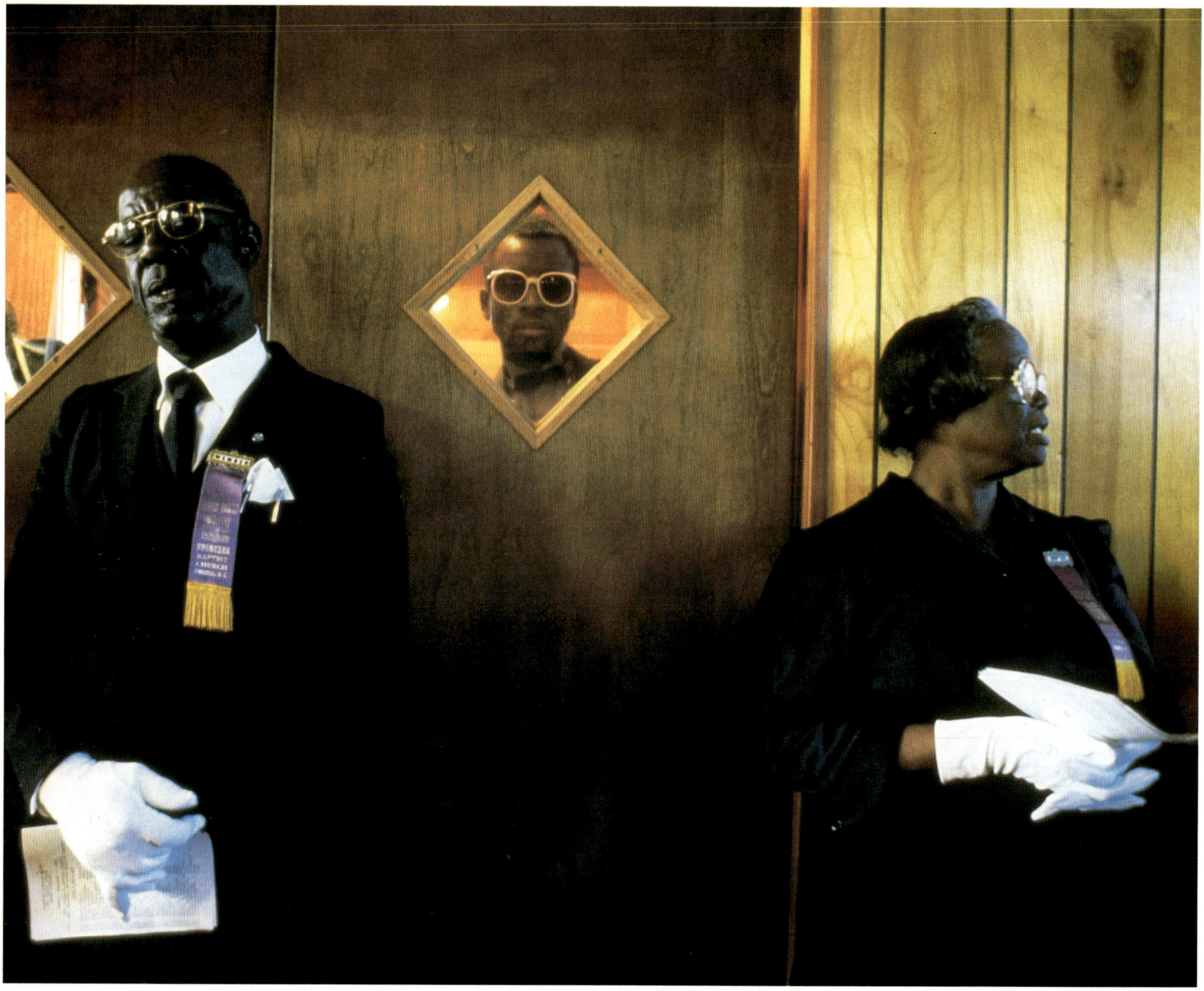

Dilip Mehta/Contact Press Images

Introduction for an article about the life of the blacks on the East Coast of the USA in a special issue of *Life* magazine devoted to the black population of the USA. This photo of ushers was shot in the Ebenezer Baptist Church on the Island of St. Helena.

Aufmacher für einen Artikel über das Leben der Schwarzen an der Ostküste der USA in einer Sondernummer der Zeitschrift *Life*, die der schwarzen Bevölkerung der USA gewidmet ist. Diese Aufnahme entstand in einer Baptisten-Kirche auf der Insel St. Helena.

Affichette-réclame pour un article sur la vie des noirs de la côte Est des Etats-Unis, publiée dans un numéro spécial du magazine *Life* sur la population noire du pays. Photo réalisée dans l'église baptiste Ebenezer sur l'île de St. Helena.

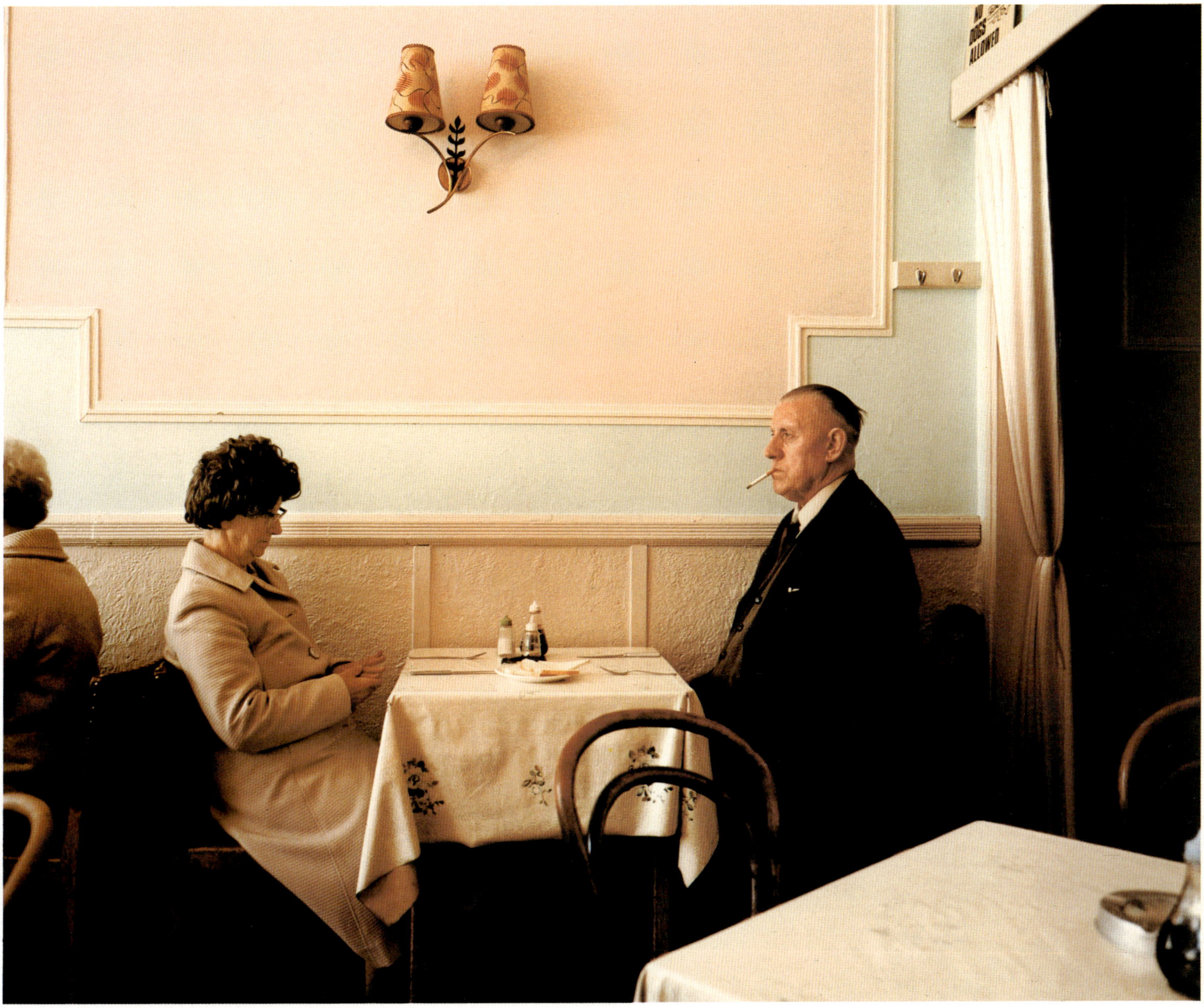

Martin Parr

Photograph from the »New Brighton« series by photographer Martin Parr.

Aufnahme aus der »New-Brighton«-Serie des Fotografen Martin Parr.

Exemple des photos de la série «New Brighton» de Martin Parr.

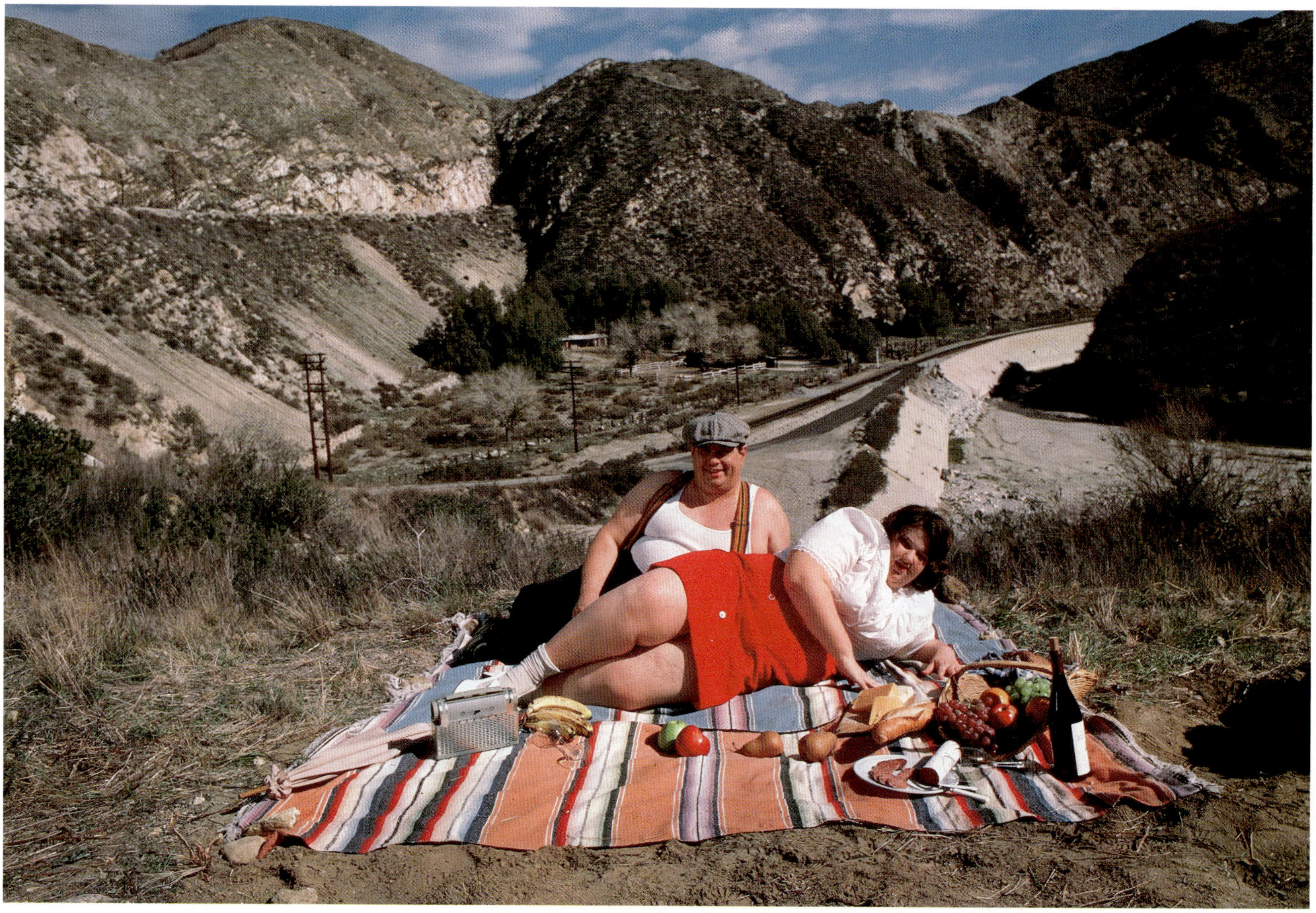

Bishin Jumonji

Photograph from a series of posters to promote artificial sweeteners.

Aufnahme für ein Plakat, mit dem für künstlichen Süßstoff geworben wird.

Photo pour une affiche vantant les mérites des édulcorants de synthèse.

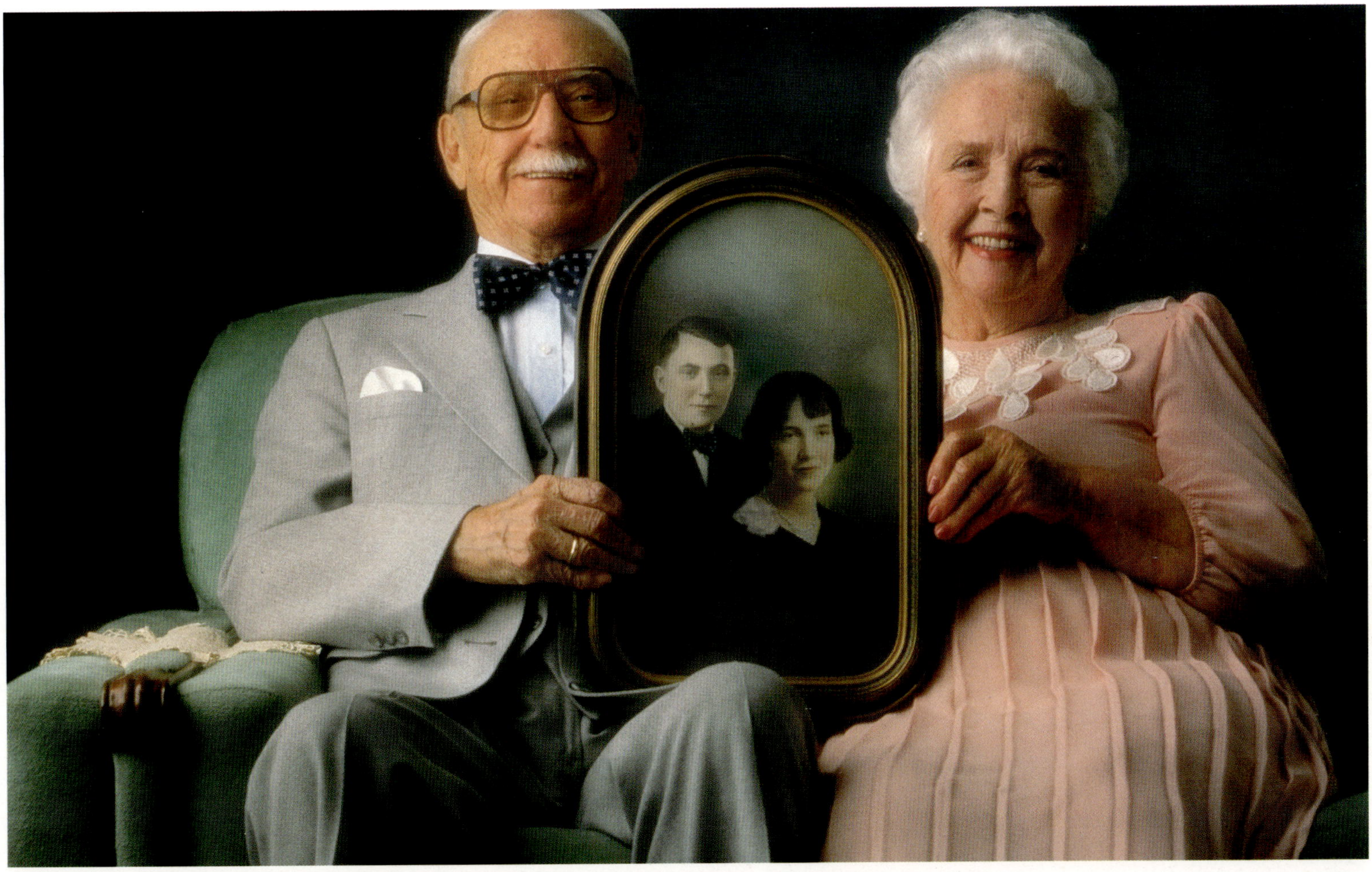

Nick Vedros

This couple proudly showing a portrait from their younger days have been married over 60 years. The photograph was shot by Nick Vedros and used in an Eastman Kodak campaign: »A professional portrait isn't expensive, it's priceless«.

Stolz zeigen die beiden, die über 60 Jahre miteinander verheiratet sind, ein Porträt aus ihrer Jugend. Diese Aufnahme stammt aus einer Kampagne für Eastman Kodak: »Professionelle Porträts sind nicht teuer, sie sind unbezahlbar«.

Ce couple, marié depuis plus de 60 ans, montre avec fierté un portrait pris au temps de leur jeunesse. Cette photo provient d'une campagne réalisée pour Eastman Kodak: «Le portrait d'un professionnel n'est pas cher, il est sans prix».

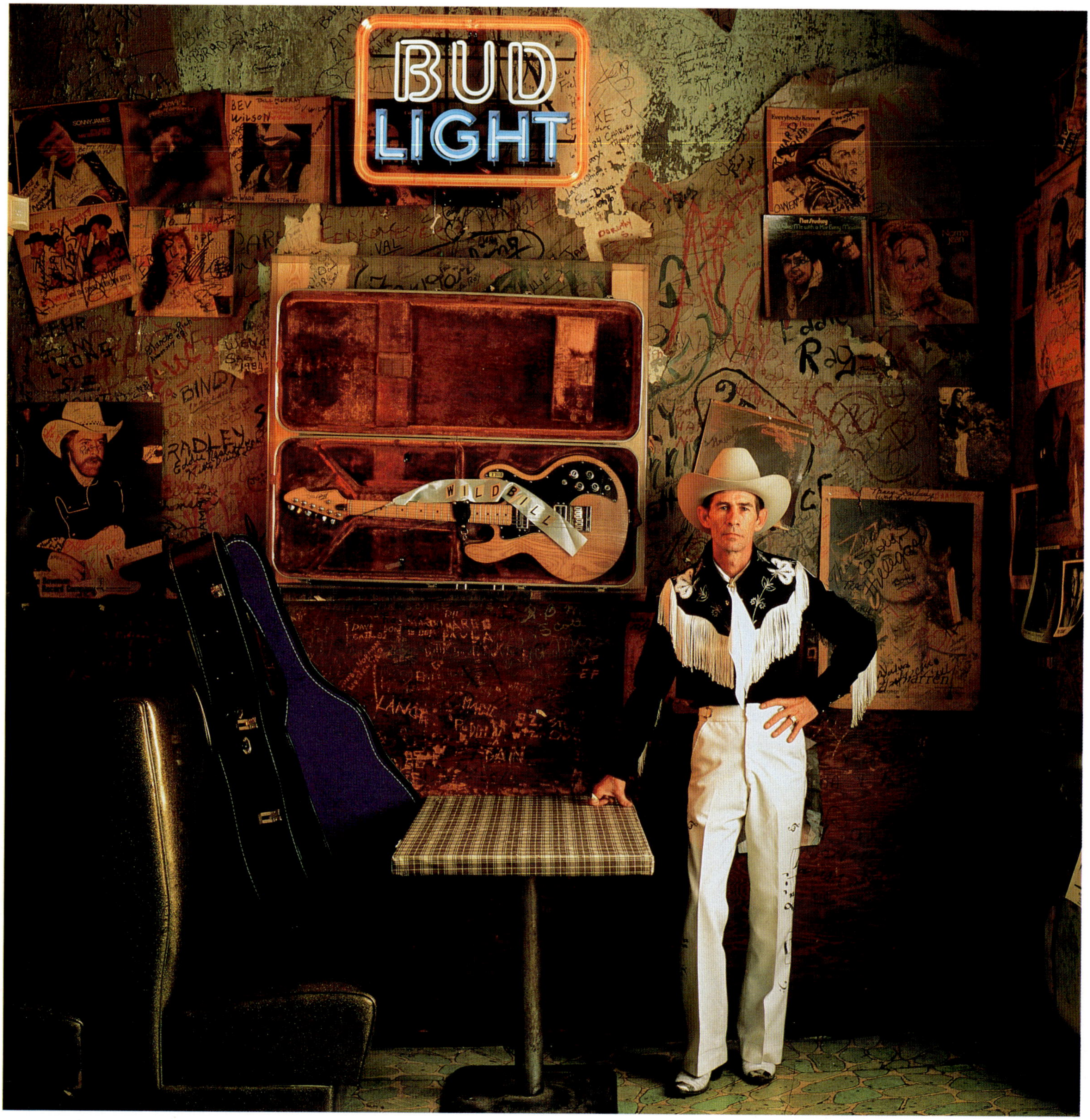

Michael O'Brien

A country singer in Tootsie's Bar in Nashville, Tennessee.

Ein Country-Sänger in Tootsie's Bar in Nashville, Tennessee.

Chanteur de country au Tootsie's Bar à Nashville (Tennessee).

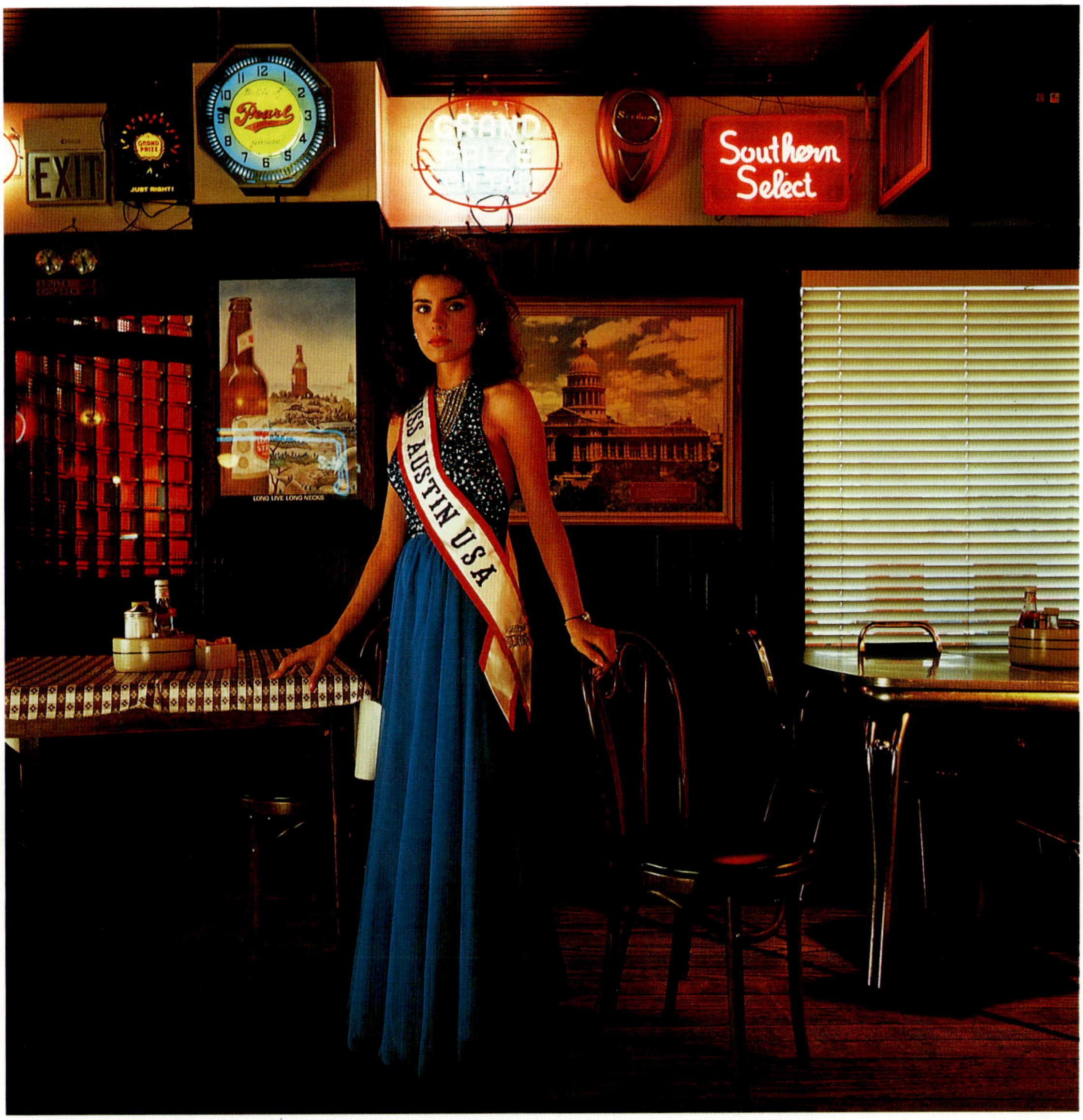

Michael O'Brien

Annabelle Lares, Miss Austin 1989, photographed in Threadgill's, a restaurant where Janis Joplin's career started. *National Geographic* magazine assigned the photographer to depict Austin, Texas, through a cross-section of its citizens.

Miss Austin, fotografiert in Threadgill's, dem Restaurant, in dem Janis Joplins Karriere begann. Der Auftrag des Magazins *National Geographic* lautete, Austin, Texas, durch einen Querschnitt seiner Bevölkerung darzustellen.

Le *National Geographic* magazine avait demandé au photographe de faire un reportage sur les habitants d'Austin, au Texas. Annabelle Lares, Miss Austin, est ici photographiée dans le restaurant Threadgill's, où Janis Joplin fit ses débuts.

Sue Bennett

A Native American, photographed with natural light.

Indianerin, mit natürlichem Licht fotografiert.

Une autochtone d'Amérique, photographiée sous une lumière naturelle.

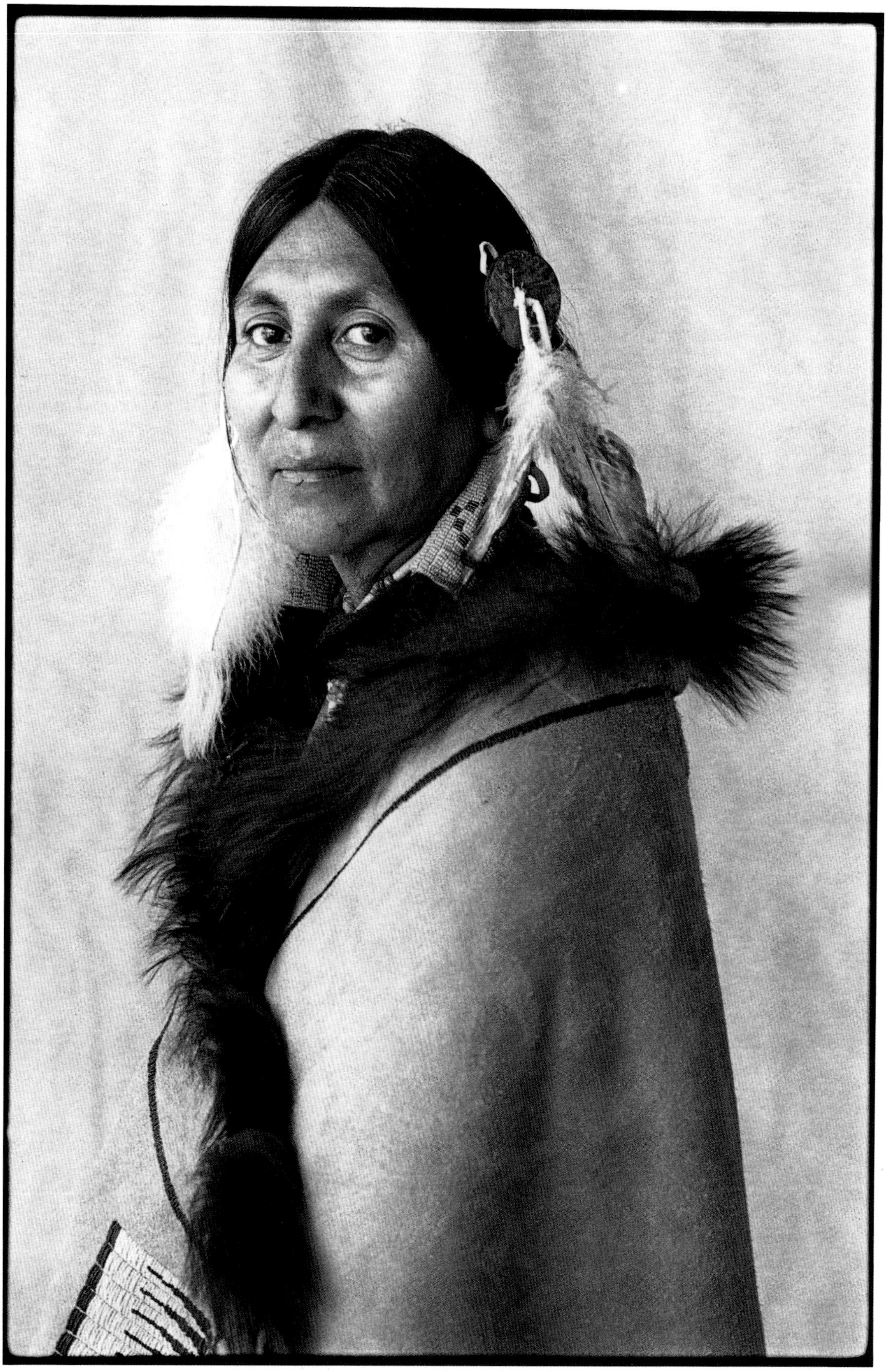

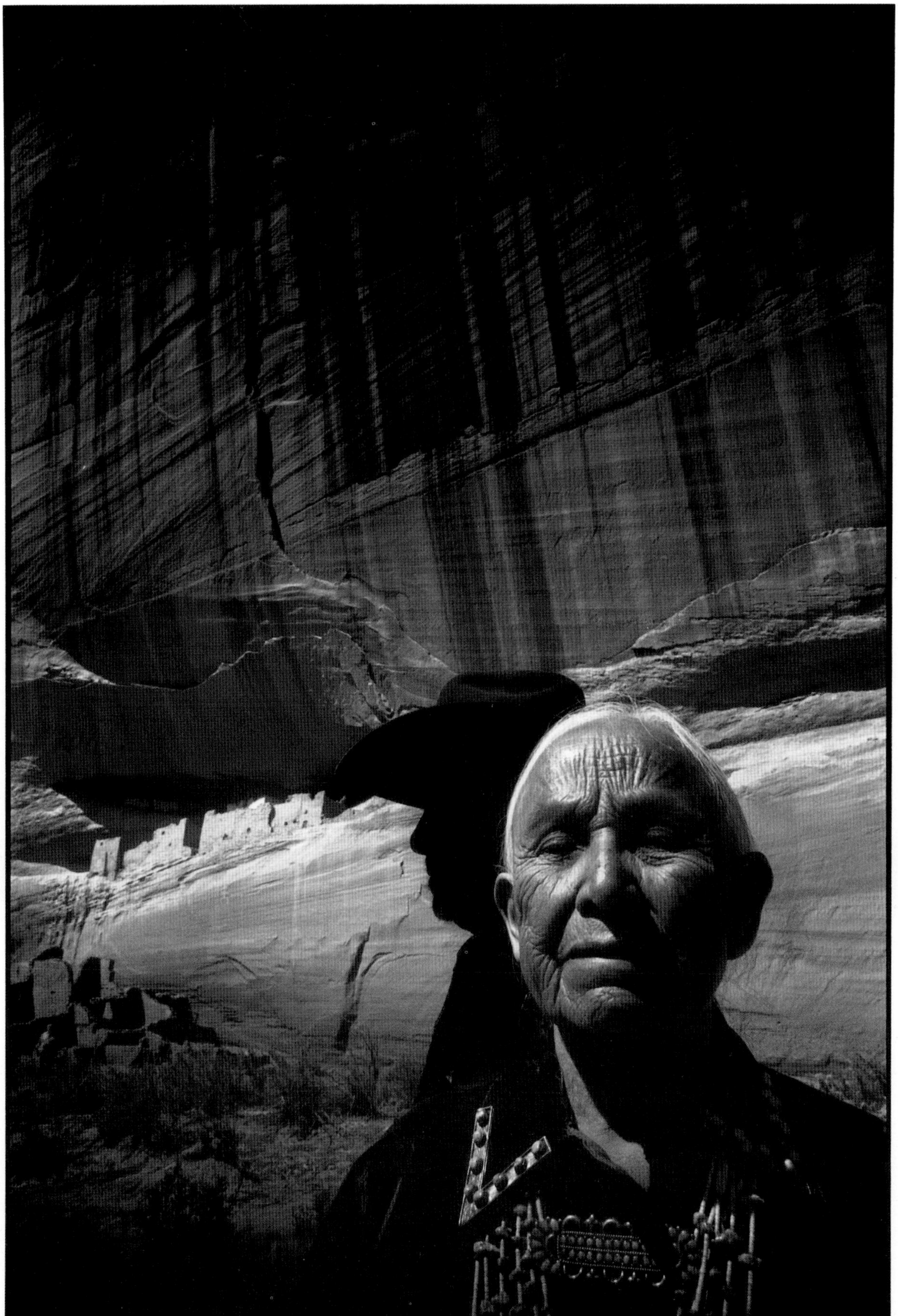

◁ Greg Booth

A young Indian guide brought the photographer, Greg Booth, to the ancient cliff dwellings of the Navaho Indians in Canyon De Chelly, Arizona. Even more than the mystical landscape, the faces of its inhabitants fascinated him, so the grandparents of his guide agreed to serve as his models. The cowboy hat of the grandfather, which he insisted on wearing despite his Indian-style clothing, cast a shadow on his figure, providing a perfect backdrop for his wife's leathery face which seemed to echo the striations of the ancient cliff beyond.

Ein junger indianischer Führer brachte den Fotografen Greg Booth zu den alten Felsbehausungen der Navajo-Indianer im Canyon De Chelly, Arizona. Noch mehr als die fast mystische Landschaft interessierten ihn die Gesichter ihrer Bewohner. Die Großeltern des Führers waren bereit, sich fotografieren zu lassen. Der Cowboyhut des Großvaters, von dem er sich trotz indianischer Tracht nicht trennen wollte, warf Schatten auf seine Gestalt. Er wurde zum perfekten Hintergrund für das sonnengegerbte Gesicht seiner Frau, auf dem sich die Furchen des Felsens zu wiederholen scheinen.

Un jeune guide indien avait conduit le photographe Greg Booth sur le site des anciennes habitations troglodytiques des Indiens Navajo, dans le Canyon De Chelly, en Arizona. Plus encore que le paysage, ce furent les visages des habitants de cette contrée qui le fascinèrent. Les grands-parents du guide acceptèrent de se faire photographier. Malgré son costume indien, le grand-père ne voulut pas ôter son chapeau de cow-boy; l'ombre de sa sihouette constitue un fond idéal, contre lequel se détache le visage buriné par le soleil de sa femme; les sillons des roches séculaires semblent s'y refléter.

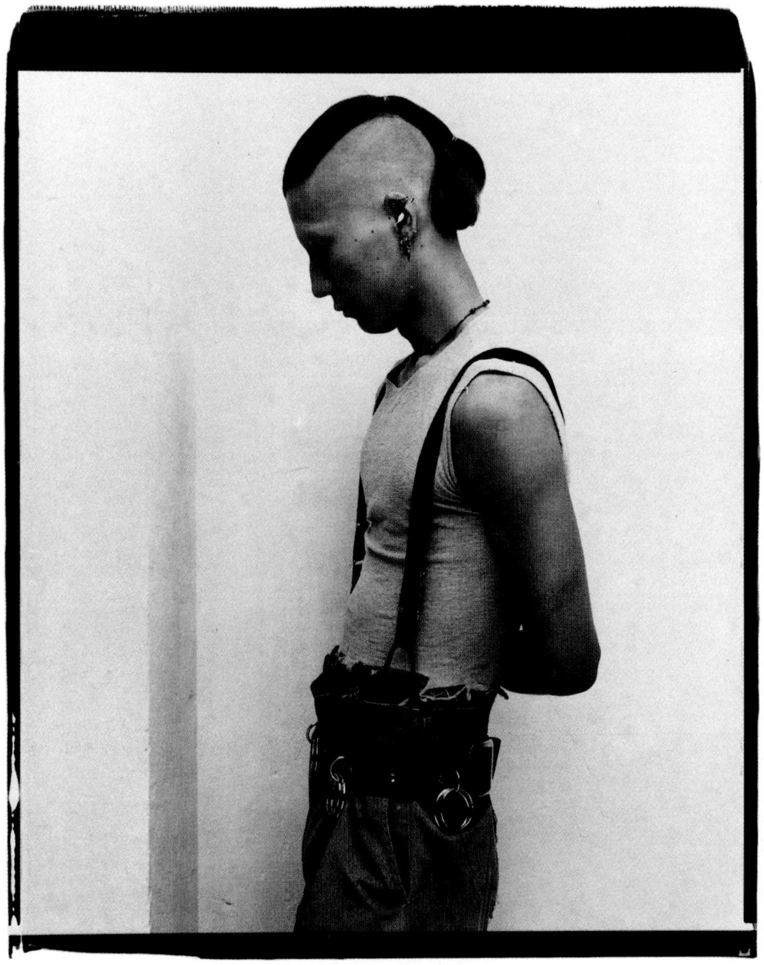

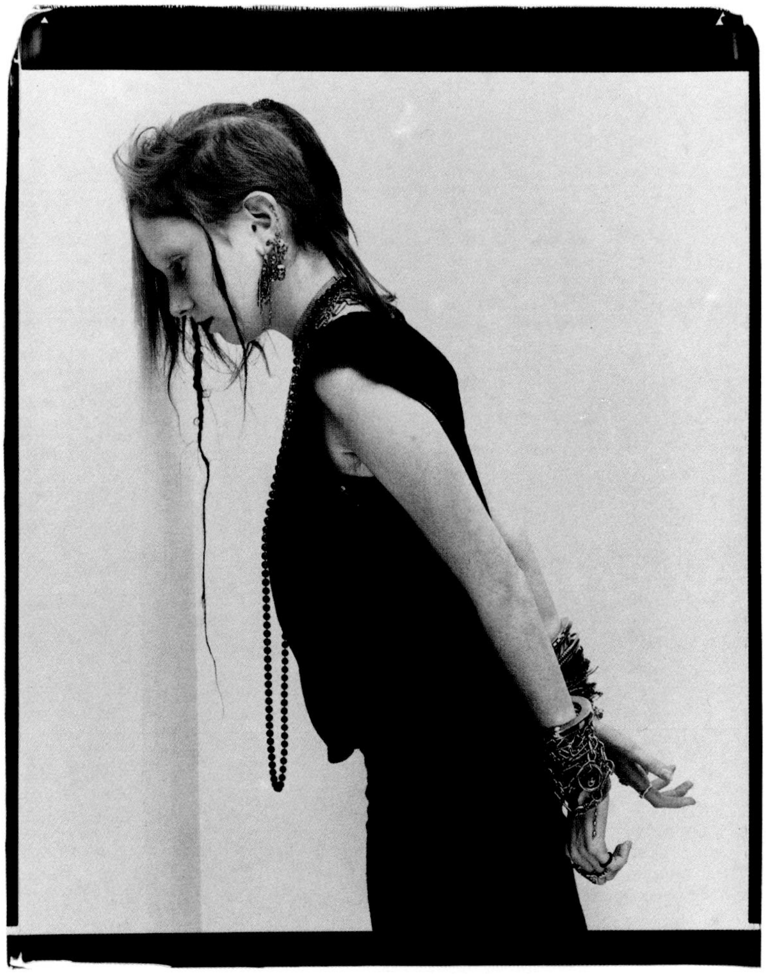

Marsha Burns

»Yaz, New York 1986« and »Kassa, New York 86«, black-and-white shots (both 61 x 50.8 cm) taken from the catalogue for an exhibition on the subject »Cities« held at the Henry Art Gallery.

Aufnahmen (beide 61 x 50,8 cm) mit dem Titel »Yaz, New York 1986« und »Kassa, New York 1986«, aus dem Katalog für eine Ausstellung zum Thema »Städte« in der Henry Art Gallery, University of Washington.

Photos noir et blanc (61 x 50,8 cm), intitulées «Yaz, New York 1986» et «Kassa, New York 1986», tirées du catalogue de l'exposition des «Villes» organisée à la Henry Art Gallery, Université de Washington.

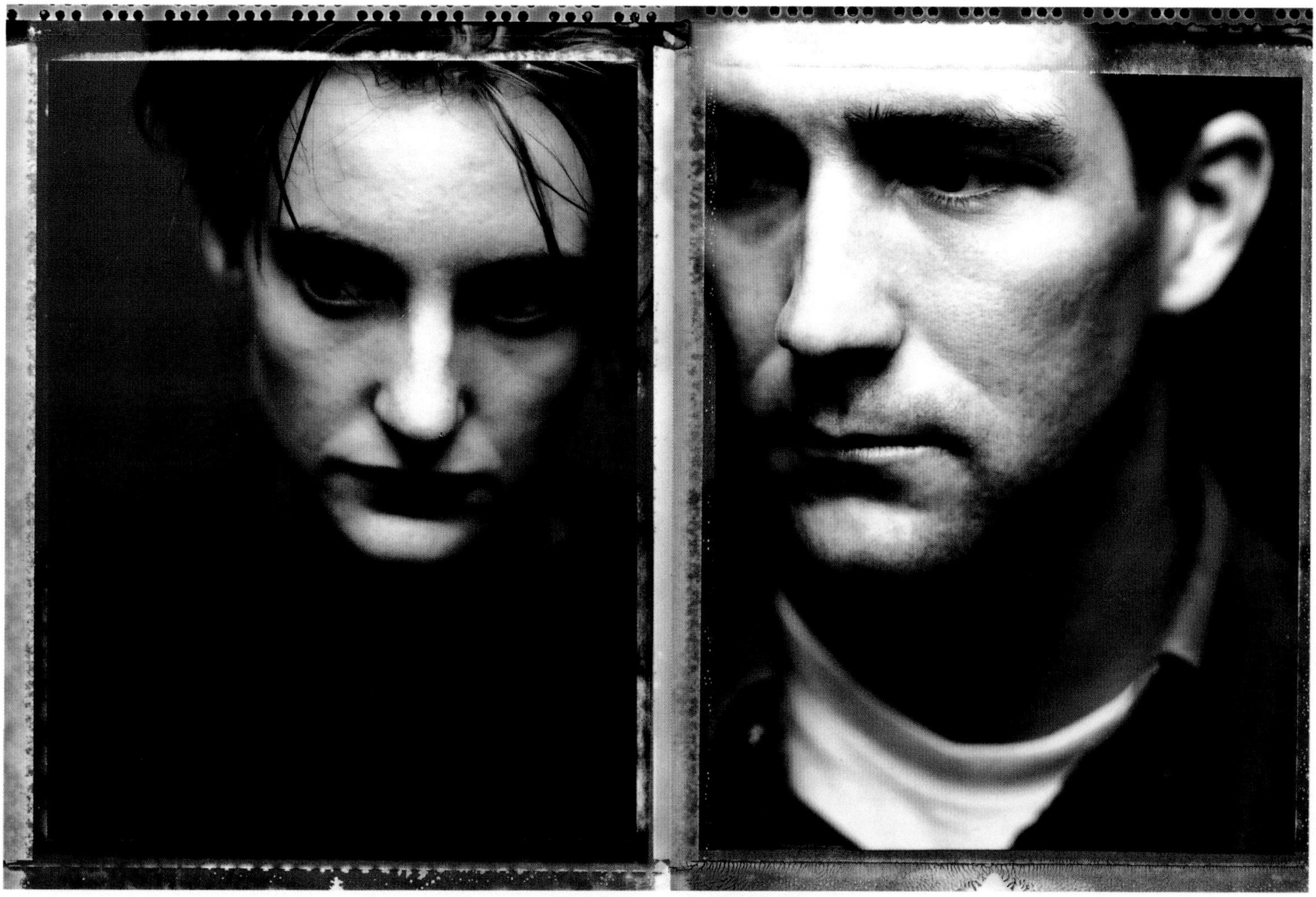

John Kolesa

Two from a self-assigned series of very close and personal portraits. The edges are an important element. Framed and accentuated by the borders of the Polaroid film.

Zwei Porträts aus einer freien Serie sehr persönlicher Porträts. Die Ränder der Aufnahmen sind ein wichtiges Element, das vom Polaroidfilm noch hervorgehoben wird.

Deux portraits tirés d'une série d'études personnelles. Les encadrements, qui sont encore mis en valeur par la bordure du film polaroïd, jouent un rôle essentiel.

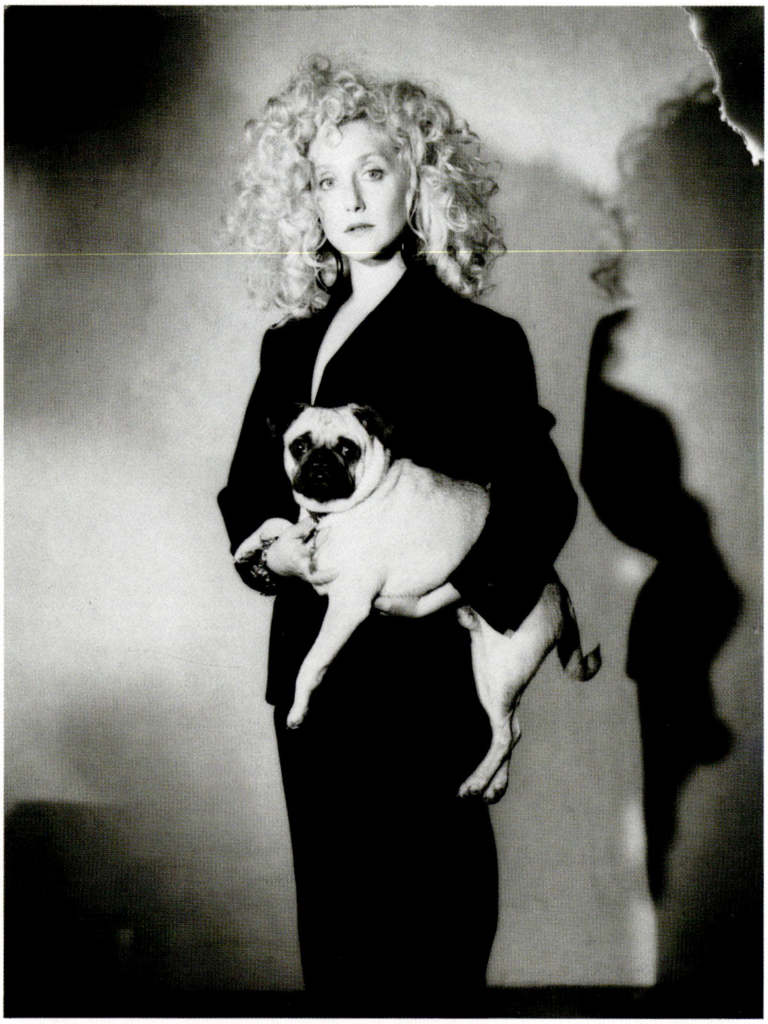

Mark Hanauer

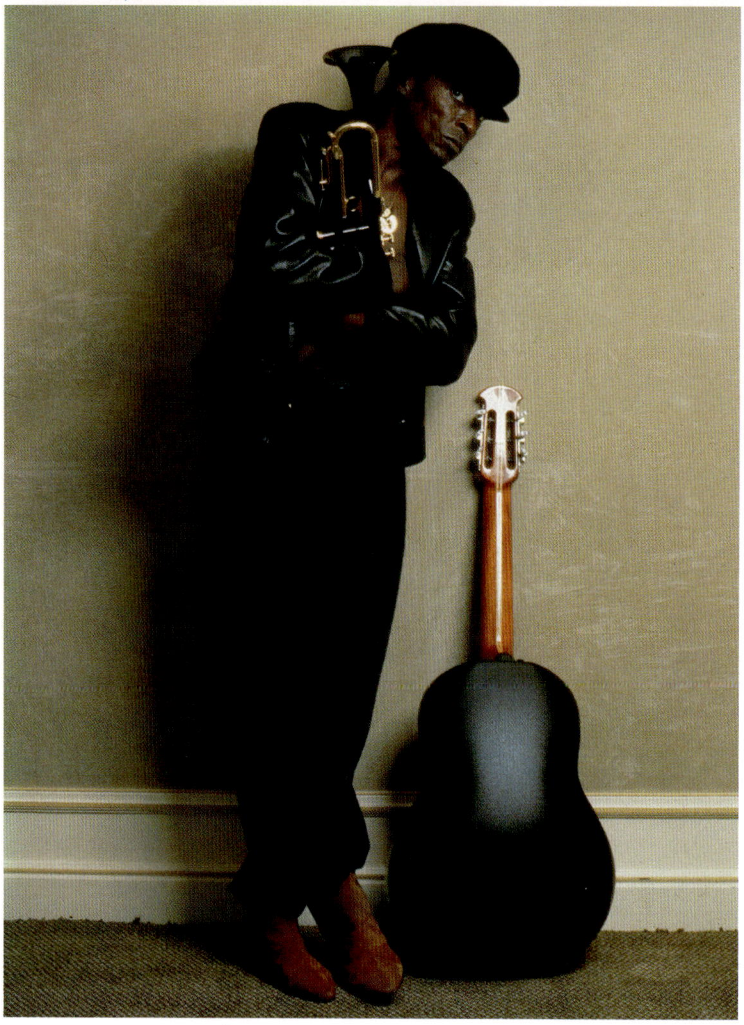

Serge Cohen

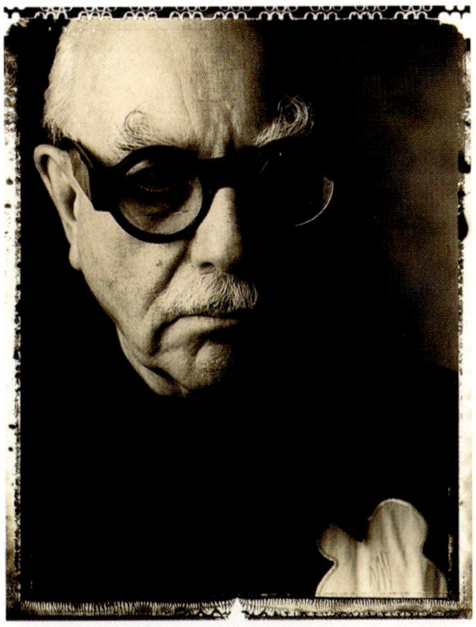
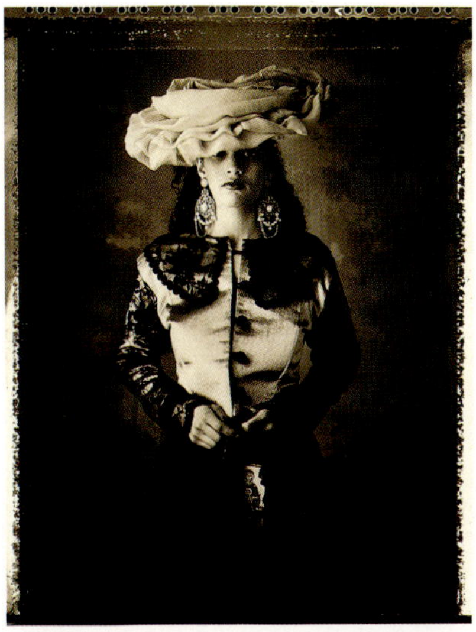
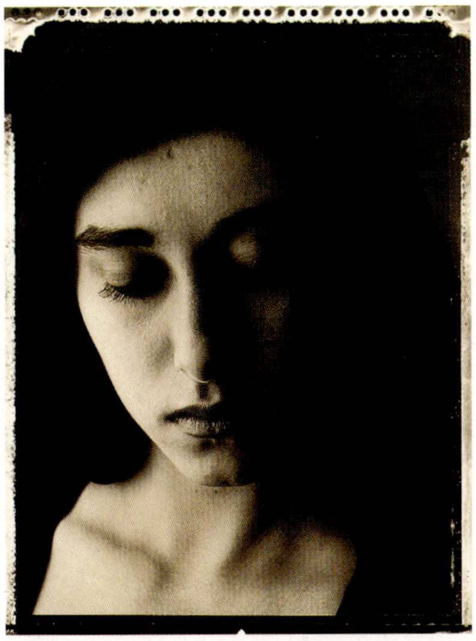
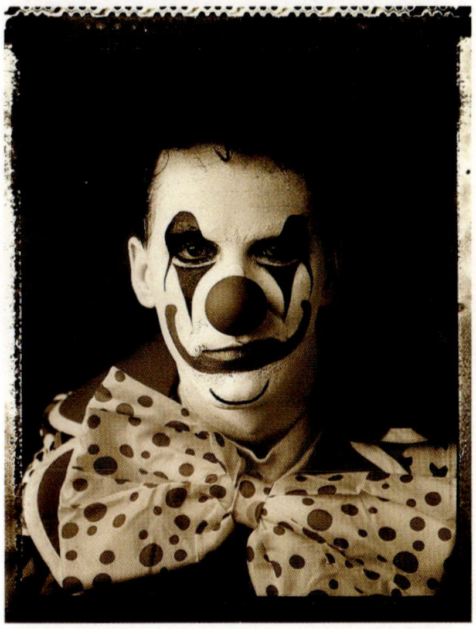
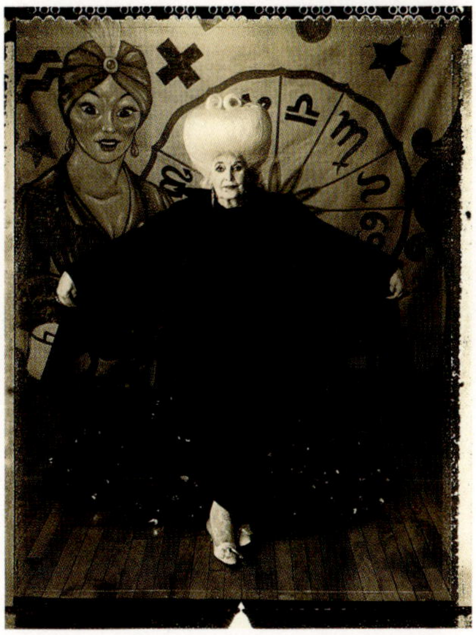
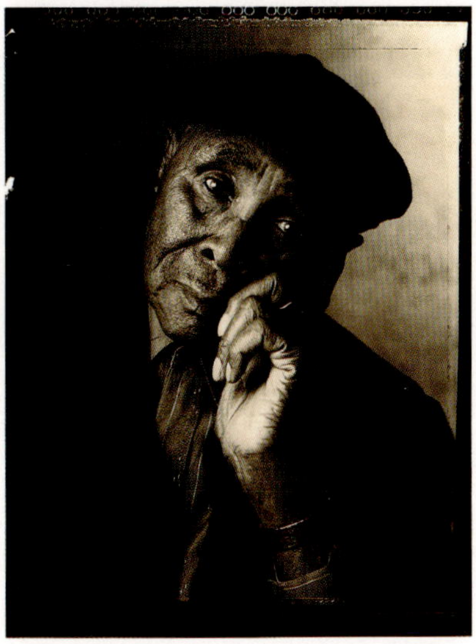

Marc Hauser

These earnest, contemplative faces were among those used in a calendar.

Ernste Gesichter, nachdenklich, versonnen. Die Porträts wurden für einen Kalender verwendet.

Des visages sérieux, méditatifs, concentrés. Ces portraits ont été reproduits dans un calendrier.

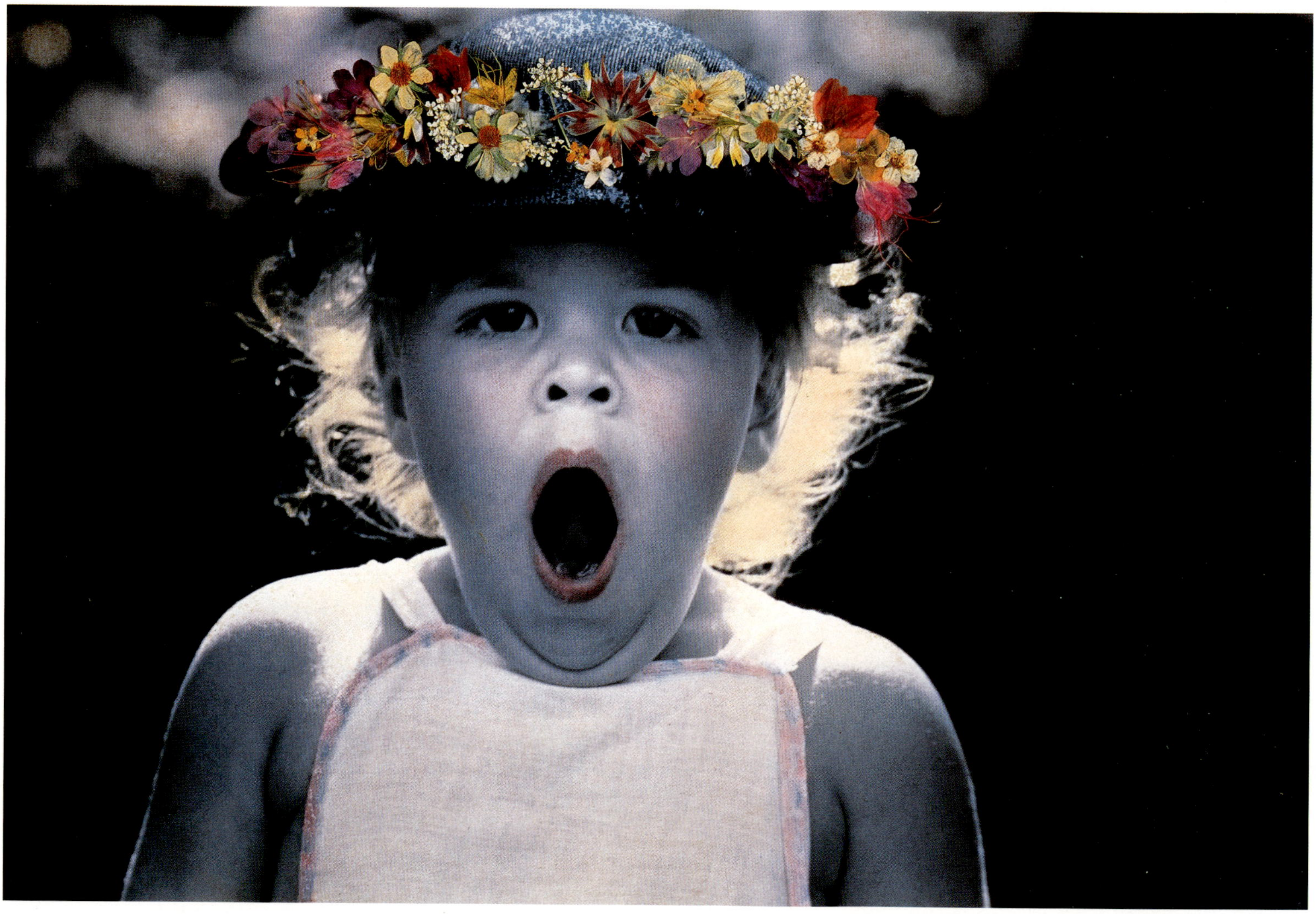

Betsy Cameron

Hand-tinted black-and-white photograph of a little girl wearing a hat with dry-pressed flowers.

Handkolorierte Schwarzweiß-Aufnahme eines kleinen Mädchens, geschmückt mit einem Blumenhut.

Photo en noir et blanc colorée à la main d'une petite fille portant un chapeau orné de fleurs.

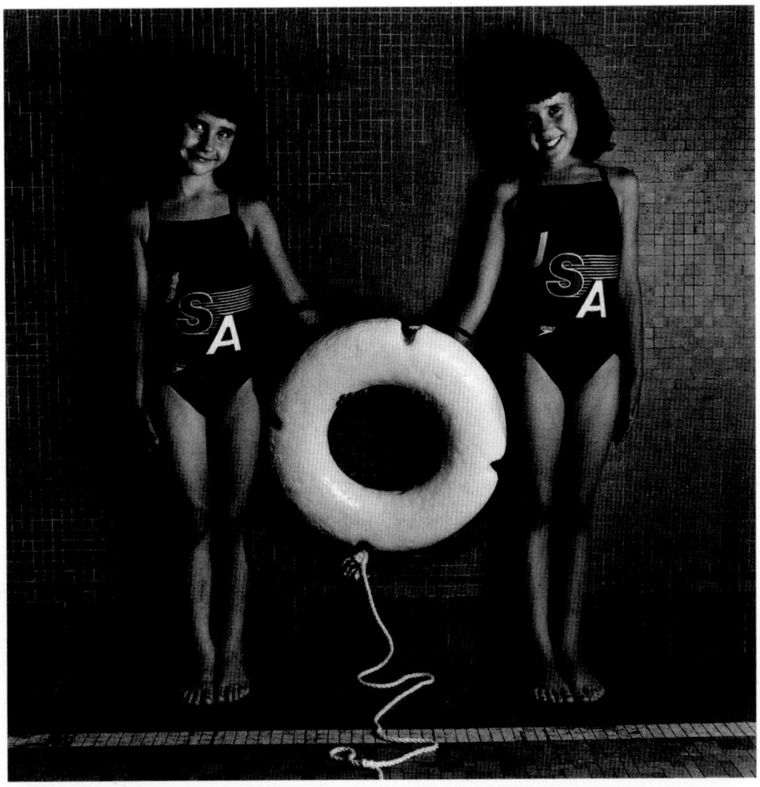

Marc Norberg

Future lifesavers – a portrait of the twins Lisa and Lauren Diloretto illustrate the annual report of the boys and girls clubs of Chicago.

Zukünftige Lebensretterinnen – ein Porträt der Zwillinge Lisa und Lauren Diloretto als Illustration eines Jahresberichtes der Boys and Girls Clubs von Chicago.

Une nouvelle génération de sauveteurs: portrait des jumelles Lisa et Lauren Diloretto illustrant un rapport annuel des boys and girls clubs de Chicago.

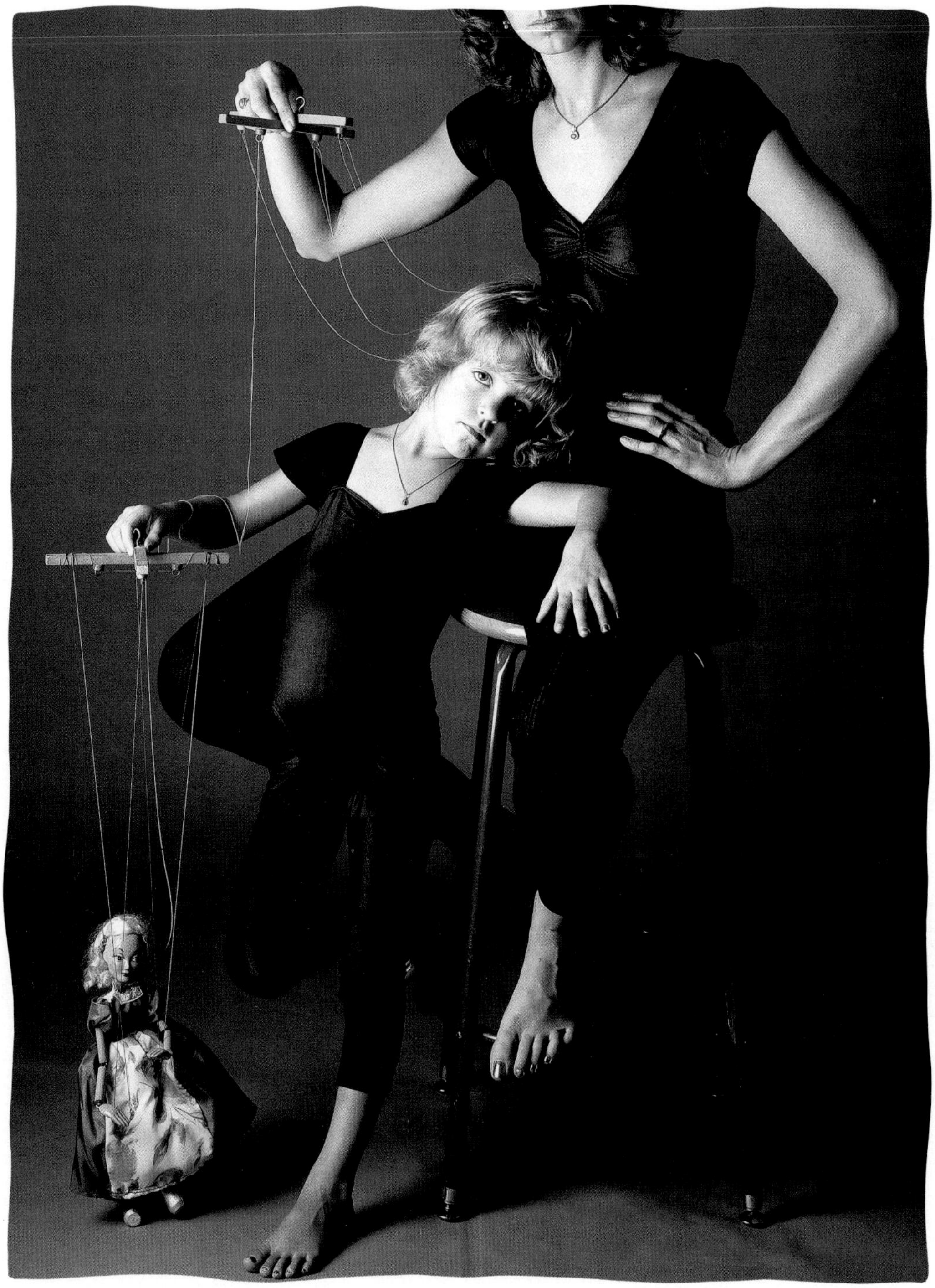

Jeffrey Muir Hamilton

Wood lithographers assigned this photograph as part of a promotional campaign, built around the theme of »toys«.

Spielzeug sollte in dieser Aufnahme für eine Lithographenanstalt eine Rolle spielen.

Interprétation personnelle sur le thème des jouets, réalisée pour des imprimeurs-lithographes.

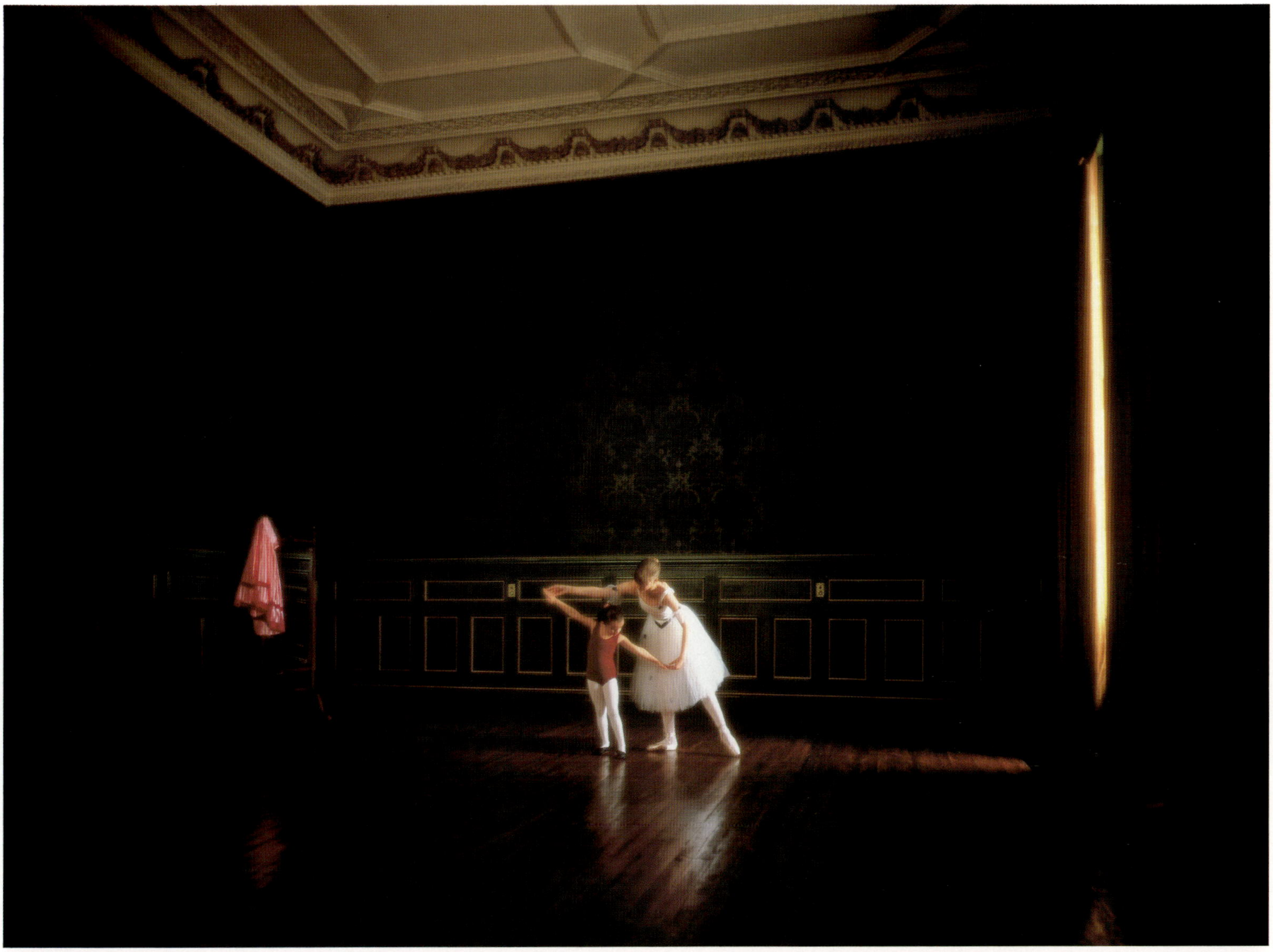

Hans Neleman

Photograph by New York photographer Hans Neleman for Kodak U.K.

Aufnahme des New Yorker Fotografen Hans Neleman für Kodak U.K.

Photo du photographe new-yorkais Hans Neleman pour Kodak U.K.

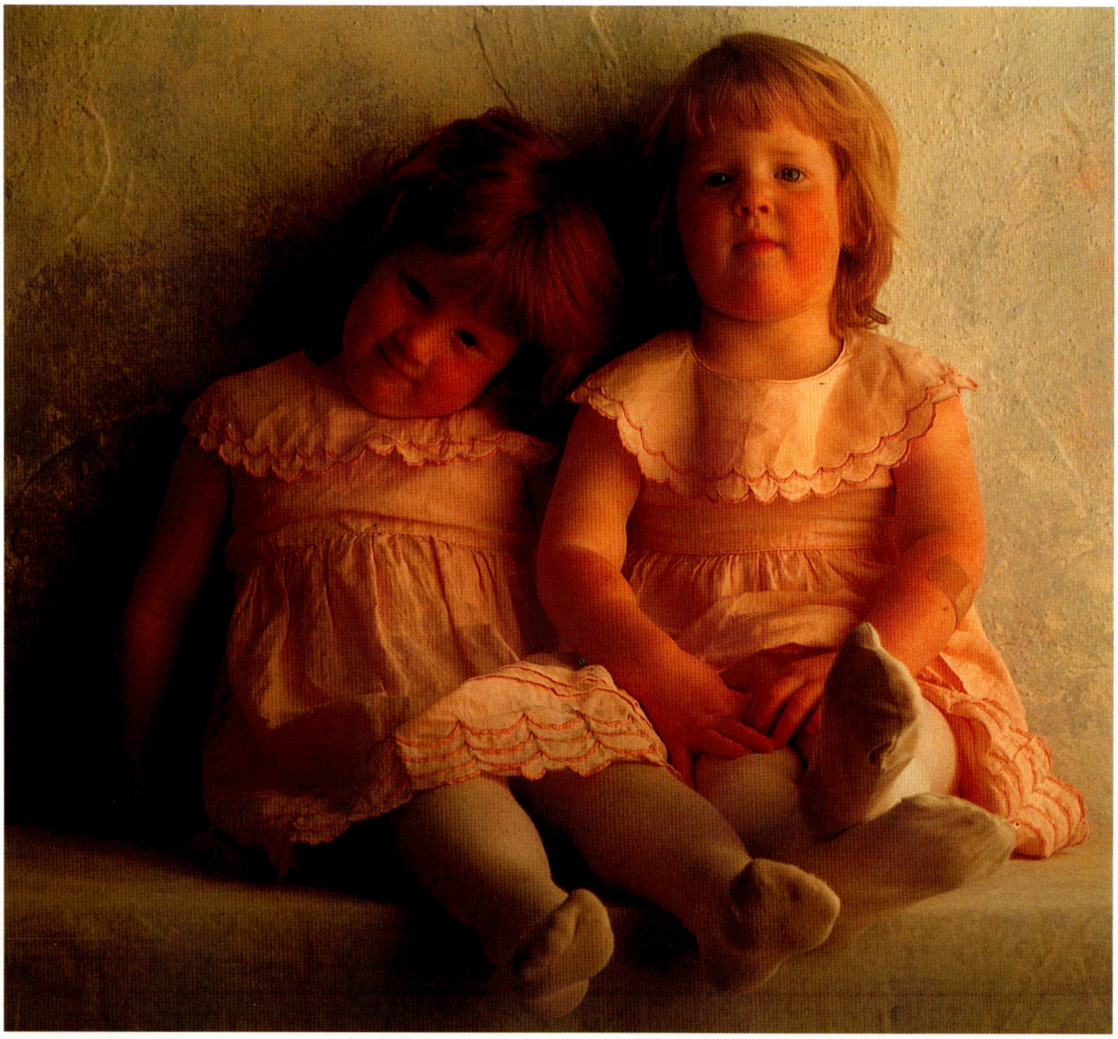

Carol Kaplan

Twin girls looking like dolls. Image used as self-promotion for photographer Carol Kaplan.

Zwei kleine Mädchen, Zwillinge, die wie Puppen aussehen. Eigenwerbung der Fotografin Carol Kaplan.

Jumelles qui ressemblent à des poupées. Autopromotion de la photographe Carol Kaplan.

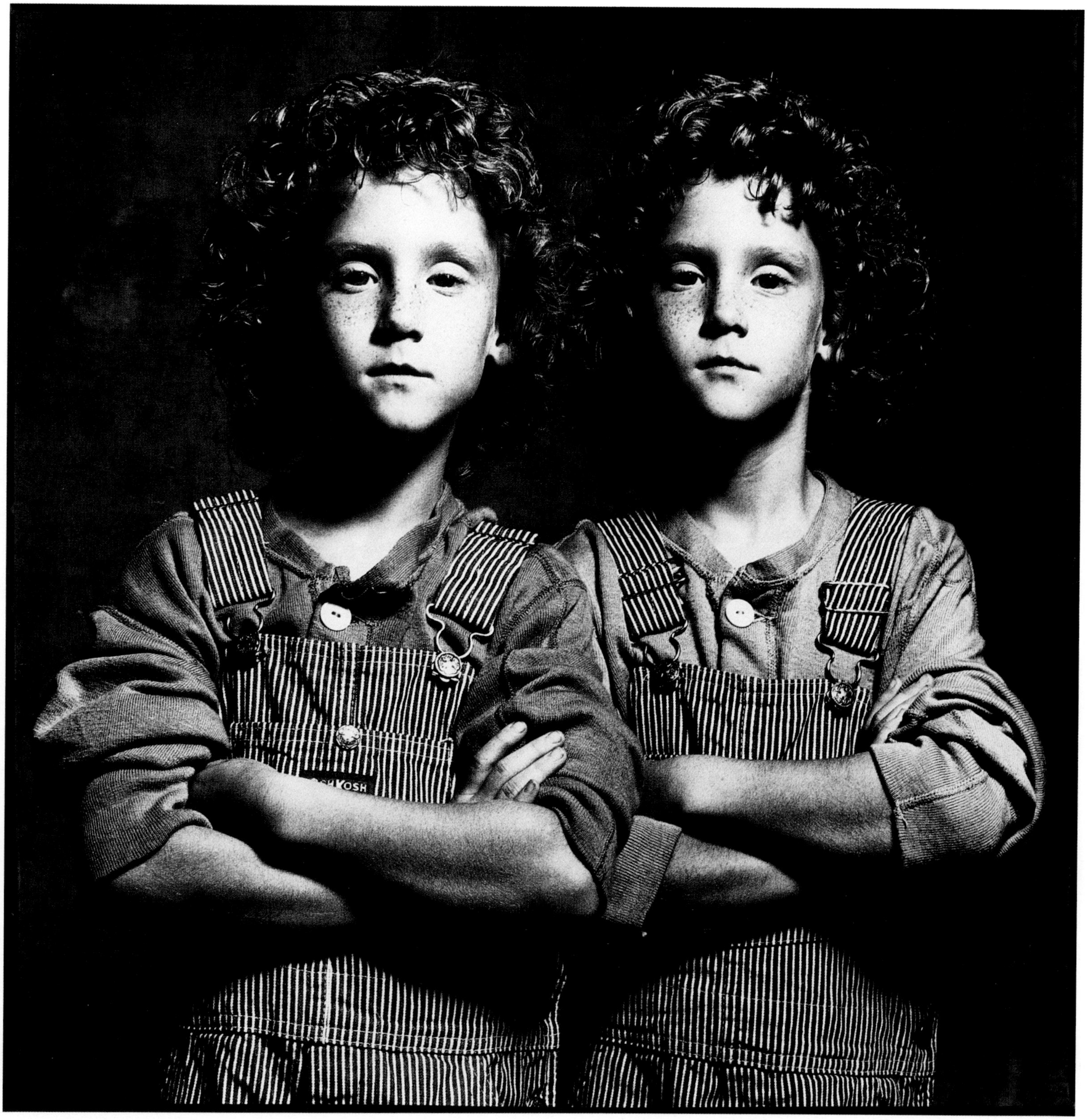

Albert Watson

From an advertising campaign for *Hasselblad* cameras. In this series photographers from all over the world had to characterize their native country in the portrait of a woman. Shown are two young American women, taken by Albert Watson.

Aus einer Werbekampagne für *Hasselblad*-Kameras. In dieser Serie hatten die aus aller Welt stammenden Fotografen den Auftrag, durch ein Frauenporträt auch deren Heimatland zu charakterisieren. Hier zwei junge amerikanische Frauen, gesehen von Albert Watson.

Campagne publicitaire des appareils photo *Hasselblad*. Les photographes requis pour cette série devaient caractériser à travers des portraits de femmes le pays d'origine de leurs modèles. Voici deux jeunes Américaines, vues par Albert Watson.

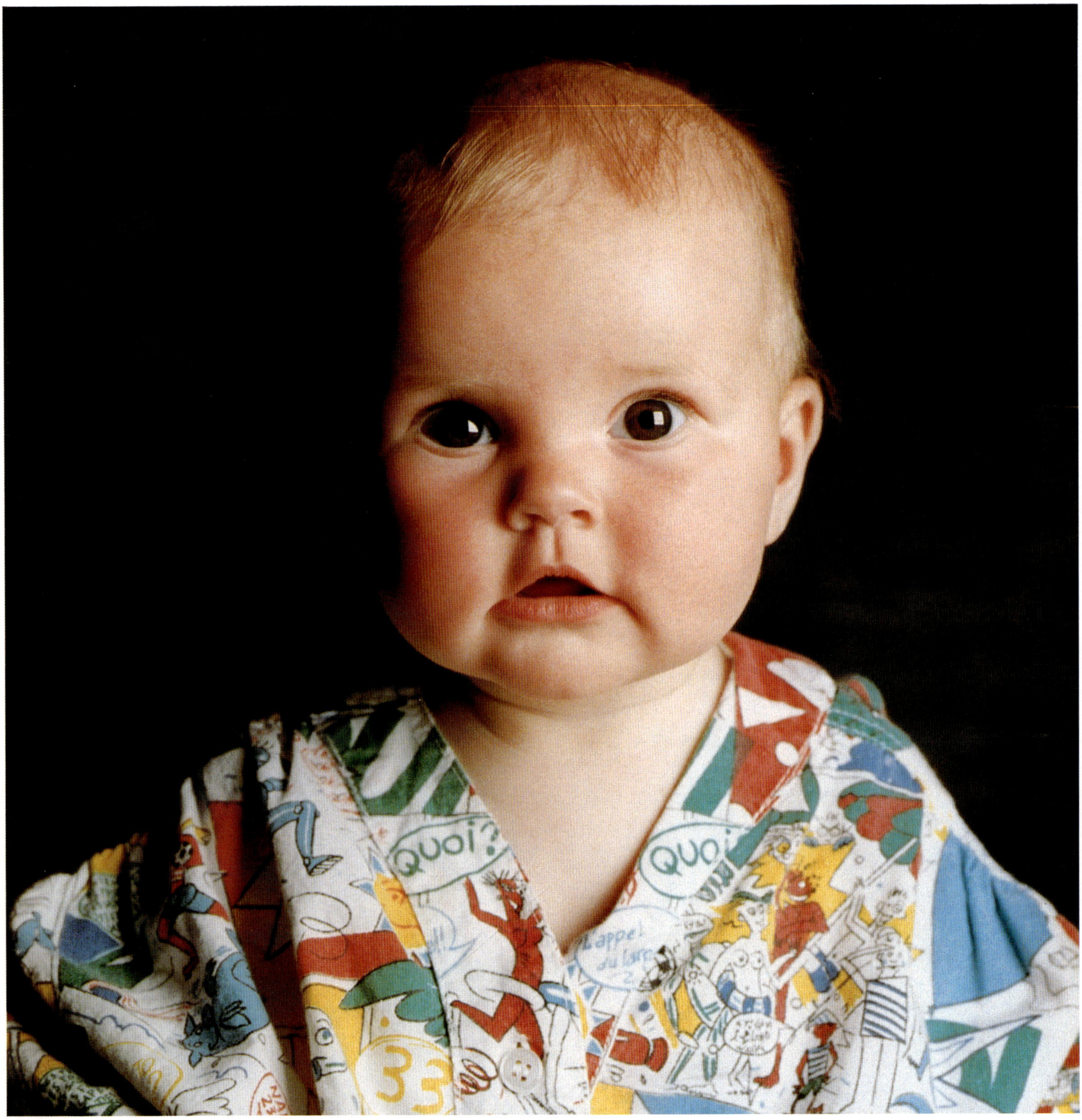

Rick English

Personal study by photographer Rick English, Palo Alto, California.

Persönliche Studie des Fotografen Rick English, Palo Alto, Kalifornien.

Etude personnelle du photographe Rick English, Palo Alto, Californie.

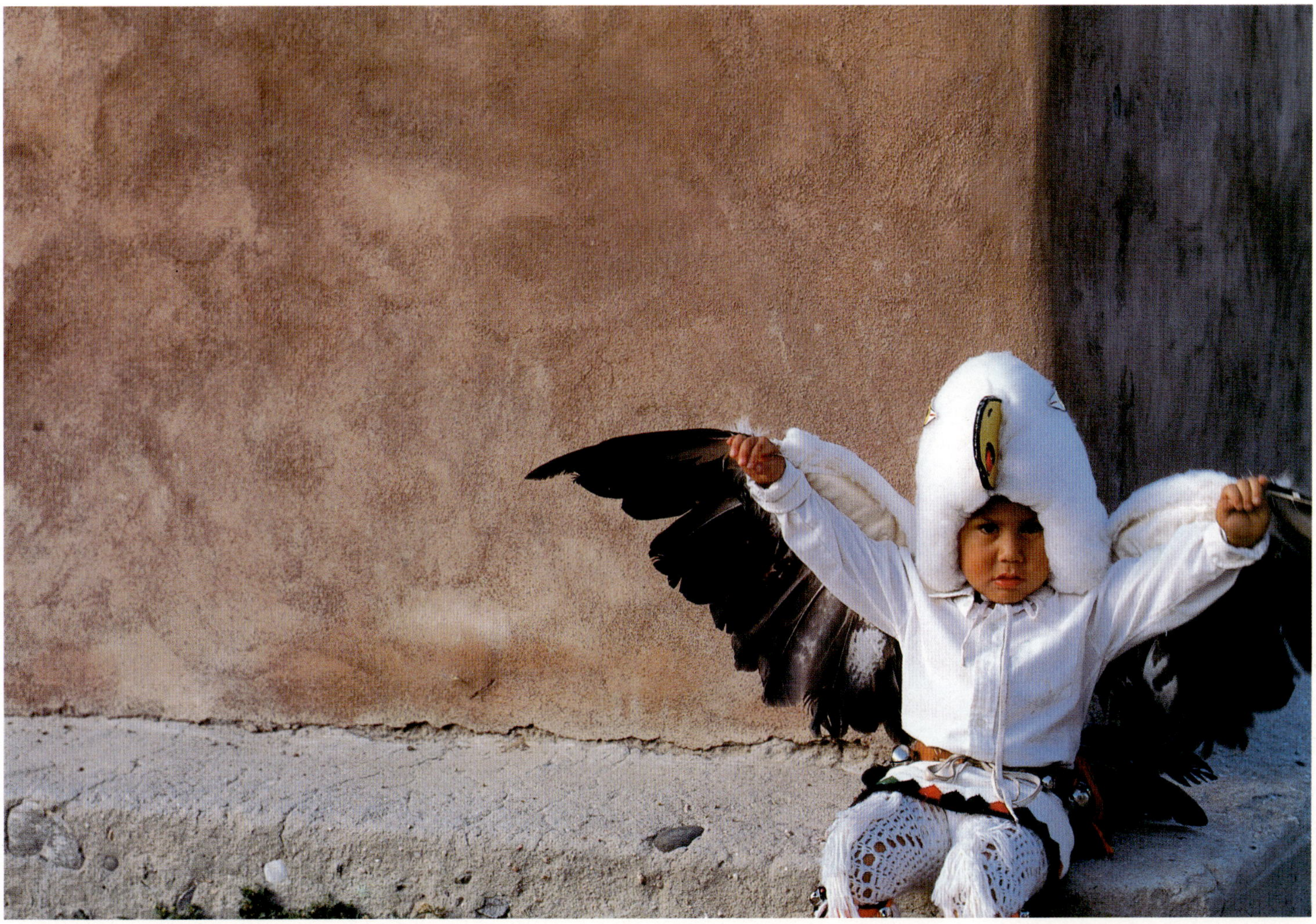

Rodney Rascona

Photograph from an article appearing in Audi of America's house magazine *Spirit of Audi*, featuring a driving tour of Albuquerque, Santa Fe and Taos, New Mexico. Shown is a shy three-year-old eagle dancer.

Albuquerque, Santa Fe und Taos in Neumexiko sind die Stationen einer Fahrt, die in der Hauszeitschrift von Audi of America beschrieben wird. Hier ein etwas schüchterner, dreijähriger Adler-Tänzer.

Albuquerque, Santa Fe et Taos au Nouveau-Mexique. Etapes d'un voyage décrit dans la revue d'entreprise d'Audi-Amérique. La photo montre un danseur aigle un peu timide, âgé de 3 ans.

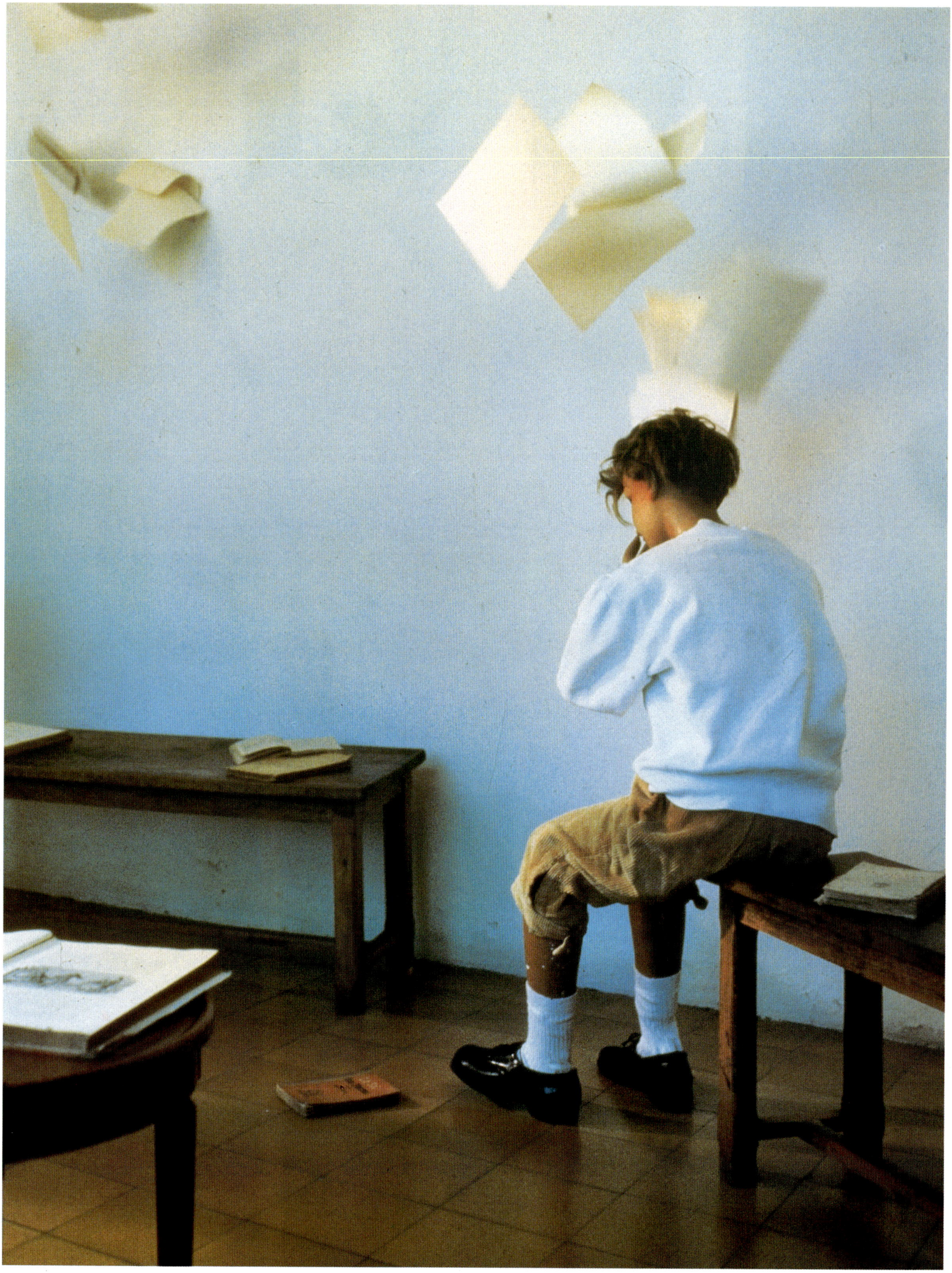

Michael Biondo

This photograph of the rap group Kris Kross by Michael Biondo was used for an album cover.

Michael Biondo fotografierte die Rap-Gruppe Kris Kross für eine Schallplattenhülle.

Michael Biondo a photographié le groupe de rap Kris Kross pour une couverture d'album.

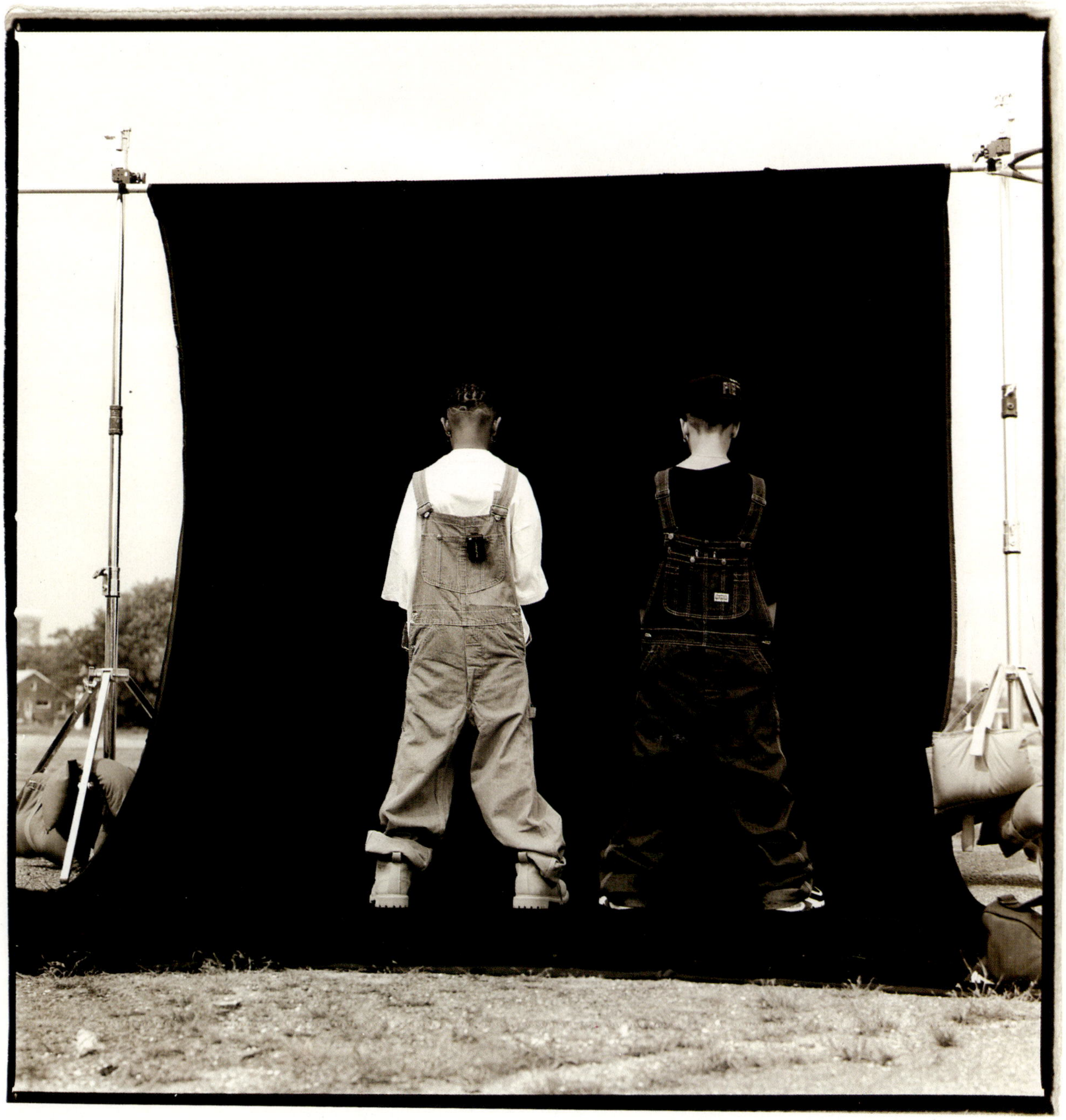

Bernard Faucon

»Flying Papers« – personal work of photographer Bernard Faucon from a series of photographs entitled »Long vacations«.

»Fliegende Papiere« – persönliche Arbeit des Fotografen Bernard Faucon aus einer Serie mit dem Titel »Der lange Urlaub«.

«Les Papiers qui volent» – œuvre personnelle du photographe Bernard Faucon, extraite de la série «Les grandes vacances».

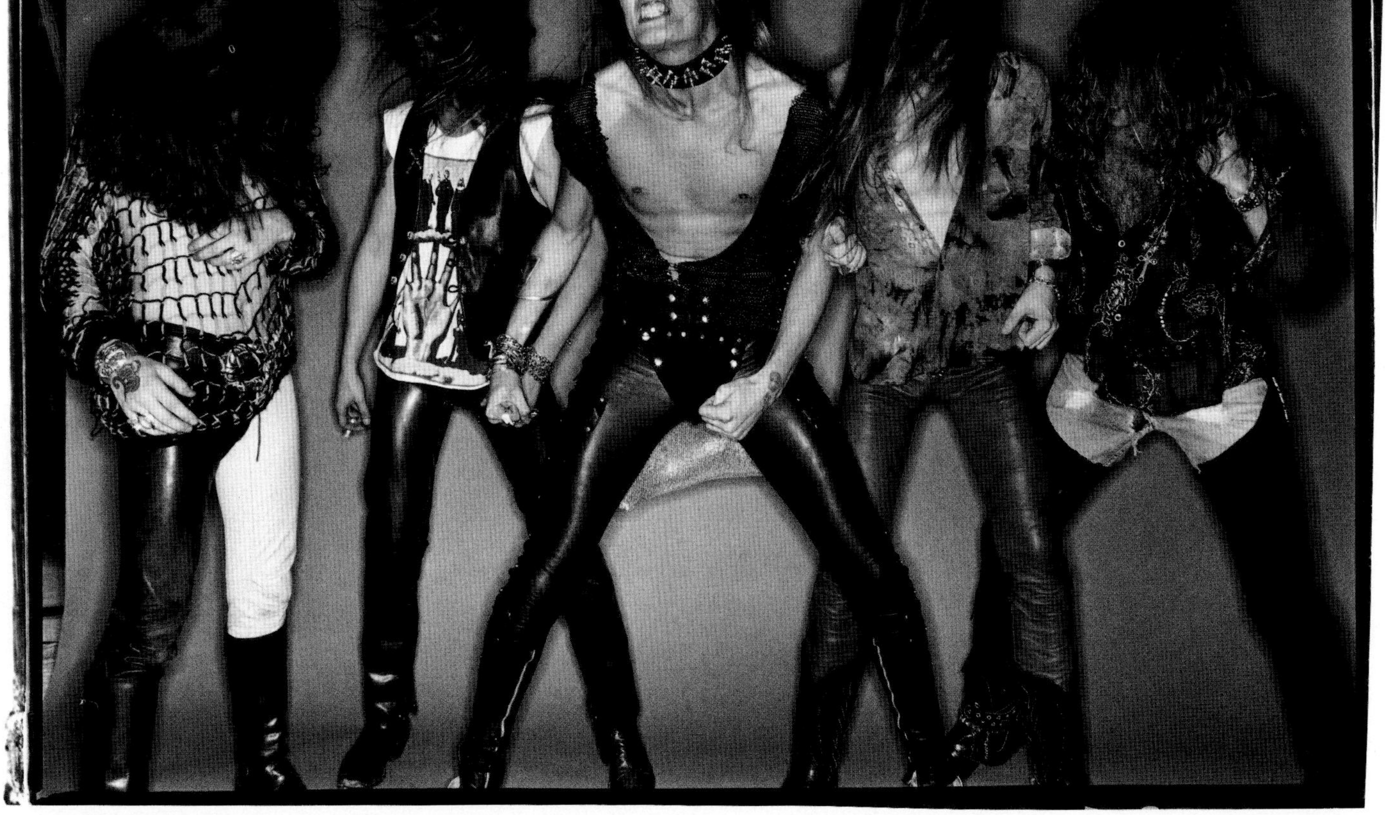

Mark Seliger

Photographs of the bands Red Hot Chili Peppers (right) and Skid Row (above) for *Rolling Stone*.

Mark Seliger fotografierte für *Rolling Stone* die Musiker der Gruppen Red Hot Chili Peppers (rechts) und Skid Row (oben).

Mark Seliger a photographié les musiciens des groupes Red Hot Chili Peppers (à droite) et Skid Row (en haut) pour le magazine *Rolling Stone*.

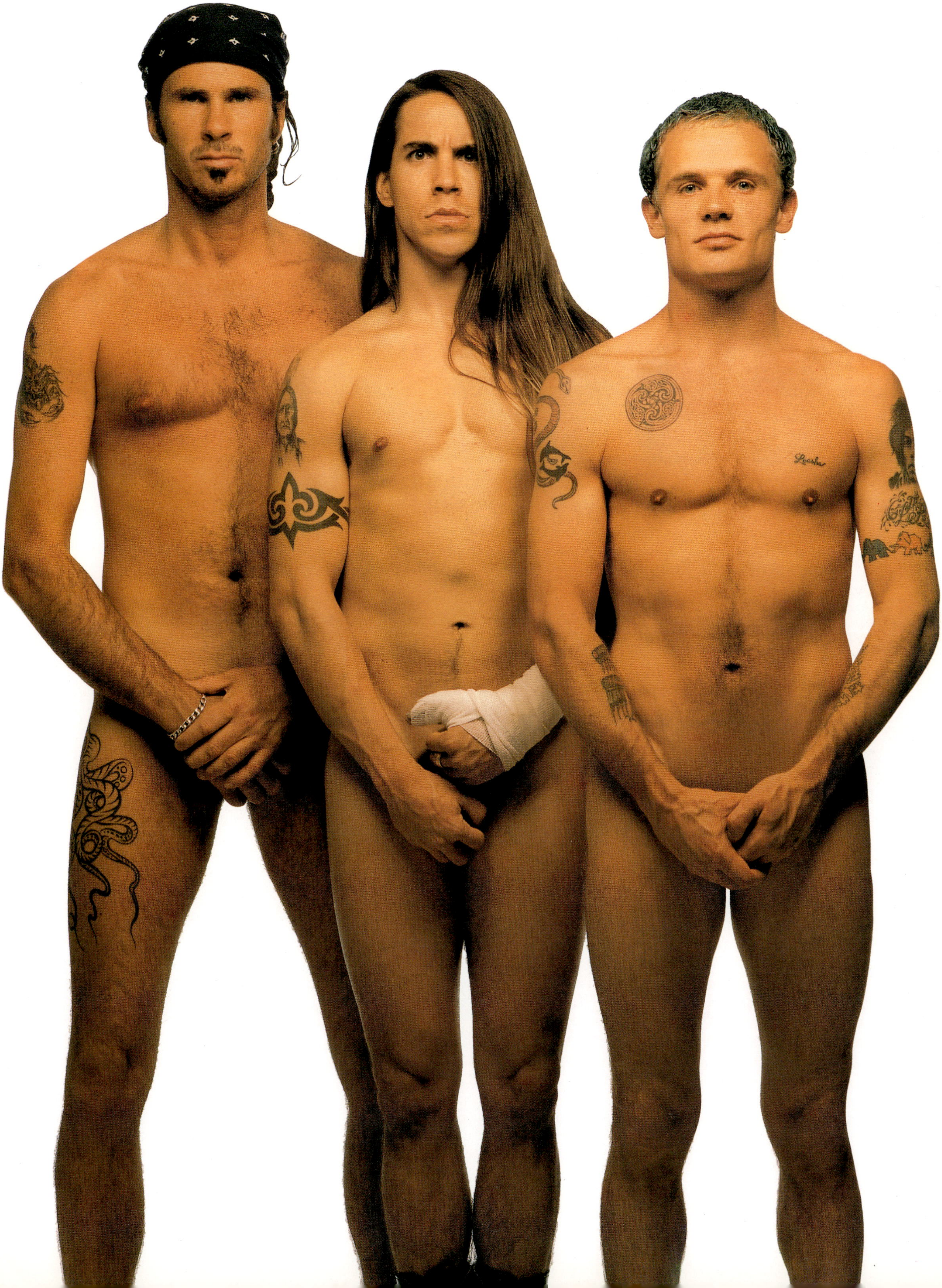

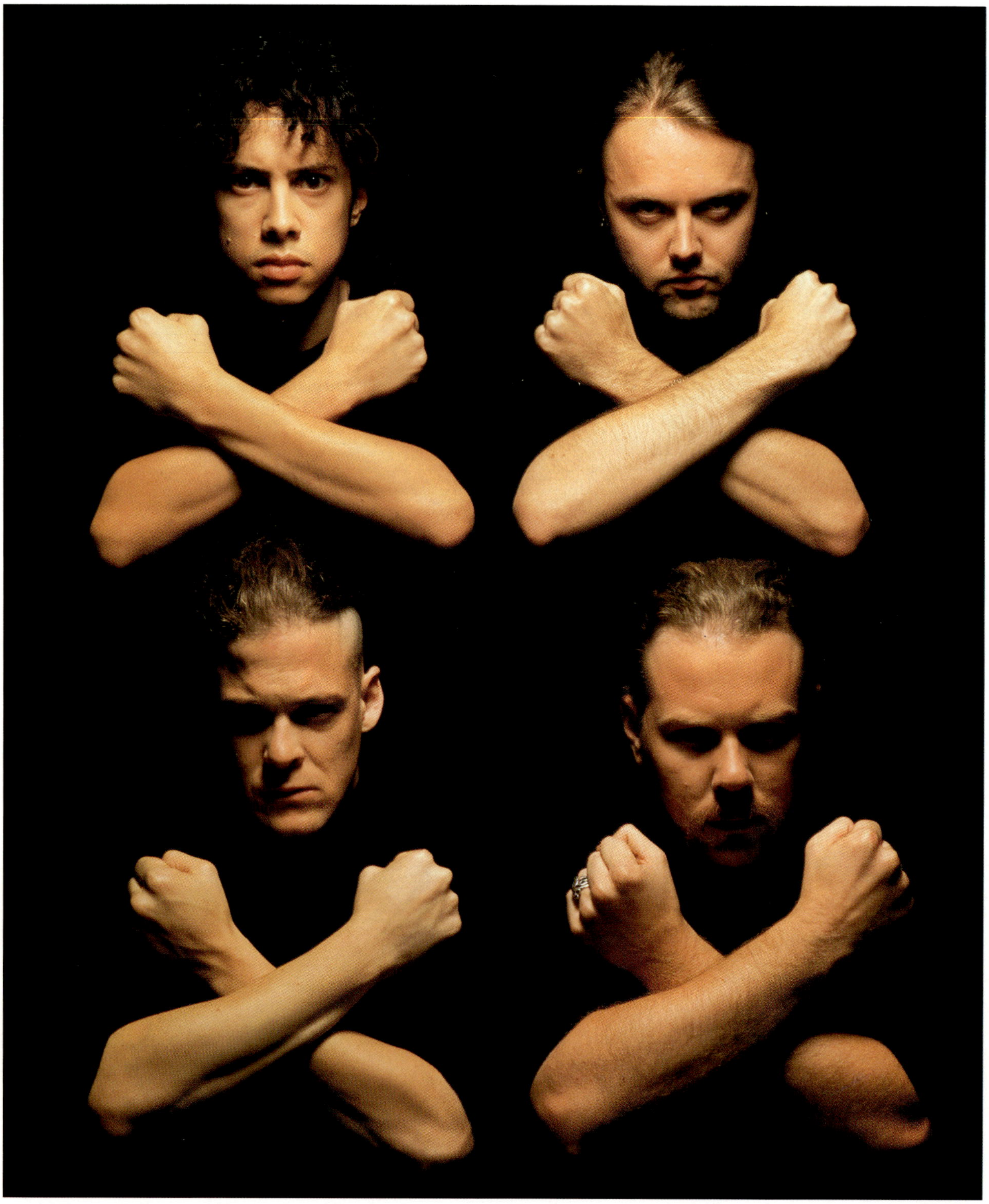

Mark Seliger

This image was used for a story on the band Metallica in *Rolling Stone.*

Rolling Stone brachte diese Aufnahme in einem Artikel über die Gruppe Metallica.

Cette photo a été utilisée pour un article de *Rolling Stone* sur le groupe Metallica.

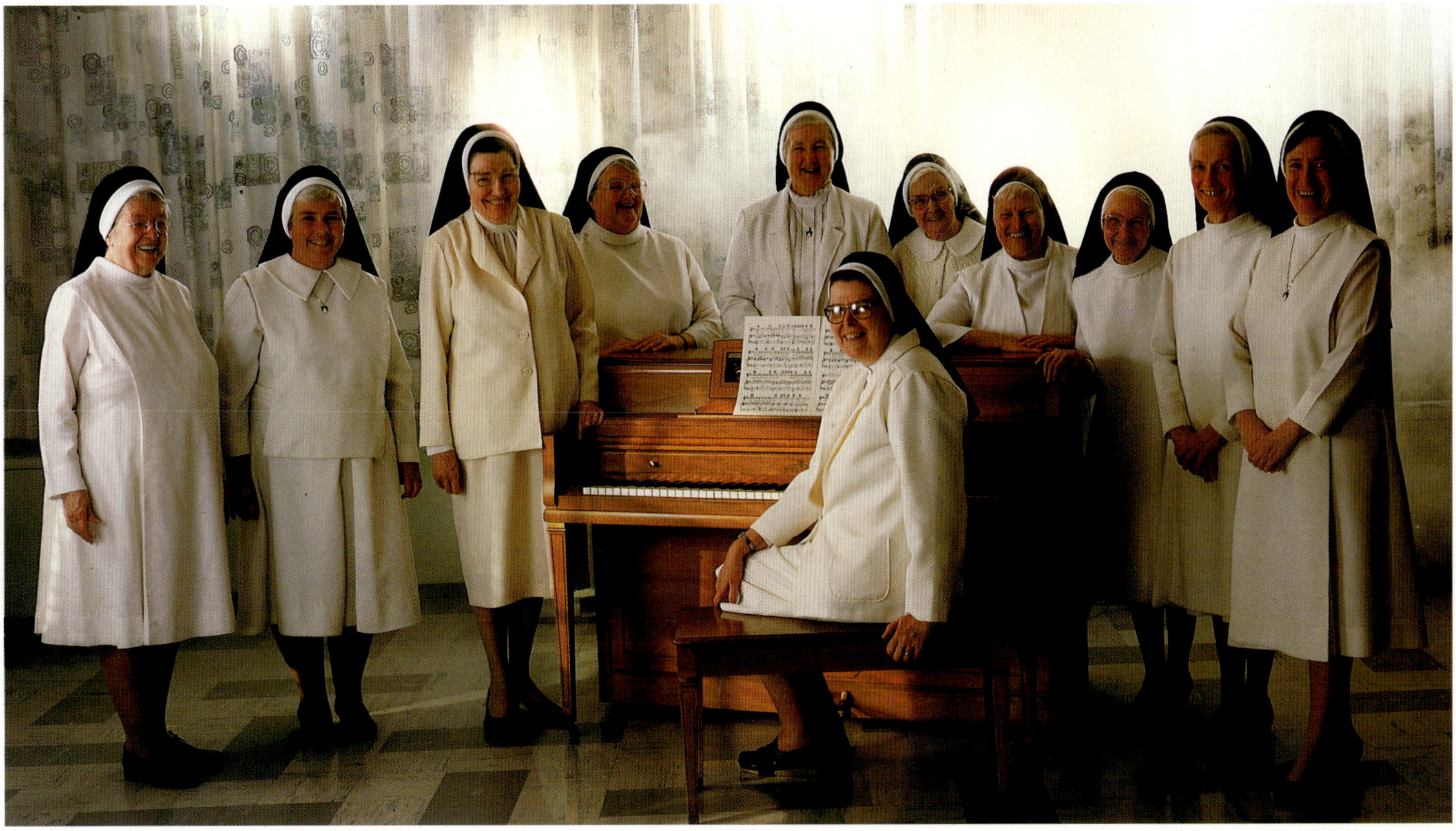

Neal Slavin

»*PC Magazine* isn't taken as gospel by all«. Photograph from an ad campaign for *PC Magazine* emphasizing that it is meant for a special readership.

Diese Aufnahme stammt aus einer Werbekampagne für *PC Magazine*, das sich als Zeitschrift für ein spezielles Publikum darstellt.

Une campagne de publicité de *PC Magazine* mettant en relief le caractère unique de cette revue, destinée à un public spécialisé.

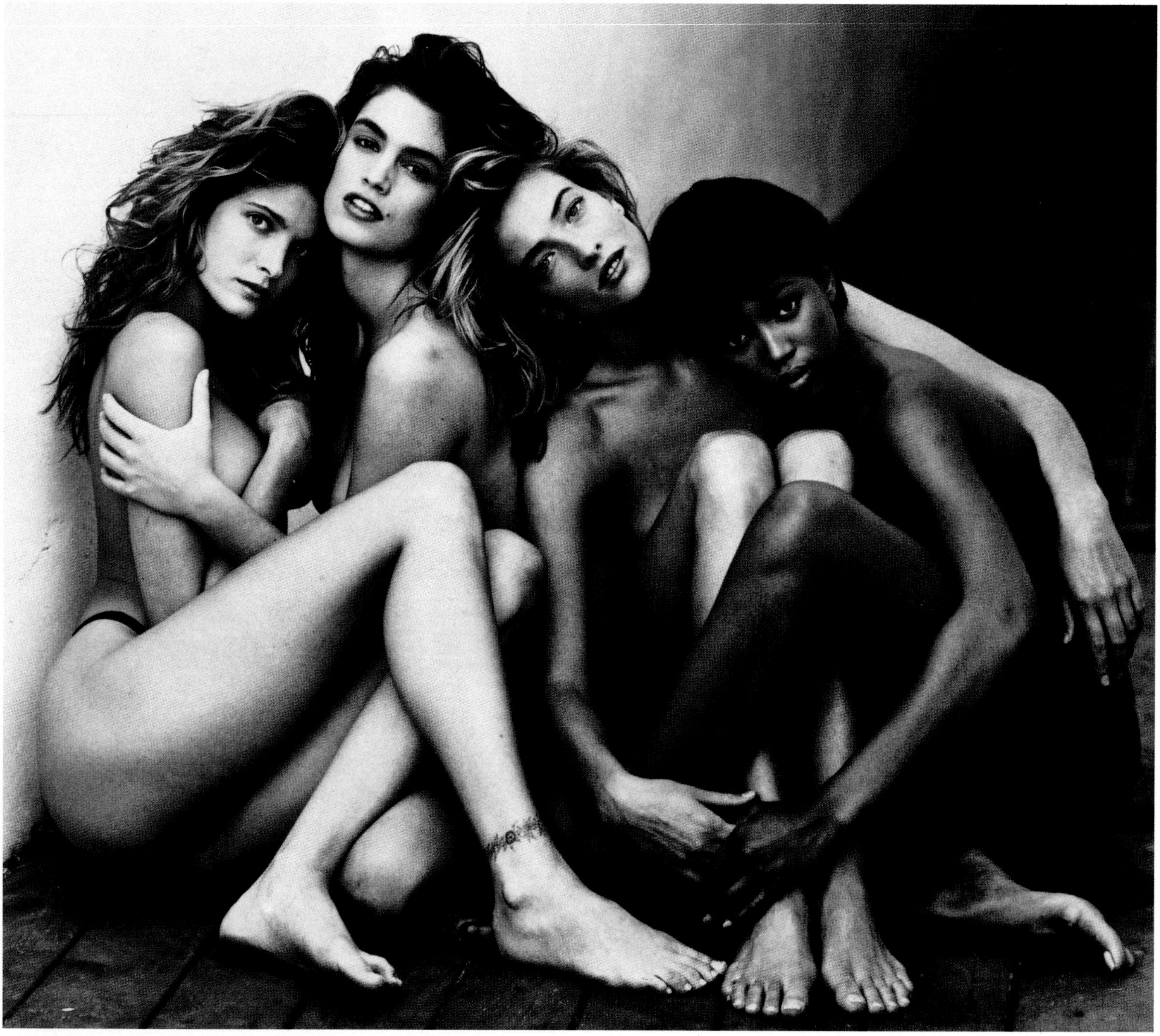

Herb Ritts

The four most expensive photo models in the world photographed by Herb Ritts for *Rolling Stone*: Stephanie Seymour, Cindy Crawford, Tatjana Patitz and Naomi Campbell (from left to right).

Die vier teuersten Fotomodelle der Welt aufgenommen von Herb Ritts für *Rolling Stone:* Stephanie Seymour, Cindy Crawford, Tatjana Patitz und Naomi Campbell (von links nach rechts).

Les quatre modèles les mieux payés du monde photographiés par Herb Ritts pour *Rolling Stone*: Stephanie Seymour, Cindy Crawford, Tatiana Patitz et Naomi Campbell (de gauche à droite).

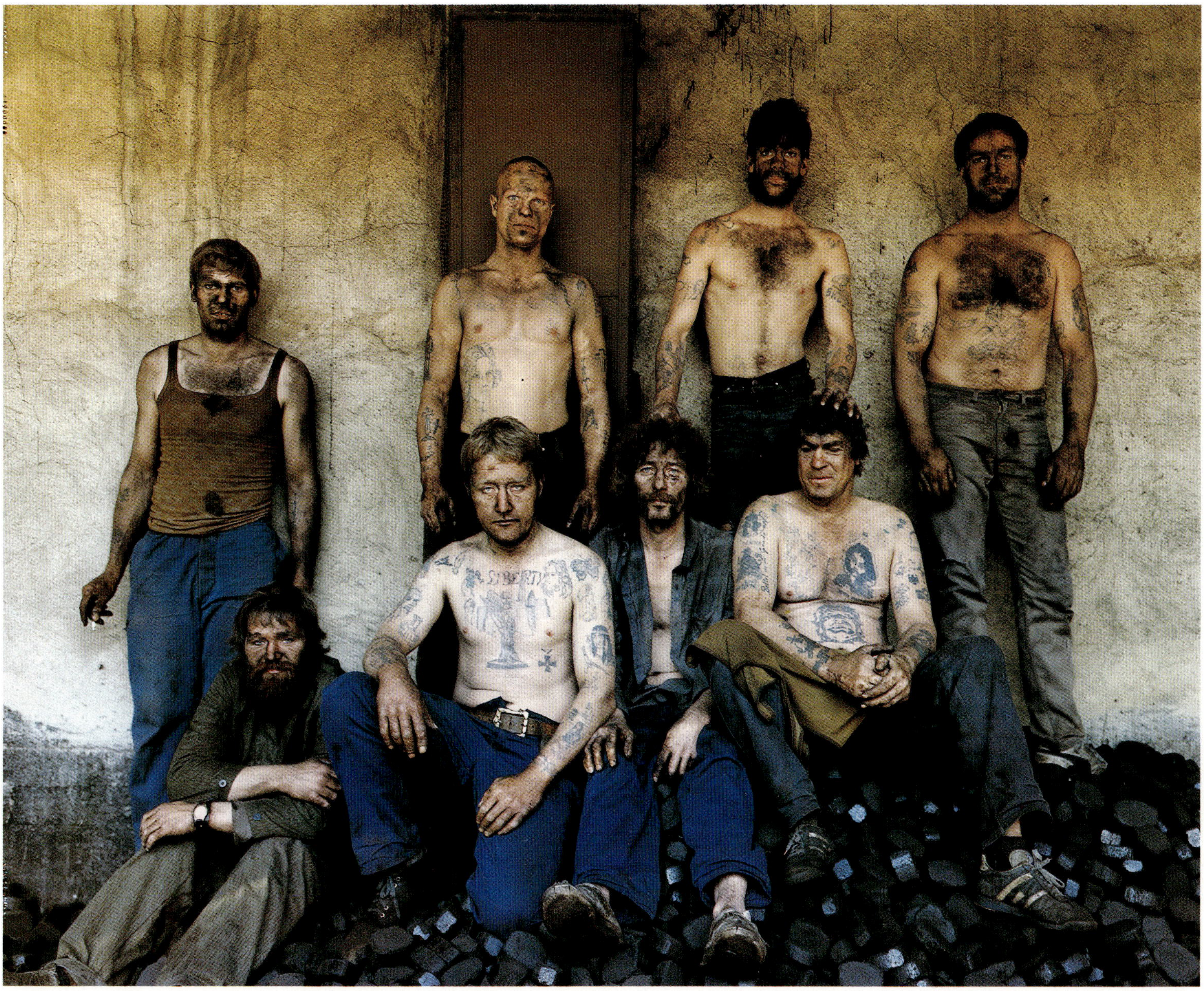

Eberhard Grames

Coal carriers in Schwerin, photographed with natural light on negative film with an 8 x 10 inch camera. Photograph from a portrait series of labourers, women and children in East Germany after the fall of the Wall.

Kohlenschlepper in Schwerin, bei Tageslicht auf Negativmaterial mit 8 x 10 inch-Kamera fotografiert. Die Aufnahme gehört zu einer Porträtreihe von Menschen im Osten Deutschlands nach der Öffnung der Mauer.

Herscheurs à Schwerin, photographiés sous un éclairage naturel sur négatif avec un appareil 8 x 10 inch. Extrait d'une série de portraits réalisés en Allemagne de l'Est, après la chute du mur.

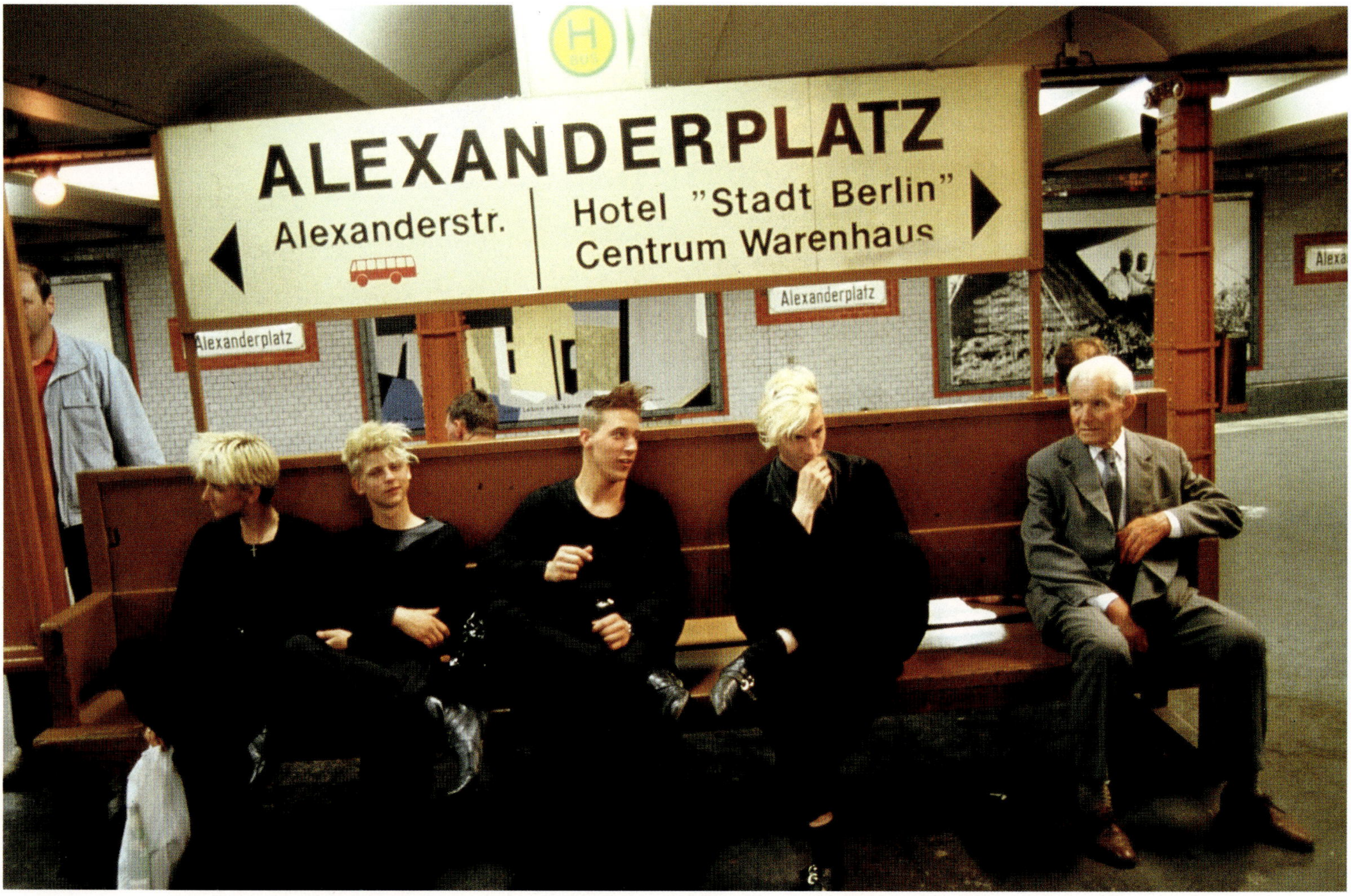

Robert van der Hilst

The contrasting lifestyle of two generations were captured in the underground station at Alexanderplatz in East Berlin prior to the reunification of Germany. The photograph appeared in the French magazine *Marie Claire*.

Der Kontrast zwischen Generationen und Lebensauffassungen, dokumentiert mit einem Foto, das vor der Wiedervereinigung in der U-Bahnstation Alexander-Platz im ehemaligen Ostberlin entstand. Es erschien in der Zeitschrift *Marie Claire*.

Cette photo, prise dans la station de Métro d'Alexanderplatz à Berlin-Est, avant la réunification allemande, montre de manière saisissante le contraste entre deux générations et deux modes de vie. Elle a été publiée dans *Marie Claire*.

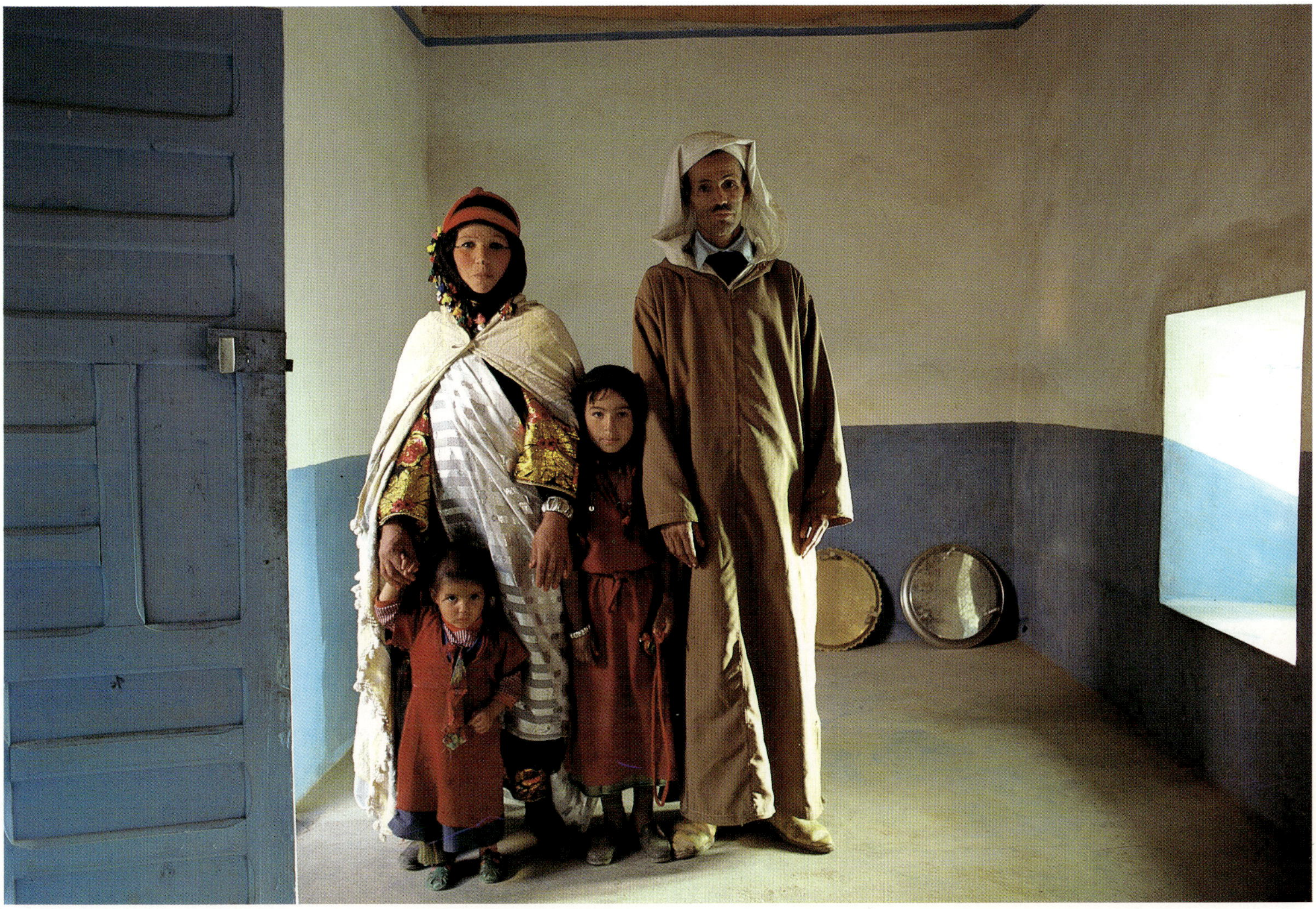

Robert van der Hilst

Example from a series of photographs by Robert van der Hilst, taken in Morocco.

Beispiel aus einer Serie von Aufnahmen des Fotografen Robert van der Hilst, die in Marokko entstanden sind.

Exemple tiré de la série de photos réalisée au Maroc par le photographe Robert van der Hilst.

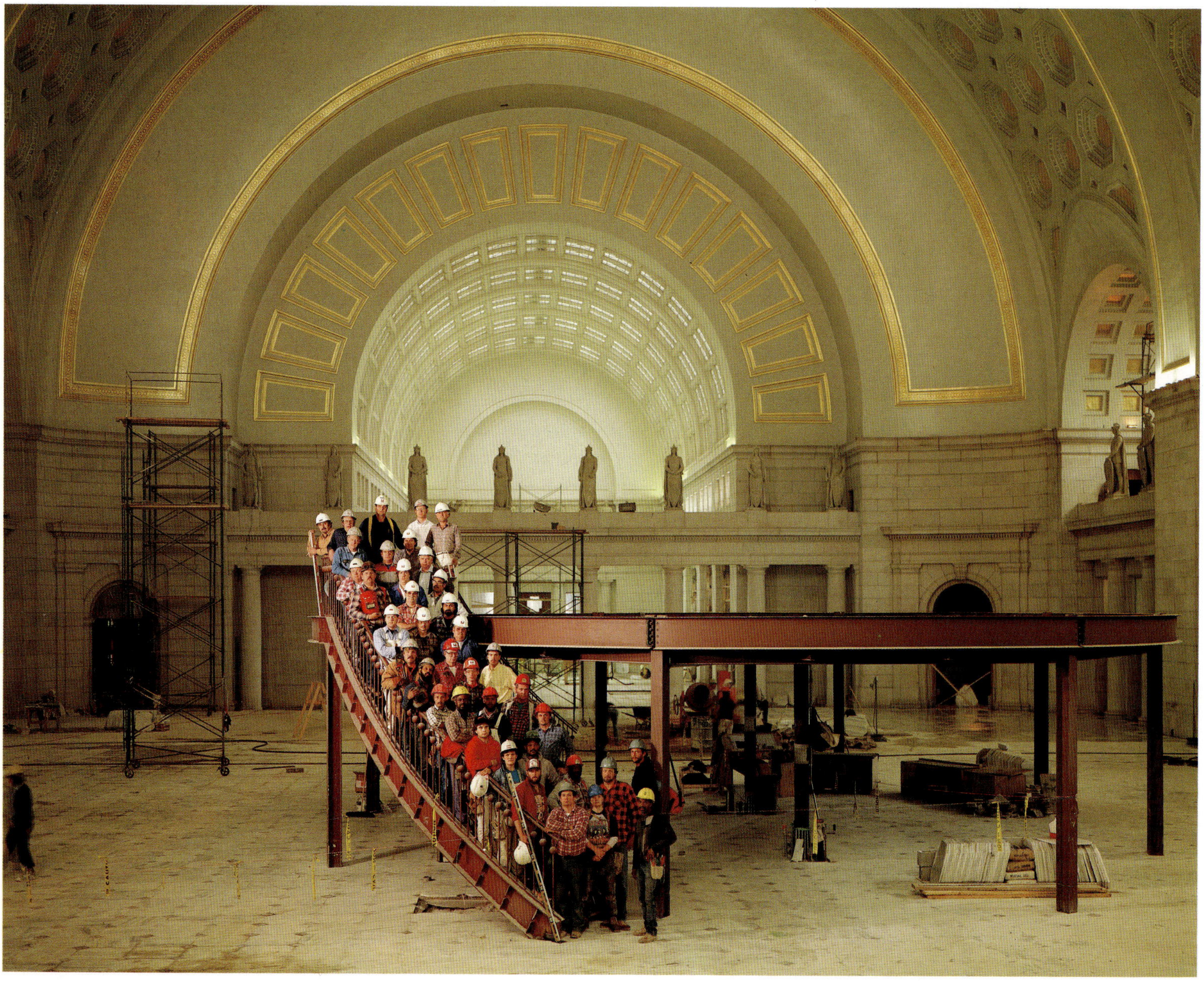

Neal Slavin

The restoration crew of Union Station, a railway station in Washington D.C. – photograph from a feature in the *Sunday Times Magazine* about Washington. It is one of a series of shots that this photographer took of groups of people in Washington. They appear regularly in the *Washington Post Magazine*.

Die Restaurierungstruppe der Union Station, eines Bahnhofes in Washington D.C. – Aufnahme aus einem Artikel im *Sunday Times Magazine* über Washington. Sie gehört zu einer Serie von Bildern, die der Fotograf von Menschengruppen in Washington machte. Sie erscheinen regelmäßig im *Washington Post Magazine*.

L'équipe de réfection de la gare d'Union Station à Washington, D.C. Photo illustrant un article du *Sunday Times Magazine* consacré à Washington. Elle fait partie d'une série de clichés d'attroupements humains réalisés à Washington, et publiés à intervalles réguliers dans le *Washington Post Magazine*.

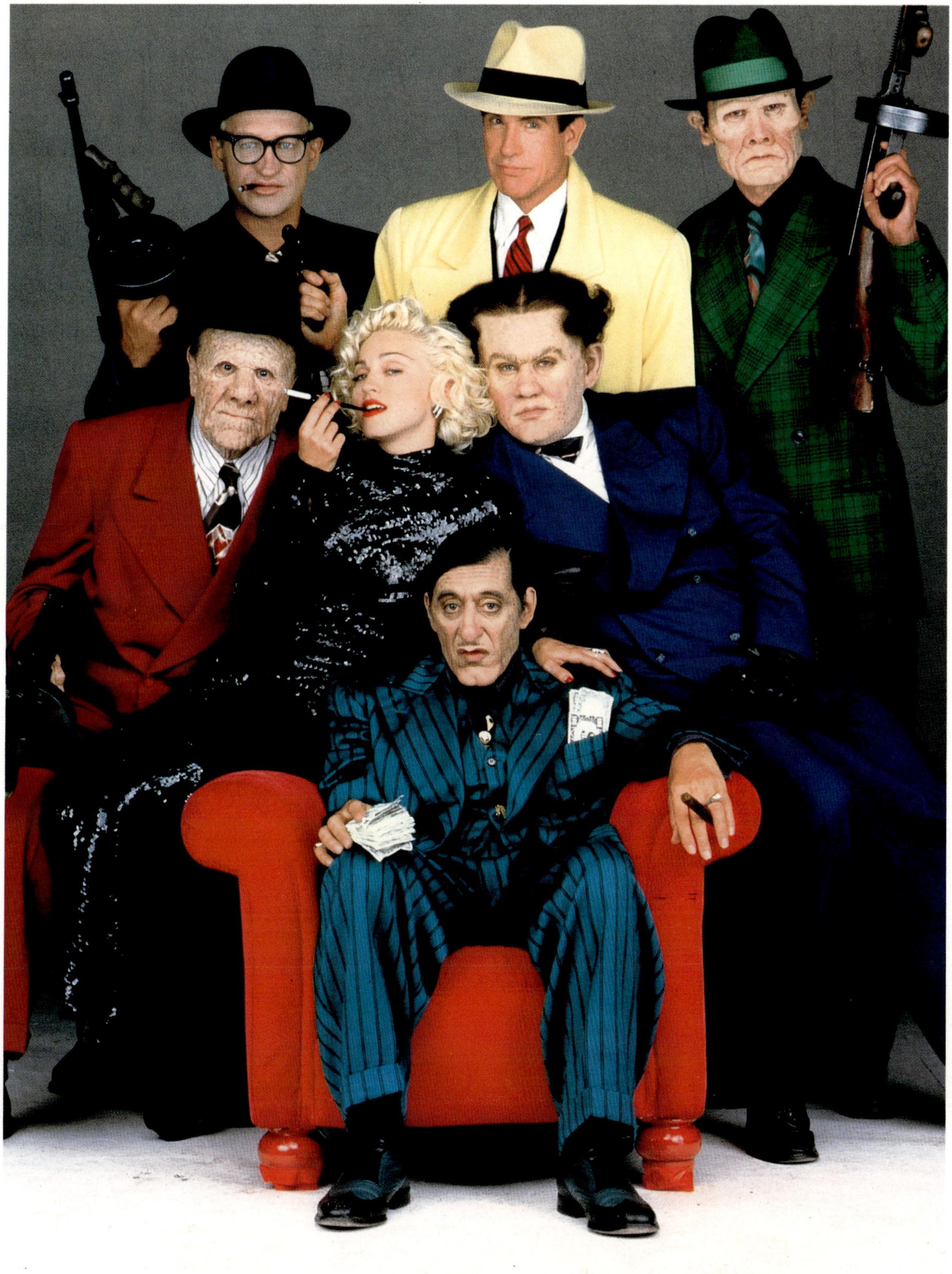

Herb Ritts

Madonna as Breathless Mahoney and Warren Beatty as Dick Tracy, in the film of the same title, are shown surrounded by their gangster foes in this publicity photograph taken for Disney Studios. It later appeared in *Rolling Stone* magazine to accompany an article on the film.

Madonna, als Breathless Mahoney, und Warren Beatty, als Dick Tracy, im gleichnamigen Film, umgeben von Gangstern. Die Aufnahme entstand im Auftrag der Disney Studios und wurde auch für einen Beitrag über diesen Film in der Zeitschrift *Rolling Stone* gezeigt.

Madonna et Warren Beatty, dans le rôle de Dick Tracy, entourées des gangsters du film du même nom. Cette photo a été réalisée pour les Studios Disney pour le lancement du film. Elle a été ensuite publiée dans *Rolling Stone* pour illustrer un article sur le film.

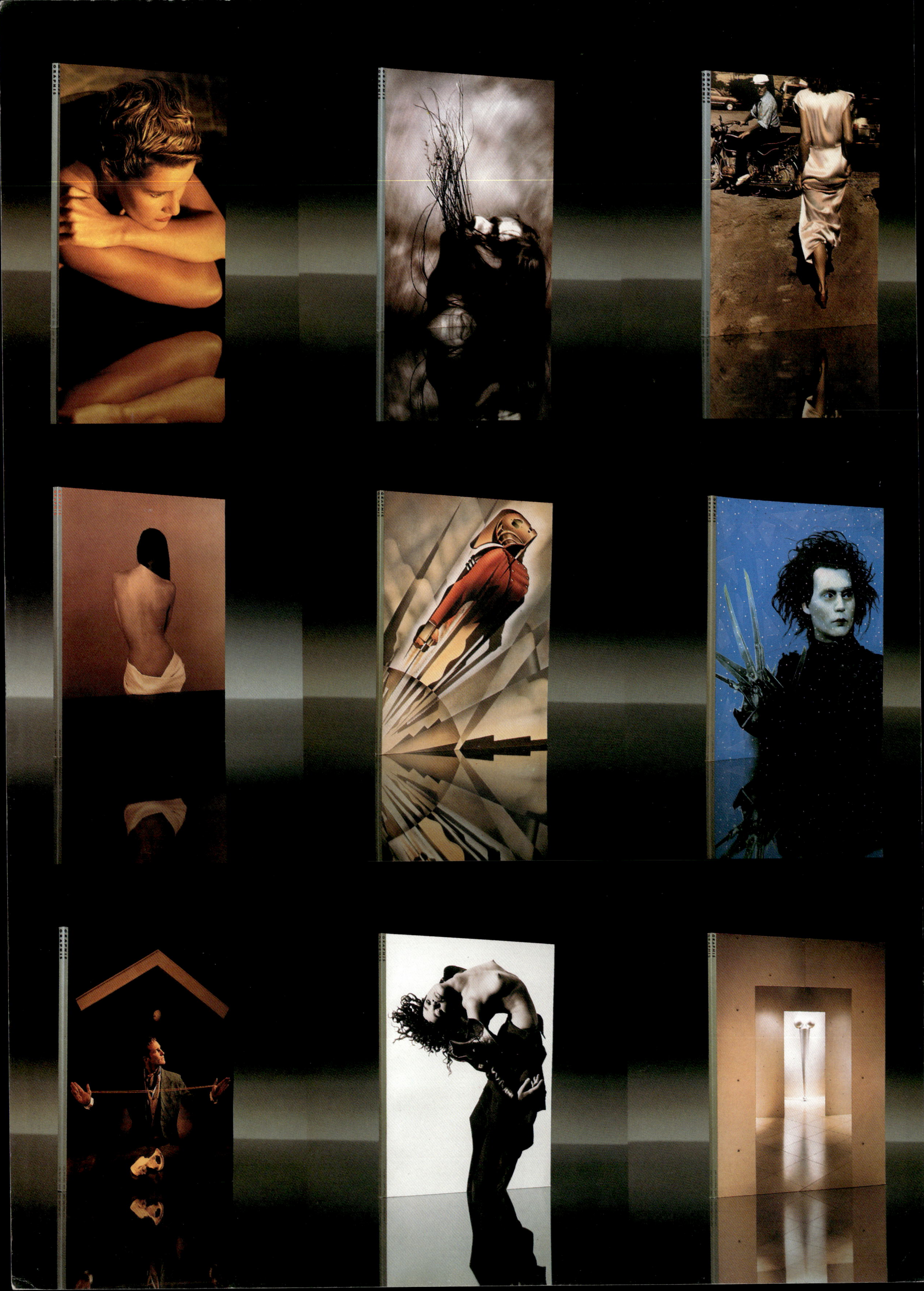

GRAPHIS PRESS CORP.
DUFOURSTRASSE 107
CH–8008 ZURICH
SWITZERLAND

GRAPHIS US INC
141 LEXINGTON AVENUE
NEW YORK NY 10157-1003